I0973231

SALAMANDERS

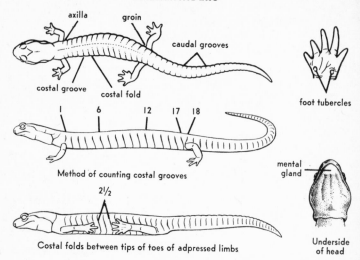

axilla

groin

caudal grooves

costal groove

costal fold

foot tubercles

Method of counting costal grooves

1 6 12 17 18

mental gland

$2\frac{1}{2}$

Costal folds between tips of toes of adpressed limbs

Underside of head

FROGS AND TOADS

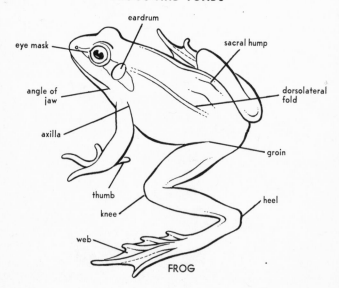

eye mask

eardrum

sacral hump

angle of jaw

dorsolateral fold

axilla

groin

thumb

knee

heel

web

FROG

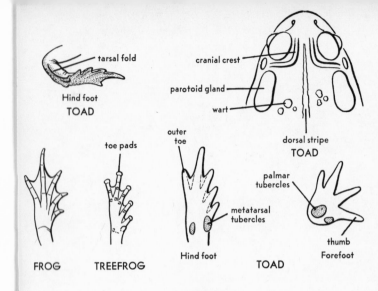

tarsal fold

Hind foot
TOAD

cranial crest

parotoid gland

wart

outer
toe

dorsal stripe
TOAD

toe pads

palmar
tubercles

metatarsal
tubercles

thumb
Forefoot

FROG

TREEFROG

Hind foot

TOAD

TURTLES

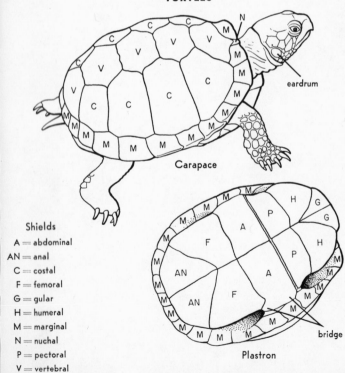

eardrum

Carapace

Shields

A = abdominal
AN = anal
C = costal
F = femoral
G = gular
H = humeral
M = marginal
N = nuchal
P = pectoral
V = vertebral

bridge

Plastron

A Field Guide to Western
Reptiles and Amphibians

THE PETERSON FIELD GUIDE SERIES

EDITED BY ROGER TORY PETERSON

THE PETERSON FIELD GUIDE SERIES

A Field Guide to Western Reptiles and Amphibians

Field marks of all species in western North America

Text and Illustrations by
ROBERT C. STEBBINS

*Professor of Zoology and Curator in
Herpetology, Museum of Vertebrate Zoology,
University of California, Berkeley*

Sponsored by the National Audubon Society
and National Wildlife Federation

HOUGHTON MIFFLIN COMPANY BOSTON

Fifth Printing v

ISBN 0-395-08211-0 hardbound
ISBN 0-395-19421-0 paperbound
Library of Congress Catalog Card Number: 66-16381

Printed in the United States of America

To

RAYMOND B. COWLES

Emeritus Professor of Zoology

University of California, Los Angeles

Editor's Note

THE BOTTLENECK in the preparation of most Field Guides is the problem of illustration. There are competent field specialists to write such guides and a lesser number of competent illustrators, but to find a man who is equally skilled both as a biologist and as a biological illustrator is extremely rare. Such a man is Robert Stebbins. The reproductions in this book, though excellent examples of the engraver's art, cannot fully record the delicacy of detail and loving care that went into the originals.

During the International Galápagos Expedition of 1964 I was privileged to share quarters with Dr. Stebbins at Academy Bay in the Galápagos Archipelago. It was there that I realized what a perfectionist he is, what a demon for work. He had chosen as one of his projects the function of the parietal, or third, eye in the Lava Lizard, *Tropidurus*. A thorough man, he spent five weeks patrolling the coral-strewn paths in the immediate vicinity of the station between the dormitories and the landing. While the rest of us were enjoying high adventure on the more remote islands and sea-girt rocks, he patiently snared 200 frisky lizards with a noose of thread suspended from a rod. He took their cloacal temperatures, marked them with dye, and then dosed them with radioactive iodine, which enabled him to locate the elusive reptiles later with a Geiger counter. From dawn to dark he charted their activities, saw them wake up in the morning, followed their daily routine, and, by means of the clicking Geiger counter, discovered where they spent the night.

He performed simple surgery on one group of lizards, deftly removing the minute "third eye," a fleck of tissue on the forehead, to observe the effect on their daily activities. Whenever a lizard with a purple leg darted across our path we knew we were seeing one of Dr. Stebbins' subjects.

It was with this same devotion to detail and relentless singleness of purpose that Dr. Stebbins tackled the long and exacting task of preparing the text, range maps, and illustrations for this manual, No. 16 in the Field Guide Series.

Recognition is step number one in any branch of natural science. That is why the Field Guide Series was launched — as a shortcut to recognizing and naming the multitude of living things which populate America, a *Who's Who* of the outdoors. The first volume to appear, *A Field Guide to the Birds*, met with instant success. This was followed by guides to other groups of animals and plants, including Roger Conant's splendid *Field Guide to Reptiles and Amphibians of the United States and Canada East of the 100th Meridian.*

This new *Field Guide* supplements Roger Conant's book, which stops at the 100th meridian. Between the eastern borders of New Mexico, Colorado, Wyoming, Montana, and Saskatchewan north (the eastern limits of the present book, or, roughly, the 103rd meridian), there is a blend zone — a "twilight zone" — an interdigitation of eastern and western influences. Here the student should carry both *Field Guides.* However, a few species west of the Pecos River in western Texas, mainly in the Big Bend area, are not included in either book at present. These will be covered in a forthcoming revision of Roger Conant's eastern *Field Guide.*

The West may not be as rich as the East in salamanders and turtles, but it makes up for this deficiency in its wealth of lizards and snakes, particularly in the diversified terrain of the arid Southwest. Some species are local and rare, all are exciting to the field naturalist.

Take this handbook with you whenever you travel. Do not leave it home on your library shelf; it is a Field Guide, intended to be used.

Roger Tory Peterson

Acknowledgments

IT IS with deep gratitude that I acknowledge the contribution of many persons to the preparation of this book. I am especially grateful to those who bore the brunt of my requests for help. These people carefully checked the distribution maps and helped procure live animals for the illustrations; some of them read parts or all of the manuscript. They are Charles M. Bogert, Paul DeBenedictis, James R. Dixon, Frederick R. Gehlbach, Charles H. Lowe, T. Paul Maslin, Hobart M. Smith, Robert M. Storm, Wilmer W. Tanner, William H. Woodin III, John Wright, and Richard G. Zweifel. Charles Bogert, Richard Zweifel, and Paul DeBenedictis read all the species accounts and Charles Lowe and John Wright the accounts of whiptail lizards.

Others who helped in the procurement of specimens, some of them making special trips to remote areas to do so, are R. Bruce Bury, Arthur E. Dammann, Philip C. Dumas, Murray M. Eells, Henry S. Fitch, Richard S. Funk, Richard Highton, Lorin Honetschlager, David Howell, Ernest L. Karlstrom, Lawrence F. La Pré, Richard B. Loomis, William L. McClure, Philip A. Medica, Dean E. Metter, Theodore J. Papenfuss, Dwight Platt, Vincent D. Roth, Charles E. Shaw, and Lewis W. Walker.

In addition to the persons mentioned at the outset, the following individuals saw copies of the distribution maps; geographic areas given special attention by them are indicated in parentheses: Paul K. Anderson (Alberta), Benjamin H. Banta (Nevada), George T. Baxter (Wyoming), W. Frank Blair (Texas), Royal B. Brunson (Montana), Pete S. Chrapliwy (all states), Ian McTaggart Cowan (British Columbia), Clifford V. Davis (Montana), William G. Degenhardt and James S. Findley (New Mexico), Raymond J. Hock (Alaska), Merritt S. Keasey (Arizona), Mervin W. Larson (Arizona), Clarence J. McCoy, Jr. (Colorado), Richard A. Pimentel (California), Gerald G. Raun (Texas), James R. Slater (Washington), Jay M. Savage (all states), Wilmer W. Tanner (Utah), E. Kenneth Teberg (Montana), and Robert G. Webb (New Mexico).

Roger and Isabelle Conant, creators of the eastern *Field Guide to Reptiles and Amphibians* kindly allowed use of their original map format in the preparation of western distributions.

For help with numerous details pertaining to a variety of topics — altitudinal range, geographic variation, locations of isolated

ix

populations, and particulars concerning certain species and species groups — I am indebted to Ralph Axtell (Lesser Earless Lizard) Arden H. Brame, Jr. (slender salamanders), Walter J. Breckenridge, Bryce C. Brown, Royal B. Brunson, W. Leslie Burger, Pete S. Chrapliwy (spadefoot toads), Roger Conant, Robert G. Crippen, Robert L. Eberhardt, Henry S. Fitch, Wade Fox, Jr., Robert A. Hendon, David L. Jameson, Kenneth B. Jones, W. Charles Kerfoot (Sagebrush Lizard), Ira La Rivers, Mervin W. Larson, John M. Legler, T. Paul Maslin, Clarence J. McCoy, Jr., Philip A. Medica, Keith Murray (slender salamanders), Kenneth S. Norris, Theodore J. Papenfuss, Michael Sabath (Sagebrush Lizard), Jay M. Savage, Fred Schuierer, Frederick A. Shannon, Hobart M. Smith, Wilmer W. Tanner (black-headed snakes), John H. Tashjian, Frederick B. Turner (Spotted Frog), Victor Twitty (newts), David B. Wake, and Roland Wauer.

The McGraw-Hill Book Company and the University of California Press generously allowed use of illustrations from *Amphibians and Reptiles of Western North America* (McGraw-Hill, 1954), *Amphibians of Western North America* (University of California Press, 1951), and *Reptiles and Amphibians of the San Francisco Bay Region* (University of California Press, 1959). These illustrations are identified on page 224. Most of the drawings of frog eggs are based on "A Synoptic Key to the Salientian Eggs of the United States" by Robert L. Livezey and Albert H. Wright (Amer. Mid. Nat. 37 [1]: 179–222). The map of natural vegetation (pp. 226–27), is adapted from H. L. Shantz and R. Zon, 1924, U.S. Dept. Agric., Atlas Amer. Agric., Sect. E.

The final manuscript was typed by Mrs. John G. O'Connor.

I am indebted to Roger Tory Peterson for his encouragement and to Paul Brooks, Helen Phillips, Katharine Bernard, Morton Baker, and Arnold Paine of Houghton Mifflin Company for their counseling throughout the preparation of the book.

Special thanks go to my children — John, Melinda, and Mary — whose interest in animals helped motivate me, and to my wife, who typed the first draft and did all the art work on the distribution maps, and who for more than twenty years has graciously coped with frogs in her refrigerator, snakes in the living room, and tortoises on the sun deck.

ROBERT C. STEBBINS

Contents

Illustrations

A Field Guide to Western Reptiles and Amphibians

MAP OF AREA COVERED IN THIS BOOK

All species of reptiles and amphibians known to occur in the areas of the United States and Canada indicated on the map by unshaded, labeled portions are included. See comments about borderline area in the Editor's Note (p. viii). Range maps are grouped at the back of the book.

Introduction

INTEREST in reptiles and amphibians is growing rapidly. Pet shops abound with scaly forms, reptile clubs are on the increase, and a small army of snake and lizard hunters roams the countryside. Along some of our desert roads collectors now may outnumber the snakes, and in some of our large municipal parks hillsides may be dotted with small boys searching for lizards on a Sunday afternoon. My *Amphibians and Reptiles of Western North America* has served mainly as a college text. Currently there is need for a guide suitable for the layman. This *Field Guide* includes 26 species of salamanders, 35 species of frogs and toads, 15 species of turtles, 61 species of lizards, and 70 species of snakes — a total of 207 species.

The primary function of the present book is identification. In this connection I have included information on methods of capture, for in contrast to birds, reptiles and amphibians must usually be in hand to be identified. Captivity should be only temporary, however, and after examination the animals should be released where they were found, unless needed for study. An attitude of "leave alone," watch, and study should be developed. The undisturbed animal in its natural setting can provide much valuable information.

When traveling through deserts and mountains, stop occasionally for roadside exploration. Armed with a lizard noose, easily improvised (see p. 9), a jar for specimens, and information supplied by this book, you may find much of interest. The desert, a forbidding place at first, will seem more hospitable after you meet some of its inhabitants. Discovery of a Long-tailed Brush Lizard, hiding camouflaged on the branch of a creosote bush, will leave a pleasant memory. The desert will never look the same again.

Area Covered: The book covers western North America from a line formed by the eastern boundaries of New Mexico, Colorado, Wyoming, Montana, and Saskatchewan north to the Arctic Circle. The area is referred to in the text as "the West."

How to Use This Book: To identify most reptiles and amphibians scales must be examined, costal grooves counted, and details of pattern studied. Fortunately, nearly all species can be caught easily and nearly all western forms are harmless. Only the rattlesnakes and coral snakes are dangerous and they are easily recognized. A few species may bite hard enough to break the skin, but such injury usually can be avoided by proper handling (see p. 9).

In making identifications there will be no difficulty in finding the appropriate major section of this book. Turtles, snakes, and frogs all are easily recognized as to group. Salamanders, although resembling lizards in form, lack claws and scales and have a soft, moist skin. Our only snakelike lizard has movable eyelids and lacks the straplike belly scutes of snakes. Those familiar with reptiles and amphibians can go directly to the proper plates; the inexperienced should consult the keys (pp. 23–31). When an identification is made, check the distribution map to see if the species is expected in the area. If not, a mistake probably has been made. Reptiles and amphibians do not have great mobility; vagrants are rare.

When range and illustration have been checked, turn to the species accounts for verification. The accounts give a more detailed description, and information on behavior, habitat, and similar species; important characteristics are in italics. So far as possible familiar terminology has been used in descriptions. However, a few technical terms were unavoidable. A brief time spent learning them will speed use of the book. The anatomical terms are explained in the figures on the endpapers inside the covers, and in the text; other terms can be found in the Glossary at the back of the book.

Although most of the characteristics mentioned in the descriptions can be seen easily, it has been necessary to refer to a few internal ones — tooth arrangements in salamanders, gill rakers in larvae, and cranial-boss structure in spadefoot toads. As regards teeth, with the exception of the Pacific Giant and Arboreal Salamanders, the mouths of salamanders can be opened without danger of being bitten. In studying the teeth of preserved specimens, you will usually have to sever the jaw on one side to free it enough to expose the teeth.

Illustrations: Most of the drawings and paintings have been made from living animals. The area designation of the specimen illustrated is usually indicated in parentheses on the legend page opposite the plate. The live animal is a far cry from the contorted specimen in the museum jar. A toad's eyes may be jewel-like and the geometry of reptilian scales is a harmony of line and shape. Life colors of some species rival the brilliance of brightly colored birds. Each species has its characteristic facial expression.

I have tried to record what I have seen in the living animals. Many of the illustrations are generalizations based not only on the subject in hand but upon long personal acquaintanceship with the species. To attempt to render a scientifically accurate drawing is time-consuming. This is especially true in illustrating reptiles with scales too large to suggest. It becomes necessary to draw them all, faithfully recording size, number, shape, and arrangement to obtain a satisfactory result.

To show details in structure, young animals and some of the

smaller species have been enlarged relative to the other illustrations. The treefrogs, ground snakes, and black-headed snakes are examples. Refer to the size scale on the legend pages opposite the plates.

Size: Range in adult size is given in inches at the beginning of the descriptions and applies to each species throughout its geographic range. Measurements are of snout to vent length in salamanders, frogs, and lizards, shell length in turtles, and total length in snakes. Sizes of young (also in inches) are included when known.

Color: Colors may vary with locality, age, sex, and color phase, and in some species may change in a few minutes. A dark frog or lizard may become pale while being handled. The brief color descriptions presented here will often be lacking, and one can expect to find individuals that fit neither description nor illustration. In such instances, special attention must be given to structure.

Young: Proportions usually differ from those of adults. Head, limbs, and eyes may be relatively larger. Young turtles may have a more rounded shell with a median ridge, and a relatively long tail. Colors may also differ. In identifying young, rely heavily on structural characteristics — scale counts and arrangement, costal-groove counts, and other traits that do not change with age.

Sex Differences: The species accounts give details pertaining to species. General remarks are set forth here.

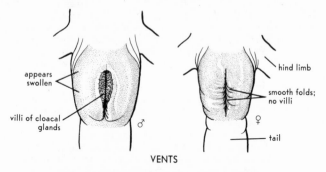

Fig. 1. Sexual characteristics of salamanders

1. Salamanders. Breeding males have a swollen vent, the lining of which is roughened by tubercles (villi) of the cloacal glands (Fig. 1). In contrast, the vent of females is not enlarged and lacks tubercles; the lips and walls are smooth or pleated. Hold the salamander in a damp cloth and spread the vent with forceps. View with hand lens or dissecting microscope. In addition to vent differences males generally have a longer tail and, in the aquatic stage, broader tail fins.

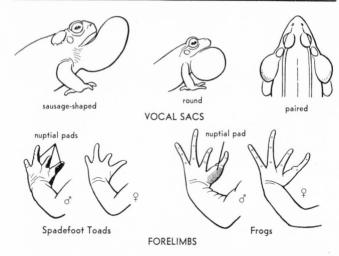

sausage-shaped   round   paired

VOCAL SACS

nuptial pads   nuptial pad

♂   ♀   ♂   ♀

Spadefoot Toads   Frogs

FORELIMBS

Fig. 2. Sexual characteristics of frogs

2. Frogs and Toads. Males usually have a voice and a well-developed vocal sac (Fig. 2); voice in females is weak or absent. When the vocal sac is deflated the skin of the throat is often dark and loose. When breeding, males develop dark nuptial pads of rough skin on one or more of the inner fingers (Fig. 2). In frogs the base of the innermost finger (or "thumb") may become enlarged. The forelimbs often become stout and muscular and webbing of the hind feet increases. Males are generally smaller than females. Amplexus may be pectoral or pelvic. In pectoral amplexus the male holds the female about her chest; in pelvic amplexus he holds her about her waist.

3. Turtles. Males typically have a concave plastron and longer tail than females. When the tail is extended full length the vent lies at or beyond the shell margin. Females have a flat or convex plastron and the vent is situated inside the shell margin.

4. Lizards. In breeding males the base of the tail usually appears swollen. The enlargement results from the hemipenes (copulatory organs) which are imbedded there. These organs can be everted by gentle squeezing with thumb and forefinger, applying pressure toward the vent opening from a point at or just behind the swollen tail base. In individuals in which eversion does not occur, probe the posterior and lateral margins of the vent with a toothpick, straightened paper clip, or bobby pin, thrusting the probe backward. If the animal is a male, the probe will pass into the opening of the inverted hemipenis.

5. *Snakes.* Males usually have longer tails than females and a broader tail base. In general, the hemipenes are less easily everted than in lizards and the probing technique will more often have to be used.

Voice: With the exception of the Tailed Frog — a mute species — males of most western frogs and toads have well-developed voices, recognition of which can be helpful in identification. Pitch, cadence, and duration of calls have been given in the accounts, but these characteristics may vary with locality, size of the individual, and temperature. In particular, individuals from the extremes of the range of some of the more widely ranging species may differ in voice quality. Young adults, as a consequence of their small size, may have higher-pitched voices than older adults. A cold frog may produce slower and lower-pitched calls than a warm one. In hybrid areas strange combinations may occur. When an unfamiliar call is heard, locate the frog by triangulation (see p. 11). Attempt to imitate the animal and write a description of both the voice and method used in imitation. Whistles, vocal sounds, tongue clicks, or combinations thereof can be used. Some calls can best be imitated mechanically. I have stimulated the Cricket Frog by striking pebbles together, one held in each hand and struck with a sliding motion. A Chorus Frog may respond to stroking the teeth of a pocket comb. Knowledge of animal sounds can greatly increase enjoyment of the outdoors, but we have become accustomed to ignoring sounds in our noisy civilized environment and awareness of animal sounds usually must be cultivated.

Knowledge of amphibian voices makes possible determination of the composition of mixed choruses. During the height of breeding it can be used to help locate the boundaries of ranges. The western border of the range of the Chorus Frog was observed one spring as I traveled at night from Wyoming into Utah. The sounds of this frog, heard for hundreds of miles throughout southern Wyoming, suddenly stopped at the western base of the central plateau, at the edge of the Great Basin. For a start in recognizing the voices of amphibians, listen to *Sounds of North American Frogs* by Charles M. Bogert (Folkway Records, FX 6166).

Time of Activity: Many amphibians and reptiles have limited periods of yearly activity. In the main descriptions or under the subheading *Voice* in the accounts, the span of months over which various species may be found has been given. Activity often reaches its peak during breeding. Some amphibians may gather in large numbers then but are scarce at other times. Breeding dates are included when information is available and reliable. Statements in the accounts are general and apply to the species over its entire range. In a widely ranging form, activity usually begins sooner and lasts longer in the south and in the lowlands than in the north and at high elevation. However, there may be local climatic effects that influence timing.

Prolonged retreat from the surface may occur in winter (hibernation), summer (estivation), or both. The former is an escape from cold; the latter an escape from heat and dryness. Hibernation occurs in most species even in the lowlands and southern desert areas. Only the smaller species there escape its grip during brief warm spells. It is universal and prolonged at high altitude and in the north. Even the cold-tolerant salamanders of the humid coastal district may disappear for short periods during cold snaps. Estivation occurs in most species in the arid and semiarid warmer areas and in most of our northwestern salamanders. In dry summers the soil and duff of even the shady forests may dry out. Exceptions are certain frogs and toads and southern populations of the Tiger Salamander which breed during the period of summer rains.

Conditions of temperature and rainfall usually will be the best guide for successful field observation. Select warm days in spring and fall for reptiles and cool (but not freezing) wet weather for salamanders. Go to the mountains in summer, when spring reaches the higher elevations or to the lowlands of the Southwest during the period of summer rainfall for reptiles and frogs. Weather, however, is not the entire story. Some seasonal activity patterns appear to be inborn and partly independent of climatic and seasonal effects. Possibly in response to internal timing mechanisms some species disappear from the surface when conditions of temperature and humidity seem favorable. Be guided by information in the accounts.

Knowledge of the pattern of daily activity is also important. Most species are diurnal and unless otherwise noted diurnality may be assumed. In many species activity is greatest in mid-morning and in mid- or late afternoon. Many amphibians, the geckos, and some snakes are nocturnal. Some species change their daily pattern with season, being diurnal when days are short and cool and nocturnal during warm summer months. Crepuscular species prowl at twilight.

Habits: Manner of locomotion, defense postures, and other aspects of behavior may aid identification. The defense pose of the salamander Ensatina (p. 44) and the tail-coiling habit of the Ringneck Snake identify these forms as surely as color. When considered helpful to identification, notes on habits and behavior have been included. With respect to reproductive habits, assume all species to be egg-laying unless otherwise noted.

Food: Amphibians will eat almost any creature that moves and can be swallowed; therefore food items have not been listed. Reptiles, on the other hand, are usually more particular in their tastes, so their food habits are described in some detail. Information on diet may be of interest to persons who wish to keep reptiles and amphibians for study.

Subspecies: The characteristics of many species differ in various parts of their ranges. Color may change with the prevailing color of soil, the scale counts and arrangement may differ with latitude, and less easily detected but important changes may occur in physiology and behavior. Many such variants have been described as subspecies and the variable species of which they are a part is referred to as "polytypic." However, professional herpetologists differ in their opinions as to the magnitude and nature of differences justifying application of subspecies names. Most persons using this book will be little interested in subspecies. Nevertheless, some of the variants are well marked and in certain respects display greater differences than exist among some species. The subspecies of the salamander Ensatina (Plates 3, 4) are an example. It would be unfortunate to disregard such distinct forms.

I have been selective in recognizing subspecies. Certain ones have been ignored pending intensive study of total species variation, others because the differences described are not easily detected. One or more subspecies described for the following species have been omitted from this book: Rough-skinned Newt; Wood, Spotted, and Leopard Frogs; Pond Slider; Zebra-tailed, Lesser Earless, Leopard, Collared, Granite Night, Crevice Spiny, Sagebrush, and Tree Lizards, and Western and Texas Blind, Checkered Garter, and Western Ground Snakes.

Distribution Maps: The range of each species is shown in pattern (dots, crosshatching, etc.) on the 190 maps at the back of the book. Only one species generally is included on each map. Subspecies that occur entirely outside our area are outlined in finely dotted grayish pattern. Specific and subspecific names on the maps can be distinguished by type size: the former are the larger and are followed by the scientific name; scientific names of subspecies are given in the text. Question marks on the maps signify doubt as to accuracy of range boundaries or whether or not the species occurs in the area.

Subspecies distributions usually fit together like the pieces of a jigsaw puzzle. At points of contact, characteristics of one subspecies usually change gradually into those of another. Such zones of change are known as areas of "intergradation." Patterns representing some subspecies overlap (Map 60), whereas others are separated by areas of solid black (Map 10). Both arrangements represent broad areas of intergradation. Black is used when the scale is small or the area of intergradation is complicated. Few areas of intergradation have been studied in sufficient detail to make such precise representation possible on all maps.

Ranges are never as continuous as shown. In the West, with its varied topography and climate, spotty or "disjunct" distributions are the rule. Supplement map information with knowledge of habitat. Fringe-toed lizards will not be found on rocky hillsides, nor Chuckwallas on sand dunes. Many miles of uninhabited territory may separate colonies of such species.

Isolated populations are represented by black dots or patches of appropriate pattern, or, when reported from a single locality, by the symbol X. Most of these isolated populations are also mentioned in the accounts. Ordinarily they are remnants of more widespread populations formerly living over a much larger area. Examples are salamanders and frogs on mountaintops in the desert. Some isolates, however, are the result of introductions, such as the Bullfrog west of the Rockies.

If a reptile or amphibian is found outside its known range, one of the following explanations may apply. (1) A new locality of occurrence may have been discovered. Many areas in the West have been little explored. Even new species still turn up: the Limestone Salamander was discovered in 1954, not far from a roadside drinking fountain on the all-year highway into Yosemite National Park. (2) An unusual individual may have been found — a hybrid or oddly marked specimen that does not fit the brief descriptions in this book. Such individuals are especially likely to occur in areas of intergradation. Consult the species accounts for remarks concerning areas of hybridization. (3) A waif may have been found, transported out of its normal range by natural or human agency. Tiger Salamanders appear in cotton fields in the desert in Arizona, having metamorphosed from escaped larvae used as fish bait. Increasing commercial and private traffic in amphibians and reptiles is a growing source of such introductions.

A map showing the distribution of natural vegetation (pp. 226–27) is included to help explain the boundaries of the species and subspecies ranges, and to aid search for new localities. Vegetation belts reflect conditions of climate and terrain that greatly influence distribution. Note how the ranges of the Chuckwalla and Desert Iguana stop at the northern limit of creosote bush in southern Nevada. With the construction of new roads and the increase in number of people entering remote areas, much new information on distribution will be forthcoming. Keep the maps up to date by adding localities from the literature and personal study. Use them as a life list by checking off species as they are encountered.

Making Captures

MANY reptiles and amphibians can simply be picked up. No special methods are needed to capture them. Individuals that have taken refuge under logs, rocks, and boards may be sluggish or momentarily light-struck. Active ones abroad on the surface often can be overtaken before they escape into a burrow or other retreat. A fast snake may be pinioned lightly underfoot while a neck hold is secured. A wrecking bar can be used as a general-purpose tool to pry open crevices, pull loose bark, scrape through leaf litter or rock rubble, and pin down snakes. Gloves will help reduce wear and tear. However, success in making captures will be greatly increased if a few standard techniques are used.

Making and Using a Snake Stick: The traditional forked snake stick is unsatisfactory for catching snakes. Instead, attach an angle iron to the end of a broom handle or a 4-foot length of ¾-inch doweling, placing the surface of the iron flush with the end of the dowel. Bevel the free edge so that it will slip easily beneath a snake when the animal is on a hard surface such as pavement. The bar can be used either as a hook to pull a snake from brush or rocks or to pin it down while a neck hold is secured. Although the bite of even our largest nonvenomous species will only superficially lacerate the skin, most people prefer to avoid being bitten. Therefore, use gloves in capturing large snakes or maneuver the snake stick to the head region so that the animal can be grasped just behind the head. Thumb and index finger should be against the rear of the jaws; if there is slack the snake may turn and bite.

Noosing: Most lizards and some snakes when warm are too fast to catch by hand. A slip noose of thread, fishline, Nylon leader, or copper wire can be used to snare them. Use No. 50 thread for lizards no larger than a fence lizard and No. 8 thread, fishline, or leader for larger species. The noose should be tied to the notched end of a slender stick or through the terminal rung of a telescopic fishing rod to prevent its pulling off. The shank should be short, usually no more than 6 inches long when the noose is open. If excessively long, it may become tangled in vegetation or be blown about so that it is hard to control. A wire noose avoids this difficulty and can be bent to thrust into small openings. Make a small loop of ¼-inch diameter at the end of a thread. Tie the loop with a square knot so that it will not close. Pass the shank through the loop and attach it to the pole. Should the noose tend to close when in use, open to the desired diameter and moisten with saliva both loop and shank where they come into contact.

To make a copper wire noose cut a 10- or 12-inch length from an electric light cord. "Zipcord," obtainable in most hardware stores, can be used. Remove the insulation and separate out a single strand of wire. Twist the ends of the remaining strands in opposite directions so that they will not separate. Coil the bundle for convenience in carrying. Since copper wire nooses must be replaced frequently, a reserve supply will be needed. Twist a small loop of $\frac{1}{8}$- to $\frac{1}{4}$-inch diameter at the end of the strand. Pass the shank through and orient the loop so that the shank moves freely; compress the sides of the loop slightly to make it somewhat elongate; then curve the loop to conform to the lizard's neck. In attaching the noose, take several turns around the end of the pole and twist the free end of the wire and shank together. Work close to the pole to make sure the attachment is firm. Then wind the free end of the wire along the shank to strengthen its base. It is here that most breakage occurs. After noosing a lizard, reduce the diameter of the noose to $\frac{1}{2}$ inch or less and carefully untwist all kinks. Pass the shank between thumb and index finger to straighten it. Re-form the noose to the desired diameter and reshape the "neck" curve in the loop.

In noosing a lizard avoid quick movements. When the noose is within 5 or 6 inches of the head, move it slowly or pause for a moment, allowing the lizard to become accustomed to the presence of a strange object nearby; then move the remaining distance gradually. When the noose has passed over the lizard's head and has reached the neck region, jerk upward and slightly backward. Remove the animal quickly, before it has a chance to wriggle free. Wary species can sometimes be noosed by creating a diversion. Gently shake a handkerchief at arm's length to one side or wriggle your fingers to attract attention away from the noose.

Snakes can also be noosed. Noosing is one of the safest ways to capture venomous species. If done properly one need not touch the snake at any time. Noose a rattler with a 3- or 4-foot length of heavy twine tied securely to the end of the snake stick, and drop the snake, at arm's length, into a large box or can (garbage can) with tightly fitting lid. With lid in place, snake resting on the bottom of the container, and twine still attached, cut the twine near the end of the snake stick and loosen the lid slightly to allow the cut end to fall free into the container. The lid should then be secured. The snake will readily crawl out of the loosened noose.

Although noosing may appear cruel, it rarely does harm. Only a heavy-bodied snake with a slender neck (such as a rattler) may be injured if it thrashes violently when suspended. Support part of the weight of such snakes by resting their hindquarters on the ground.

Night Driving: Certain snakes, geckos, toads, and salamanders can be found on highways at night. Reptiles may be attracted to the warmth of the pavement and amphibians to roadside ditches. Drive slowly (15 to 20 miles per hour) and watch both pavement and shoulders. Select roads that traverse suitable habitat. An ideal road is dark-colored, little-traveled, and without curbs or broad, bare shoulders. Roads with bordering wild-plant growth are especially favorable. Small species can easily be overlooked. On dark pavement the yellow spots of a Tiger Salamander may resemble pale-colored pebbles, a blind snake can be mistaken for a twig, and a toad for a rock. Check all suspicious-looking objects, even if it means stopping for fan-belt snakes, banana-peel lizards, and other artifacts.

Success in night collecting will depend in large part on weather conditions, particularly temperature, and not just the weather at the time but that which prevailed several days or a week before. When looking for reptiles avoid cool evenings. Air temperatures below 60° to 65° F. will usually be too low. However, if the pavement remains warm some individuals may be found. Bright moonlight and winds seem to depress activity. Warmth is less important to amphibians. Some salamanders may be abroad at a few degrees above freezing.

Wet weather is the time for amphibians. After rains in arid portions of the Southwest, the response of frogs and toads, long ensconced below dry sunbaked earth, may be dramatic. Within an hour an area powder-dry for many months may reverberate with their cries and the ground may swarm with hopping forms. Watch for thunderstorms. In open terrain where there are good roads and broad vistas, one can sometimes spot a storm and drive to it in time to arrive just after dark during or shortly after rain.

Triangulation: To locate a small, calling animal hidden in a large expanse of rough terrain would appear to be almost impossible. However, by means of triangulation it usually can be accomplished easily. The technique is particularly helpful in finding creatures whose voices are ventriloquial and thus give a deceptive impression of location. Triangulation is best done by two people. When a calling frog, for example, has been singled out of a chorus, and its approximate position determined, move 15 to 30 feet apart and listen quietly. After a few moments of listening each person should decide for himself, without discussion with his partner, the location of the sound. Then, at a signal, each should point with arm extended and sight on a distant object that will serve as a reference point. Finally, both should walk forward toward the reference point and seek the animal where pathways cross. If alone, one can listen at a position for a time, decide on direction, then move to the left or right and listen again. Triangulation is often easier to do at night than in the daytime if flashlights or headlamps with distinct beams are used; the point of intersection of the beams can be determined precisely. The lights should not be turned on, however, until direction is determined. Sudden illumination may alarm wary species and they may not call again for some time. First trials may not bring success, and it may be necessary to withdraw and repeat the procedure several times.

Eyeshines: Fortunately for the nighttime observer, many animals reflect light from their eyes. One of the pleasures in the field is to walk quietly through wild country at night, pausing occasionally to illuminate the shadows with headlamp or flashlight in search of eyeshines. Dewdrops and eyes of spiders glint silver and green, those of moths and toads yellow or red; a murky stream becomes a cascade of light. To obtain an eyeshine it is necessary to have the light source near one's eyes. A flashlight should be held at the side of the head or its base against one's forehead. A headlamp permits the hands to be free. The eyeshine method works best on toads, frogs, and turtles. Eyeshines of snakes and salamanders are too faint to be seen well and our lizards are chiefly diurnal.

Tracking: Seek areas of fine loose soil, sand, or mud — sandy flats, dunes, dusty roads, trails, fresh mud of washes, or the banks of ponds and streams. Go out when the sun is low and highlights and shadows are strong. Start early, before there is a maze of tracks, or later in the day after a wind has erased old tracks and new ones are appearing. Follow a fresh track. Direction of travel can be determined by ridges formed by backward pressure of toes, feet, or coils of a snake. Tracking demands attention to details and use of clues. From meager evidence an interesting story may unfold. I once tracked a lizard across the barren rippled surface of a sand dune. The track indicated that at first the animal had moved slowly. Marks of all four feet showed, the stride was short, the tail dragged. Then the track of a roadrunner appeared, a lizard-eating bird. The lizard's stride suddenly lengthened and marks of only two feet could be seen; the tail mark disappeared. The lizard was running now, on its hind legs with tail lifted. An occasional small dent indicated that at high speed it occasionally touched down with its front feet to maintain balance. Just over the crest of the dune, the track suddenly stopped. To one side was a faint V-shaped mark. The roadrunner track continued at full clip over the hill, then slowed and wandered. The bird seemed confused. I grabbed at the V-shaped mark and something wriggled beneath it. In my hand I held a beautiful fringe-toed lizard.

Containers for Specimens: Cloth bags are standard for transporting reptiles. Use flour or sugar sacks, inexpensive pillowcases, or bags made specifically for the purpose. Useful sizes are 24 x 10 inches and 40 x 20 inches. They may be made from unbleached muslin. Sew with French seams and hem the top. Attach a drawstring 2 to 4 inches below the hem by sewing a 12-inch length of heavy twine, at its midpoint, to the side of the bag. The bags are long and the top can be wound around one's belt to prevent the bag from working loose. The length also permits doubling back the top in tying it closed — some snakes have remarkable ability to work their way out of sacks. Inspect the sacks occasionally to detect holes or loose threads that might snarl specimens. Even small holes may give trouble, because they may be enlarged by the probing efforts of captives.

Quart or gallon glass or plastic jars with screw caps are better than bags for carrying amphibians. Place damp moss, leaves, or moist paper towels in the bottom to provide moisture. Avoid dirt and rocks. Punch a few holes in the lid for air. Punch outward so that sharp edges will not damage specimens, and file the edges to avoid personal injury in handling (or make the holes with an electric drill). In perforating lids, make only four or five $\frac{1}{8}$-inch openings. Numerous holes may result in damage to specimens through drying. A knapsack or canvas shoulder bag is convenient for carrying sacks and other collecting gear.

III

Caring for Captives

Temporary Quarters: For temporary housing, gallon mayonnaise jars with perforated lids may be used. Place sand or pea gravel in the bottom for reptiles or moist earth for amphibians. A small block of wood, propped up off the substratum, can serve as cover and a twig can be put in for climbing species.

Cages: A permanent cage can be made of wood or glass. A container approximately 15 x 30 x 18 inches deep will be adequate for most species. If of wood, one of the long sides should be of glass and the top should be screened. If screening is kept at the top, there is less chance that snakes will rub their noses raw in attempts to get out.

To make a glass cage, have a glazier cut panels for the sides, ends, and bottom. Assemble these by taping together with masking tape. Tape the outside of the joints only: if tape is placed in the corners lizards may climb out. The surface must be slippery. Tape the rim of the cage to cover sharp edges. Cover with ¼-inch hardware cloth bent to fit as a lid.

Substratum: The type of substratum will depend on the animals to be confined. Clean pea gravel can be used for amphibians that enter water — frogs, toads, newts, and ambystomid salamanders. It need not be wet if a water dish is always kept filled so that the animals can immerse themselves and a moist shelter is available. Some lizards and snakes can also be kept on such a surface. Sand should be provided species that habitually bury themselves. Examples are the horned, spiny, earless, Zebra-tailed, and fringe-toed lizards, the Rubber Boa, hognose, ground, and sand snakes. From time to time remove the soiled surface layer and replace with fresh material. Lungless salamanders should be given damp earth strewn with dead leaves. Sprinkle the surface occasionally to keep it moist. Terrariums should always offer hiding places for the confined animals. Construct crevices or tunnels by propping up boards or rocks and anchoring them so that they will not collapse. Sink a water dish in the substratum; but keep the rim aboveground to keep the water from draining away by capillary action. Lizards and snakes can be provided water from a birdcage drinking tube. Fill the trough with gravel to prevent their getting into the vertical reservoir chamber and drowning. Tape a small bar magnet at the top and bottom of the

14

tube and a metal plate to the side of the cage. The drinking container will then be held firmly in an upright position and can be refilled and replaced with ease.

Temperature: The cages of reptiles must be heated. Place a 75- to 100-watt light at one end with the bulb 8 to 10 inches above the substratum. The heat source should be at the opposite end from the shelter. Check temperature. The cool end should not go above 75° to 80° F. If it goes higher, reduce wattage. Lower temperatures will be no cause for concern. If the light has a reflector, as in a desk lamp, it will help concentrate the heat and will reduce glare.

Feeding: Most amphibians, lizards, and some of the smaller snakes will eat live mealworms, which can be purchased in pet shops, but if captives are to be maintained for long periods a mealworm colony should be established. Cut out the side of a clean 5-gallon can, leaving enough border so the edges can be turned under to form a smooth-edged overhang. Cover with window screening to keep out moths and spiders. Place 1½ to 2 inches of wheat bran in the bottom and introduce the worms. Expand the colony to other cans as needed. Occasionally place half a potato or a piece of cabbage (including the stalk) in the container to provide moisture and variety in the diet. Replace bran as necessary. When feces accumulate, sift to extract the worms and discard. Since animals on a diet of mealworms fed only bran may languish, place the worms in a container with a shallow layer of egg-layer mash or other enriched meal the day before they are to be used in feeding. Your captive animals will then get not only the worms but the enriched mash contained in their digestive tracts.

Termites can also be reared. Keep them in plastic freezer trays (8 x 11 x 4 inches) with one or two small holes bored in the tops and feed them paper toweling. Place 1 inch of coarse sand in the bottom of the tray and a 2-inch stack of towels on top. The towels should be separated and restacked so they are no longer interleaved. Moisten both sand and towels. Introduce several hundred termites. The termites will make tunnels in the towels and, by separating layers of the towels, you can remove them as needed. If winged sexual forms have been included and demands are not great, the colony will maintain itself indefinitely.

Colonies of mealworms and termites are subject to attack by ants. It may be necessary to put containers in trays of water or keep them on stands, the legs of which are placed in cans of oil or water, thereby providing moats that ants cannot cross.

Rearing Amphibian Larvae: In rearing larvae, essentials are well-oxygenated, uncontaminated water, avoidance of crowding and high temperatures, and adequate food. Suitable oxygen levels can be maintained by rearing only 3 or 4 tadpoles per gallon of water, using a tray instead of a jar to increase the amount of water surface exposed to the air, and changing the water once every few days. Use a tea strainer in handling larvae. Most species will do well at room temperature, but Olympic Salamander larvae and tadpoles of the Tailed Frog should be kept at lower temperatures and their aquarium water should be thoroughly oxygenated by vigorous air flow from an aerator.

Herbivorous tadpoles can be fed algae (green pond scum), spinach, or lettuce (boiled to help soften the tissues and reduce rate of decay), and/or egg-layer mash. Mash can be sprinkled on the surface. Bits of egg yolk or luncheon meat may be offered to provide protein. Carnivorous larvae (spadefoot tadpoles and all salamander larvae) can be fed live brine shrimp (purchased in pet shops), bits of fresh liver, luncheon meat, earthworms, and small animals shaken from the roots and leaves of pond plants. Roots of the floating water hyacinth are often rich in small organisms relished by amphibian larvae. Watch overfeeding and contamination of the water by uneaten decayed food.

As the time for transformation approaches, prepare a rocky shore for emergence on land. Imminent transformation is indicated in salamander larvae by atrophy of the gills and reduction in size of the tail fins, and in tadpoles by appearance of the forelimbs and atrophy of the tail. In general, it is best to release amphibians after transformation because of the difficulty in providing them with small live animal food. If a few transformed individuals are kept, supply food by means of a Berlese funnel. Tape a large opaque plastic funnel to the bottom of a metal cylinder (gallon can with both ends removed). Turn the cylinder upright and fill with dead leaf litter scraped from beneath trees. Before selecting the litter, remove the surface layer and look closely to be sure there are plenty of small animals present. To make certain that the contained animals can move freely, avoid compacting the litter when it is placed in the funnel. Gradually heat and dry out the upper layers with light from a desk lamp, removing the dried material as the animals move downward. By repeated drying and removal of leaves, lowering the lamp each time, the animals can be driven into a collecting tube at the spout of the funnel. A small piece of moist paper toweling should be placed in this tube and its connection with the funnel should be sealed with cotton to prevent the animals from escaping.

Rearing Reptile Eggs: Sooner or later the guardian of captive reptiles will be confronted with a batch of eggs. Until recently, the fate of such eggs was almost always assured — they would spoil. Now, however, there is an excellent technique for rearing them that results in a high rate of survival. Since the eggs and young of many reptiles are little known, here is an opportunity for obtaining new information. Keep records on the length of incubation, the process of hatching, and size and coloration of the young. Be sure to record the temperature under which the eggs developed.

Place a layer of damp earth, peat moss, or sand in the bottom of a plastic bag. Pat the surface smooth and make a dent with your index finger to hold each egg. Dents should be far enough apart so that the eggs do not touch; then if one spoils it will not contaminate the rest. Billow out the sides of the bag and draw the top together, sealing it with a rubber band. Place at room temperature. If it is kept in lighted surroundings, the light may tend to inhibit the growth of mold. Watch moisture droplets on the inside of the bag. If they disappear and the substratum seems dry, add a little water with a teaspoon.

Choice of Captives: In selecting reptiles and amphibians for laboratory or home study, consider problems of feeding and care. Some species can be kept more easily than others. If a captive does not feed well, release it — where found or in similar habitat, if possible — and get another. There may be great individual differences in feeding. Keep the number of captive animals small to facilitate observation and care.

IV

Field Study and Protection

Field Study: There is much to be learned about the distribution, habits, and behavior of western reptiles and amphibians. The many question marks on the range maps should be a challenge to filling in gaps in our knowledge of distribution. We have not even found the eggs or young of some species, and much remains to be learned about time of breeding, courtship behavior, enemies, and other matters.

A field notebook is essential. Write notes in nonfading waterproof black ink to make a permanent record. Use a hard-back (7½ x 10 inches) looseleaf notebook. Enter your name in the upper left-hand corner (Fig. 3) and head each page with the species name, entering below your observations by locality and date. Group together pages pertaining to each species. In addition to the species account, keep a journal. Describe the route traveled and general features of terrain, vegetation, and weather. When an animal is found, watch it for a time from a distance if possible. Field glasses will help. Describe the ground surface (sand, hardpan, rock), vegetation (grassland, brush, or forest — listing species of plants if possible), and moisture conditions. Note other animals present. Attempt to interpret what is seen.

If the locality can be visited frequently, opportunity is afforded for an extended study. Individuals of a species can be marked, measured, sexed, and released at points of capture. The area can be mapped, using as reference points rock outcrops, trees, and other natural features, or numbered stakes set out in a grid (Fig. 4). Movements of individuals, their interrelationships, activity patterns, growth rate, and other facts can be ascertained.

Mark salamanders, lizards, and frogs by removing two or more toes in different combinations, but avoid removing two toes on the same foot. Toes can be snipped quickly with sharp scissors. This is of little disturbance to the animal; a lizard that has just been toe-clipped may accept food, and thus pain does not appear to be severe or prolonged. Salamanders regenerate their toes, and reclipping from time to time may be necessary. Snakes can be marked by cutting out small wedges of skin from the ventral scutes and recording scute number, counted forward from the anal scale. By making two cuts, one on each side and including the caudal scutes, many combinations are possible. Cuts must be entirely through the skin, down to the quick, if they are to form a recognizable scar. Mark turtles by notching the margin of the shell with a file. Two or more marginal shields should be used, counting posteriorly from the nuchal. A large number of combinations are possible. Notches should be deep enough to scar the underlying bone.

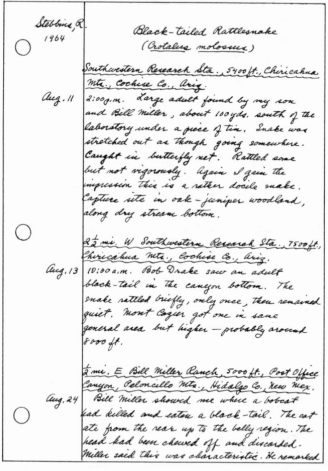

Fig. 3. Sample page from field notebook

Small temporary marks, recognizable at a distance, can be applied to lizards and snakes, but they may have the disadvantage of spoiling the concealing effect of the normal pattern and may thus reduce the animal's chances of survival. Such marks, however, can be inconspicuous and, if applied in diagnostic arrangements, can save one the trouble of frequent recaptures and disturbance of the marked animals. The marks also make possible determination of the frequency of shedding. Mongol water-color pencils are excellent, and the colors can be put on in the field by moistening with saliva the surface to be marked. Each marked animal should be given a number in the field notebook and the date and place of captures, sex, and size (snout-vent length) recorded.

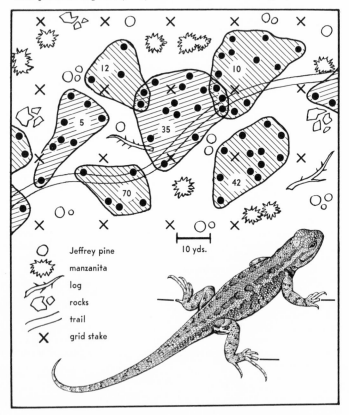

Fig. 4. Map of study area, showing home ranges of marked lizards

Locations of captures should be plotted on the map of the study area.

Figure 4 illustrates the kind of results that can be obtained. The home ranges of six Sagebrush Lizards are shown. The lizards were given identification numbers and were permanently marked by removal of two or more toes in different combinations (see illus.). Recaptures (black dots) were plotted with reference to numbered stakes (X) arranged in a grid at 20-yard intervals, and were located by pacing the distance to the two nearest stakes. Toes removed from the lizard shown are right fore 4, right hind 3, left hind 5, expressed as RF4-RH3-LH5.

Such field studies are recommended rather than the amassing of large numbers of hapless captives. The animals remain little disturbed in their natural setting. Since they are marked and under study, they appeal in much the same way as one's pets, yet do not demand care. Information obtained is more likely to be reliable than that procured under artificial conditions, and there is always the excitement of the hunt and the anticipation of meeting an old friend.

Protection: Reptiles and amphibians are important to us in many ways. They play a part in the balance of nature; they are a storehouse of unexplored scientific information that can benefit us; they have contributed enormously to the advance of vertebrate physiology and embryology, and they enhance the outdoor experiences of a growing number of people who gain pleasure from observing them. Yet at a time of growing awareness of their value, their numbers are declining. The greatest destructive force is habitat disturbance. Most species of wild animals are adapted to a specific and complex set of conditions which must be met if they are to survive. Growth of the human population brings great and rapid changes. Marshes are drained, streams are placed in concrete troughs, canyons are dammed and inundated, the ground is cleared for subdivisions and highways, agriculture spreads into marginal lands and, spurred on by water developments, reaches out even into deserts, the stronghold of reptiles. Air, water, and soil are contaminated. Although a few species may be temporarily benefited by some of these changes, most are not and the list of creatures rendered extinct in historic times can be expected to grow. The trend is toward an ordered, domesticated world, reduced in organic variety and crowded with people and their possessions. Interest in wildlife preservation cannot be separated from concern with efforts to limit human population growth and prevent careless exploitation of remaining natural areas.

Throughout this book I have given particular attention to methods of collecting, because it is often necessary to have the animals in hand for identification. This information can be misused. Some populations of reptiles and amphibians have been severely damaged by overcollecting and by disruption of habitat.

Commercial traffic in reptiles and amphibians has sometimes been damaging and increases the probability of the establishment of exotics. Amateur trading of live specimens has a similar effect. This practice and the development of private collections should, in general, be discouraged. Establishment of study collections is better left to educational and scientific institutions. The number of animals kept as pets should be small, and when they are released they should be returned to their area of origin or given to a scientific institution. In obtaining specimens treat the habitat with special care. Replace rocks, logs, and other objects turned over in the search, to minimize disturbance to the microenvironment and in consideration of people who will follow. Some populations are so small that they should not be collected at all. Many of the isolated populations represented on the maps by the symbol X are examples.

V

Identification Keys

THESE FOUR KEYS are designed to help locate the plates illustrating the species. All major groups of reptiles and amphibians are included except the turtles — they are easily recognized and there are few western species (see Plates 14, 15, and 16).

To aid recognition, species have been grouped by means of easily observed characteristics, sometimes without regard for relationships. For example, the kingsnakes, Long-nosed Snake, and coral snakes are grouped because they are banded; the Vine, hook-nosed, leaf-nosed, and Western Hognose Snakes because they have modified snouts. Those interested in taxonomic relationships will find such information in the text.

At each step in a key a choice must be made between two alternatives. To illustrate: in the salamander key below, decide first whether or not the animal has a nasolabial groove (furrow between the nostril and edge of lip), alternatives 1A and 1B. Examine also its teeth and skin. If 1A is selected, go to alternative 3A or 3B, where again a choice must be made. If 1B is chosen, go to 2A or 2B, thence to the plates.

Drawings illustrating key characteristics accompany each key. Numbers in parentheses in the keys refer to the numbered parts of each drawing; the right-hand column leads to the next step in the key or else to the identification plate(s). Consult also the illustrations on the endpapers of the book.

SALAMANDERS

Salamanders are lizardlike but lack scales and claws and have a moist, soft skin. See Fig. 5 for numbers in parentheses.

1A. Nasolabial groove present (1); clusters of teeth at back of roof of mouth (2); skin always smooth
Lungless Salamanders   3

1B. Nasolabial groove and tooth clusters absent; skin smooth or rough   2

2A. Teeth in roof of mouth in 2 diverging longitudinal rows (3); skin rough, except in breeding males   **Newts**   Pl. 1

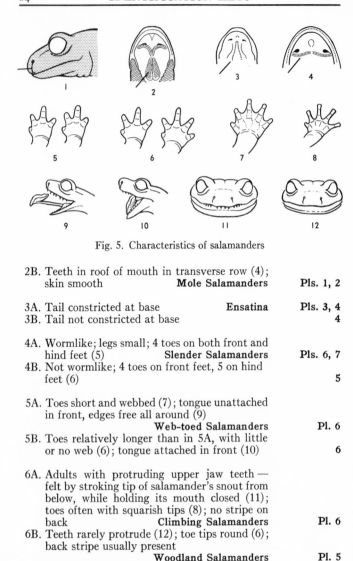

Fig. 5. Characteristics of salamanders

2B. Teeth in roof of mouth in transverse row (4);
skin smooth   **Mole Salamanders**   **Pls. 1, 2**

3A. Tail constricted at base   **Ensatina**   **Pls. 3, 4**
3B. Tail not constricted at base   **4**

4A. Wormlike; legs small; 4 toes on both front and
hind feet (5)   **Slender Salamanders**   **Pls. 6, 7**
4B. Not wormlike; 4 toes on front feet, 5 on hind
feet (6)   **5**

5A. Toes short and webbed (7); tongue unattached
in front, edges free all around (9)
     Web-toed Salamanders   **Pl. 6**
5B. Toes relatively longer than in 5A, with little
or no web (6); tongue attached in front (10)   **6**

6A. Adults with protruding upper jaw teeth —
felt by stroking tip of salamander's snout from
below, while holding its mouth closed (11);
toes often with squarish tips (8); no stripe on
back   **Climbing Salamanders**   **Pl. 6**
6B. Teeth rarely protrude (12); toe tips round (6);
back stripe usually present
     Woodland Salamanders   **Pl. 5**

FROGS AND TOADS

1A. 5th toe of hind foot broader than other toes (1)
                                   Tailed Frog   Pl. 13
1B. 5th toe not broadened (2)   2

2A. Fold of skin across head behind eyes (8)   3
2B. No skin fold on head   5

3A. Small brown or gray toad, adult body length
       under $1\frac{1}{2}$ in.; small black eyes; extreme s.
       Arizona   **Great Plains Narrow-mouthed Toad**   Pl. 13
3B. Adults larger than in 3A, eyes not small and
       black   4

Fig. 6. Characteristics of frogs and toads

4A. Eardrum conspicuous, partly transparent;
       many tubercles on underside of toes (4); back
       blotched   **Barking Frog**   Pl. 10 ·
4B. Eardrum not transparent; toes without tuber-
       cles; back has large spots with definite borders
                             Burrowing Treefrog   Pl. 13

5A. Parotoid glands present (9)   **True Toads**   Pls. 8, 9, 10
5B. Parotoid glands absent   6

6A. Single sharp-edged black "spade" on under-
       side of hind foot (5); eye with vertical pupil —

    except when pupil dilated (11)

                               Spadefoot Toads   **Pl. 8**

6B. No sharp-edged black "spade" on hind foot; rounded pale or brownish tubercle(s) sometimes present on hind foot; pupil not vertical (12)   **7**

7A. Extra joint at tips of toes (6); toe pads often present (3); no dorsolateral folds

                          Treefrogs and Allies   **Pl. 13**

7B. No extra joint at tip of toes (7); no toe pads; dorsolateral folds often present (10)

                                True Frogs   **Pls. 11, 12**

LIZARDS

All have scales and, with the exception of the snakelike legless lizard, clawed toes; movable eyelids distinguish the latter from the snakes.

1A. Eye with a fixed transparent covering; no movable eyelids   **2**

1B. Movable eyelids present   **3**

2A. Tips of toes very broad, with pair of large scales (1)   **Leaf-toed Gecko**   **Pl. 29**

2B. Toe tips not broadened   **Night Lizards**   **Pl. 26**

3A. Large, pale yellow catlike eyes with vertical pupil   **Banded Gecko**   **Pl. 29**

3B. Eyes not unusually large and pupil round or not easily seen (eyes dark)   **4**

4A. Snakelike, legless, but tiny eyes with movable lids   **California Legless Lizard**   **Pl. 29**

4B. Limbs present   **5**

5A. Scales cycloid, very smooth and shiny all over body (2)   **Skinks**   **Pl. 24**

5B. Scales not cycloid all over body   **6**

6A. Horns at back of head (11a, 11b); usually 1 or 2 rows of enlarged fringe scales at sides of body

                               Horned Lizards   **Pl. 18**

6B. No horns or fringe scales   **7**

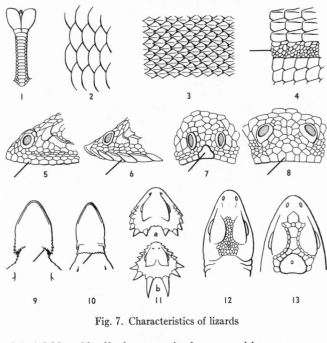

Fig. 7. Characteristics of lizards

7A. A fold on side of body, separating large squarish
    scales on back and belly (4) **Alligator Lizards**   **Pl. 25**
7B. No fold on side of body separating squarish
    back and belly scales   **8**

8A. 4th and 5th toes about same length; tail stout,
    much shorter than body, often sausage-shaped
    Gila Monster   **Pl. 17**
8B. 4th toe much longer than 5th; tail as long or
    longer than body, not swollen   **9**

9A. Great difference between back and belly scales
    — those on back fine and granular, those on
    belly many times larger and arranged in
    straight transverse and longitudinal rows
    Whiptails Pls. 27, 28, 29
9B. Back and belly scales not greatly different in
    size — those on belly usually overlap like
    shingles   **10**

10A. A single enlarged row of scales down middle
     of back   **Desert Iguana**   Pl. 20
10B. No enlarged row of scales down middle of back   11

11A. Rostral absent (8)   **Chuckwalla**   Pl. 17
11B. Rostral present (7)   12

12A. All scales on back keeled and pointed (3); an
     incomplete gular fold (9)   **Spiny Lizards**   Pls. 22, 23
12B. Some or all scales on back granular, if keeled
     often not pointed; complete gular fold (10)   13

13A. Labials separated by diagonal furrows (6);
     usually with distinct black crossbars or spots
     on underside of tail
     Fringe-toed, Zebra-tailed, and Earless Lizards   Pl. 19
13B. Labials separated by vertical furrows (5);
     underside of tail without black crossbars   14

14A. Scales on top of head between and behind eyes
     small (12); large, robust lizards
     Leopard and Collared Lizards   Pl. 20
14B. Scales on top of head between and behind
     eyes enlarged (13); slim lizards of small to
     medium size
     Side-blotched, Tree, and Banded Rock Lizards   Pl. 21

SNAKES

All are legless and lack eyelids; our single legless lizard has
movable eyelids and small ventral scales.

1A. Cycloid scales completely encircling body (1);
    no large ventrals; eyes pigmented spots under
    head scales.   **Slender Blind Snakes**   Pl. 30
1B. Belly scales (2) more than twice as broad as
    those on back and sides; eyes well developed   2

2A. Tail with rattle (3)   **Rattlesnakes**   Pls. 38, 39
2B. Tail without rattle   3

3A. Only small scales on underside of lower jaw
    between labials (4)   **Boas**   Pl. 30
3B. Large scales on underside of lower jaw between
    labials (5)   4

4A. Rostral modified — much enlarged, turned up,

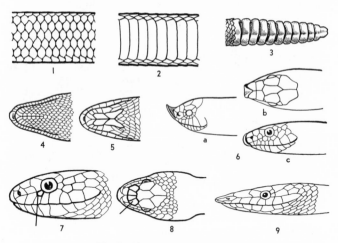

Fig. 8. Characteristics of snakes

and pointed (6a), or flat and attached patchlike to tip of snout (6b, 6c)   **Hognose,**
Hook-nosed, Patch-nosed, Leaf-nosed Snakes   Pl. 34
4B. Rostral normal, not greatly enlarged or shaped
   as in 4A   5

5A. Dorsal scales smooth   10
5B. Some or all dorsal scales keeled   6

6A. Scales weakly keeled along middle of back
   only, becoming smooth on sides   **Rat Snakes**   Pl. 32
6B. All dorsal scales keeled   7

7A. Plain green above and plain white or pale
   yellow below   **Rough Green Snake**   Pl. 33
7B. Not colored as in 7A   8

8A. 4 prefrontals (8)   **Gopher Snake**   Pl. 33
8B. 2 prefrontals (6b)   9

9A. Anal single; no scale pits
                     Garter and Lined Snakes Pls. 35, 36, 37
9B. Anal divided; scale pits present; in our area
   found only in e. Colorado and se. New Mexico
                                 Water Snakes   Pl. 37

10A. Plain green above (gray in preservative) and
plain white or pale yellow below   11
10B. Not colored as in 10A   12

11A. Lower preocular wedged between upper labials
(7)   **Racer**   Pl. 30
11B. Lower preocular not wedged between upper
labials   **Smooth Green Snake**   Pl. 33

12A. Lower preocular wedged between upper
labials (7)   **Racers and Whipsnakes**   Pl. 30
12B. Lower preocular not wedged between upper
labials   13

13A. Extremely slender, vinelike; head and snout
very long (9)   **Vine Snake**   Pl. 34
13B. Not vinelike; head not extremely long   14

14A. All ventral scales marked with regular narrow
black crossbands, a band at base of each scale;
tail with sharp point   **Sharp-tailed Snake**   Pl. 33
14B. All ventrals not uniformly marked with black
crossbands; markings, when present, more
widely spaced, confined to sides, or in less
regular arrangement; tail with or without
sharp point   15

15A. Plain-colored, without pattern on dorsum.
Uniformly colored head cap, often darker than
body and sometimes set off from body color by
whitish, yellow, or orange collar
Ringneck and Black-headed Snakes   Pls. 31, 35
15B. Body with dorsal pattern of spots, blotches,
crossbands, or stripes   16

16A. Belly pale and plain-colored or with dusky
bars, scattered dots or fine speckling, usually
confined to sides   17
16B. Belly marked with bold crossbands or bars or
sometimes plain black with pale spots
Coral, Long-nosed, and Kingsnakes   Pl. 31
**Ground, Shovel-nosed, and
Banded Sand Snakes**   Pl. 32

17A. Dorsal scales in 17 or fewer rows at midbody   18
17B. Dorsal scales in more than 17 rows   19

18A. Dorsal pattern of spots; vertical pupils
                              Night Snake   **Pl. 33**
18B. Dorsal surface plain or with pattern of cross-
     bands or a broad longitudinal stripe; pupils
     round or not visible   **Ground, Shovel-nosed,
                              and Banded Sand Snakes**   **Pl. 32**

19A. Head much broader than neck, with lyre-
     shaped marking; pupils vertical **Lyre Snakes**   **Pl. 33**
19B. Head only slightly broader than neck, no lyre-
     shaped marking; pupils not distinctly vertical
                              Glossy Snake   **Pl. 33**

VI

Salamanders

Mole Salamanders and Relatives:
Family Ambystomatidae

THESE salamanders vary greatly in size, proportions, and coloration but can be distinguished from all other western species by their teeth, which form a continuous or broken row across the roof of the mouth (Fig. 5, No. 4, p. 24). Typically they have a broad head, small eyes, prominent costal grooves, and the tail is flattened from side to side. Males usually have a bulbous vent and longer tail than females.

Except for the Pacific Giant and Olympic Salamanders, which may be found in or near water most of the year, ambystomatids are rarely seen except during their brief breeding season. Then they crawl over land to ponds, lakes, and streams and sometimes stumble into cellars or light wells. Migrations usually occur at night, during or after rains.

Most species breed in winter or spring. Breeding may start early, soon after ice melts from lakes and ponds, but at high altitudes and in the north it may be delayed until summer. Throughout the rest of the year, except occasionally during rains, these salamanders stay inside rotten logs and animal burrows, or in other moist places underground.

Larvae may be found all year. At high elevations and in the north, where temperatures are low and the growing season short, they may not transform until their second season. Some larvae (neotenics) may fail to transform and may breed in the larval condition.

To find ambystomatids go out at night, during or shortly after the first hard rain at the start of the breeding season, and drive slowly or walk through favorable habitats. Carry a gasoline lantern or other light that will illuminate a large area. Seine breeding ponds with a dip net or search under objects in moist places on land. Large larvae sometimes can be caught on a hook baited with meat, worms, or salmon eggs, or even on artificial flies floated nearby. Bait should be dropped in front of the salamanders or placed on the bottom near openings under rocks and logs.

A New World family ranging from se. Alaska and s. Labrador

to the southern part of the Mexican plateau. About 24 species — 5 in the West, some 15 in Mexico, and the remainder in the East.

TIGER SALAMANDER *Ambystoma tigrinum* **Pl. 2**

Identification: 3–6½. A large stocky salamander with *small eyes*, broad rounded snout, and *tubercles on underside of the feet*. No parotoid glands. Color varies greatly, depending upon locality. Over much of its range (California, e. and s. U.S. and Mexico) markings consist of spots and bars of white, cream, or yellow on a black background. Elsewhere the black ground color may be reduced to dusky spots or a more or less broken network of "tiger" markings. In the north-central part of its range the dorsal color may be plain olive or yellowish.

Frequents quiet water of ponds, reservoirs, lakes, temporary rain pools, and streams from arid sagebrush plains and rolling grassland to mountain meadows and forests. Adults found under objects near water or crawling at night to and from breeding sites. Migrations generally occur during or shortly after rains, in cold areas soon after the ice begins to melt from ponds. Adults spend much time underground in the burrows of ground squirrels, gophers, and badgers and usually emerge only for brief periods to breed. In the north and at high altitudes breeding occurs March through June, in the lowlands (California) mid-Dec. through Feb., and in the arid Southwest in July and Aug., during the period of summer rains. In California migrations occur with the first hard rains in Nov. In cold areas larvae may overwinter and are sometimes neotenic. Neotenics, known as axolotls (a Mexican Indian name), reach total length of 7 to 12 in.

Similar species: (1) Northwestern Salamander has parotoid glands, a glandular ridge on the tail, and lacks foot tubercles. (2) Black Salamander (p. 49) has a more rounded tail and projecting upper-jaw teeth, felt by stroking tip of snout.

Range: Eastern to western coasts of N. America; s. Canada to Puebla, Mexico. Absent from Great Basin, most of Pacific Coast, Mojave and Colorado Deserts, Appalachian region, and s. Florida. Near sea level in California to above 11,000 ft. in Rocky Mts.

Subspecies: GRAY TIGER SALAMANDER, *A. t. diaboli* (Fig. 10, opposite Pl. 2). Light olive, with scattered dusky spots. UTAH TIGER SALAMANDER, *A. t. utahensis* (Fig. 10). Above gray, brown, or blackish-brown with dark spots, or without definite markings; no yellow spots. BLOTCHED TIGER SALAMANDER, *A. t. melanostictum* (Fig. 10). Numerous light markings with indefinite borders; dark ground color often reduced to network. In Montana, barred individuals occur on the plains and mottled to solid green ones in the mountains. ARIZONA TIGER SALAMANDER, *A. t. nebulosum.* Above yellow-spotted, with less than 25 (usually 10 to 20) spots on back between front and hind limbs. Belly boldly marked with yellow. Isolated ponds in yellow pine forest on the South Rim of Grand Canyon contain salamanders of both the Utah and Arizona types. SONORA TIGER SALAMANDER, *A. t. stebbinsi.* Above spotted with usually more than 25 (20 to 30) spots on back between front and hind limbs. Belly brownish, not boldly marked with yellow, with only a few small yellowish spots. Parker Canyon, 5000 ft., Huachuca Mts., Santa Cruz Co., Arizona. CALIFORNIA TIGER SALAMANDER, *A. t. californiense* (illus.). Black above, with oval to bar-shaped white, cream, or yellow spots. Open woodland and grassland of California west of Sierra Nevada crest, from Sonoma Co. to Santa Barbara Co. and east to Sierran foothills. BARRED TIGER SALAMANDER, *A. t. mavortium* (illus.). Above black, with yellow spots and bars; neotenic larvae to 12 in.

In Arizona the native salamander populations of the central plateau may soon be thoroughly mixed because of the seining activities of bait dealers and the importation, as live fish bait, of larvae from Texas, New Mexico, and Colorado. Canals in the lowlands south of the plateau, formerly uninhabited by salamanders, now contain larvae; adults turn up in cotton fields.

Map 5

NORTHWESTERN SALAMANDER   *Ambystoma gracile*   **Pl. 2**
Identification: 3–4½. A brown or black salamander with broad head and relatively small eyes, *parotoid glands*, and a glandular thickening along the upper border of the tail. The glandular areas are pitted with openings of poison glands and the skin there is rougher than elsewhere. No tubercles on underside of feet. In northern part of the range, back flecked with cream or yellow.

Inhabits open grassland, woodland, or dense forest under rocks, boards, and logs near water. Look under driftwood on streambanks after storms, when water is receding. Spawns in ponds, lakes, and streams Jan.–July, late in the season in the north and at high altitude. In cold areas larvae may overwinter and some may be neotenic. When molested, adults close their eyes, assume a butting pose, elevate the tail, and secrete a sticky white poison from the glands on the head, back, and tail.
Similar species: See Tiger Salamander.
Range: Humid coast from extreme se. Alaska, chiefly west of crest of Cascade Mts., to mouth of Gualala River, California. Sea level to over 10,000 ft.
Subspecies: BROWN SALAMANDER, *A. g. gracile.* Plain brown above, often with touches of rust on head and tail; 2 joints in 4th toe of hind foot. BRITISH COLUMBIA SALAMANDER, *A. g. decorticatum.* Light flecks on dorsal surfaces; 3 joints in 4th toe.   Map 2

LONG-TOED SALAMANDER *Ambystoma macrodactylum* **Pl. 2**
Identification: 2⅛–3¼. A dusky or black salamander usually
with a *dorsal stripe* of tan, yellow, or olive-green. Stripe often
with irregular borders and in some subspecies more or less broken
into a series of spots. Usually a sprinkling of fine white flecks
on the sides. Belly dark brown or sooty. Foot tubercles present.

Frequents a great variety of habitats from the semiarid sagebrush and cheatgrass plains east of the Cascade Mts. to alpine
meadows and the barren rocky shores of high mountain lakes.
Found in piles of rotten wood, under bark, rotting logs, rocks,
and other objects near quiet water of ponds, lakes, or streams.
When in the water adults seem to prefer shallows near shore.

Breeds early, sometimes entering ponds not yet free of ice.
The time depends on elevation and latitude. In the lowlands to
the south breeding occurs in late Jan. or Feb. and in the mountains, or in the far north, from April to July. In cold areas larvae
may overwinter, transforming the following summer or fall. In
warmer areas, as in the lowlands of the Willamette Valley,
Oregon, adults migrate to breeding ponds in late Oct. and early
Nov. with the onset of fall rains and, except for cold spells,
remain active all winter.

Similar species: Striped plethodons have nasolabial grooves,
(Fig. 5, No. 1, p. 24), a different tooth pattern, and no foot
tubercles.

Range: Se. Alaska to Spicer Reservoir, Tuolumne Co., California, east to Rocky Mts. In Rockies south to cent. Idaho and
w. Montana. Isolated populations near Aptos, Santa Cruz Co.,
California. Near sea level to about 9000 ft. in Sierra Nevada,
California.

Subspecies: WESTERN LONG-TOED SALAMANDER, *A.
m. macrodactylum* (illus.). Dorsal stripe greenish to yellowish,
with indefinite edges, diffuse on head. Sides heavily sprinkled
with small white flecks, sometimes appearing whitewashed.
Dorsal ground color gray. EASTERN LONG-TOED SALA-
MANDER, *A. m. columbianum*. Dorsal stripe bright yellow to
tan, usually unbroken on body, even-edged or irregularly indented, its width exceeding distance between nostrils. Stripe
broken into well-defined spots on head. SOUTHERN LONG-
TOED SALAMANDER, *A. m. sigillatum* (illus.). Dorsal stripe
bright yellow, with irregular borders and often broken into
smooth-edged spots, its greatest width less than distance between
nostrils. Small distinct yellow spots on head. SANTA CRUZ
LONG-TOED SALAMANDER, *A. m. croceum* (illus.). Similar
to Southern Long-toed but stripe color yellow-orange and ground
color of back darker, usually black. Known from only two
localities: Valencia Lagoon near Aptos and ½ mi. northwest of
Ellicott Railroad Station, Santa Cruz Co., California. NORTH-
ERN LONG-TOED SALAMANDER, *A. m. krausei* (illus.).

Dorsal stripe yellow and unbroken, continuous onto snout and widest behind eyes; a large patch of stripe color on each eyelid; stripe narrow, its edges nearly parallel. Map 3

PACIFIC GIANT SALAMANDER *Dicamptodon ensatus* **Pl. 1**
Identification: 4½–6. A large, formidable-looking salamander with massive head and marbled coloration. Skin smooth and costal grooves inconspicuous. Above with a *network or irregular spots of black* on brown, gray, or purplish ground color. Three segments in the 4th toe of the hind foot; no foot tubercles.

Frequents damp forests in or near clear, cold streams or seepages and the rocky shores of mountain lakes. Found under logs, bark, rocks, and other objects near streams or crawling exposed in damp woods, even in daytime. Occasionally climbs, and has been recorded in trees and bushes to a height of 8 ft. In spring adults may be found in the vicinity of springs in the headwaters of streams, where they lay their eggs. Larvae frequent clear cold rivers, creeks, and lakes and can be found by carefully turning stones in shallow water or caught on a baited hook (see p. 32). In the south they hatch in winter but may not transform until their 2nd summer. Neotenic individuals may reach total length of nearly 12 in.

Voice: May emit a low-pitched rattling sound when molested.
Similar species: Mole salamanders (*Ambystoma*) lack marbled pattern and have 4 segments in the 4th toe of the hind foot.
Range: Extreme sw. B.C. to Santa Cruz Co., California. Inland in n. California to headwaters of Sacramento River. Rocky Mts. of Idaho and Montana. Some Rocky Mt. localities are: headwaters of Palouse River, Latah Co.; Mannering Creek, 12.2 mi. north of Harvard, Benewah Co.; Rock Run Creek, west of Monument Peak, Shoshone Co.; and South Fork of Salmon River, 5 mi. north of Knox, Valley Co., Idaho. Near sea level to over 7000 ft. Map 1

OLYMPIC SALAMANDER *Rhyacotriton olympicus* **Pl. 1**
Identification: 1⅔–2½. *Small size and large eyes* are distinctive. The diameter of the eye opening is about equal to the distance between the anterior eye corner and the tip of the snout. In other species, eye diameter only ½ to ⅓ this distance. Head small, body long, limbs and tail short. Above plain brown, or olive mottled with dusky; below orange or yellow. *Male:* Prominent, *squarish vent lobes.*

Inhabits cold mountain streams, springs, and seepages. When on land, usually found under stones within the splash zone, and in moss-covered talus where water trickles among the rocks; streams tend to be well shaded and the banks are often grown to moss and ferns. Probably breeds in spring and early summer. Larvae have short gills and adult proportions and are found in clear shallow water, in the muck of seepages, and in accumulations of dead leaves in creeks.

Range: West of Cascade crest from Olympic Peninsula, Washington, to 10 mi. south of Elk, Mendocino Co., California.

Subspecies: NORTHERN OLYMPIC SALAMANDER, *R. o. olympicus* (illus.). Above plain brown, speckled on sides with white; below yellow-orange, sparsely flecked with black. SOUTHERN OLYMPIC SALAMANDER, *R. o. variegatus* (illus.). Above olive, mottled with dusky; below yellowish green, heavily spotted with black.   Map 4

Newts: Family Salamandridae

IN North America this family is represented by the Pacific and eastern newts, with 3 species in each genus. The former ranges from Alaska to s. California, the latter chiefly east of the Great Plains. The family is also represented in Europe, North Africa, and Asia.

Pacific newts are plain brown or black above, yellow, orange, or red below. During much of the year they are terrestrial and rough-skinned, but they must enter ponds and streams to breed. Breeding males develop a smooth skin and flattened tail. Eastern newts are more aquatic and change directly from the larval stage into water-dwelling adults or into rough-skinned, round-tailed red efts that live on land for a while and then return to water.

Pacific Newts: Genus *Taricha*

READILY distinguished from all other western salamanders by their distinctive tooth pattern (Fig. 9, opposite Pl. 1), lack of costal grooves, and rough skin (except in breeding males). The latter have a smooth skin, flattened tail, swollen vent, and dark patches of roughened skin (nuptial pads) on the underside of the feet (Fig. 9).

Newts are the most familiar salamanders on the Pacific Coast. They are less disturbed by light than other species and are often seen crawling over land in the daytime or moving about fully exposed on the bottom of ponds, lakes, and streams. Their potent skin secretion repels most predators. When slapped on the back or seized, newts assume a characteristic swayback defense pose with eyes closed, head and tail bent upward, limbs extended, and toes flexed. The bright color of the ventral surface is brought into view and perhaps serves as a warning.

During or after rains in fall, winter, and spring (except during cold weather), these salamanders are often seen moving in large numbers to breeding sites. Summer is spent under bark, inside decayed logs, in rock crevices, and in the burrows of other animals.

ROUGH-SKINNED NEWT *Taricha granulosa*   **Opp. Pl. 1**
  Identification: 2¼–3½. A newt with *dark lower eyelids*. Above black to dark brown, sometimes tan. Below yellow to reddish orange. Dark color of the back stops abruptly on the sides or grades into the belly color. Eyes relatively small, usually not extending to outline of head when viewed from above. Teeth in roof of mouth in V-shaped arrangement. *Breeding male:* Above, brown to olive; a broad dusky patch on each side, smooth skin, bulbous vent, flattened tail, dark pads on feet.
  Frequents grassland, woodland, and forest, breeding from late Dec. to July in ponds, lakes, reservoirs, or slowly flowing streams. Our most aquatic newt. When on land, may be found crawling in the open or hiding under rocks, logs, bark, and in rotten wood. The Rough-skinned differs from other western newts in laying its eggs singly and, in some parts of its range, in curling the tip of its tail when in the extreme defense pose (see p. 37).
  Similar species: The California Newt usually has light-colored lower eyelids, larger eyes, and teeth in Y-shaped arrangement.
  Range: Humid coast from se. Alaska to s. Santa Cruz Co., California, chiefly west of crest of Cascade Mts.; south in foothills of Sierra Nevada to Magalia, Butte Co.; Moscow Mts., Idaho, and Thompson Falls, Sanders Co., Montana. Sea level to around 9000 ft.
  Subspecies: NORTHERN ROUGH-SKINNED NEWT, *T. g. granulosa*. Ventral surface with little or no dark blotching. CRATER LAKE NEWT, *T. g. mazamae*. Ventral surface heavily blotched with dusky. Crater Lake, Oregon.   Map 6

CALIFORNIA NEWT *Taricha torosa*   **Pl. 1**
  Identification: 2¾–3½. Similar to Rough-skinned Newt, but usually lighter brown above, less contrast between the dorsal and ventral color on the sides, *light-colored lower eyelids*, larger eyes, the corneal surfaces extending to or beyond outline of head when viewed from above, and teeth in roof of mouth usually in Y-shaped arrangement. *Breeding male:* Smooth skin, bulbous vent, flattened tail, dark pads on feet.
  Habitat similar to Rough-skinned Newt's but generally less humid. Breeds in ponds, reservoirs, and slowly flowing streams. In the Sierra Nevada and in the mountains of s. California, it enters the larger rivers and streams where it may frequent fast water. Goes to water during the first fall rains, breeding Dec. to May, with a peak from Feb. to April. In the Sierra, migrations start in Jan. or Feb. and breeding lasts until the end of April.
  Similar species: See Rough-skinned Newt.
  Range: Coast Ranges of California from Mendocino to San

Diego Co. (Boulder Creek) and western slope of Sierra Nevada. Isolated population at Squaw Creek, Shasta Co., California. Near sea level to 5000 ft.

Subspecies: COAST RANGE NEWT, *T. t. torosa*. As described above. Grotesquely warty individuals, known as the "Warty Newt," occur in the southern part of the range; the warts are thought to be caused by disease. Coexists with the Rough-skinned Newt from Santa Cruz to Mendocino Cos. SIERRA NEWT, *T. t. sierrae*. More orange above and below than Coast Range Newt; eyes paler yellow.   Map 8

RED-BELLIED NEWT *Taricha rivularis*   Pl. 1
Identification: 2¾–3¼. A *dark-eyed newt*. Eyes larger, head narrower, and snout longer than in other western species. Above brown to nearly black; below tomato-red. Dark color conspicuous on undersurfaces of limbs. A *prominent dark band across the vent*, especially broad in males. Less sex difference in skin texture than in other species.

A stream- or river-dwelling newt of coastal woodlands, entering water as early as the first week in Feb. and breeding from March to May in flowing water of rivers and creeks.
Similar species: (1) California and (2) Rough-skinned Newts have yellow eyes and less dark pigment on the underside of the limbs.
Range: Coastal region of California from Russian River, Sonoma Co., and Lower Lake and Kelsey Creek, Lake Co., north to Honeydew, Humboldt Co. Coexists with the Rough-skinned Newt but generally breeds in flowing water.   Map 9

Lungless Salamanders:
Family Plethodontidae

LARGEST family of salamanders; more than 130 species. Confined to the New World — s. Canada to n. Bolivia and e. Brazil — except for the web-toes (*Hydromantes*), which are represented by 2 species in Europe and 3 in California. Most are terrestrial, living under rocks, bark, logs, in rotten wood and animal burrows, but in e. America many species live in and near streams. Terrestrial forms rarely enter water, and lay their eggs in moist places on land. They lack a free-living larva and the young emerge fully formed. All western species are terrestrial.

All plethodontids are lungless. They breathe through their thin moist skin, which is smooth and slippery. All have a nasolabial groove (see Fig. 5, No. 1, p. 24), a hairline furrow that extends from the nostril to the edge of the upper lip and sometimes out onto a lobe (or palp). Tooth pattern is distinctive (Fig. 5, No. 2). The family name means "many teeth."

Mating occurs in fall, winter, and spring. Eggs are usually deposited in spring and summer (slender salamanders may lay in winter).

Woodland Salamanders: Genus *Plethodon*

SLIM-BODIED short-legged salamanders, usually with a dorsal stripe of reddish, tan, or yellow. Some 19 species in the U.S. and Canada; 6 in the Pacific Northwest, 1 in n. New Mexico, and the remainder in e. and s. U.S.

There are 4 toes on the front and 5 on the hind feet, the edges of the tongue are free except in front, the tail is round or oval and without a basal constriction, and the upper jaw teeth extend to the angle of mouth. Males typically have a broader head, more pointed lower jaw, and longer tail than females. Costal-groove counts are useful in distinguishing species. Count the groove over the front limb (even if not well developed) and all dorsolateral grooves anterior to the hind limb (even when 2 grooves join ventrally on the groin).

These salamanders usually frequent damp woods, where they are found by day under bark, logs, moss, in moist leaf litter, rotten wood, rock outcrops, and talus. They are active on the surface at night, usually during or shortly after rains.

DUNN'S SALAMANDER *Plethodon dunni* **Pl. 5**
  Identification: 2–3. *Dorsal stripe tan, yellow, or greenish-yellow,* brightening on the tail but *not reaching its tip.* Stripe flecked with dusky, the flecks sometimes nearly concealing it. Occasional melanics are dark-colored and unstriped; found in Benton Co., Oregon. Sides dark brown or black, spotted with yellowish or tan and speckled with white. Upper surface of base of limbs yellow, flecked with dusky, like the dorsal stripe. Below slaty, with small spots of yellowish or orange. Tail slightly flattened from side to side. Costal grooves 15 (rarely 16). *Male:* A small lobe on each side of rear margin of vent.

  Lives in moss-covered rock rubble of seepages and under rocks and logs on shady streambanks, preferring wetter locations than other western plethodons except Van Dyke's Salamander. Sometimes found in water trickles beneath stones and occasionally, when frightened, enters water and swims with eel-like movements.
  Similar species: Western Red-backed Salamander usually has 16 costal grooves, a network of light and dark markings on the belly (Fig. 11, opposite Pl. 5), and the stripe color extends to tip of the tail; in yellow-striped individuals, stripe lacks greenish-yellow tone of Dunn's Salamander.

Range: From near South Bend, Pacific Co., Washington, west of Cascade crest, to California border. Map 12

WESTERN RED-BACKED SALAMANDER Pl. 5
Plethodon vehiculum

Identification: 1½–3¼. Dorsal stripe usually well defined, tan, reddish brown, orange, yellow, or dusky edged with black. *Stripe with even edges*, extending to tip of tail. Tan or reddish-brown colors are most common, but sometimes all stripe colors are present at the same locality. Sides of body dusky, sprinkled with white. Occasionally all dark color is subdued and the stripe color suffuses the entire body. Such plain-colored individuals may be orange, pale yellow, or sooty. Below blue-gray with varying amounts of yellowish or orange flecking, which sometimes reduces the dark ventral color to a network or to scattered spots and blotches. *Costal grooves 16*, occasionally 15 or 17.

Found under rocks, logs, bark, and boards in damp locations in humid forests, but generally in drier locations than Dunn's Salamander, which shares its range in Oregon.

Similar species: See (1) Dunn's and (2) Larch Mountain Salamanders.

Range: Chiefly west of Cascade crest from sw. B.C., including Vancouver I., to Coos Co., Oregon. Map 11

VAN DYKE'S SALAMANDER *Plethodon vandykei* Pl. 5

Identification: 2–3. Dorsal stripe of yellowish, tan, or reddish with even or scalloped edges, bordered with black or dark brown. *Throat pale yellow*, contrasting in dark-bellied individuals with belly color, which is black or dusky, flecked with white. Large adults from Washington may be nearly plain dull yellow, tan, or pinkish rose (Willapa Hills), and the dark color of the sides and belly faint or absent. *Costal grooves 14*, rarely 15. *Young:* A conspicuous yellow dorsal stripe, black sides, black venter, and large *yellow throat patch*. *Male:* Nasolabial groove ends in a tubercle on upper lip.

Found under rocks, logs, and bark near lakes, rivers, and streams, often in seepages where the soil is thoroughly wet. Occurs in both wooded and open areas from the lowlands well up into the mountains.

Similar species: (1) Dunn's and (2) Western Red-backed Salamanders lack the pale throat. (3) The Larch Mountain Salamander has reddish ventral color. (4) Lack of a constriction at base of the tail distinguishes unstriped individuals from plain-colored Ensatina (p. 44).

Range: W. Washington, n. Idaho, and nw. Montana. To around 5000 ft.

Subspecies: WASHINGTON SALAMANDER, *P. v. vandykei*

(illus.). Broad, usually even-edged dorsal stripe of yellow or tan; some adults plain-colored; stripe color on upper surface of base of limbs. Willapa Hills, Olympic, and Cascade Mts., Washington. Coexists with Dunn's Salamander southeast of South Bend, Pacific Co., Washington. COEUR D'ALENE SALAMANDER, *P. v. idahoensis* (illus.). Dorsal stripe narrower and usually with scalloped borders, contrasting sharply with black of upper sides; upper surface of base of limbs dark-colored; below sooty, yellow throat conspicuous. Southern shore of Wolf Bay, Coeur d'Alene Lake, Kootenai Co., 5.5 mi. south of Emida, Benewah Co., and Lochsa River east of Lowell, Idaho Co., Idaho; Big Hoodoo Mt., Lincoln Co. and Cascade Creek, 6.5 mi. south of Paradise, Mineral Co., Montana. Map 16

LARCH MOUNTAIN SALAMANDER *Plethodon larselli* **Pl. 5**
Identification: 1½–2. A close relative of Van Dyke's Salamander. Dorsal stripe of reddish, tan, or yellowish tending to become obscure on head, edged with black or dark brown, and often speckled or heavily mottled with small dark flecks. Sides black or dark brown sprinkled with white. *Below red to reddish orange or salmon-pink*, brightest on tail, lightly and irregularly speckled with black. Underside of feet usually reddish; throat cream or dull yellow. Toes partly webbed as in Van Dyke's Salamander and only 1 segment in 5th toe. Costal grooves 15 (rarely 14 or 16). *Young:* Dorsal stripe well defined; below with less reddish and more dark color than adult.

Inhabits lava talus of the Columbia River gorge, chiefly in dense stands of Douglas fir, where there is considerable moss and humus. Found in rotten wood and under rocks and bark.
Similar species: Differs from all other woodland salamanders in having reddish color on belly and underside of feet and tail. (1) Dorsal stripe heavily mottled with small dark flecks, darker than in Van Dyke's Salamander; latter typically has 2 segments in the 5th toe. (2) Edges of dorsal stripe more irregular and belly pattern less variegated than in Western Red-backed Salamander.
Range: Lower Columbia River gorge between Troutdale and Hood River, Oregon; Archer Falls, Skamania Co., Washington. Some Oregon localities are northern slope of Larch Mt., 3 mi. from summit on Multnomah Falls Trail, Multnomah Co., and Starvation Falls between Wyeth and Hood River, Hood River Co. To 3900 ft. Map 14

JEMEZ MOUNTAINS SALAMANDER **Pl. 5**
Plethodon neomexicanus
Identification: 2–3. Our slimmest plethodon, approaching the slender salamanders in proportions. *Costal grooves usually 19* (rarely 18 or 20). Legs short, in adults 7½ to 8½ costal folds

between tips of toes of adpressed limbs. *Fifth toe absent or with only 1 segment.* Above, brown with fine brassy-colored stippling. Below, sooty, lightening on throat and tail. *Young:* A faint gray or brassy dorsal stripe.

Frequents moss-covered rockslides, especially on north-facing slopes in and near mixed forests of fir, spruce, aspen, and maple above 8000 ft. in the Jemez Mts., New Mexico. A subterranean salamander that spends little time on the surface except during the period of summer rains. Turn rocks, pieces of bark, and rotting logs; peel back moss on rocks and logs. Eggs laid in early July. May be locally abundant.

Similar species: Del Norte Salamander has 2 segments in the 5th toe and usually 18 costal grooves.

Range: Reported from only 3 localities in the Jemez Mts., New Mexico: 12 mi. west and 4 mi. south of Los Alamos (8750 ft.), 6 mi. northwest of Bland (8500 ft.), and East Fork of Rito de los Frijoles (8920 ft.), Sandoval Co. **Map 15**

DEL NORTE SALAMANDER *Plethodon elongatus* **Pl. 5**
Identification: 2–3. A long-bodied dark brown or black plethodon with *18* (occasionally 17 or 19) *costal grooves* and short limbs. *Toes short and partly webbed.* Adults with 6 to 8 costal folds between tips of toes of adpressed limbs. Sides sprinkled with fine white flecks. Belly black or slaty, flecked with light gray. Pale orange-yellow flecks on underside of head. *Young:* Reddish-brown or tan dorsal stripe usually fades with age, but adults striped at Boise Creek and other inland localities in Humboldt Co., California.

A rock-rubble salamander, found among rocks of old river-beds, road fills, outcrops, and moss-covered talus. At some localities in s. Oregon it coexists with Dunn's Salamander, but generally occurs in drier locations.

Similar species: (1) Might be mistaken for a dark-colored Dunn's Salamander; latter, however, has 15 (rarely 16) costal grooves, less webbing of toes, and 2½ to 4 costal folds between tips of toes of adpressed limbs. (2) Siskiyou Mountain Salamander has longer legs, 2 to 7 costal folds between tips of toes of adpressed limbs, lighter ground color, no dorsal stripe, and light-colored flecking on dorsum. (3) See also Jemez Mountains Salamander.

Range: Humid coastal forest from northern side of Rogue River, Oregon, to near Orick and inland to vicinity of Willow Creek, Humboldt Co., California. **Map 13**

SISKIYOU MOUNTAIN SALAMANDER **Pl. 5**
Plethodon stormi
Identification: 2–3. A close relative of the Del Norte Salamander. Above chocolate-brown, often *profusely speckled with whitish or yellowish.* Below purplish gray, with whitish speckling encroach-

ing on ventral surfaces. Costal grooves 18 (occasionally 17).
Adults with 2 to 7 costal folds between tips of toes of adpressed
limbs.

   Habitat resembles that of the Del Norte Salamander.

Similar species: See Del Norte Salamander.

Range: Headwaters of Applegate River, ½ mi. north of California line along Applegate River Road, 1¼ mi. south of Copper
and 0.3 mi. south of McKee Bridge, Jackson Co., and on
Oregon Caves Road, 14.6 mi. east of junction with U.S. Highway
199 at Cave Junction, Josephine Co., Oregon. Found recently
in California at Hutton Guard Station, Rogue River Nat'l
Forest, ½ mi. south of Oregon border, Siskiyou Co.   Map 13

Ensatina: Genus *Ensatina*

ENSATINA   *Ensatina eschscholtzi*   **Pls. 3, 4**

Identification: 1½–3. A smooth-skinned salamander with 12 or
13 costal grooves and a *"swollen" tail, constricted at its base.*
The defense posture is characteristic: when tapped on the back,
an ensatina may stand stiff-legged and sway-backed, with tail
arched. Color varies greatly (see plates), but nearly all ensatinas
have yellow or orange limb bases. *Male:* Enlarged upper lip;
tail slimmer and longer than in female.

   Found in both deciduous and evergreen forests under rotting
logs, bark, and rocks. To the south, frequents well-shaded canyons, with or without permanent water. In the north may be
found in clearings as well as wooded areas. During cold or dry
weather, ensatinas retreat to the interior of rotten logs and
woodrat nests, or enter rotted-out root channels and the burrows
of gophers and meadow mice. In California, surface activity
occurs from the first rains in Oct. or Nov. to the end of April,
and occasionally during summer rains in the southern mountains. At high altitude and to the north, activity may last until
May or June.

Similar species: See Van Dyke's Salamander (p. 41).

Range: Sw. B.C. to s. California, chiefly west of Cascade-
Sierran crest. Absent from Great Valley of California. Sea
level to above 10,000 ft. (Mt. San Gorgonio), California.

Subspecies: MONTEREY SALAMANDER, *E. e. eschscholtzi*
(Plate 4). Reddish brown above; whitish below; eyes black.
Ranges inland in s. California to Sawmill Canyon, headwaters
of San Gorgonio River above Banning, Riverside Co., where
it hybridizes with the Yellow-blotched Salamander. YELLOW-
EYED SALAMANDER, *E. e. xanthoptica* (Plate 4). Orange-
brown above; orange below; yellow patch in eye. Hybridizes
with Sierra Nevada Salamander in the Sierran foothills. ORE-
GON SALAMANDER, *E. e. oregonensis* (Plate 4). Brown to

nearly black above; whitish to pale yellow below, with very fine black speckling. PAINTED SALAMANDER, *E. e. picta* (Plate 4). Dwarf form, ⅔ size of ensatinas to south. Above brown, blotched with black, yellow, or orange; tail often variegated with black and yellow. Young Oregon Salamanders often similarly blotched. SIERRA NEVADA SALAMANDER, *E. e. platensis* (Plate 3). Gray to brown above, with prominent orange spots. YELLOW-BLOTCHED SALAMANDER, *E. e. croceater* (Plate 3). Blackish above, with large greenish-yellow, yellow, or cream blotches. Tehachapi Mts., Mt. Pinos, and vicinity of Fort Tejon, California. LARGE-BLOTCHED SALAMANDER, *E. e. klauberi* (Plate 3). Blackish above, with large orange or pale salmon blotches. Coexists with Monterey Salamander on Mt. Palomar, California.   Map 10

Slender Salamanders: Genus *Batrachoseps*

SLENDER salamanders are confined to the Pacific Coast. They are sometimes called "worm salamanders" because of their slim form, conspicuous costal and caudal grooves that give them a segmented appearance, and their small limbs. They have 4 toes on both front and hind feet, whereas all other western salamanders typically have 5 toes on the hind feet. They usually have a dorsal stripe of reddish, tan, or buff. Young individuals have relatively long limbs, a large head, and short tail. Males have a blunt snout and their premaxillary teeth perforate the upper lip.

Found in damp woods, under logs, bark, and rocks, in leaf litter, termite galleries, and crevices of logs and stumps. When first exposed they may remain motionless, sometimes coiled like a watchspring. Occasionally, when first picked up they may slip away and bounce randomly over the ground.

OREGON SLENDER SALAMANDER   Pl. 7
Batrachoseps wrighti

Identification: 1½–2¼. A long-legged, broad-headed slender salamander with a *black belly marked with large white blotches*. Costal grooves 16 or 17, counting one each in axilla and groin. Above dark brown, often with a reddish or yellowish-brown stripe; in some, back color contrasts with brick-red tail.

Frequents moist woods of Douglas fir, maple, hemlock, and red cedar. Found under boards, rocks, wood, or bark at the base of stumps, under the bark and moss of logs, and inside logs in crevices or termite burrows. Generally scarce, occurring in scattered and often widely separated colonies, but sometimes locally common. Becomes active on the surface of the ground in April or May.

Similar species: (1) California and (2) Pacific Slender Salamanders have 18 or more costal grooves and lack large white blotches on belly.

Range: Northern base of Mt. Hood, along Columbia River from Starvation Falls, Hood River Co., to near Crown Point, Multnomah Co.; south on western slope of Cascade Mts. to 15 mi. northeast of Westfir, Lane Co., Oregon. Some additional localities: 8⁷⁄₁₀ mi. southeast of Sandy, ½ mi. east and ¼ mi. south of Wemme, and near Cherryville, Clackamas Co.; near mouths of Moose and Trout Creeks, tributaries of Quartzville Creek, Middle Santiam River, Linn Co.; and 2 mi. south McKenzie Bridge, Lane Co. To around 3000 ft.   Map 18

PACIFIC SLENDER SALAMANDER   Pl. 7
Batrachoseps pacificus

Identification: 1⅔–2½. Typically a pale brown light-bellied salamander with eyelids, snout, and upper surface of tail often tinged with reddish orange or rust. The throat and underside of the tail are pale, often suffused with yellowish or tan; *belly whitish or slate-colored*, frequently *without enough dark pigment to form a continuous network*, under magnification seen to be sprinkled with black and white flecks. Mainland populations usually lack white speckling along midline of underside of tail. Costal grooves 18 to 21, counting one each in the axilla and groin. *Young:* Often with a brown or reddish-brown dorsal stripe; belly dusky.

Inhabits coast live-oak woodland and open chaparral of washes, canyon bottoms, and lower mountain slopes, usually where the soil is sandy or gravelly. On the Los Angeles coastal plain it is most common on alluvial deposits at the mouths of canyons. Found under rocks, bark, and logs in oak woods, and in gardens beneath stones, boards, and potted plants.

Similar species: See (1) California and (2) Oregon Slender Salamanders.

Range: Exists in most typical form in scattered colonies west of desert from Pasadena, Los Angeles Co., to Escondido, San Diego Co., California. Channel islands off coast s. California; Los Coronados Is., Baja California. In addition, slender salamanders at following isolated mainland localities are tentatively assigned to this species: 6 mi. northeast of Three Rivers (2700 ft.), Tulare Co.; 6.3 mi. southeast of Keene, along U.S. Highway 466, Kern Co. (locality buried under highway fill, X, Map 21); and south side of San Gorgonio Pass near Cabazon and Banning, Riverside Co., California. Tulare and Kern Co. animals are black-bellied and flat-bodied and may represent a new species. **Subspecies:** CHANNEL ISLANDS SLENDER SALAMANDER, *B. p. pacificus*. Long-legged; hind limb of adult when extended along side overlaps 5½ to 6½ costal folds. San Miguel,

Santa Rosa, Santa Cruz, and Anacapa Is. SANTA CATALINA
SLENDER SALAMANDER, *B. p. catalinae*. Hind limb of
adult when extended along side overlaps 3½ to 4½ costal folds;
18 to 20 costal grooves. Sides of belly with fine black network.
Catalina I. GARDEN SLENDER SALAMANDER, *B. p.
major*. Limb length resembles Catalina I. form, but 20 to 22
costal grooves and sides of belly usually with fine black flecks.
Coastal s. California from base of San Gabriel Mts. south at
least to Escondido, San Diego Co., California. East and North
Coronado Is., Baja California.   Map 21

CALIFORNIA SLENDER SALAMANDER   Pls. 6, 7
Batrachoseps attenuatus

Identification: 1–2. A slender salamander with a *black or dusky
belly, the dark pigment usually arranged in a fine unbroken network*. Underside of the tail often lighter than the belly and
tinged with yellow. Ventral surfaces finely speckled with white.
Dorsal stripe often present — brick-red, brown, tan, buff, or
yellow, the frequency of the colors varying with locality. Red
to reddish brown predominates in the redwood belt in the Northwest; dull brown in foothills of the Sierra Nevada. A variety of
stripe colors is found in the vicinity of San Francisco Bay. The
remaining dorsal ground color is sooty to black. Eighteen to 21
costal grooves, counting one each in axilla and groin. *Male:* More
pointed lower jaw and more truncate and broader snout than
female's. Premaxillary teeth project slightly beyond closed
margin of mouth.

Most abundant salamander in California, frequenting grassland (usually where there are scattered trees), woodland, and
forest. Found under logs, boards, bark, in damp leaf litter and
rotting logs, from the time of the first fall rains to the beginning
of the dry period in late spring or summer.

In s. California the California Slender Salamander tends to
occur in the uplands and the Pacific Slender Salamander on the
plains, the two species coming into contact along drainage
channels at the base of the mountains.

Similar species: (1) Pacific Slender Salamander is generally
larger and paler; dorsal stripe often faint or lacking in adults;
black network on belly tends to be broken up and replaced by
black speckling. (2) See also Oregon Slender Salamander.

Range: Coastal areas from extreme sw. Oregon to San Pedro
Mártir Mts., Baja California; western slope of Sierra Nevada;
Santa Cruz I., California, and Todos Santos I., Baja California.

Salamanders included here as members of the California
slender salamander group vary greatly in proportions and coloration. Some in s. California south of Los Angeles display traits
usually attributed to the Pacific Slender Salamander. Mingling
of characteristics may be the result of interbreeding. A popula-

tion 6.5 mi. south-southeast of Redlands, San Bernardino Co., for example, seems to be hybrid. On the other hand, the two forms are clearly distinct in some areas (at several localities in Pasadena, Los Angeles Co., and near Irvine Park, Orange Co.).

The situation is further complicated by the scattered occurrence of what appear to be relict populations. Some of these live with or near *attenuatus*. The relictual forms are black-bellied, broad-headed, long-legged, and have low costal-groove counts, resembling in proportions the Pacific Slender Salamander. They occur at Cow Flat Creek (1800 ft.), Kern Co., on the Monterey Peninsula, Monterey Co., at Pine Mt., San Luis Obispo Co. (in association with *attenuatus*), Santa Cruz I. (in association with *pacificus*), and above 7000 ft. in San Pedro Mártir Mts., Baja California. The Cow Flat Creek animals are unusual in being semiaquatic. Relictual populations also occur in the Sierra Nevada from Kern River area north to Briceburg, Mariposa Co. Those differing most from *attenuatus* occur in the south, where they reach an elevation of 8000 ft. At Briceburg (2000 ft.) differences are less marked. In general, Sierra Nevada relictual forms occur at higher elevation than typical *attenuatus*. A comparable situation seems to exist along the coast, where relictual populations range from mountains in n. San Luis Obispo Co. (coexisting with and clearly distinct from *attenuatus*) northward along the western slope of the Santa Lucia Mts. to the Monterey lowlands.   Map 17

Climbing Salamanders: Genus *Aneides*

THERE ARE 4 western species but not all climb. The Black Salamander spends most of its time on the ground. A 5th climbing species, the rock-dwelling Green Salamander, occurs in the Appalachian Mts.

These salamanders have prominent jaw muscles, especially well developed in males, which give the head a triangular shape. The teeth in the front of the upper jaw project beyond the lip when the salamander's mouth is closed, and can be felt by stroking the tip of its snout; there are no teeth at the back of the upper jaw. In counting costal grooves, count one each in axilla and groin. See front endpaper for difference between costal groove and costal fold. Males have an oval or heart-shaped mental gland and broader head than females.

SACRAMENTO MOUNTAIN SALAMANDER   Pl. 7
Aneides hardyi

Identification: 1¾–2¼. A slim-bodied, short-legged climbing salamander, with 4 to 4½ costal folds between tips of toes of adpressed limbs. Toe tips rounded. Above light to dark brown with varying amounts of greenish-gray to bronze mottling. Belly light brown, throat cream-colored, and underside of tail slate. *Young:* Throat whitish; dorsal stripe brown or bronze.

Found during period of summer rains under bark and inside rotting logs, in old rockslides, and beneath logs, bark, and boards in forests of Douglas fir, white fir, and spruce. Most abundant on north- and east-facing slopes. Emerges late June and July. Brooding females with eggs have been found in hollows in Douglas fir logs in summer.

Range: Mts. of s. New Mexico. Sacramento Mts. — Cloudcroft and vicinity, Agua Chiquite, Wofford Lookout; Capitan Mts. — ½ mi. north of Summit Spring and 1¼ mi. southeast of Koprian Springs; White Mts. — 1½ mi. southwest of Monjeau Lookout. From around 8000 to 9600 ft. Map 22

BLACK SALAMANDER *Aneides flavipunctatus* **Pls. 6, 7**
Identification: 2⅝–3. Dorsal coloration varies greatly depending upon locality (see below). *Below black or slaty.* Projecting upper jaw teeth, felt by stroking the salamander's snout when its mouth is closed, and the triangular head will distinguish it as a climbing salamander. Limbs short, 3 to 5 costal folds between tips of toes of adpressed limbs. *Toe tips rounded. Young:* Above black, often suffused with olive or green — brilliant green (in light phase) in redwood country of the Northwest coast; limb bases yellow. *Male:* Heart-shaped mental gland; small gray glands on belly.

Frequents mixed deciduous woodland and coniferous forests. Chiefly ground-dwelling. Found under rocks along streams, in talus of road cuts, under logs, bark, boards, and other objects, and occasionally beneath bark and in fissures of logs. More tolerant of wet soil than other climbing salamanders, often occurring under rocks in seepages but rarely completely immersed.
Similar species: (1) Tiger Salamander (p. 33) has a flattened tail, widely set small eyes, and lacks projecting teeth. (2) Arboreal and (3) Clouded Salamanders have less than 2 costal folds between tips of toes of adpressed limbs, and squarish toe tips; Arboreal Salamander has a whitish belly and Clouded Salamander a brown or gray belly.
Range: Coastal mts. of California from w. Humboldt to s. Santa Cruz Cos., and interiorly, in northern part of range, to near southern base of Mt. Shasta. Headwaters of Applegate River, Jackson Co., Oregon.
Subspecies: SANTA CRUZ BLACK SALAMANDER, *A. f. niger* (Plate 6). Uniformly black above or black with very small white flecks. San Mateo, Santa Clara, and Santa Cruz Cos., California. SPECKLED BLACK SALAMANDER, *A. f. flavipunctatus* (Plate 6). This name currently applies to all Black Salamanders north of San Francisco Bay, but within this region there are at least 4 unnamed color varieties, as follows:

(1) black with large white spots — interior coast range from Alder Springs, Glenn Co., and Lucerne, Lake Co. south; (2) black with pale yellow spots — outer coast range from Sonoma to middle Mendocinos Cos.; (3) unspotted, with black ground color frosted with gray, olive, or green — redwood country of Mendocino and Humboldt Cos.; (4) black with numerous small white spots — Klamath Mts. east to near Mt. Shasta.   Map 23

CLOUDED SALAMANDER   *Aneides ferreus*   Pl. 7

Identification: 2–3. Slim, long-legged, and agile, the best climber among western salamanders. *Tips of toes of adpressed limbs separated by no more than 1½ costal folds and sometimes overlapping as much as 1½ folds.* Usually 16 costal grooves. The toes have slightly broadened and squarish tips. Above brown clouded with ash, greenish gray, or pale gold; ventral surfaces dusky. In the dark phase these salamanders may be nearly plain dark brown above; in the light phase, pale gray color may predominate and the brown pigment is reduced to a network. *Young:* Hatchlings have a copper or brassy dorsal stripe which soon becomes reduced to patches on the snout, shoulders, and tail; stripe color on upper surface of base of limbs. *Male:* Heart-shaped mental gland.

Occurs in forests of Douglas fir, cedar, alder, and redwood, often at the borders of clearings. Found chiefly under the bark of standing or fallen dead trees, and occasionally among rocks. May climb to above 20 ft. in trees. Seems to prefer logs with a firm interior and bark separated ¼ in. or so from the heartwood. Search piles of leaf litter on top of sawed stumps and peel bark from logs, especially Douglas fir. In summer, colonies occur deep inside decayed logs.

Similar species: See (1) Arboreal and (2) Black Salamanders.

Range: Coast Ranges of California and Oregon, from middle Mendocino Co. to Columbia River; lower western slope of Cascade Mts., Oregon; Vancouver I.   Map 19

ARBOREAL SALAMANDER   *Aneides lugubris*   Pls. 6, 7

Identification: 2½–3¾. A plain brown salamander, usually spotted with yellow. Spotting conspicuous in San Benito and Monterey Cos. and on South Farallon I. off San Francisco Bay; weak or absent in Sierra Nevada. *Below whitish, unmarked.* Enlarged jaw muscles give head a triangular shape; toes have slightly enlarged squarish tips. *Tips of toes of adpressed limbs overlap, or fail to meet as much as 1 costal fold.* Usually 15 costal grooves. The tail is somewhat prehensile and usually coiled when the salamander is at rest. *Young:* Dark ground color of dorsal surfaces clouded with light gray or brassy color and a rust or brassy mark on the snout, on each side above the forelimbs, on upper surface of bases of the limbs, and along upper surface of the tail. *Male:* Chunky, broad head with powerful jaw muscles; heart-shaped mental gland.

Occurs chiefly in coastal live-oak woodland but in the Sierra Nevada ranges into forests of yellow pine and black oak. Found both on the ground and in trees. In summer, during dry weather it enters damp caves and mine shafts; large numbers may aggregate in tree hollows and are sometimes encountered by tree surgeons. Found under logs, boards, and rocks and under the bark of standing or fallen dead trees. Examine tree trunks, rock surfaces, and crevices of rock walls at night with a flashlight. A slender wire with a "shepherd's" hook can be used to remove salamanders from cracks. Sometimes squeaks when first caught.

Similar species: (1) Clouded Salamander usually has 16 costal grooves, mottled dorsal coloration, and a dark belly, finely speckled with white. See also (2) Black and (3) Limestone Salamanders.

Range: Coast Ranges of California from Humboldt Co. to n. Baja California. Foothills of Sierra Nevada from Calaveras to Madera Cos., California. South Farallon, Catalina, and Los Coronados Is. off coast of California and Baja California. Map 20

Web-toed Salamanders: Genus *Hydromantes*

WEBBED toes, a mushroomlike tongue with free margin, and a flattened body are distinctive. Tongue very long. When prey is being captured, the tongue can be extended ⅓ the length of the body, excluding tail. Males have projecting upper jaw teeth and an oval mental gland.

Web-toes are excellent climbers, moving with ease over smooth rock surfaces. When on a steep slope, the California species use the tail as an aid in locomotion, curling the tip forward and placing it against the ground as the hind foot is lifted, a habit that alone will distinguish them from other western salamanders.

These salamanders live in rocky habitats, hiding by day under stones and in crevices and caves. They frequent cliff faces, vertical walls of caverns, and occasionally level ground.

There are 5 species, so much alike that they might be considered varieties of a single species; yet 2 occur in Europe and 3 in California.

MOUNT LYELL SALAMANDER   Pl. 6
Hydromantes platycephalus

Identification: 1¾–2¾. Easily recognized by its flattened head and body, *granite-matching coloration*, blunt webbed toes, and short tail. The ventral surface is dusky, flecked with white. Usually ½ to 1½ costal folds between tips of toes of adpressed limbs. *Young:* Black ground color above overlain with greenish suffusion, under magnification seen to consist of pale gold flecks.

Confined to granite exposures of the Sierra Nevada of California. Typical habitat includes rock fissures, seepages from streams or melting snow, shade, and low-growing plants. Look under rocks near cliffs, cave openings, melting snow banks, and in the spray zone of waterfalls. Seems to favor north-facing slopes. Found from Feb. to Oct., the time depending upon altitude and local moisture conditions.

Similar species: (1) The adult Shasta Salamander is often tan to reddish above, without granite markings, usually has white blotches on chest, and toes overlap $\frac{1}{2}$ to $1\frac{1}{2}$ costal folds. (2) Limestone Salamander is uniformly brown above and whitish or yellowish below; young pale green or yellowish.

Range: Sierra Nevada from Sonora Pass to Twin Lakes, Silliman Gap, Sequoia Nat'l Park, California. Low altitude records are from the upper edge of the talus on the south side of Yosemite Valley (Staircase Falls and base of Cathedral Rocks). 4000 to 11,000 ft.   Map 7

SHASTA SALAMANDER *Hydromantes shastae*   **Pl. 6**
Identification: $1\frac{3}{4}$–$2\frac{1}{2}$. Primarily a cave dweller, less specialized for climbing and crevice-dwelling than the Mount Lyell Salamander. Body not so flat, toes less webbed, and limbs longer. Toes of adpressed limbs overlap $\frac{1}{2}$ to $1\frac{1}{2}$ costal folds. *Above gray-green, beige, tan, or reddish, usually with yellow on tail.* White blotches on chest and abdomen. *Young:* Above gray-green, olive, tan, or reddish on body, yellowish on tail.

Found in moist limestone fissures and caves, and in wet weather under rocks in the open, in mixed forest of Douglas fir, Digger pine, black and canyon oak. Enters moist caves in summer, where it lays and broods its eggs.

Similar species: See (1) Mount Lyell and (2) Limestone Salamanders.

Range: Known only from limestone country in n. California south of Mt. Shasta in headwaters of Shasta Reservoir — Low Pass Creek, McCloud River, Brock Mt., and Samwell Cave. 1000 to 2500 ft.   Map 7

LIMESTONE SALAMANDER *Hydromantes brunus*   **Pl. 6**
Identification: 2–$2\frac{3}{4}$. *Uniformly brown above and pale below;* underside of tail yellowish. Eye size, and length of the limbs, toes, and tail are greater than in the Mount Lyell Salamander. The tips of the toes of the adpressed limbs overlap $1\frac{1}{2}$ costal folds. *Young:* Pale yellowish green above, changing with age through pale yellow and beige to brown.

Frequents limestone in the Digger pine – chaparral belt of the lower Merced Canyon, living in crevices of cliffs and ledges and in talus, especially where overgrown with moss. Active during period of fall, winter, and spring rains, except during cold spells. Often coils body when molested.

Similar species: (1) See Mount Lyell Salamander. (2) Shasta Salamander usually has a tan or reddish dorsal coloration and a dusky belly. (3) Arboreal Salamander has a triangular head, tongue attached in front, and unwebbed toes with broadened, squarish tips.

Range: Vicinity of Briceburg, Mariposa Co., California, at confluence of Bear Creek and Merced River and along tributaries of Bear Creek. 1200 to 2500 ft. Map 7

VII

Frogs and Toads

Tailed Frogs: Family Ascaphidae

THE FAMILY gets its name from the tail-like copulatory organ in the male of our single North American species, the Tailed Frog. In this species fertilization is internal, a method of breeding unique among frogs. In the other members of the family, three New Zealand species of the genus *Leiopelma*, the organ is lacking. The Tailed Frog inhabits cold streams, where its tadpole lives in torrents or quiet water and clings to rocks with its large suckerlike mouth. The other species are terrestrial. Amplexus is pelvic.

TAILED FROG *Ascaphus truei*   **Pl. 13**
   Identification: 1–2. Above olive, brown, gray, or reddish, usually with a pale yellow or greenish triangle on the snout and a dark eyestripe. Flat-bodied and toadlike; skin rather rough. Eye with vertical pupil. *Outermost hind toe broader than the rest. Male:* Tail-like copulatory organ, vent opening at tip. Palmar and forearm tubercles darken in fall and a patch of small, horny, black pads develops on each side of the pectoral region. No "tail" or pads in female.
   Frequents clear, cold, rocky, streams in humid forests of Douglas fir, pine, spruce, redwood, maple, alder, and bay. Trees sometimes absent. In dry weather found on streambanks or under stones on the bottom of streams. Look for eyeshine near water's edge at night. Usually stays close to water but after rains may venture into damp woods. Adults abroad from April to early September, but time varies with locality. Breeds in early fall; eggs laid from late June to early Aug., hatching in Aug. and Sept. (n. Idaho and se. Washington). Eggs unpigmented, in rosary-like strings under stones.
   Similar species: (1) Yellow-legged Frog, which may share the habitat in Oregon and California, has a horizontal pupil and no enlargement of the 5th toe. (2) Pacific Treefrog has toe pads.
   Voice: Apparently absent.
   Range: Chiefly west of crest of Cascade Mts. from sw. B.C. to near Albion, Mendocino Co., California. Rocky Mts. of Idaho and Montana; extreme se. Washington and ne. Oregon. Many isolated populations. Sea level to over 6500 ft.   Map 28

Leptodactylid Frogs:
Family Leptodactylidae

A LARGE FAMILY of chiefly Australian and New World frogs, well represented in the American tropics. Land-dwelling, aquatic, and arboreal. Most lay their eggs in water, and the tadpoles develop in the usual fashion, but some lay eggs in foamlike masses in pockets in the ground and rains wash the tadpoles into nearby pools. Others, members of the genus *Eleutherodactylus*, are completely terrestrial, lay their eggs on land and guard them; young emerge fully formed.

Frog or toadlike. The underside of the toes usually has prominent tubercles at the joints, teeth are present in the upper jaw, and the eardrums generally are smooth and semitransparent. Some have a circular fold of skin on the belly.

Five species in the U.S., 1 introduced.

BARKING FROG *Eleutherodactylus augusti*   **Pl. 10**
   Identification: 2–3¾. Toadlike, but toes slender, unwebbed, and with prominent tubercles beneath the joints. Walks in stilted fashion with hindquarters and heels well off the ground. *Fold of skin across back of head and circular fold on belly.* Eardrum smooth and semitransparent. Above purplish gray, sometimes clouded with cream, brown, or greenish, and marked with dark blotches that often have light borders. Conspicuous dark brown eyes. *Male:* Much smaller than female. *Young:* Light-colored band across back which rapidly fades with age.

   A secretive, terrestrial, rock-dwelling species often found in limestone areas. Hides by day under rocks and in mines, wells, caves, and fissures. Ranges from treeless, dry yucca-covered hills into open forests. In Texas in juniper–live-oak association; in Sonora in large, low, dense, clumps of cactus. Eggs, large-yolked and unpigmented, laid in caves, fissures, or under rocks, during period of summer rains.
   Voice: Resembles bark of dog. A series of explosive notes given at intervals of 2 or 3 secs.
   Range: Extreme s. Arizona, New Mexico, and cent. Texas (escarpment of Edwards Plateau), south to Isthmus of Tehauntepec. Distribution spotty.
   Subspecies: EASTERN BARKING FROG, *E. a. latrans.* Adults of both sexes usually over 2⅖ in.; dorsal coloration in preservative often light brown; dark bars on dorsal surface of femur, relatively weak and poorly defined. Carlsbad, Eddy Co., New Mexico; cent. Texas. WESTERN BARKING FROG, *E. a. cactorum.* Adults usually under 2⅖ in.; dorsal coloration in preservative often dark purplish gray, olivaceous in life; leg bars darker than in Eastern Barking Frog. Old record for Madera Canyon, Santa Rita Mts., Arizona.   **Map 30**

Spadefoot Toads: Family Pelobatidae

DISTINGUISHED from the true toads (genus *Bufo*) by their catlike eyes, single black sharp-edged "spade" on the hind foot, teeth in the upper jaw, rather smooth skin, and absence of parotoid glands. Pupils vertical in bright light, round at night. Males may have a dusky throat and dark nuptial pads on the innermost front toes; amplexus is pelvic. True toads typically have horizontal pupils and 2 rounded brown foot tubercles, are toothless and warty, and have large parotoid glands; amplexus is pectoral.

Spadefoot toads breed in pools that form after heavy rains or in slow streams, reservoirs, or irrigation ditches. Their voices are audible for a great distance and are important in bringing the sexes together for breeding in arid country where the number, location, and suitability of breeding sites is uncertain. A parched region may reverberate with their cries within an hour after rain begins.

Dry periods are spent in burrows of gophers, squirrels, kangaroo rats, or in self-made burrows. Active chiefly at night during spring and summer rains. When burrowing, spadefoot toads back into the ground by means of their spades and rotation of the body, the hind feet moving alternately in circular fashion, a motion like that for stamping out a cigarette.

Canada to s. Mexico and from coast to coast; 5 species, all members of the genus *Scaphiopus*. Representatives also in Europe, w. Africa, Asia, and East Indies.

COUCH'S SPADEFOOT *Scaphiopus couchi*   **Pl. 8**
  Identification: 2¼–3½. A large greenish-yellow or brownish-yellow spadefoot with an irregular network or blotches of black, brown, or dark green. Below whitish. Width of eyelids about the same as or less than the distance between them. No boss between the eyes and no pug-dog profile. *Spade* on hind foot black, *sickle-shaped*. *Male:* Greenish yellow; dorsal dark markings usually subdued or absent; throat pale.
    Frequents shortgrass plains, mesquite savannah, creosote bush desert, and other areas of low rainfall.
  Similar species: Other spadefoots have a wedge-shaped spade, shorter distance between the eyelids, and pug-dog profile.
  Voice: A plaintive cry, declining in pitch, like the anxious bleat of a sheep, a drawn out *ye-ow*, lasting ¾ to 1¼ secs. Breeds July to Sept., during period of summer rains.
  Range: From sw. Oklahoma, cent. New Mexico, and Arizona to tip of Baja California, Nayarit, and s. San Luis Potosí; se. California to cent. Texas. Northern record in Arizona is in vicinity of Petrified Forest Nat'l Monument. Isolated California populations at Glamis, Imperial Co., and 15 mi. north of Vidal Junction, San Bernardino Co.   Map 27

WESTERN SPADEFOOT *Scaphiopus hammondi* **Pl. 8**
Identification: 1½–2½. *No boss between the eyes.* Above dusky green, gray, or brown, often with 4 irregular longitudinal light-colored stripes on back, the central pair sometimes setting off an hourglass shape of dark color. Generally less contrast between light and dark markings than in Plains Spadefoot, and "hourglass" usually less evident or absent. Skin tubercles tipped with orange or yellow. Below whitish, without markings. A wedge-shaped glossy-black spade on the hind foot. Width of eyelids usually greater than distance between them.

Primarily a species of the lowlands, frequenting washes, floodplains of rivers, alluvial fans, playas, and alkali flats, but ranges into the foothills and mountain valleys. Prefers areas of open vegetation and shortgrass, where the soil is sandy or gravelly. Breeds in quiet streams and temporary pools. When handled, may smell like roasted peanuts and the skin secretion may cause sneezing.
Similar species: (1) Plains and (2) Great Basin Spadefoot toads have a boss between the eyes. (3) Couch's Spadefoot has an elongate sickle-shaped spade and widely spaced eyes.
Voice: Hoarse, snore-like, lasting ½ to 1¼ secs., resembling the sound made by stroking the teeth of a pocket comb. Often calls from floating position. A distant chorus suggests a man cutting wood with a handsaw. In California breeds Jan. to May; to the east during the period of summer rains.
Range: Great Valley, bordering foothills, and Coast Ranges south of San Francisco Bay, into nw. Baja California. N. Arizona, sw. Colorado, New Mexico, and w. Oklahoma south to Oaxaca. Mostly below 6000 ft. Hybridizes with Plains Spadefoot in se. Arizona and probably w. Texas. **Map 26**

GREAT BASIN SPADEFOOT *Scaphiopus intermontanus* **Pl. 8**
Identification: 1½–2. Ash-gray streaks usually set off an hourglass marking of gray or olive on the back. Spade on hind foot wedged-shaped. *Glandular boss between eyes.*

An inhabitant of the Great Basin, ranging from sagebrush flats and piñon-juniper woodland to high elevations in the spruce-fir belt (Cedar Breaks, Utah). Enters permanent and semi-permanent water, often in response to rain. In dry-weather burrows into the ground or uses the burrows of other animals.
Similar species: (1) Western and (2) Couch's Spadefoot toads lack the boss; (3) in the Plains Spadefoot it is hard and underlain with bone.
Voice: A hoarse *wa-wa-wa*, a series of short rapid calls, each lasting about ⅕ to ⅛ sec. Rounded, slightly bilobed vocal sac. Breeds in July.
Range: Great Basin from extreme s. B.C. to n. Arizona and from eastern base of Cascade-Sierran mt. system to Rockies. To 8500 ft. **Map 24**

PLAINS SPADEFOOT *Scaphiopus bombifrons*   **Pl. 8**
  Identification: 1½–2½. A spadefoot with a *prominent boss*
between the eyes and a pug-dog profile. Boss underlain with
bone. Above usually with 4 light stripes of irregular outline, the
middle pair often setting off an hourglass shape in the middle of
the back. General color dusky, purplish brown, dark brown, or
greenish flecked with orange- to yellow-tipped tubercles. Below
white. A single glossy-black, wedge-shaped spade on the hind
foot. Width of eyelids usually greater than the distance between
them.
  The prairie spadefoot. Inhabits plains, hills, and river bottoms
in shortgrass prairie and farmland chiefly east of the Rocky
Mts., in regions of low rainfall. Prefers loose, sandy or gravelly
soil suitable for burrowing. Frequents both permanent and
temporary water. Tadpoles sometimes cannibalistic.
  Similar species: (1) Western and (2) Couch's Spadefoot toads
lack the boss between the eyes. (3) The boss in the Great Basin
Spadefoot is glandular, rather than bony. Couch's Spadefoot
has a sickle-shaped spade and widely spaced eyes. (4) The
Great Plains Toad (p. 63) has 2 brown foot tubercles.
  Voice: A short, distinct ducklike note lasting about ⅕ sec.,
shorter than the Western Spadefoot's and less often given from
floating position. In the southern part of its range it breeds in
July during the period of summer rains, but in the north (Alberta)
as early as the latter part of May.
  Range: Eastern and southern outwash plains of Rocky Mts.
from s. Alberta and Saskatchewan to nw. Texas and Chihuahua,
east to extreme w. Missouri and e. Oklahoma. Isolated populations in extreme s. Texas. Old record for Dauphin, Manitoba.
To above 6000 ft. Coexists with the Western Spadefoot in the
southern part of its range and apparently hybridizes with it in
se. Arizona.   Map 25

True Toads: Family Bufonidae

WORLDWIDE but absent from extremely cold or dry areas, remote
oceanic islands, and Australia, where the Marine Toad has been
introduced. Toads are able to live under adverse conditions. They
range from below sea level in Death Valley, California, to above
16,000 feet in the Andes of S. America and from the tropics nearly
to the Arctic Circle. Ten species occur in the West.
  Typical toads (genus *Bufo*) are chunky, short-legged, and warty
and have parotoid glands that distinguish them from all other
tailless amphibians (See spadefoot toads, p. 56). The parotoids
and warts secrete a sticky white poison, which in some species can
paralyze or kill dogs and other predators. Many animals, however,
eat toads with no ill effect. If gotten into one's eyes or mouth the

skin secretion may cause irritation, and if swallowed in quantity can cause illness. However, there is no danger in ordinary handling; and toads do not cause warts.

Western species differ in size, shape of the parotoids, conspicuousness and arrangement of the cranial crests (ridges that frame the innerside of the upper eyelids), wartiness, appearance of the foot tubercles, and color. Color may change from light to dark, in response to temperature.

Breeding occurs in spring and summer, usually after rains. Adult males of most species have a dark throat. Exceptions are the Western, Yosemite, Southwestern, and Colorado River Toads. All develop brown nuptial pads on the thumb and inner fingers which help them to cling to the slippery body of the female. Amplexus is pectoral.

COLORADO RIVER TOAD *Bufo alvarius*   **Pl. 9**
   Identification: 3–6. Our largest western toad. Dark brown or olive above, with smooth skin, long kidney-shaped parotoids, and prominent cranial crests. *Several large warts on the hind legs stand out conspicuously against the smooth skin.* An enlarged whitish wart near angle of the jaw. Below cream. *Young:* Warts light-colored, set in dark spots. *Male:* Throat pale like female's.
   Ranges from arid mesquite-creosote bush lowlands into the oak-sycamore-walnut association in mountain canyons. Usually found near permanent water of springs, reservoirs, and streams, but occasionally frequents temporary pools and has been reported several miles from water. Nocturnal; activity stimulated by rainfall. When molested, assumes a butting pose with its parotoid glands directed toward the intruder. A dog may be temporarily paralyzed (rarely, killed) if it mouths one of these toads.
   Voice: Weak, low-pitched, resembling a ferryboat whistle. Hoots last ½ to 1 sec. Vocal sac absent or inconspicuous. Most active May to July.
   Range: Lower Colorado and Gila Rivers of Arizona and extreme sw. New Mexico, south to nw. Sinaloa; extreme se. California. Sea level to above 4000 ft.   **Map 39**

WESTERN TOAD *Bufo boreas*   **Pl. 9**
   Identification: 2½–5. The common garden toad of the West. *The white or cream-colored dorsal stripe and lack of cranial crests will usually identify it.* The parotoid glands are oval, well separated, and slightly larger than the upper eyelids. Well-developed tarsal fold. The general color is dusky, gray, or greenish, with warts set in dark blotches and often tinged with rust. *Young:* Recently transformed, ¼ in.; dorsal stripe weak or absent. Larger young have prominent spotting and undersides of feet are yellow. *Male:* Throat pale like female's.
   Frequents a great variety of habitats, desert streams and springs, grassland, woodland, and mountain meadows. Found

in and near ponds, lakes, reservoirs, rivers, and streams. In warm, low-lying areas active at night; diurnal at high elevations and in the north. Buries itself in loose soil or seeks shelter in the burrows of gophers, ground squirrels, and other animals. Tends to walk rather than hop.

Similar species: (1) Woodhouse's Toad has conspicuous cranial crests or a cranial boss and the male has a dark throat. (2) See also Yosemite Toad.

Voice: A mellow chirruping, suggesting the peeping of a baby chick. No vocal sac. Active Jan. to Oct., breeding late Jan. to July, the time depending on latitude, elevation, and local conditions.

Range: S. Alaska to n. Baja California; Rocky Mts. to Pacific Coast. Absent from most of arid Southwest. Sea level to around 10,000 ft.

Subspecies: BLACK TOAD, *B. b. exsul.* Size small; heavily mottled above and below with black; skin smooth. Deep Springs Valley, Inyo Co., California. Active late May to mid-Sept.; breeds late March to late April; diurnal. AMARGOSA TOAD, *B. b. nelsoni.* Head narrow, snout long; elbows and knees do not touch when placed along sides. Amargosa River Valley in vicinity of Springdale and Beatty, Nye Co., Nevada. Breeds mid-March to early April; diurnal in spring, becoming nocturnal in summer. BOREAL TOAD, *B. b. boreas.* Considerable dark blotching on both dorsal and ventral surfaces. CALIFORNIA TOAD, *B. b. halophilus.* Less dark blotching than in Boreal Toad; head wider, eyes larger (less distance between upper eyelids), and feet smaller.   Map 31

YOSEMITE TOAD *Bufo canorus*   **Pl. 9**
Identification: 1¾–3. The toad of the high Sierra Nevada, a close relative of the Western Toad. Differs in having a smoother skin, *large flat parotoids less than width of a gland apart,* and closely set eyes, the distance between them less than the width of the upper eyelid (as viewed from above). Sexes differ greatly in color. Females and young have numerous dark blotches on a pale background, the parotoids are usually tan-colored, and the dorsal stripe is narrow or absent. *Male:* Above pale yellow-green or dark olive, with blotches virtually absent or reduced to small scattered flecks. Throat pale like female's.

Frequents high mountain meadows and forest borders, emerging soon after the snow melts. Active April to Oct., breeding in shallow pools and lake margins, or in the quiet water of streams. Chiefly diurnal. On cool days may not be active until afternoon. Seeks shelter in burrows of gophers and meadow mice and in clumps of grass, sedges, or willows near water.

Similar species: Immatures are colored like the Western Toad but parotoids of the latter are separated by about twice the width of the gland. The Western Toad is present at high altitude in the s. Sierra Nevada south of Kaiser Pass, Fresno Co., where the habitat resembles that occupied by the Yosemite Toad farther north.

Voice: A mellow, sustained musical trill of 10 to 20 or more notes, usually uttered rapidly and at frequent intervals. Breeds mid-May to mid-July.

Range: High Sierra of California from vicinity of Ebbetts Pass, Alpine Co., to south of Kaiser Pass and Evolution Lake, Fresno Co. Above 6000 to over 11,000 ft., mostly above 9000 ft. Coexists and apparently hybridizes with Western Toad in Blue Lakes region (around 8000 ft.), Alpine Co.   Map 32

WOODHOUSE'S TOAD *Bufo woodhousei*   **Pl. 10**
Identification: 2–5. *The whitish dorsal stripe, prominent cranial crests*, and elongate divergent parotoids should distinguish this toad. Ground color above gray, yellowish brown, olive, or nearly black. Dorsum usually dark-blotched. Yellow and black network on rear of thighs. Below cream to beige, with or without dark flecks. *Male:* Throat sooty, setting off pale yellow lower-jaw margin.

Frequents a great variety of habitats — grassland, sagebrush flats, woods, desert streams, valleys, floodplains, farms, and even city backyards. It seems to prefer sandy areas, breeding in quiet water of streams, marshes, lakes, freshwater pools and irrigation ditches, usually during or soon after rains.

Similar species: (1) Southwestern Toad lacks the dorsal stripe, lacks or has weak cranial crests, has more rounded parotoids, and males have a pale throat. (2) Dakota Toad (p. 64) has a narrow parallel-sided cranial boss, is heavily spotted below, and the dark pigment of the throat of males is confined to the underlying muscles rather than the skin; the call is softer and more musical. (3) See also Western Toad.

Voice: Has been compared to a snore, an infant's cry, and the bawling of a calf — a nasal *w-a-a-a-ah*. An explosive, wheezy sound lasting 1–2½ secs., often suddenly dropping in pitch at the end. Vocal sac round. Breeds March to July.

Range: N. Montana to Durango; Atlantic Coast to arid West. To 8500 ft. Hybridizes with Southwestern Toad.

Subspecies: ROCKY MOUNTAIN TOAD, *B. w. woodhousei.* Dorsal stripe complete; no boss between eyes. SOUTHWESTERN WOODHOUSE'S TOAD, *B. w. australis.* Tends to lack dorsal stripe on snout and to have well-developed black markings on sides of chest. S. Arizona, s. New Mexico, sw. Texas, into n. Mexico. Hybridizes with Texas Toad in Texas.   Map 34

SOUTHWESTERN TOAD *Bufo microscaphus*   **Pl. 10**
Identification: 2–3. A rather uniformly warty, stocky toad with

a light-colored stripe across the head, including the eyelids. *Parotoid glands* oval-shaped and widely separated, *pale anteriorly.* Above greenish gray, buff, brown, or salmon, the color harmonizing with the general color of soil and rocks. *Usually a light area on each sacral hump and in middle of back.* Below buff, often unspotted. Cranial crests weak or absent. *Young:* Ash-white, light olive, or salmon with or without prominent black spots; red-tipped tubercles on back; underside of feet yellow. *Male:* Throat pale like female's.

A toad of washes, streams, and arroyos of semiarid parts of the Southwest. Breeds in brooks or streams; does not depend directly on rainfall. In California frequents sandy banks grown to willows, cottonwoods, or sycamores and in Arizona and New Mexico rocky streams in the pine-oak belt. Adults nocturnal except during the breeding season. More often hops than walks.
Similar species: See (1) Woodhouse's and (2) Texas Toads.
Voice: A melodious trill usually lasting 8 to 10 secs., often rising in pitch at first and usually ending abruptly. Vocal sac round. In California breeds March to July but may be abroad until Sept. Height of breeding season in June in sw. Utah.
Range: S. Nevada to s. Durango; coastal s. California to w. New Mexico. Many isolated populations. To around 6000 ft.
Subspecies: ARIZONA TOAD, *B. m. microscaphus* (illus.). Usually little or no dorsal dark spotting; skin relatively smooth. Scattered localities in headwaters of tributaries of Colorado River in sw. Utah, s. Nevada, cent. Arizona, w. New Mexico; Sierra Madre Occidental. Hybridizes with Woodhouse's Toad along Virgin River and in cent. Arizona. ARROYO TOAD, *B. m. californicus* (illus.). Above dark-spotted; skin rough. S. California chiefly west of desert from near Santa Margarita, San Luis Obispo Co., to nw. Baja California. Desert population along Mojave River, San Bernardino Co., California.   Map 33

RED-SPOTTED TOAD *Bufo punctatus*   **Pl. 10**
Identification: 1½–3. A small toad with *flattened head and body and round parotoids*, about same size as eye. Snout pointed; cranial crests weak or absent. Above light gray, olive, or reddish brown, with reddish or orange warts. Below whitish to buff, with or without spotting. *Young:* Numerous orange-tipped warts; below dark-spotted; underside of feet yellow. *Male:* Throat dusky.

A toad of desert oases, open grassland, rocky canyons and arroyos. Although sometimes seen on the floodplains of rivers, it is more often associated with rocks, which it climbs with ease and in the crevices of which it seeks shelter. Breeds in springs, reservoirs, and temporary pools of intermittent streams. Chiefly nocturnal, but may be diurnal when breeding.
Voice: A prolonged clear musical trill, less rapid and clearer than

the Green Toad's, lasting about 6 to 10 secs. Pitch high, often nearly constant but occasionally dropping toward the end. Vocal sac round. Breeds April to Sept., during or after rains.

Range: S. Nevada and s. Kansas to Hidalgo and tip of Baja California. Cent. Texas to se. California. To 6500 ft.   Map 40

GREAT PLAINS TOAD *Bufo cognatus*   **Pl. 9**
   Identification: 2–4½. A toad with large well-defined *dark blotches in symmetrical pairs on its back.* Blotches with pale borders. Cranial crests diverge widely posteriorly and are more or less united on the snout to form a boss. Inner tubercle on the hind foot usually sharp-edged. General color above light brown, olive, or gray, and blotches dusky, olive, or green. Sometimes a narrow dorsal stripe down middle of the back. *Young:* Numerous small brick-red tubercles; crests form a V. *Male:* Dark loose skin of deflated vocal sac often partly concealed by pale flap of skin.
   Inhabits prairies or deserts, usually breeding after heavy rains in summer in shallow temporary pools or quiet water of streams and irrigation ditches, where it may gather in large numbers. Primarily a grassland species but frequents creosote bush desert, mesquite woodland, and sagebrush plains in the West. Nocturnal. A proficient burrower.
   Similar species: (1) Texas Toad may have pairs of spots on its back but they are smaller and less well defined; cranial crests and boss on snout are weaker; voice a series of short trills rather than a prolonged clatter. (2) See also Plains Spadefoot (p. 58).
   Voice: A harsh explosive clatter, lasting 5 to 50 (Texas) or more secs., almost deafening when large numbers of the toads are heard at close range. When inflated, vocal sac sausage-shaped, ⅓ size of body. Breeds April to Sept.
   Range: Great Plains from extreme s. Canada to San Luis Potosí; w. Texas to extreme se. California and s. Nevada.   Map 36

TEXAS TOAD *Bufo speciosus*   **Pl. 10**
   Identification: 2–3½. A close relative of the Great Plains Toad. *A rather plain-colored, uniformly warty species without a dorsal stripe. Cranial crests weak or absent.* Tubercles on hind foot usually blackish and sharp-edged, the inner one sickle-shaped. Parotoid glands oval and widely separated. Above greenish gray to brown, sometimes with dark blotches on the back arranged in symmetrical pairs; below white to cream, unmarked or with dark spots. *Young:* Above gray-brown, blotched with green and flecked with black; warts tipped with red. *Male:* Olive-colored skin of deflated vocal sac overlain by pale skin fold.
   A nocturnal, burrowing species of mesquite woodland and prairie. Breeds in quiet water of rain pools, ˙eservoirs, and cattle tanks.

Similar species: (1) Southwestern Toad has a light-colored band across the head and a light-colored patch at the anterior end of each parotoid gland and on each sacral hump. Hind foot tubercles brown, not sharp-edged. (2) See also Great Plains Toad.

Voice: A continuous series of explosive, shrill trills each lasting ½ to 1 sec., often given at intervals of about 1 sec. After some minutes of calling there may be a distinct drop in pitch followed by a return to the original pitch. Vocal sac sausage-shaped. Breeds after rains, April to Sept.

Range: Extreme sw. Kansas, se. New Mexico, and Texas, into n. Mexico.   Map 37

DAKOTA TOAD   *Bufo hemiophrys*   Pl. 10
Identification: 1¾–3. Dorsum generally brownish to light gray with reddish tubercles situated in dark spots. Some individuals may be rust-red to reddish brown and some may be tinged with greenish. Whitish stripe on back. *A parallel-sided boss on the head,* slightly convex, flat, or with a median furrow. Below whitish, spotted with dusky. *Young:* Crests appear with age and eventually unite to form a boss. *Male:* Dark-colored throat.

A prairie toad found close to water. Frequents lakes, ponds, streams, marshes, and roadside ditches, where it usually breeds in the shallows. May swim well out from shore when frightened. Chiefly diurnal during the breeding season, retiring to sandy banks to bury itself at night. May be active on warm nights.

Similar species: See Woodhouse's Toad (p. 61).

Voice: A clear, soft trill uttered about twice a minute and lasting about 1½ to 5 secs. Vocal sac round. Season, late March to Sept., with most breeding probably occurring in May, June, and early July.

Range: District of Mackenzie, Canada, to e. South Dakota; se. B.C. to e. Manitoba. Isolated population in se. Wyoming along Big and Little Laramie Rivers to about 15 mi. north and 15 mi. west of Laramie, Albany Co.   Map 35

GREEN TOAD   *Bufo debilis*   Pl. 8
Identification: 1½–2. A small, flat, vivid *green or yellow-green* toad with black spots and bars on its back. The black markings may be more or less united to form a network. Large, elongate, widely separated parotoids. Cranial crests weak or absent. Below white. *Male:* Throat dark; yellow or cream in female.

A species of arid and semiarid plains, valleys, and foothills — treeless or with scattered shrubs and trees and grass around the pools usually sought as spawning sites. Ordinarily not found on steep slopes or in barren rocky areas. A secretive, burrowing, nocturnal toad, generally abroad for only brief period during and after rains. Breeds in temporary streams and pools that form during the summer rainy season; occasionally in irrigation ditches and reservoirs. When trilling, Green Toads often hide under clumps of grass or other growth near water, and are difficult to see. Use triangulation to find them (see p. 11).

Similar species: See Sonoran Green Toad.

Voice: A wheezy buzz lasting 2 to 7 secs., with intervals of 5 secs. or more. Vocal sac round. Breeds April through Aug.

Range: W. and s. Kansas to Zacatecas; se. Arizona to e. Texas. To above 6000 ft., but mostly around 4000 ft.

Subspecies: The WESTERN GREEN TOAD, *B. d. insidior*, occurs in our area. Map 38

SONORAN GREEN TOAD *Bufo retiformis* **Pl. 8**
Identification: 1½–2¼. Similar to the Green Toad but *vividly marked above with network of black*, setting off oval areas of greenish-yellow ground color. *Male:* Throat dark.

A secretive nocturnal species of rolling mesquite grassland and creosote bush desert. Breeds in rainwater sumps and wash-bottoms bordered by fresh grass and scattered shrubs. Males begin to call at nightfall after rains, usually from among grass within a foot or so of the water's edge, but occasionally from more distant sites.

Similar species: The Green Toad has a more broken black network, often represented by scattered spots and bars which enclose areas of light ground color usually only half the size of those of the Sonoran Green Toad.

Voice: A combined buzz and whistle, a wheezy call lasting 1 to 3⅓ secs., gradually lowering in pitch or remaining constant and ending abruptly. May be highly ventriloquial, sounding as if 20 ft. away when within 5 ft. Voice resembles the Great Plains Narrow-mouthed Toad's. Vocal sac round. Breeds in July during period of summer rains.

Range: S.-cent. Arizona south to w.-cent. Sonora. In s. Arizona from Organ Pipe Cactus Nat'l Monument to vicinity of Kitt Peak, Pima Co. To 1500 ft. Map 38

Treefrogs and Their Allies:
Family Hylidae

A LARGE FAMILY of usually slim-waisted, long-legged frogs, mostly of small size. Many hylids are arboreal and have well-developed toe pads set off from the rest of the toe by a small, extra segment (see Fig. 6, No. 6, p. 25). These frogs are found on all continents but are most abundant and varied in the New World tropics. Treefrogs (*Pternohyla* and *Hyla*), the Cricket Frog (*Acris*), and the Chorus Frog (*Pseudacris*) occur in our area. Amplexus is pectoral.

CRICKET FROG   *Acris crepitans*   **Pl. 13**

Identification: ⅝–1⅜. A small slim-waisted frog with slender webbed toes and a triangular mark on the head (occasionally lacking). In the West, dorsal coloration is gray or light brown, with dark markings on back and dark bands on legs. White bar from eye to base of foreleg. *A dark stripe on the rear of the thigh.* *Male:* Throat dusky, suffused with yellow; more ventral spotting than in female.

Ranges widely over e. and middle U.S., entering the short-grass plains of e. Colorado and New Mexico along rivers. Basks on sunny banks of shallow pools. Often found in groups, individuals scattering when frightened, leaping high and fast or skittering over the surface of water.

Similar species: Young frogs (*Rana*) may be mistaken for a Cricket Frog. Look for the thigh stripe, triangular mark on the head, and facial bar.

Voice: A metallic *gick, gick, gick* — resembling the sound made by striking two stones together, about 1 call a second, the rate gradually increasing. Vocal sac round. Active all year except midwinter in the north. Breeds from winter through summer; choruses as late as Oct. in the south.

Range: Michigan to ne. Mexico; Long Island to e. Colorado and se. New Mexico.

Subspecies: BLANCHARD'S CRICKET FROG, *A. c. blanchardi*, occurs in our area.   **Map 43**

CHORUS FROG   *Pseudacris triseriata*   **Pl. 13**

Identification: ⅝–1½. A small, slim frog *without toe pads* and little webbing. Dorsal coloration highly variable — gray, brown, olive, or green. A dark stripe from snout through eye to groin, contrasting with a white stripe on the upper jaw. Usually 3 dark stripes on the back, sometimes broken or replaced by spots, occasionally absent. Often a triangular spot on the head. Below whitish, yellowish, or pale olive, unmarked or with a few dark spots on throat and chest. *Male:* Greenish-yellow to dark olive throat, with longitudinal folds of loose skin.

A frog of grassy pools, lakes, and marshes of prairies and mountains. Usually breeds in shallow, temporary pools in the open, but also uses deep, more permanent water in dense woods. Has adapted well to human habitation, occurring on farms and in cities.

Similar species: (1) Pacific and (2) Arizona Treefrogs have toe pads; the eyestripe in the Pacific Treefrog stops at the shoulder.

Voice: A vibrant *prreep, prreep* with rising inflection, lasting ½ to 1½ secs.; 30 to 70 calls a minute. To imitate, stroke the teeth of a pocket comb. Vocal sac round. Breeds Dec. to July, earliest in the south. Choruses occur night and day during the height of the breeding season.

Range: Great Bear Lake in nw. Canada to Gulf of Mexico; New Jersey to cent. Arizona and eastern border of Great Basin. To above 11,000 ft. (Uintah Mts., Utah).
Subspecies: WESTERN CHORUS FROG, *P. t. triseriata* (illus.). Ground color above pale gray, dark brown, dull green, or olive; markings dark gray or brown. Tibia not notably short-ened. BOREAL CHORUS FROG, *P. t. maculata* (illus.). Ground color above brown or greenish. Tibia shortened — so much so that this frog usually hops rather than leaps.   Map 41

BURROWING TREEFROG *Pternohyla fodiens* **Pl. 13**
Identification: 1–2. A *casque-headed frog*, the upper surface of the head very hard and the skin firmly attached. Prominent ridge between eye and nostril and *fold of skin at back of head.* No toe pads. *Single large whitish tubercle on hind foot.* Above brown or pale yellow, with large dark brown spots edged with black; below plain white. *Male:* Dark patch on each side of throat.

A terrestrial, burrowing, nocturnal frog of open grassy terrain. Occurs in mesquite grassland in extreme s. Arizona. The first hard rain in July brings them forth, choruses quickly forming about pools.
Voice: A loud, low-pitched *walk, walk, walk,* 2 or 3 calls a second each lasting ⅕ to ½ sec. and given on one pitch. Resembles Pacific Treefrog's but its sounds are lower-pitched, hoarser, shorter, faster, and without rising inflection. Large vocal sac, slightly bilobed from in front. Breeds July and Aug. during period of summer rains.
Range: San Simon Valley between Sells and Ajo, Pima Co., Arizona. Widespread in w. Mexico from Sonora to Michoacán.
Map 42

Treefrogs: Genus *Hyla*

ON ALL continents, but in Africa only north of the Sahara; head-quarters in the American tropics. Fifteen species in the U.S., most in the Southeast; only 4 in the West.

Typically, frogs with a rather large head, rounded snout, large eyes, slim waist, and prominent toe pads. Most are jumpers and climbers and are able to cling to twigs or climb a vertical surface by means of their adhesive toe pads. They range in size from less than ½ in. (Little Grass Frog of se. U.S.) to over 5 in.

CANYON TREEFROG *Hyla arenicolor* **Pl. 13**
Identification: 1¾–2¼. A brown or olive-gray treefrog *usually without an eyestripe,* blotched or spotted with dark brown or

olive, but sometimes with little or no pattern (sw. Utah). Below cream, grading to yellow on hind legs. Large toe pads; webbing of hind foot moderately well developed. Skin rather rough. *Male:* Throat dusky.

A small camouflaged frog that often huddles in niches on the sides of boulders or streambanks, within easy jumping distance of water. Favors intermittent or permanent streams with rocky pools. Essentials seem to be a firm substratum (sandstone, conglomerate, granite) and proximity to quiet water. Frequents arroyos in semiarid grassland and streams in pine-oak woods. Chiefly a ground-dwelling frog but occasionally climbs trees.

Similar species: See California Treefrog.

Voice: An explosive whirring sound on one pitch, lasting 1 to 3 secs. Vocal sac weakly bilobed from above. Breeds May through July.

Range: W. Colorado and s. Utah to n. Oaxaca; w. Texas to Colorado River in nw. Arizona. Isolated populations in Mogollon highlands of Arizona and Davis and Chisos Mts. in w. Texas. Old record for Mesa de Maya, Las Animas Co., Colorado. To around 9000 ft.   Map 46

CALIFORNIA TREEFROG *Hyla californiae*   Pl. 13

Identification: 1–2. Typically a *gray treefrog with dark blotches and usually no eyestripe*, its coloration blending with background. Frogs on granite tend to be dark-blotched, those on sandstone are usually plain. Below whitish with yellow on underside of hind legs, in groin, and on lower abdomen. Toes with well-developed web and conspicuous pads. *Male:* Throat dusky.

A frog of canyon streams and washes where there are rocks, quiet pools, and shade. Ranges from the desert to the pine belt in the mountains.

Similar species: (1) Canyon Treefrog tends more toward brown than pale gray, the webbing of the hind foot is reduced and the voice differs. (2) See also Pacific Treefrog.

Voice: A ducklike quack — short, low-pitched, ending abruptly and given repeatedly, lacking the whirring quality of the Canyon Treefrog's. Calls last $\frac{1}{5}$ to $\frac{1}{2}$ sec., have little or no inflection, and are only occasionally two-parted. Heard day and night at the peak of the breeding season. Vocal sac round. Breeds March to May.

Range: Mts. of s. California, including western fringe of desert along streams and at oases (Forty-nine Palms, Indian Cove), south into n. Baja California. From near sea level to around 5500 ft.   Map 46

PACIFIC TREEFROG *Hyla regilla*   Pl. 13

Identification: $\frac{3}{4}$–2. A small frog with toe pads and *black eye-*

stripe. The stripe is always present but difficult to see in dark individuals. Dorsal coloration highly variable — green, tan, gray, brown, or black. May change color from dark to light phase in a few minutes. Often a triangular dark spot on the head; dark spots on back and legs. Markings change in clarity with color phase. Below cream, yellowish on hindquarters. *Male:* Throat dusky, wrinkled.

Frequents a variety of habitats from sea level high into mountains. Breeds in marshes, lakes, ponds, roadside ditches, reservoirs, and slow streams in woods, meadows, and grassland. Chiefly a ground dweller found among low plant growth near water.

Similar species: (1) California Treefrog usually has no eyestripe, has larger toe pads, more fully webbed hind toes, and is rarely green. (2) Eyestripe of the Arizona Treefrog extends well beyond the shoulder; webbing is reduced.

Voice: The most commonly heard frog on the Pacific Coast. Calls often uttered in sequence, about 1 a second, a loud two-parted *kreck-ek*, the last syllable with rising inflection. Resembles California Treefrog's but call longer, higher-pitched, inflected, more musical, and more often two-parted. Vocal sac round. Breeds Jan. through July.

Range: Southern B.C. to tip of Baja California, east to w. Montana and e. Nevada. Only native frog on islands off coast of s. California. Sea level to 11,000 ft. in Sierra Nevada.

Map 44

ARIZONA TREEFROG *Hyla wrightorum* **Pl. 13**
Identification: $\frac{3}{4}$–$2\frac{1}{4}$. A close relative of the Pacific Treefrog. An eyestripe extends beyond the shoulder, sometimes to the groin; posteriorly it may be replaced by spots. Spotting on head and upper back usually scarce or absent. There is more often a triangular spot between the eyes in the Pacific Treefrog, but in the Arizona Treefrog there may be a spot on each upper eyelid and longitudinal bars on the lower back. Toe pads distinct; webbing reduced. *Male:* Throat dusky.

Frequents meadows in oak-pine or pine-fir forests, generally above 5000 ft. Found both on the ground and in shrubs and trees, usually near grassy shallow pools and along the slower parts of streams.

Similar species: See Pacific Treefrog.

Voice: A low-pitched harsh metallic clack lasting about $\frac{1}{4}$ sec. Lacks two-part quality of Pacific Treefrog's voice. Frequency may vary from 1 to 3 calls per second, all essentially on one pitch. Vocal sac round. Breeds June to Aug., during and after rains.

Range: Mts. of cent. Arizona and w. New Mexico, south in Sierra Madre Occidental. Isolated population in Huachuca

Mts., Cochise Co., Arizona. Old record for Nutria, McKinley
Co.(?), New Mexico. A single specimen, perhaps escaped fish
bait, has been taken at Island Lake, near Picacho, lower Colorado
River, Yuma Co., Arizona. From 5000 to over 7000 ft.   Map 45

True Frogs: Family Ranidae

TYPICALLY slim-waisted, long-legged, smooth-skinned jumpers
with webbed hind feet, and often with dorsolateral folds (glandular
ridges) that extend from behind the eyes to the lower back. Any
western tailless amphibian with dorsolateral folds is a true frog.
Family headquarters in Africa but representatives on all continents.
Only the large, widespread genus *Rana* (with some 250 species)
occurs in the New World. There are 16 species in N. America
north of Mexico, about equally divided between East and West,
and a dozen more in the New World tropics. Two introduced
species, the Bullfrog and the Green Frog, bring the western total
to 10. The Leopard Frog and the Wood Frog range across the
continent. A number of our western frogs are difficult to identify;
rely heavily on the range maps.

In males during the breeding season, forelimbs and thumb bases
become enlarged and webbing increases; a dark nuptial pad appears
on the thumb. Amplexus pectoral. Vocal sac paired or single,
generally inconspicuous.

RED-LEGGED FROG *Rana aurora*   Pls. 11, 12
  Identification: 2–5. Our largest western native frog. Red on
  lower abdomen and underside of hind legs, often overlying
  basic yellow coloration. Usually has a *dark mask bordered by a
  whitish jaw stripe.* Back with numerous small black flecks and
  larger, irregular, dark blotches of indistinct outline on brown,
  gray, or reddish ground color. In some individuals flecks join
  to form a more or less continuous network of black lines. Dark
  bands on legs. *Usually with coarse black (or gray), red, and yellow
  mottling in groin.* Relatively long legs; heel of adpressed hind
  limb extends to or beyond nostril. Eyes turned outward, well
  covered by lids as viewed from above; prominent dorsolateral
  folds. *Young:* May have yellow instead of red on underside of
  legs and in groin. *Male:* Enlarged forelimbs, thumb base, and
  webbing.
    Frequents marshes, slow parts of streams, lakes, reservoirs,
  ponds and other, usually permanent, water. A pond frog. Most
  common in wooded areas in the lowlands and foothills, but also
  occurs in grassland. Attracted to places where cattails and other
  plants provide good cover. Generally found in or near water but

disperses after rains and may appear on highways at night. When not breeding, may be found in damp woods.

Similar species: (1) In the Spotted Frog the light jaw stripe usually extends to the shoulder, the groin is usually unmottled, and the eyes are turned slightly upward and are less completely covered by the lids. (2) Cascades Frog, a mountain species, has distinct black dorsal spots, yellowish color on the lower abdomen and underside of the legs, a yellowish, lightly mottled groin, and generally rougher skin. (3) See also Foothill Yellow-legged Frog.

Voice: A stuttering accelerating series of gutteral notes on one pitch — *uh-uh-uh-uh-uh-rowr*, the last resembling a growl. Calls last about 3 secs. but are weak and easily missed. Occasionally only 3 or 4 chuckles are given. When the frogs are in chorus a continual low clucking is heard. Vocal sac single or absent, only moderately expandable. Breeding period short, often lasting only one or two weeks, usually Jan. to March, the time depending on locality.

Range: West of Cascade-Sierran crest from B.C. to n. Baja California. Perhaps formerly present in parts of Great Valley of California but now apparently absent. Introduced into Smoky Valley (Millett) and reported at Duckwater, Nye Co., Nevada. From near sea level to about 8000 ft.

Subspecies: NORTHERN RED-LEGGED FROG, *R. a. aurora*. Dorsal spots usually without light centers. To 3 in. CALIFORNIA RED-LEGGED FROG, *R. a. draytoni*. Dorsal spots usually with light centers. Skin rougher, limbs shorter, and eyes smaller than in the Northern Red-legged Frog.

Map 48

WOOD FROG *Rana sylvatica* Pl. 12

Identification: 1⅜–3¼. A relative of the Red-legged Frog. A black or *dark brown mask* ending abruptly just behind the eardrum and bordered below by a *white jaw stripe*. Dorsal ground color brown, pink, gray, or greenish. Back often with 2 broad longitudinal light-colored stripes separated by a dark one, which may or may not be bisected by a whitish line. Dark spot on each side of chest near base of foreleg. Prominent dorsolateral folds. Individuals in the Northwest are short-limbed and toadlike.

In the East it is truly a wood frog, inhabiting damp shady woods in the vicinity of clear streams and leafy pools. It favors shade but when breeding it may move out of the forests. In the Northwest, in the colder parts of its range, it is chiefly diurnal and less a forest dweller. There it may be found in open grassy areas bordered by thickets of willow and aspen, and in tundra ponds. Spruce or other forest trees are often present nearby. Its coloration blends well with fallen leaves and the mottled light and shade of the forest floor.

Similar species: (1) Spotted Frog has red, orange, or yellow on the ventral surfaces. (2) Red-legged Frog has less well defined mask and reddish color on underside of hind legs.

Voice: Resembles the Leopard Frog's but shorter, higher-pitched, and weaker. A series of rather high grating notes lasting 1 sec. or less, like the clucking of a domestic duck. Paired vocal sacs over forelimbs. Breeds Jan. to July, usually soon after the ice begins to melt from ponds, in the southern part of its range (s. Appalachians and the Ozarks) in Jan. and Feb., at the coldest time of the year. Breeding lasts 1 or 2 weeks, after which the frogs usually disperse.

Range: W. Alaska to Labrador, south in e. U.S. to s. Appalachian Mts., following closely the distribution of spruce. Ranges farther north than any other North American amphibian. Isolated populations in Ozarks, e. Kansas, n. Colorado (vicinity of Rand, Jackson Co., 5 mi. northwest of Grand Lake, Grand Co., and Chambers' Lake, Larimer Co.), s. Wyoming (Foxpark, Woods Creek, Albany Co.), and n. Idaho (1 mi. west of Bonner's Ferry, Boundary Co.). Records for Havre, Hill Co., and Billings, Yellowstone Co., Montana, require confirmation. Sea level to 10,000 ft. (Wyoming).   Map 47

SPOTTED FROG   *Rana pretiosa*   Pl. 11

Identification: 2–4. Light or dark brown above, with varying numbers of spots often having rather indistinct borders and generally light centers. Mask present, sometimes faint. Light-colored *jaw stripe.* Below red, salmon, or yellow, depending on locality and age. In contrast to the Red-legged Frog, the color appears to be more superficial, almost painted on. Throat, and sometimes entire ventral surface, spotted and mottled with dusky. Legs relatively short, heel of adpressed hind limb seldom reaching nostril. *Eyes turned slightly upward.* Dorsolateral folds usually present. *Young:* Yellow or orange ventral color faint or absent.

Populations in Nevada, Utah, Idaho south of Salmon River, and se. Oregon usually have yellowish ventral color; elsewhere red or salmon predominates.

A highly aquatic species found in the vicinity of cold, permanent water — streams, rivers, marshes, springs, pools, and small lakes. Seems not to occur in warm stagnant ponds grown to cat-tails. Frequents both woods and meadows. Rather sluggish. Migrates to upland areas in May and returns to permanent water in July (Yellowstone Nat'l Park).

Voice: Unknown. In Yellowstone at 7800 ft. breeds in late May and June and at lower elevations as early as March.

Similar species: Distinguished from (1) Cascades and (2) Red-legged Frogs by usual lack of mottling on sides, shorter legs, greater webbing, and rougher skin. (3) See also Wood Frog.

Range: Extreme se. Alaska to w. Alberta, nw. Wyoming, n. Utah, cent. Nevada west to near Pacific Coast in Oregon and Washington. Isolated populations west of Cascade Mts. and in southern part of range — Deep Creek near Ibapah, Tooele Co., Utah; Humboldt drainage and headwaters of Reese River, Nevada. Map 50

CASCADES FROG *Rana cascadae* Pl. 11

Identification: 1¾-2½. A relative of the Spotted Frog. Brown above, with *sharply defined inky black spots on back* and dark spotting on legs. Black flecking between the spots scarce or absent. Yellow on lower abdomen and underside of hind legs. Groin somewhat mottled; lower sides yellowish or cream. Dorsolateral folds present.

A mountain frog, closely restricted to water. Frequents small streams, potholes in meadows, ponds, and lakes. Found in the water or among grass, ferns, and other low herbaceous growth nearby. Ranges to near timberline. A rather sluggish frog, often allowing close approach. When frightened it usually attempts to escape by swimming rather than seeking refuge on the bottom. It may swim to the opposite bank or return to the same bank downstream. Diurnal.

Similar species: (1) Spotted Frog, with which it overlaps slightly in range, has a more conspicuous light-colored upper jaw stripe, lacks a mask, and has the nostrils closer together and higher on the snout. (2) See also Red-legged Frog.

Voice: A low-pitched grating, chuckling sound, resembling the Red-legged Frog's. Four or 5 notes per second. Breeds late May to mid-Aug.

Range: Cascade Mts. from n. Washington to vicinity of Lassen Peak, California; Olympic Mts., Washington. Coexists with Red-legged Frog at intermediate elevations in w. Oregon and Washington. From about 3000 to 9000 ft. Map 49

FOOTHILL YELLOW-LEGGED FROG *Rana boylei* Pl. 12

Identification: 1¾-2¾. Dorsal coloration gray, brown, reddish, or olive, usually harmonizing with the prevailing color of rocks and soil. Truly *yellow-legged*, the yellow extending from the underside of the hind legs onto the lower abdomen. Sometimes plain-colored above, but more often spotted and mottled with dusky. *Snout with a triangular buff-colored patch* from its tip to a line connecting the eyelids; no mask. Throat and chest often dark-spotted. Skin, including the eardrums, granular; indistinct dorsolateral folds. *Young:* Yellow on hind legs faint or lacking. *Male:* Swollen and darkened thumb base.

A stream or river frog of woodland and forest. Usually found near riffles where there are rocks and sunny banks. When frightened, it dives to the bottom and takes refuge among stones, silt, or vegetation. Closely restricted to water.

Similar species: (1) Red-legged Frog has red on underside of hind legs, usually a dark mask, well-defined dorsolateral folds, and smooth eardrums. (2) Mountain Yellow-legged Frog has a smoother skin, generally heavier spotting and mottling dorsally, usually lacks the snout patch, and often has dark toe tips. (3) See also Tarahumara Frog.

Voice: Seldom heard. A gutteral, grating sound on one pitch or with rising inflection, a single croak lasting $\frac{1}{2}$ to $\frac{3}{4}$ sec. Four or 5 croaks may be given in rapid series followed by a rattling sound, the entire sequence lasting about $2\frac{1}{2}$ secs. Inconspicuous vocal sac on each side of throat, anterior to the forelimbs. Breeds mid-March to May after high water of streams subsides.

Range: West of crest of Cascade Mts., Oregon, south in coastal mts. of California to San Gabriel River, Los Angeles Co.; Sierra Nevada foothills to about 6000 ft. (near McKessick Peak, Plumas Co.); San Pedro Mártir (lower end of La Grulla meadow, 6700 ft.), Baja California. Isolated populations in Elizabeth Lake Canyon and San Gabriel River drainage (vicinity of Camp Rincon), Los Angeles Co., California. Single record for 5 mi. north of Lodi, San Joaquin Co., California. Coexists with Mountain Yellow-legged Frog along North Fork of San Gabriel River. Map 55

MOUNTAIN YELLOW-LEGGED FROG   Pls. 11, 12
Rana muscosa

Identification: 2–3¼. The only frog of the Sierran highlands, a close relative of the Foothill Yellow-legged Frog. Generally a spotted or blotched species with *dusky toe tips*. Underside of the hind legs and sometimes the entire belly yellow or orange, usually more opaque than in Foothill Yellow-leg. Yellow often extends forward to level of forelimbs. Dorsolateral folds present but frequently indistinct. When handled these frogs smell like garlic. *Male:* Swollen darkened thumb base.

A frog of well-illuminated riverbanks, meadow streams, isolated pools, and lake borders in the high Sierra Nevada and rocky stream courses in the mountains of s. California. Seems to prefer sloping banks with rocks or vegetation to the water's edge. Seldom found more than 2 or 3 jumps from water. Chiefly diurnal. Tadpoles may overwinter.

Similar species: See (1) Foothill Yellow-legged and (2) Tarahumara Frogs.

Voice: No record of mating call. At high altitudes breeds June to Aug. after meadows and lakes are free of snow and ice. In s. California breeds March to May when high water in streams subsides.

Range: Sierra Nevada, mostly above 6000 to over 12,000 ft.; mts. of s. California from Pacoima River south, 600 to 7500 ft. Southernmost population isolated on Mt. Palomar.   Map 54

TARAHUMARA FROG   *Rana tarahumarae*   Pl. 11
Identification: 2½–4½. The Mexican counterpart of the Mountain Yellow-legged Frog. Above rust, olive, or dark brown with dark spots on back, often with light centers; prominent dark banding on hind legs. Below whitish to cream *often clouded with dusky. No mask or light jaw stripe.* Dorsolateral folds and eardrums indistinct, the latter frequently granular.

A species of the Sierra Madre Occidental barely entering the U.S. in the Pajarito Mts. of extreme s. Arizona. Frequents oak woodland along rocky, gravelly stream courses grown to willows and sycamores. Like its close relative the Foothill Yellow-legged Frog it is a stream dweller, usually staying within one or two jumps of water, on the banks of pools, under stones, or in niches in cliffs. Although these frogs apparently prefer moving water, individuals gather at quiet pools and springs in dry weather.

Similar species: The Yellow-legged Frogs are smaller and usually have a spotted throat.

Voice: Unknown. Breeds July and Aug., during the period of summer rains.

Range: Near Pena Blanca and Alamo Springs and in Sycamore and Tinajas Canyons, Pajarito Mts., Santa Cruz Co., Arizona, south in Sierra Madre Occidental to Jalisco.   Map 56

LEOPARD FROG   *Rana pipiens*   Pl. 12
Identification: 2–5. Typically a slim green frog with a dorsal pattern of well-defined *oval or round dark spots with pale borders.* The dorsal ground color varies — green, brownish, gray, or rarely almost black; sometimes the spots are faint, lack the pale borders, or are absent. There are well-defined, usually pale, dorsolateral folds and a white stripe on the upper jaw. Below cream or yellowish. In arid parts of its range it tends to be pale — gray or dull green and spotting is less vivid. *Young:* Spotting may be reduced or absent. *Male:* Loose skin between the jaw and shoulder during the breeding season.

The most widely distributed amphibian in N. America, ranging from brackish marshes along the eastern and southern coasts north to the District of Mackenzie and from desert lowlands high into the mountains. Frequents springs, creeks, rivers, ponds, canals, and reservoirs where there is permanent water and growth of cattails or other aquatic vegetation. May forage far from water in damp meadows. When frightened on land, it often seeks water in a series of zigzag jumps. Most easily found at night by its eyeshine (see p. 12).

Voice: A low "motor boat" sound interspersed with grunting and chuckling, lasting about 1 to 3 secs. Choruses are a medley of moaning, grunting, and chuckling suggesting the sounds made by rubbing an overinflated balloon. Individuals may squawk when they jump into the water and may scream when caught. Paired vocal sacs expand over the forelimbs. Breeds any month in the south, Feb. to Sept. in the arid Southwest, and May or later in the far north. In arid parts of its range it is an opportunistic breeder, ready to spawn whenever it rains, almost any time of year.

Range: Great Slave Lake, District of Mackenzie, Canada, south to Panama; Atlantic Coast to western edge of Great Basin. Introduced near Yettem, Tulare Co., San Joaquin Valley, California. An isolated population near San Felipe Creek, San Diego Co., California, may also have been introduced. Many scattered populations in arid Southwest.

Subspecies: VEGAS VALLEY LEOPARD FROG, *R. p. fisheri*. Dorsal spots small and faint, without sharp outline. Isolated at Las Vegas, Nevada. Probably now extinct. LEOPARD FROG, *R. p. pipiens*. Usually with well-defined oval or round, even-edged, black spots with pale yellow borders.

Map 51

BULLFROG *Rana catesbeiana*   Pl. 12

Identification: 3½–8. Our largest frog. Olive, green, or brown above, often grading to light green on the head — but sometimes light green confined to the upper jaw. Legs banded and blotched with dusky and usually some spotting on the back. Below whitish mottled with gray, a tinge of yellowish on the chin and hindquarters. A fold of skin extends from the eye around the eardrum. No dorsolateral folds. Eardrums conspicuous. *Male:* Yellow throat; eardrum larger than eye (about same size as eye in female).

Highly aquatic, remaining in or near permanent water, its activities largely independent of rainfall. Frequents marshes, ponds, lakes, reservoirs, and streams — usually quiet water where there is thick growth of cattails or other aquatic vegetation. Wary by day but readily found at night by its eyeshine. Often easily caught when dazzled by light. When first seized, it may "play possum" — hanging limp and motionless; be alert for sudden recovery!

Similar species: The Green Frog has dorsolateral folds.

Voice: A deep-pitched bellow suggesting *jug-o-rum* or *br-wum*. Frightened individuals may give a catlike *miaow* when they leap into water. Vocal sac single and internal. In the East, where native, breeds Feb. to Aug., earliest in the South; in the West, March to July. Tadpoles may overwinter.

Range: Atlantic Coast to e. Colorado and e. New Mexico; s.

Canada to ne. Mexico. Introduced at many localities west of Rockies (see Map 53) and in Hawaiian Is., Mexico, Cuba, Japan, and Italy.   Map 53

GREEN FROG *Rana clamitans*
Identification: 2⅛–4. Resembles Bullfrog (Plate 12). A green, brown, or bronze frog with plain or dark-spotted back and green on sides of head. Below white with irregular dusky lines or blotches. *Prominent dorsolateral folds* that fail to reach the groin. Eardrum conspicuous. *Young:* Usually profusely dark-spotted above. *Male:* Eardrum larger than eye, and throat usually yellow.

Closely restricted to water of marshes, ponds, lakes, streams, and springs. Introduced in West.
Similar species: See Bullfrog.
Voice: An explosive *bung* or *c'tung*, a low-pitched note resembling the sound made by plucking the lowest string of a banjo, often repeated several times in succession. When startled emits a high-pitched squawk as it leaps. Vocal sacs paired and internal, the throat forming a flattened pouch when inflated. In the East, where native, breeds March to Aug. Tadpoles may overwinter.
Range: Maritime Provinces to n.-cent. Florida, west to Minnesota and e. Texas. In the West introduced at Hope (Fraser Valley) and vicinity of Victoria, B.C., at Toad Lake, Whatcom Co., Washington, and along lower Weber River, Ogden, Utah.
                                                                      Map 52

Narrow-mouthed Toads:
Family Microhylidae

A LARGE diverse family of burrowing, terrestrial, and arboreal frogs with representatives in the Americas, Africa, Madagascar, Asia, and the Indo-Australian Archipelago. Arboreal species often have adhesive toe pads. Some microhylids lay their eggs on land and the young hatch fully formed.

Two closely related genera, *Gastrophryne* (narrow-mouthed toads) and *Hypopachus* (sheep frogs), primarily tropical with headquarters in Cent. America, are the sole ones reaching the U.S., and only 1 species, the Great Plains Narrow-mouthed Toad (*Gastrophryne olivacea*), occurs in our area. Another species, the Eastern Narrow-mouthed Toad, occurs in se. U.S., and the sheep frog reaches extreme s. Texas. New World forms are small, stout amphibians with small pointed head, tiny eyes, a fold of skin across the back of the head, short legs, and a smooth, tough skin, which probably helps protect them against ants, upon which they feed.

GREAT PLAINS NARROW-MOUTHED TOAD   Pl. 13
Gastrophryne olivacea

Identification: ⅞–1⅜. A tiny brown or gray, smooth-skin toadlike amphibian with *small pointed head* and broad waist. Hind legs short and stout. A fold of skin across the back of the head. *Male:* Dark throat; small tubercles on lower jaw and chest.

A secretive toad, hiding by day in damp burrows, crevices, and under rocks, bark, and boards, in the vicinity of streams, springs, and rain pools. Look under the bark and in the interior of rotten termite-infested stumps and under flat rocks near ant nests. In Arizona this toad ranges from mesquite grassland in San Simon Valley, Pima Co., to oak woodland in the Pajarito and Patagonia Mts. Narrow-mouths are difficult to find because of their small size and habit of calling from sites hidden in grass. Use triangulation (see p. 11).

Voice: A short *whit* followed by a low nasal buzz lasting 1 to 3 secs. and declining in pitch. At a distance a chorus sounds like a band of sheep; nearby it resembles a swarm of bees. Vocal sac round, about the size of a pea. Breeding occurs during the period of summer rains; and calling is stimulated by rainfall. Eggs laid in July.

Range: In the West occurs in extreme s. Arizona from vicinity of Patagonia, Santa Cruz Co., to San Simon Valley between Quijotoa and Ajo, Pima Co.; Pena Blanca Springs and Sycamore Canyon, Pajarito Mts., thence south, west of crest of Sierra Madre Occidental, to n. Nayarit. East of Continental Divide, it ranges from se. Nebraska to s. Coahuila and Chihuahua to e. Texas.

Subspecies: The SINALOA NARROW-MOUTHED TOAD, *G. o. mazatlanensis*, occurs in our area.   Map 29

Although numbered page 81 follows page 78 there is no omission of text. Necessity of relocating the plates resulted in this gap of pagination.

VIII

Turtles

Snapping, Musk, and Mud Turtles: Family Chelydridae

Snapping Turtles: Subfamily Chelydrinae

TWO SPECIES in the subfamily, the Common Snapping Turtle and the Alligator Snapping Turtle. The former reaches our area, ranging from Canada to Ecuador; the latter occurs from ne. Missouri to the Gulf Coast. Both are large freshwater turtles with long tail, powerful hooked jaws, and small plastron, less than half the width of the carapace.

SNAPPING TURTLE *Chelydra serpentina*   **Pl. 14**
   Identification: 8–18. A turtle that seems too large for its shell. Chunky head with powerful hooked jaws, *long tail* with saw-tooth crest, and a *small, narrow plastron*. Tail usually longer than half the length of the carapace. Carapace black, brown, or horn-colored. *Young:* 1¼ in. at hatching. Three prominent, longitudinal sawtooth ridges on the carapace, becoming reduced with age. Tail as long or longer than shell. General coloration dusky; carapace margin and plastron with white spots.
   Inhabits marshes, ponds, lakes, rivers, and slow streams, especially where aquatic plants are abundant. Closely restricted to water. Well camouflaged when resting on the bottom among plants, its concealment sometimes enhanced by growth of algae on its shell. Individuals bask on land or float at the water's surface. Often ill-tempered and prone to bite, but can be carried safely suspended by its tail if held well out from one's body. Emerges from hibernation March to May; eggs laid May to Oct., most nesting occurs in June and July. Feeds on crayfish, snails, insects, fish, frogs, salamanders, reptiles, birds, mammals, and aquatic plants.
   Similar species: The small plastron distinguishes it from all other western species.
   Range: Extreme s. Canada to Ecuador; western base Rocky Mts. to Atlantic Coast. To above 5000 feet in Colorado.

Subspecies: The COMMON SNAPPING TURTLE, *C. s. serpentina*, occurs in our area.   Map 57

Musk and Mud Turtles: Subfamily Kinosterninae

IN THE U.S. represented by 2 genera, each with 4 species — the musk turtles (*Sternothaerus*) and mud turtles (*Kinosternon*). Other members of the subfamily occur in Cent. and S. America. These turtles give off a musky odor when handled, hence they are sometimes called "stinkpots" or "stinking-jims." The odor glands are located on each side of the body where the skin meets the underside of the carapace. There are barbels (nipple-like projections) on the throat; the tail is short (prehensile in males), and there are 23 marginal shields, including the nuchal. Most other turtles have 25 marginals.

Two species of mud turtles (*Kinosternon*) occur in our area.

YELLOW MUD TURTLE   *Kinosternon flavescens*   **Opp. Pl. 14**
  Identification: 4–5¾. *Head and neck brown or olive above, contrasting with plain yellow or cream below.* Barbels present. Carapace elongate and high, flat or slightly concave on top, without flaring margin — olive or brown with occasional black seam borders. *Ninth and 10th marginal shields, counting from front of shell, usually distinctly higher than 8th.* Tail short, without saw edge above and ending in nail. Musky odor when handled. *Young:* Carapace nearly round, with weak-middorsal ridge. Ninth and 10th marginals not enlarged. *Male:* Two patches of horny scales on inner surface of each hind leg. Tail with horny, hooked tip.

  A highly aquatic turtle of semiarid grasslands and open woodland, frequenting both permanent and intermittent streams. Seems to prefer mud bottoms. Often only its snout is seen when it rises to the surface for air. Spends most of its time in the water but comes on land to feed, lay eggs, and bask, or when forced to leave a drying pool.
  Similar species: Distinguished from all western turtles except the Sonora Mud Turtle by single gular and 5 pairs of plastral shields. The latter lacks supraorbital ridges, the 9th marginal shield is not enlarged, and the head and neck are mottled.
  Range: S. Nebraska and Illinois to Durango and Tamaulipas; e.-cent. Texas to near mouth of Colorado River. In Arizona in Swisshelm Mt. area, Cochise Co.; San Simon Valley, Pima Co.; Big Sandy River, Mohave Co.; and Tempe–Mesa area, Maricopa Co. Reported at Yuma, Yuma Co., Arizona, and at Pyramid Canyon, Clark Co., Nevada.   Map 62

SONORA MUD TURTLE   *Kinosternon sonoriense*   **Pl. 14**
  Identification: 4–6½. Resembles the Yellow Mud Turtle but

lacks supraorbital ridges; 9th marginal shield unenlarged, and *head and neck heavily mottled. Male:* As in Yellow Mud Turtle.

Chiefly a woodland turtle that frequents ponds, springs, creeks, and waterholes of intermittent streams. Inhabits woodland of oaks and piñon and juniper or forests of ponderosa pine and Douglas fir. Less often found in the lowlands than the Yellow Mud Turtle, but occurs in the lower Colorado River. Closely restricted to water.

Similar species: See Yellow Mud Turtle.

Range: Cent. Arizona to Durango; w. Texas to se. California. In Arizona in Gila River drainage of central and southeastern part, to slightly over 5000 ft., and at Quitobaquito Spring, Pima Co. In New Mexico in headwaters of Gila River east to Taylor Creek, Catron Co., 6700 ft. Old records for Palo Verde and Yuma Indian Reservation, Imperial Co., California, along the Lower Colorado River.   Map 61

Water and Box Turtles, Tortoises, and Allies: Family Testudinidae

Water and Box Turtles: Subfamily Emydinae

NEARLY worldwide but absent from high latitudes and the Australian region, Madagascar, and Africa south of the Sahara. Many species are aquatic and have webbed toes, but the box turtles are mainly terrestrial. Well represented in e. N. America; 5 species in the West.

WESTERN POND TURTLE *Clemmys marmorata*   **Pl. 14**
   Identification: 3½–7. Carapace low — olive, dark brown, or blackish, occasionally without pattern but usually with a *network of spots, lines, or dashes of brown or black that radiate from the growth centers of the shields.* Plastron with 6 pairs of shields — yellowish, blotched with blackish or dark brown, occasionally unmarked. Limbs with prominent scales, flecked and lined with black. Head with spots or network of black. Crushing surface of upper jaw usually smooth or undulating. *Young:* Hatchlings 1 in.; tail nearly as long as shell. Carapace uniformly brown or olive above with yellow markings at edge of marginals; shields with numerous small tubercles. Plastron yellow, with large irregular central black figure; head, limbs, and tail marked with dusky and pale yellow. *Male:* Shell usually flatter and less heavily marked than in female.

A thoroughly aquatic turtle of ponds, marshes, rivers, streams, and irrigation ditches that typically have a rocky or muddy bottom and are grown to watercress, cattails, water lilies, or other aquatic vegetation. May be seen basking on logs, cattail mats, and mudbanks. Found Feb. to mid-Nov. in the north; all year in the south. Nests May to Aug., mostly June to mid-July, the time varying with locality. Food consists of aquatic plants, insects, and carrion.

Similar species: (1) Painted Turtle has yellow lines on head and limbs. (2) See also Pond Slider.

Range: Extreme sw. B.C. to nw. Baja California, chiefly west of Cascade-Sierran crest. Outlying areas are Mojave River, California, and Truckee and Carson Rivers, Nevada. Old record for Eagles Nest near Shoshone Falls, Jerome Co., Idaho. To around 6000 ft.

Subspecies: NORTHWESTERN POND TURTLE, *C. m. marmorata*. A pair of triangular inguinal plates; neck markings dull. SOUTHWESTERN POND TURTLE, *C. m. pallida*. Inguinal plates small or absent; neck markings contrast with light ground color.   Map 59

PAINTED TURTLE *Chrysemys picta*   **Pl. 15**

Identification: 3½–9⅞. Carapace low, smooth, unkeeled, generally black or olive with *front edge of shields bordered with yellow* or sometimes shell with an open network and vertebral stripe of yellow. *Yellow lines on head and limbs* and a red blotch or bar behind the eye. Usually plastron marked with a large dark central figure with branches extending along the furrows between the scutes. Crushing surface of upper jaw often with a ridge or row of tubercles parallel to the jaw margin. Rear of carapace with smooth border. *Young:* Plastron red or orange, the central dark figure well developed. *Male:* Much smaller than female; very long fingernails.

An aquatic turtle that frequents ponds, marshes, small lakes, ditches, and streams where the water is quiet or sluggish and the bottom muddy, grown to aquatic plants. Often seen sunning on mudbanks, logs, or rocks near water, sometimes in groups of a dozen or more. May not emerge from hibernation until March or April in the north. Nests May to Aug. Feeds on aquatic plants, insects, spiders, earthworms, mollusks, crayfish, fish, frogs, and tadpoles. Sometimes scavenges.

Similar species: See (1) Western Pond Turtle and (2) Pond Slider.

Range: Widely distributed in e. and n. U.S. south to Chihuahua and along Mississippi River to Gulf of Mexico. Isolated populations in San Juan River drainage of sw. Colorado and nw. New Mexico; Rio Grande and Pecos Rivers, New Mexico; Thurston Co., Washington. Reported from Labyrinth Canyon, Kane Co., Utah   Map 63

POND SLIDER *Pseudemys scripta*   **Pl. 15**

Identification: 5–14¼. Carapace usually with longitudinal wrinkles and streaks and bars of yellow on an olive or dusky background; yellow markings sometimes more or less hidden by black pigment and some individuals almost completely black. Streaking on 2nd and 3rd costal shields tends to parallel the long axis of the shields. Head and limbs striped with yellow; usually a *broad red stripe* or yellow spot *behind the eye.* Underside of carapace and plastron yellow, with dusky blotches, or "eye-spots," usually in symmetrical arrangement. Lower jaw appears rounded when viewed from front. Rear of carapace with saw-tooth margin. *Young:* Carapace green, streaked with yellow; usually a red or yellow postocular stripe; plastron with many dark eyelike spots. *Male:* More often dark-colored than female. Long nails on front feet.

A thoroughly aquatic turtle that seldom ventures far on land. Often seen basking singly or in groups on logs or other objects in the water. Prefers quiet water with mud bottom and abundant aquatic vegetation. Young widely sold as pets. Feeds on aquatic plants and crayfish, snails, tadpoles, and fish.

Similar species: (1) The carapace of the Painted Turtle is usually marked with red and lacks longitudinal wrinkles and saw-toothed rear margin. (2) Cooter usually has a maze of light and dark lines on the 2nd and 3rd costal shields rather than vertical streaking, and a flattened lower jaw as viewed from in front. (3) Western Pond Turtle has spotted head and limbs.

Range: Michigan to Panama; Atlantic Coast to s. New Mexico, s. Sonora, and s. half of Baja California.   Map 65

COOTER *Pseudemys concinna*

Identification: 9–16. Resembles the Pond Slider (Plate 15). Generally brown to olive above, carapace of adults with longitudinal furrows and *whorls and circles of brown or black on a lighter ground color.* Yellow streaks on head. The Texas Slider, the subspecies in our area, has intricate whorls and the head markings are highly variable, consisting of broad stripes, spots, or vertical bars variously joined together or separated by dark pigment. Underside of shell with eyelike markings on marginals and narrow dark lines along plastral sutures. Plastral markings fade with age. Upper jaw notched in front, flanked by a cusp on each side. *Young:* 1–1¾. Pattern vivid, in our subspecies carapace marked with tight whorls, head and neck striped. *Male:* Forelimbs with elongate toenails; shell flatter than in female. Old males may become uniformly mottled on shell, head, and limbs; ridges may extend downward from the nostrils, terminating in the jaw cusps.

Chiefly a river turtle but also enters ditches, cattle tanks, and saltwater near the mouths of rivers. Fond of basking and usually slides into the water at the first sign of danger.

Similar species: See Pond Slider.

Range: Virginia and s. Illinois to Gulf Coast and nw. Florida. Atlantic Coast to w. Texas, se. New Mexico, and Nuevo León.

Reported at Bitter Lakes Wildlife Refuge, 12 mi. northeast of
Roswell, Chaves Co., New Mexico.
Subspecies: The TEXAS SLIDER, *P. c. texana*, occurs in our
area.   Map 64

WESTERN BOX TURTLE   *Terrapene ornata*   **Pl. 14**
Identification: 4–5¾. A land turtle that can completely enclose
itself in its shell. *The front of the plastron is hinged* and can be
drawn up tightly against the carapace. Shell high, rounded,
and typically marked with radiating lines or a series of dots of
black or dark brown on a yellow background. Similar markings
may be found on plastron. Occasional individuals have a plain
yellow or horn-colored shell. *Male:* First hind toenail turned
inward. Iris and spots on forelegs reddish (yellowish in female)
and head sometimes greenish.
    Primarily a prairie turtle. Over much of its range it inhabits
treeless plains and gently rolling country grown to grass or
scattered low bushes where the soil is sandy. Also occurs in open
woodland. In some areas tortoise "sign" consists of disturbed
piles of cow dung into which they have dug in search of beetles
and other insects; they also eat berries, tender shoots, and
leaves. Seeks shelter under boards, rocks, and other objects or
in self-made burrows. Active March to Nov. Breeds both spring
and autumn and nests May through July. Activity stimulated
by rainfall.
Range: Sw. South Dakota, s. Michigan, and Indiana south to
Gulf Coast of Texas and extreme n. Mexico; e. Texas across s.
New Mexico to se. Arizona and Sonora. To 6000 ft.
Subspecies: YELLOW BOX TURTLE, *T. o. luteola*. Pale
radiating lines on shell more numerous than in the Ornate Box
Turtle, 11 to 14 on 2nd costal shield. Markings become less
distinct with advancing age and eventually are lost; shells of
most old individuals are uniform straw color or pale greenish
brown. ORNATE BOX TURTLE, *T. o. ornata*. Pale radiating
lines fewer than above, 5 to 8 on 2nd costal shield. Usually no
obvious fading of shell with advancing age.   Map 60

Gopher Tortoises: Subfamily Testudininae

LAND-DWELLING chelonians with domed shell and elephantlike
limbs, ranging into some of the most arid parts of the world. The
majority are herbivorous, feeding on leaves, soft stems, and fruits,
but some occasionally eat animal matter. On all continents except
Australia. Includes the giant tortoises of the Galápagos Islands
and islands in the Indian Ocean. The Desert Tortoise, the only
species in our area, is a member of the genus *Gopherus*, of which
there are 4 species, all in N. America.

DESERT TORTOISE *Gopherus agassizi*   **Pl. 15**
Identification: 6–14½. *A high-domed shell usually with prominent growth lines on shields* of both carapace and plastron. Carapace brown or horn-colored, usually without definite pattern. Plastron yellowish, without a hinge. Front limbs covered with large conical scales. When drawn in, the limbs completely close opening of shell. Limbs stocky. Tail short. *Young:* Hatchlings 1½ in.; flexible shell; claws longer and sharper than in adult. Carapace dull yellow to light brown, the shields usually with dark borders. *Male:* Gular shields longer than in female; lump on each side of lower jaw.
   A completely terrestrial desert species, requiring firm, but not hard, ground for construction of burrows (banks of washes or compacted sand), adequate ground moisture for survival of eggs and young, and grass, cactus, or other low growth for food. Frequents desert oases, riverbanks, washes, dunes, and occasionally rocky slopes. Creosote bush is often present in its habitat; in Mexico it occurs in thorn scrub. Tortoise tracks consist of parallel rows of rounded dents, the direction of travel indicated by sand heaped up at the rear of each mark. Burrows, often found at the base of bushes, have half-moon shaped openings and may be 3 to 30 ft. long and be occupied by one to many individuals. Short tunnels afford temporary shelter; longer ones, called dens, are used for estivation and hibernation. Nests in late spring and summer.
Range: S. Nevada and extreme sw. Utah to n. Sinaloa; se. Arizona (vicinity of Benson, Cochise Co.) to Mojave Desert and eastern side of Salton Basin, California; absent from Coachella Valley, California, although habitat seems suitable.   Map 58

Sea Turtles: Families
Cheloniidae and Dermochelyidae

LARGE marine turtles, primarily of tropical and subtropical seas. Low, stream-lined shell and powerful flippers. The cold Alaskan current usually keeps them south of s. California, but occasional individuals range far north. Both the Leatherback and Green Turtle have been recorded off s. B.C. Five species, with representatives in both Atlantic and Pacific Oceans.

Family Cheloniidae

GREEN TURTLE *Chelonia mydas*   **Pl. 16**
   Identification: 30–60+ (usually 120–200 lbs., record 850 lbs.).

Carapace smooth, with *4 costal shields on each side*, the 1st not touching the nuchal. *A pair of large scales (prefrontals) between the upper eyelids.* Carapace olive; plastron without pattern, pale yellow or whitish. Head plates olive, edged with yellowish. *Young:* About 2 in. at hatching. Carapace scutes overlap slightly and flippers are relatively larger than adult's. Generally dark brown to blackish, the shell and flippers edged with cream. Below pale. *Male:* Longer, narrower carapace than female's; very long, prehensile tail, tipped with a horny nail. Enlarged curved claw on front flipper.

A thoroughly aquatic turtle that seldom comes on land. It basks and sleeps on remote rocky shores and lays its eggs on gently sloping sandy beaches, in breeding rookeries. May be seen in the vicinity of mangroves, beds of eelgrass, or seaweed, where it comes to graze. In migration may occur far at sea. A rare visitor to our shores, although formerly common in San Diego Bay. Commercially valuable, its flesh highly esteemed. The common name comes from the color of its fat.

Similar species: See Loggerhead.

Range: Worldwide in warm seas. On Pacific Coast, common as far north at San Quintín Bay, Baja California; occasional along coast of s. California. Single record for Ucluelet Inlet, B.C.

Subspecies: The PACIFIC GREEN TURTLE, *C. m. agassizi*, occurs in our area.

LOGGERHEAD *Caretta caretta*   **Pl. 16**

Identification: 28–84 (large individuals, 300–400 lbs.; some to over 900 lbs.). Shell high in front; *costal shields 5 or more on each side*, not overlapping, the 1st touching the nuchal. Broad head with 2 pairs of prefrontals. Carapace usually reddish brown, the shields often edged with yellow. Head shields yellowish brown to olive-brown, grading to yellowish at their margins. Below cream, more or less clouded with dusky. *Young:* About 1½–2 in. at hatching. Carapace yellowish buff, brown, or grayish black, with 3 longitudinal ridges and a tendency toward slight overlapping of shields. Plastron creamy white to grayish black mottled with white.

A widely ranging turtle of the open ocean. Enters bays, lagoons, estuaries, salt marshes, and river mouths to forage and breed. Nests on gently sloping sandy beaches singly or in groups. Feeds on crabs, mollusks, sponges, jellyfish, fish, and eelgrass.

Similar species: (1) Green Turtle has 4 costal shields and 1 pair of prefrontals. (2) See also Pacific Ridley.

Range: Warmer parts of Pacific, Indian, and Atlantic Oceans and throughout Mediterranean Sea. Pacific Coast from s. California and upper end of Gulf of California to Chile.

Subspecies: The PACIFIC LOGGERHEAD, *C. c. gigas*, occurs in our area.

PACIFIC RIDLEY   *Lepidochelys olivacea*   **Pl. 16**
   Identification: 24–28 (to around 80 lbs.). A relatively small sea
   turtle with uniformly olive-colored heart-shaped carapace,
   nearly round from above and rather flat-topped from the side.
   Usually 6 to 8 (occasionally 5 to 9) *costal shields on each side,* the
   1st pair in contact with the nuchal. Head large, with *2 pairs of
   prefrontals. Four pairs of inframarginals on the bridge,* each perforated by a pore. Plastron light greenish yellow or greenish
   white. *Young:* 1½–1¾ in. Nearly uniform grayish black, except
   for lighter shade on ventral keels, which are strong and sharp
   from the humeral to anal shields. Carapace with longitudinal
   keels.
   Evidently more a bottom dweller than other marine turtles.
   Frequents protected and relatively shallow water of bays and
   lagoons, but also ranges well out to sea. Nests on beaches.
   Feeds on seaweed, mollusks, and sea urchins.
   Similar species: The 2 pairs of prefrontals, high costal shield
   count, and 4 enlarged inframarginals will distinguish it from
   other marine turtles.
   Range: Warmer parts of the Pacific and Indian Oceans. Off
   western Coast of Baja California and in Gulf. Single record
   from beach near Table Bluff, Humboldt Co., California.

Family Dermochelyidae

LEATHERBACK   *Dermochelys coriacea*   **Pl. 16**
   Identification: 48–96 (700–1600 lbs., possibly to a ton). Largest
   living turtle. *Carapace and plastron with smooth leathery skin
   (no horny shields) and prominent longitudinal ridges.* Carapace
   dark brown, slaty, or black, unmarked or blotched with whitish
   or pale yellow, in profile often having a toothed outline imparted
   by some 30 tubercles. *Young:* Hatchlings covered with small
   scales; tail rudderlike, with thin, high dorsal keel. Scales and
   keeling soon shed. Flipper margins and shell ridges light-colored.
   A widely ranging species that may be encountered far out at
   sea. Females ascend gently sloping sandy beaches of tropical
   and subtropical shores to lay their eggs. These turtles sometimes gather in schools to feed on jellyfish.
   Range: Worldwide, chiefly in warm seas but occasionally enters
   cold water. On Pacific Coast recorded north to Sedgwick Bay,
   Queen Charlotte Is.
   Subspecies: The PACIFIC LEATHERBACK, *D. c. schlegeli,*
   occurs in our area.

Softshell Turtles:
Family Trionychidae

THESE are the "pancake" turtles, named for their round, flat, flexible shell. The neck is long and the nostrils open at the end of a proboscis-like snout; feet broadly webbed and paddle-like. Although thoroughly aquatic, they venture on land to bask and nest. Softshells actively seek prey (insects, crayfish, worms) or ambush it as they lie with shell buried in mud or sand. When in the shallows the long neck and snout can be extended to the surface from time to time for air while the turtle remains concealed. Handle with care; they are quick and can inflict a painful bite.

Three species in the U.S.; others in Mexico, s. Asia, Malay Archipelago, and Africa.

SPINY SOFTSHELL *Trionyx spiniferus*   **Pl. 15**
  Identification: 3½–12½. An extremely flat turtle with *flexible pancake-like shell covered with leathery skin* rather than horny shields. Anterior edge of shell often with tubercles, or "warts" (occasionally smooth in Texas Softshell). Limbs flat and toes broadly webbed. A flexible proboscis. Each nostril with a median ridge. Lips fleshy, concealing sharp-edged jaws. Above olive-brown or grayish, variously flecked with black, sometimes with dark eyelike spots on shell; carapace with cream-colored border. Below cream or yellowish, unmarked. Markings tend to fade with age. *Young:* About 1½ to 1¾ in. at hatching. Carapace border conspicuous. Shell often spotted with black, sometimes profusely so. Prominent dark markings on head and limbs. *Male:* Averages smaller than female and has more contrasting pattern, retaining juvenile markings. Carapace with sandpaperlike texture. Tail thick and fleshy, extending beyond edge of shell. *Female:* Tends to become blotched and mottled with age; carapace smoother than in male and with well-developed warts on anterior edge.

  In the West, it is primarily a river turtle and is attracted to quiet water with bottom of mud, sand, or gravel. It also enters ponds, canals, and irrigation ditches, but generally avoids temporary water. Agile both in water and on land. Can retract head out of sight beneath its shell, among folds of neck skin. Active April to Sept. in the north, all year in the south. Nests May to July on sandy banks. Feeds on earthworms, snails, crayfish, insects, fish, frogs, tadpoles, and occasionally aquatic plants. Sometimes scavenges.
  Similar species: The Smooth Softshell has less-contrasting marks on the dorsal surface of the limbs, a more pointed snout, and lacks a whitish ridge on each side of the septum between the nostrils; the tip of the snout is wedge-shaped and the nostrils can

be seen in both side and ventral view. The snout of the Spiny Softshell is less pointed and the nostrils open to the front.

Range: Widespread throughout Mississippi basin and se. U.S. In West in western tributaries of Mississippi; Rio Grande and Pecos Rivers, New Mexico; Gila and lower Colorado Rivers. Introduced into Colorado River system from New Mexico about turn of century.

Subspecies: WESTERN SPINY SOFTSHELL, *T. s. hartwegi*. Retains juvenile pattern of small ocelli, or solid black dots, on carapace. Only 1 dark marginal line separates pale border of carapace from dorsal ground color; pale border not conspicuously widened posteriorly. Bold pattern of dark and light markings on head and limbs. TEXAS SOFTSHELL, *T. s. emoryi*. Juvenile pattern of white dots confined to rear 3rd of carapace. Pale border conspicuously widened, 4 to 5 times wider at rear than at sides. Pattern on head and limbs reduced.

Map 66

SMOOTH SOFTSHELL   *Trionyx muticus*

Identification: 3¼–8½. Resembles the Spiny Softshell (Plate 15). *Nostrils round, no median ridges,* and front end of carapace smooth. Juvenile pattern of large dusky spots (sometimes eyelike) or small dark dots and bars persistent in males. A pale, usually unbroken stripe behind the eye; otherwise side of head unpatterned. No contrasting marks on dorsal surface of limbs. *Young:* Hatchlings 1⅛–1¾ in. Carapace brown or olive-gray, marked with dots and dashes only a little darker than the ground color. *Male:* Tends to be colored like the young. *Female:* Mottled with various shades of gray, brown, or olive.

Chiefly a river turtle, apparently more restricted to running water than the Spiny Softshell. Frequents large rivers and streams but also lakes and impoundments, the latter principally in the southern part of its range. Nests May to July on small islands or gently sloping muddy or sandy shores.

Similar species: See Spiny Softshell.

Range: Chiefly in Mississippi drainage from extreme w. Pennsylvania, s. Minnesota, and South Dakota to Gulf Coast; from western end of panhandle of Florida to cent. Texas. In our area known only from Canadian River drainage of Conchos River to above Conchos Dam, 4250 ft., San Miguel Co., New Mexico.

Subspecies: The MIDLAND SMOOTH SOFTSHELL, *T. m. muticus*, occurs in our area.   Map 67

IX

Lizards

Geckos: Family Gekkonidae

A LARGE FAMILY of tropical and subtropical lizards found on all continents and widespread on oceanic islands. Most are nocturnal and therefore limited in distribution by low night temperatures. Geckos communicate by chirping and squeaking. The name is based on the sound made by an oriental species. They are excellent climbers. They crawl with ease on walls and ceilings and are often found in houses and public buildings in the tropics.

Typically, they have a soft skin with fine granular scales, large eyes with vertical pupils and without movable lids, a fragile tail easily lost but readily regenerated, and toes with broad flat tips and well-developed claws. The undersides of the toes are covered with broad plates which bear numerous villi, microscopic hairlike structures with spatulate tips. The villi and the sharp claws, which anchor in surface irregularities, make possible the remarkable climbing ability.

In the U.S. there are at least 4 native species, 3 of which enter our area. The banded geckos differ from most geckos in having movable eyelids and slender toes. In addition, several species have been introduced in the U.S. at port cities in s. Florida and along the Gulf Coast.

BANDED GECKO *Coleonyx variegatus* **Pl. 29**
Identification : 2½–3. The *soft pliable skin, vertical pupils, and movable eyelids* will distinguish this lizard from all others except its close relative the Texas Banded Gecko. Scalation finely granular, *toes slender*, and tail constricted at its base. When seized, the tail usually breaks off at the constriction. Chocolate-brown bands on both body and tail, on a pink to pale yellow background. The bands tend to break up with age into a blotched or variegated pattern. Below pale whitish. May squeak when caught. *Young:* Above with brown bands, usually well defined and unbroken. *Male:* Prominent spur on each side at base of tail; spurs weak or absent in female. Preanal pores present. Corresponding scales in female usually enlarged and sometimes pitted.

Although it appears delicate, this lizard is able to live in extremely dry parts of the desert because of its nocturnal and subterranean habits. It is chiefly a rock dweller, ranging from creosote bush flats to the piñon-juniper belt, and from catclaw, cedar, grama grass association in the eastern part of the range to chaparral areas in the West. In some parts of its range it occurs in barren dunes. (Algodones Dunes, California). To find these lizards, drive slowly along blacktop roads and watch for a small pale twiglike form. In the daytime turn rocks, boards, and dried cow dung; remove cap rocks and pry open rock crevices, particularly in outcrops on the lower slopes and bottoms of canyons in the vicinity of intermittent or permanent streams. Feeds on insects and spiders.

Range: S. Nevada to tip of Baja California and s. Sonora; coastal s. California to sw. New Mexico. Ranges from desert across s. Sierra Nevada via Kern River Canyon to Granite Station, Kern Co., on eastern side of San Joaquin Valley, California.

Subspecies: DESERT BANDED GECKO, *C. v. variegatus.* Preanal pores in males usually 7 or fewer; dark body bars equal to or narrower than interspaces; bars with light centers or replaced by spotting; light collar mark indistinct. TUCSON BANDED GECKO, *C. v. bogerti.* Pattern resembles above but preanal pores in males usually 8 or more. SAN DIEGO BANDED GECKO, *C. v. abbotti.* Dark body bars uniform in color and equal to or narrower than interspaces; distinct narrow light-colored collar mark. UTAH BANDED GECKO, *C. v. utahensis.* Dark body bars in adult wider than interspaces, and with their edges highly irregular and often confluent with spots in the interspaces. Map 69

TEXAS BANDED GECKO *Coleonyx brevis*
Identification: 1¾–2¼. Closely resembles the Banded Gecko (Plate 29) but usually averages fewer preanal pores, seldom more than 4 (3 to 6), which are interrupted by 1 or more small scales at the midline. Dark body bars in adult wider than the interspaces and often replaced by spotting.

Like its western relative, it is primarily a rock dweller, frequenting outcrops and canyons in arid environments where it may be found under cap rocks and exfoliating flakes. Nocturnal. Found on roadways at night.

Similar species: See Banded Gecko.

Range: S. New Mexico to s.-cent. Texas, south to Zacatecas. Old record for Santa Fe, New Mexico. Map 69

LEAF-TOED GECKO *Phyllodactylus xanti*   Pl. 29
Identification: 2–2½. A typical gecko with *enlarged toe pads* and large *eyes without movable eyelids.* Pupils vertical. Toe tips with 2 large flat scales having claw between. Scales on dorsal surfaces

of body mostly granular, a few keeled. Above flesh-colored, brown, or gray marked with dark brown. Below pale.

A desert rock dweller, often inhabiting canyons with massive boulders. Attracted to water; especially likely to occur in the vicinity of streams and springs. An excellent climber closely restricted to rocks, hence rarely found on roadways at night. Search for it by prying open crevices with a crowbar. Often squeaks when caught. Tail readily lost.

Similar species: See Granite Night Lizard (p. 118).

Range: Lower desert slope of mts. of s. California, from vicinity of Palm Springs to tip of Baja California. On islands in the Gulf and off western coast of Baja California.

Subspecies: The LEAF-TOED GECKO, *P. x. nocticolus*, occurs in our area.   Map 68

Iguanids: Family Iguanidae

INCLUDES most North American lizards, lizards of greatly varied form and habits. Dorsal scales range from smooth and granular to spiny and keeled; body rounded or broad and flat (horned lizards); habits arboreal, ground-dwelling, and marine (Marine Iguana of the Galápagos). Restricted to the New World except for a few species in the Madagascan region and a single species in the Tonga and Fiji Is.

A noteworthy structural feature in our species is the presence of 3 to 5 longitudinal keels on the underside of the toes. Males often have enlarged postanal scales and, when breeding, a swollen tail base, from which the copulatory organs (hemipenes) can usually be extruded by gentle squeezing with thumb and forefinger.

DESERT IGUANA *Dipsosaurus dorsalis* **Pl. 20**
  Identification: 4–5½. A large pale round-bodied lizard with long tail and rather small rounded head. Scales small, granular on sides, smooth and overlapping on belly. *A row of slightly enlarged, keeled scales down middle of back.* Above pale gray, with barring or network of brown on sides; variously spotted and blotched with light gray. Below pale, with pinkish areas on sides of belly in both sexes during breeding season.

Typical habitat in the northern part of its range consists of creosote bush desert with hummocks of loose sand and patches of firm ground with scattered rocks. In the south it frequents subtropical scrub. Most common in sandy habitats but also occurs along rocky streambeds, on bajadas, silty floodplains, and on clay soils. May be seen basking on rocks or sand hummocks, near a burrow in which it may take refuge. Tolerant of high temperatures, remaining abroad on hot, sunny days when most other lizards seek shelter. Chiefly herbivorous. Climbs among the branches of the creosote bush and other plants to obtain fresh leaves, buds, and flowers. It also eats insects, carrion, and its own fecal pellets. Usually easily noosed when it is feeding or resting. Breeds April and early May.

Range: From s. Nevada to tip of Baja California and n. Sinaloa. Desert side of mts. in s. California to cent. Arizona. To around 4000 ft. Its range in the U.S. coincides closely with that of the creosote bush, a staple food.

Subspecies: The DESERT IGUANA, *D. d. dorsalis*, occurs in our area.   Map 73

CHUCKWALLA *Sauromalus obesus*   **Pl. 17**
Identification: 5½–8. A large, flat, dark-bodied lizard with *loose folds of skin on neck and sides*, often seen sprawled on a rock in the sun. Skin with sandpaper texture. Tail with blunt tip and broad base. *Rostral scale absent. Young:* Crossbands on body and tail. Those on tail conspicuous, black on an olive-gray or yellow background. *Male:* Foreparts and limbs usually black, sometimes spotted and flecked with pale gray. Remainder of body usually red or light gray, depending on age and locality; tail pale yellow. Female tends to retain juvenile crossbands. Adults of both sexes usually banded in sw. Utah.

A rock-dwelling herbivorous lizard widely distributed in the desert. The creosote bush, a staple food occurs throughout its range. Nearly every lava flow, rocky hillside, and outcrop will have its chuckwallas. Rocks provide shelter and basking sites. In hunting this lizard, drive on desert roads in late morning and afternoon to locate basking individuals. When one is found approach on foot as close as possible and take note of the crevice it enters or listen for the sandpaperlike sound made when the animal slides into a crack. Search may be aided by discovery of droppings (elongate cylinders containing plant fibers), which mark basking sites and favored retreats. When a "chuck" is located, darken a portion of the crevice opening with a collecting sack or garment and *gently* probe the animal with a slender stick to guide it into position under the sack. Then quickly remove the cover and grab. Even if you obtain a firm grasp on leg or tail, a crowbar may be needed to pry open the crevice to get the "chuck" out. When disturbed, chuckwallas gulp air, distend their body, and wedge themselves in place.

Range: S. Nevada to Guaymas, Sonora; desert side of mts. in s. California to cent. Arizona; drainage of Colorado River in s. Utah to vicinity of Hite.

Subspecies: WESTERN CHUCKWALLA, *S. o. obesus*. Single row of femoral pores. Tail bands, when present, 3 to 5 dark, alternating with 2 to 4 light. End of tail usually light-colored.

UPPER COLORADO RIVER CHUCKWALLA, *S. o. multi-foraminatus*. Most individuals with secondary row of femoral pores. Tail bands 5 to 6 dark, alternating with 4 to 5 light. End of the tail usually dark. Young often brick-red, speckled with cream and with light-to-dark bands across back. Colorado River from Glen Canyon Dam at Page, Arizona, to a few miles above Hite, Garfield Co., Utah. ARIZONA CHUCKWALLA, *S. o. tumidus*. Differs from other subspecies in having fewer than 50 scales encircling the middle of the forearm.   Map 71

LESSER EARLESS LIZARD *Holbrookia maculata*   **Pl. 19**
Identification: 2–2½. A small ground-dwelling lizard *lacking ear openings;* above with *smooth granular scalation.* The upper labials overlap and are separated by diagonal furrows. A fold of skin across the throat. Tail short; no black bars on underside. Ground color above brown, tan, gray, or whitish, usually resembling the soil color of the habitat. Back usually with scattered light spots and several longitudinal rows of dark blotches with light posterior margins. A pair of black marks on sides of belly. Often a yellow or orange spot on the throat. *Male:* Enlarged postanal scales. Dark dorsal blotches often faint, when present usually light-edged. Belly marks more conspicuous than in female and set off by blue border. During the breeding season females develop vivid orange or yellow color on throat.

Primarily a plains lizard, most common where there are exposed patches of sand or gravel. Frequents washes, sandy streambanks, sand dunes (White Sands, New Mexico), short-grass prairie, mesquite woodland and farmland. Not a particularly fast runner; can sometimes be caught by hand. Where there is little shade, throw a collecting sack (or hat) on the ground, under which the lizard may seek shelter. Pin the animal beneath, then carefully roll back the edges to capture it. Feeds on insects and spiders.
Similar species: (1) Side-blotched Lizard (p. 110) has ear openings, lacks overlapping upper labials, and usually has a dark spot behind the axilla. (2) Greater Earless and (3) Zebra-tailed Lizards have black bars on the underside of the tail, and the latter has ear openings.
Range: Great Plains and cent. Mexican plateau from s. South Dakota to Guanajuato, across southern part of Continental Divide to se. Utah and n. and cent. Arizona.   Map 74

GREATER EARLESS LIZARD *Holbrookia texana*   **Pl. 19**
Identification: 2–3¼. A slim-legged lizard with long flat tail cross-barred on the underside with black. Dorsal coloration tends to blend with the soil color of the habitat and may be gray, brown, or reddish, with numerous small light flecks. *Each side of belly marked with 2 black bars set in a blue patch. No ear open-*

ings. Black markings behind midpoint of body. Dorsal scalation granular; diagonal furrows between upper labials; gular fold present. *Male:* Enlarged postanal scales. Blue belly patches with conspicuous black bars, faint or absent in female. During the breeding season, females may develop pinkish markings and a vivid orange throat patch.

A lizard of middle elevations, avoiding extreme desert lowlands and the higher mountains. Plants indicative of environments occupied are cactus, mesquite, ocotillo, creosote bush, and palo-verde. Seems to prefer the sandy gravelly soil of flats, washes, and intermittent streambottoms where plants are sparse and there are open areas for running. Occasionally found on rocky hillsides. Often curls and wags tail when preparing to run and upon coming to rest. When running, the tail is curled upward and forward, revealing the conspicuous black and white mark-ings which may divert attack of predators to an expendable part. Insectivorous.

Similar species: (1) Zebra-tailed Lizard has ear openings, and the black belly bars are located at midpoint of body. (2) See also Lesser Earless Lizard.

Range: Cent. Arizona, New Mexico, and n. Texas south to San Luis Potosí and s. Tamaulipas. Cent. Texas west to eastern edge of Mojave Desert at Williams River, Arizona.

Subspecies: SOUTHWESTERN EARLESS LIZARD, *H. t. scitula.* Total number of femoral pores usually 28 or more; back with numerous small orange, red, or yellow flecks and a series of large prominent paired dark spots down middle of back. TEXAS EARLESS LIZARD, *H. t. texana.* Total number of femoral pores usually 27 or fewer. Usually no orange or yellow spots dorsally, and vertebral dark spots, when present, not prominent. Map 75

ZEBRA-TAILED LIZARD *Callisaurus draconoides* **Pl. 19**
Identification: 2½–3½. A slim-bodied lizard with long, flat tail and extremely long slender legs, adapted for running at high speed. *Ear openings present. Black crossbars on white under-surface of tail* ("zebra" markings). Dorsal scalation granular. Upper labials separated by diagonal furrows. Gular fold present. A gray network on the back and dusky crossbars on the tail; sides usually lemon-yellow. A pair of black bars set in a blue area on each side of belly, conspicuous when the lizard flattens its sides. *Black belly markings at or in front of midpoint of body.* Throat dusky, often with pink or orange spot at center. *Male:* Enlarged postanal scales. Belly markings conspicuous; faint or absent in female.

Frequents washes, desert "pavements" of small rocks, and hardpan, where plant growth is scant and there are open areas for running. Occasionally found on fine windblown sand but usually not far from firm soil. When about to run, curls and wags tail. Runs at great speed, with banded tail curled forward. As with the Greater Earless Lizard, the tail markings may divert the attack of hawks or other predators to the tail, which can be regenerated. To catch zebra-tails, noose them in the morning when they are sluggish. Food consists of insects, spiders, other lizards, and occasionally plants.

Similar species: See (1) Greater Earless, (2) Fringe-toed, and (3) Lesser Earless Lizards.

Range: W.-cent. Nevada south to s. Sinaloa and tip of Baja California; extreme sw. New Mexico to desert slope of mts. in s. California and on coastal slope along Cajon and San Jacinto washes (X marks on map).   Map 76

COLORADO DESERT FRINGE-TOED LIZARD   Pl. 19
Uma notata

Identification: 2¾–4½. A flattened sand-dwelling lizard with velvety skin, *toes fringed* with projecting pointed scales, countersunk lower jaw, and well-developed earflaps — adaptations to life in sand. Well camouflaged, the dorsal ground color and pattern of black flecks and eyelike markings (ocelli) harmonizing with background. Ocelli tend to form broken longitudinal lines over the shoulders. Below white with dark *diagonal lines on throat*, black bars on underside of tail, and a *conspicuous black spot on each side of the belly*. Sides of belly orange, pinkish, or white. *Young:* Belly color faint or absent. *Male:* Enlarged postanal scales.

Completely restricted to fine, loose, windblown sand of dunes, flats, riverbanks, and washes in some of the most arid parts of the desert. Vegetation is usually scant, consisting of creosote bush or other scrubby growth. When frightened, fringe-toes often dart suddenly to the opposite side of a sand hummock or bush, where they freeze, plunge into the sand, or disappear into a burrow. When running at high speed they are primarily bipedal. Their tracks are distinctive, consisting of alternating large round dents made by the hind feet and occasional smaller ones made by the front feet in maintaining balance. The help of a companion may be needed to catch these wary lizards. Walk abreast, 25 or 30 ft. apart, keeping sand hummocks and bushes between. Hiding places can then be kept in view as the lizards dash to the opposite side of hummocks. Chiefly insectivorous, but occasionally feeds on buds and leaves.

Similar species: (1) Mojave Fringe-toed Lizard has black gular crescents and usually a greenish-yellow wash on the ventral surfaces. (2) Coachella Valley Fringe-toed Lizard lacks the black belly spots or has them reduced to one or several small dots. (3) Zebra-tailed Lizard lacks fringed toes, is slimmer and less often found in areas of fine windblown sand.

Range: Vicinity of Salton Sea, California, south across Colorado River delta, around head of Gulf of California to Tepoca Bay, Sonora.

Subspecies: COLORADO DESERT FRINGE-TOED LIZARD, *U. n. notata.* A conspicuous black spot set in an orange patch on each side of belly. COWLES'S FRINGE-TOED LIZARD, *U. n. rufopunctata.* No orange on belly; pinkish belly patches in breeding season.   Map 77

COACHELLA VALLEY FRINGE-TOED LIZARD   Pl. 19
Uma inornata

Identification: $2\frac{3}{4}$–$4\frac{1}{2}$. It should perhaps be considered a subspecies of the Colorado Desert Fringe-toe. The lateral *black belly spots are absent or reduced to a single small dot or cluster of dots*, and streaks on throat are paler. Breeding coloration consists of a pinkish wash on the sides of the belly and orange on the lips and posterior portion of the eyelids.

Habits and habitat as in the Colorado Desert Fringe-toe.

Similar species: (1) Mojave Fringe-toed Lizard has black crescents on the throat, the dorsal ocelli fail to form longitudinal lines over the shoulders and breeding color consists of a ventral yellow-green wash. (2) See also Colorado Desert Fringe-toed Lizard.

Range: Coachella Valley, Riverside Co., California.   Map 77

MOJAVE FRINGE-TOED LIZARD   *Uma scoparia*   Pl. 19
Identification: $2\frac{3}{4}$–$4\frac{1}{2}$. Resembles the Colorado Desert Fringe-toe but dorsal pattern of ocelli do not form broken longitudinal lines over the shoulders and *throat markings are crescent-shaped*. A conspicuous black spot on each side of the belly. Breeding coloration consists of a yellow-green ventral wash that becomes pink on sides of body.

Habits and habitat as in the Colorado Desert Fringe-toe.

Similar species: See (1) Colorado Desert and (2) Coachella Valley Fringe-toed Lizards.

Range: Mojave Desert, California; barely enters Arizona along Bouse Wash, southeast of Parker, Yuma Co.   Map 77

COLLARED LIZARD   *Crotaphytus collaris*   Pl. 20
Identification: 3–$4\frac{1}{2}$. A robust lizard with massive head and long tail slightly flattened from side to side. *A conspicuous black and white collar.* "Leopard" spots on face, limbs, and tail. Scalation mostly smooth, granular. Broad crossbands and numerous light spots on body. Dorsal ground color varies — greenish, bluish, olive, pale brown, or yellowish, depending on locality, sex, age, and color phase. Markings tend to fade with age, the collar least. Strikingly colored green individuals with

yellow head are found in w. Colorado and e. Utah, south unto
the central plateau of Arizona. *Young:* Hatchlings about 1½
in. Broad dark crossbands or transverse rows of dark spots on
body and tail. Sometimes with red markings like breeding
female's (see below). *Male:* Throat green, bluish, orange, or
yellow, often with black pigment which may extend to chest,
sides of belly, groin and even base of hind legs; bluish belly
patches. *Female:* When not breeding, less vividly marked than
male. Throat unmarked or lightly spotted with brown or gray.
In breeding season develops spots and bars of orange on sides
of neck and body, which fade after the eggs are laid.

A rock-dwelling lizard that frequents canyons, rocky gullies,
mountain slopes, and boulder-strewn alluvial fans, usually where
vegetation is sparse. Essentials appear to be boulders for basking
and lookouts, open areas for running, and adequate warmth.
Collared Lizards jump nimbly from rock to rock and seize their
lizard and insect prey with a rush, often running with forelimbs
lifted off the ground and tail raised. Most easily caught in the
morning when basking at the top of boulders. To avoid being
bitten, handle these lizards by the sides of the head. Do not
cage with smaller animals.

Similar species: See (1) Leopard, (2) Crevice Spiny (p. 103),
and (3) Banded Rock (p. 113) Lizards.

Range: Great Basin south to cent. Baja California and Sonora;
desert slope of mts. in s. California, east across Continental
Divide to e. Missouri and cent. Texas, south to n. Zacatecas. On
coastal side of mts. in s. California in headwaters of East Fork
of the San Gabriel River, Los Angeles Co.   Map 79

LEOPARD LIZARD *Crotaphytus wislizenii*   **Pl. 20**
Identification: 3½–5. *A large lizard with "leopard" spots,*
rounded body, long round tail, and large head. Capable of
marked color change. When in the dark phase the spots are
nearly hidden and light crossbars are conspicuous on both body
and tail. Dorsal ground color gray or brown; throat streaked or
spotted with gray. Scales on top of head small, including interparietal. *Young:* In light phase, yellowish with tan crossbars
and spots. Spots red in *C. w. silus. Male:* Ventral surfaces may
become suffused with salmon or rust during the breeding season
(San Joaquin Valley, California). *Female:* During the breeding
season, orange color appears on underside of tail and orange
spots and bars on sides of neck and body.

Inhabits arid and semiarid plains grown to bunch grass, alkali
bush, sagebrush, creosote bush, or other scattered low plants.
The ground may be hardpan, gravel, or sand; rocks may or may
not be present. Avoids dense grass and brush, which interfere
with running. Often lies in wait for insect or lizard prey in the
shade of a bush where its spotted pattern blends. In hunting

Leopard Lizards, tap bushes with a stick to cause the lizards to reveal themselves by movement. Bipedal when running fast. May bite when caught. Do not cage with smaller animals. Feeds on insects (cicadas, grasshoppers, crickets), spiders, lizards, small mammals, blossoms, and seeds.

Similar species: The Collared Lizard has collar markings and a laterally flattened tail.

Range: Great Basin south to tip of Baja California, Sonora, and Zacatecas; desert base of mts. of s. California east to se. New Mexico and w. Texas. San Joaquin Valley, California; Hat Rock, Umtilla Co., and The Dalles, Wasco Co., Oregon.

Subspecies: LONG-NOSED LEOPARD LIZARD, *C. w. wislizenii.* Snout long. Throat with gray longitudinal streaks. BLUNT-NOSED LEOPARD LIZARD, *C. w. silus.* Snout blunt. Throat with dark gray blotches. San Joaquin Valley and surrounding foothills, California. Map 78

Spiny Lizards: Genus *Sceloporus*

THESE ARE the "blue-bellies" or "swifts." Males of most species have a blue patch on each side of the belly and on the throat, enlarged postanal scales and, when breeding, a broad tail base. Blue color reduced or absent in females. All have keeled, pointed, overlapping scales on the dorsal surfaces, which along with the incomplete gular fold will distinguish them from the utas (*Uta* and *Urosaurus*). Spiny lizards are usually gray or brown above with a pattern of crescents or stripes, are round-bodied or somewhat flattened, and the tail is longer than the body; limbs are of moderate length.

Below sea level to above 13,500 feet, s. Canada to Panama. Habitats vary from steaming tropical forests to the sparse growth of timberline. Some are ground dwellers; others climb, ascending rocks, stumps, tree trunks, and sides of buildings with ease. Confirmed baskers, they are frequently seen on top of rocks, fence posts, stumps, or other objects in full sun. Some species are live-bearing.

BUNCH GRASS LIZARD *Sceloporus scalaris* **Pl. 22**
Identification: 1¾–2½. A mountain form distinguished from all other spiny lizards by the arrangement of the femoral-pore rows and scales on the sides of the body. The femoral rows are separated at the midline by only 1 or 2 scales rather than 3 or more, and the *lateral scale rows parallel the dorsal rows.* In other species lateral rows extend diagonally upward. Above usually with brown blotches, edged posteriorly with black. A white or orange dorsolateral stripe on each side. Black blotch at base of front legs. *Male:* Usually has orange dorsolateral stripes and

blue belly patches; dorsal blotches faint or absent. *Female:* Blotched pattern; blue markings reduced or absent.

Found in our area chiefly in isolated mountains, mostly above 6000 ft., where it occupies sunny patches of bunch grass in open coniferous woods, but it also occurs as low as 4300 ft. Search for these lizards in late morning on warm, bright days. Walk softly through grass. Individuals may be seen or heard scurrying into grass clumps or to hiding places under rocks, logs, or pieces of bark. Catch them by trapping them by hand in the grass tangles. Peak activity during period of summer rains. Food includes insects and spiders.

Similar species: The Striped Plateau Lizard (p. 108), with which it coexists in some areas, has the lateral scales in diagonal rows and lacks blue belly markings.

Range: Huachuca, Dragoon, Santa Rita, and Chiricahua Mts., Arizona; Animas Mts., New Mexico; Sierra Madre Occidental (including Sierra del Nido) to Puebla. To around 10,000 ft. "Lowland" occurrences are Empire Valley, 11 miles north-northeast of Sonoita, 4300 ft., Santa Cruz Co., Arizona; upper Animas Valley, 10 mi. east of Cloverdale, 5200 ft., New Mexico; and grassy plains between the desert and the Sierra Madre, Chihuahua, Mexico.   Map 88

YARROW'S SPINY LIZARD *Sceloporus jarrovi*   **Pl. 22**
Identification: 2½–3½. *Above with black lace-stocking pattern* consisting of whitish scales with flesh or bluish-green sheen, edged with black. Head with sooty markings or nearly all black in adult males. Broad black neck band edged with white along rear margin, often connected anteriorly with the dark head markings. *Outer row of supraoculars small;* usually over 40 scales between interparietal and rear of thighs. *Young:* Usually a blue patch on posterior part of throat, on each side of venter behind axilla, and in front of groin. *Male:* Sides of belly and throat patch blue; blue colors subdued in female.

A mountain species, attracted to rocky canyons and hillsides in the oak and pine belts, mostly above 5000 ft. On lower mountain slopes it lives in the more humid portions in the vicinity of streams, canyon pools, or damp sand. Occasionally climbs trees, but more often seen perched on boulders or climbing nimbly over rocks. When these lizards first emerge they are nearly black and when on light-colored rocks are conspicuous. Food consists of insects and spiders. Live-bearing.

Similar species: The Crevice Spiny Lizard has larger scales (usually less than 40 between the interparietal and rear of thighs) and a collar band with whitish anterior border.

Range: Chiricahua, Dos Cabezas, Dragoon, Graham (to 10,700 ft.), Huachuca, Santa Rita, Quinlan, and Baboquivari Mts., Arizona; Peloncillo, Pyramid, San Luis, Animas, and Hatchet

Mts., New Mexico; Sierra Madre Occidental and Oriental to
State of Mexico and s.-cent. Veracruz. To around 11,000 ft.
Subspecies: YARROW'S SPINY LIZARD, *S. j. jarrovi*,
occurs in our area.   Map 89

CREVICE SPINY LIZARD *Sceloporus poinsetti*   **Pl. 23**
Identification: 3¾–4⅝. A large flat-bodied, spiny, rock dweller.
The *conspicuously banded tail and broad black collar* can be seen
from a great distance. Collar bordered in front and back with
whitish. Ground color above yellowish, olive, or reddish. Below
beige to pale orange, grading to pinkish orange on underside of
tail. *Scales large, keeled and pointed*, usually less than 40 between
interparietal and rear of thighs. Outer row of supraoculars
about same size as inner row. *Young:* Crossbands on body and
tail often more conspicuous than in adult; sometimes a narrow
dark stripe down middle of the back. *Male:* Sides of belly and
throat blue; belly markings bordered with black toward midline.
Crossbands on back indistinct or absent. Blue color weak or
absent in female and crossbands usually retained.

A wary lizard, inhabiting rocky canyons, gullies, hillsides, and
outcrops of limestone, granite, or lava in arid and semiarid
regions. Usually retreats to the opposite side of a rock or into
a crevice when approached. These lizards can sometimes be
extracted from crevices with a wire noose. Use a mirror or
flashlight for illumination. Food consists of insects and occasionally buds and leaves.
Similar species: (1) Collared Lizard (p. 99) has a double black
collar, no dark bands on tail, and small, smooth scales. (2) See
also Yarrow's Spiny Lizard.
Range: S. New Mexico south to Zacatecas; sw. New Mexico to
cent. Texas. To above 8000 ft. in Mexico.   Map 82

DESERT SPINY LIZARD *Sceloporus magister*   **Pl. 23**
Identification: 3½–5½. A stocky, usually light-colored lizard
with large pointed scales and a *black wedge-shape mark on each
side of the neck.* Rear edge of neck markings whitish or pale
yellow. Above straw-color, yellowish brown, or brown with
crossbands or spots of dusky, which usually fade with age. Sides
often tinged with rust. Head sometimes orange. Five to 7
pointed ear scales; supraorbital semicircles incomplete. *Young:*
About 1¼–1½ in. Crossbands usually conspicuous. *Male:*
Enlarged postanals and swollen tail base. Blue patch on throat
and on each side of belly. Belly patches edged with black and
sometimes joined at midline. Blue markings weak or absent in
female.

An inhabitant of plains and the lower slopes of mountains in
arid and semiarid regions. Avoids high elevations. Found in
Joshua tree, creosote bush, and shad-scale deserts, juniper and

mesquite woodland, and along river courses grown to willows and cottonwoods. A good climber, ascending rocks and trees, but also found on the ground. Seeks shelter in crevices, under logs and other objects on the ground, in woodrat nests, and in rodent burrows. Often bites when captured. Feeds on insects, lizards, and occasionally on buds and leaves.

Similar species: (1) Clark's Spiny Lizard is gray, greenish, or bluish above, has dark crossbands on wrists and forearms and usually 3 ear scales. (2) Granite Spiny Lizard is darker, lacks conspicuous neck markings, and has more rounded, less spiny scales.

Range: W. Nevada and s. Utah to tip of Baja California, n. Sinaloa, and n. Durango; inner Coast Ranges and desert of s. California to New Mexico and w. Texas. In Coast Ranges north to Panoche Pass.

Subspecies: DESERT SPINY LIZARD, *S. m. magister.* Adult male with black or deep purple middorsal stripe approximately 4½ to 5 scales wide. Stripe extends from behind head to middle of back or to base of tail and is bordered by light stripe on each side. Dark shoulder patch usually extends upward to meet anterior edge of stripe. TWIN-SPOTTED SPINY LIZARD, *S. m. bimaculosus.* Adult male with 2 parallel longitudinal rows of blotches on back, each blotch 1½ to 2 scales wide. Usually a well-defined dark stripe behind eye. BARRED SPINY LIZARD, *S. m. transversus.* Adult male (and sometimes female) with 6 or 7 dark crossbars on back, usually 1½ scales wide. Dark shoulder patch often extends well up on neck, nearly forming a collar. Ground color usually yellow. YELLOW-BACKED SPINY LIZARD, *S. m. uniformis.* Back of adult male often uniformly light yellow or tan, grading into darker brown on sides. Faint blotches usually present on back of adult female and occasionally in juveniles and adult males. ORANGE-HEADED SPINY LIZARD, *S. m. cephaloflavus.* In most adult males 5 or 6 chevron-shaped bars on dorsum from shoulders to base of tail. Adults of both sexes with yellowish orange on head.   Map 80

CLARK'S SPINY LIZARD   *Sceloporus clarki*   **Pl. 23**
Identification: 3–5. A large, extremely wary lizard, usually only glimpsed as it scrambles to the opposite side of a limb or tree trunk. *Gray, bluish green, or blue above, with dusky or black bands on wrists and forearms.* Black shoulder mark as in Desert Spiny Lizard. Irregularly crossbanded with dark and light markings, which may become faint or disappear, especially in old males. Projecting spine-tipped scales on body; incomplete supraorbital semicircles; usually 3 ear scales. *Young:* Crossbands on body and tail. *Male:* Enlarged postanals and swollen tail base. Throat patch and sides of belly blue. Belly markings usually weak or absent in female.

Inhabits chiefly lower mountain slopes in the pine-oak belt. Prefers more humid environments, generally at higher elevation, than the Desert Spiny Lizard. Chiefly a tree dweller but also occurs on the ground among rocks. Often heard before seen. Two people are usually required to keep these lizards in sight because they tend to stay on the opposite side of rocks and tree trunks. Watch for a bright eye furtively peering from behind cover. To noose them usually requires careful stalking while a companion diverts their attention. Food consists of insects and occasionally leaves, buds, and flowers.

Similar species: See (1) Desert and (2) Granite Spiny Lizards.
Range: Cent. Arizona and sw. New Mexico to n. Jalisco. In s. Arizona ranges west to Kitt Peak and Ajo Mts. To above 6000 ft.
Subspecies: SONORA SPINY LIZARD, *S. c. clarki.* Juvenile pattern lost in adult males. PLATEAU SPINY LIZARD, *S. c. vallaris.* Juvenile pattern retained even in adult males. Lake Watson and Granite Dells, near Prescott, Yavapai Co., Arizona.   Map 81

GRANITE SPINY LIZARD *Sceloporus orcutti*   **Pl. 23**
Identification: 3¼–4. *A large, spiny, dark-colored rock dweller.* Dark wedge-shaped mark on each side of neck and crossbands on body and tail often hidden by general dark coloration. Scales with rounded rear margins, weakly keeled on the body, strongly keeled and pointed on the tail. Incomplete supraorbital semicircles. *Young:* Hatchlings 1¼–1½ in. Head rusty; crossbands and neck markings evident. *Male:* When in the light phase, one of our most beautiful lizards. Dorsal scales marked with yellow-green and bluish, a broad purple stripe down middle of the back, entire ventral surface vivid blue. *Female:* Lacks the gaudy blue and purple markings; crossbands more distinct than in male.

On the coastal side of the mountains in s. California it frequents granite outcrops in areas of oak and chaparral, ranging into the yellow pine belt below 5500 ft.; on the desert side it is found in rocky canyons and on the rocky upper portions of alluvial fans where there is sufficient moisture for growth of chaparral, palms, or mesquite. In Baja California it occurs in piñon-juniper woodland. Conspicuous on light-colored rocks, but wariness makes up for lack of camouflage. Hunt them when they first emerge; once warm, they will seldom allow close approach. Feeds on insects, lizards, and occasionally on buds and fleshy fruits.

Similar species: (1) Clark's Spiny Lizard has a well-defined black neck patch, is paler, and has more pointed and prominently keeled scales. (2) See also Desert Spiny Lizard.
Range: Lower slopes of mts. of s. California from southern side of San Gorgonio Pass south to tip of Baja California. To above 7000 ft.

Subspecies: The GRANITE SPINY LIZARD, *S. o. orcutti,*
occurs in our area.   **Map 83**

WESTERN FENCE LIZARD   *Sceloporus occidentalis*   **Pl. 22**
   Identification: 2¼–3½. A black, gray, or brown lizard with
   blotched pattern. Dark-striped individuals are occasionally
   found in s. California. Sides of belly blue. Rear surfaces of
   limbs yellow or orange. Scales of dorsal surfaces keeled and
   pointed, relatively smaller than in Desert, Clark's, and Granite
   Spiny Lizards; *35 to 51 scales between interparietal and rear of
   thighs.* Complete supraorbital semicircles. Scales on back of
   thigh mostly keeled. *Young:* No blue on throat; blue belly
   markings faint or absent; no yellow or orange on limbs in
   hatchlings. *Male:* Enlarged postanals, swollen tail base. Blue
   patch on throat, sometimes partly or completely divided; blue
   belly patches edged with black. When in light phase the dorsal
   scales become blue or greenish. *Female:* No blue or green color
   dorsally. Dark crescents or bars on back. Ventral blue markings
   usually less vivid or absent.
       One of the most common western lizards, popularly known as
   "swift" or "blue-belly," seen on fence posts, rocks, logs, piles of
   lumber, and the sides of buildings. Occupies a great variety of
   habitats from sea level to above 9000 feet, but absent from
   extreme desert. Although it occasionally ascends trees, it is
   more often found on or near the ground. Usually noosed easily.
   Feeds on insects and spiders.
   Similar species: In sw. Utah, nw. Arizona, and s. Nevada, where
   the ranges of the Western and (1) Eastern Fence Lizards approach one another and perhaps overlap, the two species may
   be distinguished as follows: male Western Fence Lizard has a
   single blue throat patch that occasionally covers entire throat
   to edge of chin — females usually have 2 patches; both sexes in
   the Eastern Fence Lizard have 2 small lateral blue throat patches
   tipped with black anteriorly — in females they are more laterally situated than in the female Western Fence Lizard. (2)
   Sagebrush Lizard, with which the Western Fence Lizard sometimes coexists, has rust on side of neck and body, usually a black
   bar on the shoulder, lacks yellow color on the rear of the limbs,
   and has smaller dorsal scales; blue throat patch of male flecked
   with white or pink. (3) Side-blotched Lizard (p. 110) has small
   unpointed scales on the back, usually a black spot behind the
   axilla, and a complete gular fold.
   Range: Cent. Washington to nw. Baja California; Pacific Coast
   to w. Utah. Absent from desert except in mts.
   Subspecies: NORTHWESTERN FENCE LIZARD, *S. o.
   occidentalis.* Males usually have 2 blue throat patches connected
   at the midline by a narrower, lighter blue band; rarely, throat
   patch single; ventral surfaces, excluding blue areas, light-

colored or with scattered dark flecks. GREAT BASIN FENCE LIZARD, *S. o. biseriatus*. Similar to the Northwestern Fence Lizard but blue of throat in male usually in a single patch; ventral surfaces, excluding blue areas, often gray or black. SIERRA FENCE LIZARD, *S. o. taylori*. Large size, males 3¼ in. or more in snout-vent length; venter blue throughout, the belly patches not separated by a pale area. Small males resemble the Northwestern Fence Lizard in ventral coloration. Sierra Nevada, mostly above 7000 ft., from Yosemite Nat'l Park to Tulare Co. ISLAND FENCE LIZARD, *S. o. becki*. Throat patch black, extending across gular region from shoulder to shoulder. Chin light blue, with lines of blue-black radiating from black patch. Santa Cruz, Santa Rosa, and San Miguel Is. off coast of s. California.   Map 84

EASTERN FENCE LIZARD   *Sceloporus undulatus*   **Fig. 27**
   Identification: 2⅛–3¼. Similar to the Western Fence Lizard. Gray, brown, or nearly black above, with pattern of crossbars, crescents, or longitudinal stripes. Striped patterns are prevalent in the Great Plains area. *Blue of throat usually divided*, often into 2 widely separated patches, a characteristic that distinguishes this lizard from the Western Fence Lizard where the ranges of the two species are contiguous (see Maps 84 and 85).
   Like its western relative, it lives in a great variety of habitats

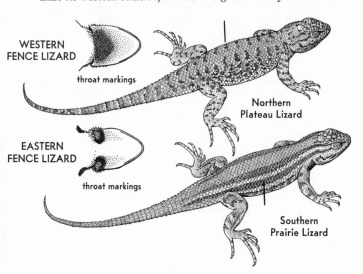

WESTERN FENCE LIZARD
throat markings

Northern Plateau Lizard

EASTERN FENCE LIZARD
throat markings

Southern Prairie Lizard

Fig. 27. Pattern variation in Eastern Fence Lizard

— forests, woodland, prairie, brushy flatlands, sand dunes, rocky hillsides, and farmlands. Shelter is sought in bushes, trees, old buildings, woodpiles, rodent burrows, and under rocks, logs, or other objects on the ground. In forested parts of its range it climbs trees, and when frightened keeps to the opposite side of the trunk. Where trees are scarce it is primarily a ground dweller. Active throughout the year in the southern part of its range. Feeds on insects, spiders, millipedes, snails, and other small animals.

Similar species: See Western Fence Lizard.

Range: S. South Dakota, s. Illinois, and se. New York to cent. Florida, Gulf Coast, and Zacatecas; sw. Utah and cent. Arizona to Atlantic Coast.

Subspecies: NORTHERN PLATEAU LIZARD, *S. u. elongatus* (Fig. 27). High dorsal-scale count — 45 or more scales between interparietal and rear of thighs. Other subspecies generally have lower counts, 44 or less. Narrow crossbars or wavy crosslines usually present on back in both sexes; blue throat and belly patches. SOUTHERN PLATEAU LIZARD, *S. u. tristichus*. Dorsal light stripes usually present; males with blue on throat and sides of belly; females often have blue belly patches; 45 or more scales between interparietal and rear of thighs. SOUTHERN PRAIRIE LIZARD, *S. u. consobrinus* (Fig. 27). Resembles Southern Plateau Lizard but females usually lack blue belly patches. RED-LIPPED PLATEAU LIZARD, *S. u. erythrocheilus*. Dorsolateral light stripes weakly developed, discontinuous, or lacking; blue throat patches connected at midline in both sexes; in breeding season lips bright rust-red. A rock dweller, usually below 7000 ft., rarely above 9000 ft. Not known to overlap the range of the Northern Prairie Lizard, although the latter occurs nearby to the east. NORTHERN PRAIRIE LIZARD, *S. u. garmani*. Dorsolateral light stripes distinct in both sexes; blue belly patches but no blue on throat in males. A prairie species. COWLES PRAIRIE LIZARD, *S. u. cowlesi*. Above pale gray to nearly white; dorsal pattern obscure. White Sands, New Mexico. Map 85

STRIPED PLATEAU LIZARD *Sceloporus virgatus* **Pl. 22**
Identification: 2–2¾. Striped pattern. *An unbroken dorsolateral and lateral whitish stripe on each side separated by a broad dark brown band.* Each dorsolateral stripe bordered by a row of brown or brown and white spots which are separated along the midline by a broad pale gray area. Usually some dark flecking on throat and chest. *Belly plain white or cream,* without blue markings. Small blue patch on each side of throat. *Young:* Stripes well defined; blue patches on throat faint or absent. *Male:* Enlarged postanals; swollen tail base. Blue throat patches more prominent than in female and dorsal dark spots usually

absent or reduced, each dorsolateral light stripe instead bordered medially by a brown stripe. *Female:* When breeding, blue throat patches surrounded or replaced by orange.

A mountain form, most abundant in mixed pine and oak woods from 5300 to 7000 ft., but ranges upward into coniferous forest and downward in oak woodland along streams to 4900 ft. Although it has been found within a mile of the Eastern Fence Lizard, which occurs in the lowlands, it is not known to overlap the range of this species. Most abundant in the vicinity of rocky and sandy intermittent streams where there is shade and water or damp sand. Chiefly a ground dweller but climbs readily, ascending boulders, logs, and trees. Feeds on insects, centipedes, and other arthropods.

Similar species: Differs from (1) the Eastern Fence Lizard in lacking blue belly patches and usually having notches on the femoral pore scales. (2) See also Bunch Grass Lizard (p. 101). **Range:** Mts. of extreme se. Arizona and sw. New Mexico, south in Sierra Madre Occidental at least to s. Chihuahua. In the U.S., in the Chiricahua, Peloncillo, Guadalupe, and Animas Mts. From 4900 to 8400 ft. Map 87

SAGEBRUSH LIZARD *Sceloporus graciosus* **Pl. 22**
Identification: 2–2½. Resembles the Western Fence Lizard but is smaller and has relatively smaller scales (42 to 68 between interparietal and rear of thighs). Gray or brown above, usually with blotches or crossbars and dorsolateral light stripes. Often a *black bar on the shoulder. Rust in axilla and on sides of neck and body.* No yellow or orange on rear surfaces of limbs. Blue belly patches. *Scales on back of thigh mostly granular. Young:* Orange on neck, ventral blue markings subdued or absent. *Male:* Enlarged postanals; swollen tail base. Blue throat with white or pink flecks, but throat patch sometimes absent. Belly patches darker blue than throat, edged with black. In light phase, blue or blue-green flecks appear in the dorsal scales. *Female:* Little or no blue ventrally, none dorsally, and orange more vivid on neck and sides.

A sagebrush lizard over much of its range, but also occurs in manzanita and ceanothus brushland, piñon-juniper woodland, yellow pine and fir forests, and along river bottoms in the coast redwood forests. West of the Great Basin it lives chiefly in the mountains, generally occurring at higher elevations than the Western Fence Lizard, but often overlapping it in range at intermediate altitudes. Requirements seem to be good illumination, open ground, and scattered low bushes. A ground dweller, usually found near bushes, brush heaps, logs, or rocks. When frightened it retreats to rocks, thick brush, or occasionally climbs trees. Food includes insects, spiders, mites, ticks, scorpions, and snails.

Similar species: See Western Fence Lizard.
Range: Cent. Washington, s. Idaho, and s. Montana to nw. New Mexico, n. Arizona, and n. Baja California; w. Colorado to coast in n. California and s. Oregon, to eastern slope Cascade Mts. farther north. Isolated populations in se. New Mexico, w. Texas, and in California at Sutter Buttes, Mt. Diablo, San Benito Mt., Telescope Peak, and higher mts. of s. California; also North Unit of Theodore Roosevelt Nat'l Memorial Park, North Dakota. Old record for Pullman and Almota, Whitman Co., Washington. From 500 to above 10,000 ft.
Subspecies: NORTHERN SAGEBRUSH LIZARD, *S. g. graciosus.* In male, blue belly patches usually do not meet at midline and blue (or black) of ventral color fails to join blue throat patch. A pale variety, with both dorsal blotching and blue on throat reduced or absent, occurs in sandy habitats in extreme se. New Mexico and w. Texas. SOUTHERN SAGE-BRUSH LIZARD, *S. g. vandenburgianus.* Much more ventral blue color in male than in Northern Sagebrush Lizard. Blue belly patches may meet at the midline or are separated by a narrow white or black stripe. Blue (or black) of ventral color often joins blue throat patch. Venter of female often dusky.

Map 86

SIDE-BLOTCHED LIZARD   *Uta stansburiana*   **Pl. 21**
Identification: 1½–2⅛. A small brownish lizard with a *bluish or black blotch on the side of the chest behind the axilla.* Side blotch occasionally absent. Dorsal surfaces blotched or speckled. A gular fold. Scales on back small, unpointed. Frontal divided. *Male:* Slightly enlarged postanals; swollen tail base. In light phase, speckled above with pale blue. *Female:* Blotched with brown and whitish, occasionally striped; no blue speckling.
One of the most abundant lizards in the arid and semiarid regions of the West. The habitat varies — sand, rock, hardpan, or loam with vegetation of grass, bushes, and scattered trees. Often found along sandy washes where there are scattered rocks and low-growing bushes. A ground dweller, active all year in the south. Food includes insects, scorpions, spiders, mites, ticks, and sowbugs.
Similar species: See (1) Lesser Earless (p. 96), (2) Western Fence (p. 106), and (3) Tree Lizards.
Range: Cent. Washington to tip of Baja California, n. Sinaloa, and Durango; Pacific Coast to w. Colorado and w. Texas. Mostly below 5000 ft. but ranges to around 9000 ft. on the Colorado Plateau.
Subspecies: CALIFORNIA SIDE-BLOTCHED LIZARD *U. s. hesperis.* Dorsum of both sexes with prominent, coarse dark blotching set off by pale spots and bars. Generally 2 rows of postrostrals. Dorsal scales change rather abruptly dorso-

laterally from large central keeled scales to smooth granular ones. DESERT SIDE-BLOTCHED LIZARD, *U. s. stejnegeri.* This and the following subspecies usually have 1 row of postrostrals. Males, with subdued dorsal dark blotching. When in light phase numerous small blue flecks on dorsal surfaces. Females normally are striped. Dorsal scales usually 93 or less from just behind large scales on head to rear of thighs; prefrontals typically in contact on midline. NORTHERN SIDE-BLOTCHED LIZARD, *U. s. stansburiana.* Resembles Desert Side-blotched Lizard but females lack or have broken striped pattern. Dorsal scales smaller and more numerous, generally numbering 94 or more; prefrontals usually not in contact on midline.   Map 92

LONG-TAILED BRUSH LIZARD *Urosaurus graciosus* **Pl. 21**
  Identification: 1⅞–2¼. A well-camouflaged bush-dwelling lizard that often lies motionless, its slim body aligned with a branch. *The tail is long and slender, often twice as long as the body.* Above gray, with dusky crossbars, but when captured this lizard may change color from dark gray to pale beige in less than 5 min. Usually a pale lateral stripe extends from the upper jaw along the sides of the neck and body. *A broad band of enlarged scales down middle of the back.* Well-developed gular fold. Frontal usually divided. *Male:* A pale blue or greenish patch flecked with white on each side of the belly, lacking in female. Both sexes may have a reddish, orange, or lemon-yellow throat.
  A desert species. Habitat requirements are loose sand and scattered bushes and trees, creosote bush, burrow bush, galleta grass, catclaw, mesquite, and paloverde. Creosote bushes with exposed roots seem to be especially favored, perhaps because of the shelter afforded by the root tangle. Being more heat-tolerant than its relative the Tree Lizard, it can live in sparser growth. At night and on windy days it may seek shelter in the sand or in burrows of other animals. At Palm Springs, California, it thrives about human habitation in olive trees and Washington palms. Since these lizards resemble bark and tend to remain motionless when approached, the collector usually must examine carefully branches of bushes and trees to find them. Although diurnal, after a hot day they may sleep aloft and can be found by searching terminal branches at night. Food consists of insects, spiders, and occasionally plants.
  Similar species: See (1) Tree and (2) Small-scaled Lizards.
  Range: Extreme s. Nevada to nw. Sonora and ne. Baja California; desert slope of mts. of s. California to cent. Arizona. Coexists with Tree Lizard near Wickenburg in Hassayampa River drainage and along Verde River near Tempe, Arizona.
  Subspecies: WESTERN BRUSH LIZARD, *U. g. graciosus.* Pale coloration; greatly subdued pattern, some individuals nearly

patternless. Frequents both small and large desert shrubs.
ARIZONA BRUSH LIZARD, *U. g. shannoni*. Males with
highly contrasting dorsal pattern of black and gray; 6 or 7 bold
black crossbars on back, often connected with paired black
blotches; 6 to 8 blackish oblique lateral bars, which may form
chevrons. Bold black collar usually incomplete middorsally.
Frequents chiefly the larger desert trees — mesquite, catclaw,
and occasionally paloverde.   Map 91

TREE LIZARD   *Urosaurus ornatus*   **Pl. 21**
   Identification: 1⅞–2¼. A slim dark brown, tan, sooty, or gray
   lizard with small scales and long slender tail. Often a rusty area
   at the base of the tail. A gular fold. *Band of enlarged scales down
   middle of back, separated into 2 or more parallel rows by center
   strip of small scales.* Above usually blotched or cross-barred
   with dusky. A fold of skin on each side of body. *Male: Vivid
   blue or blue-green belly patches,* sometimes united and occasionally
   connected with blue throat patch. Throat sometimes yellow,
   greenish, or pale blue-green. *Female:* Throat whitish, orange,
   or yellow; no belly patches.
   A climbing lizard that spends much of its time in trees and on
   rocks; sometimes seen clinging head downward. Its color usually
   blends with background. Frequents mesquite, oak, pine, juniper,
   alder, cottonwood, and non-native trees such as tamarisk and
   rough-bark eucalyptus. Appears to be especially attracted to
   riparian habitats. When encountered on the ground it may run
   to a rock or tree and climb upward, keeping out of sight. Feeds
   on insects and spiders.
   Similar species: (1) Differs from the spiny lizards in having a
   complete gular fold and enlarged scales down the middle of the
   back. (2) Side-blotched Lizard is a ground dweller, has a dark
   blotch behind the axilla, back scales of uniform size, and lacks
   blue belly patches. (3) Long-tailed Brush Lizard has a broad
   band of enlarged scales down the back, unbroken by small
   scales. (4) See also Small-scaled Lizard.
   Range: Sw. Wyoming to cent. Sinaloa and n. Coahuila; lower
   Colorado River to cent. Texas. Sea level to 9000 ft.   Map 90

SMALL-SCALED LIZARD   *Urosaurus microscutatus*   **Pl. 21**
   Identification: 1½–2. Resembles the Tree Lizard. Above gray,
   with dark blotches on the back. Dorsal scales granular, usually
   enlarging gradually toward the midline. Gular fold present. A
   skin fold on the side of the body. Frontal usually single. *Young:*
   Hatchlings about 1 in., often with pale yellow-orange throat
   patch. *Male:* Blue throat with center spot of yellow or orange;
   a blue patch on each side of the belly. *Female:* Lacks blue
   markings.
   In our area frequents rocky habitats grown to oak, sycamore,
   desert willow, and chaparral in arid and semiarid regions.

Search rocks and the trunks and branches of trees along permanent or intermittent streams. Feeds on insects and spiders.

Similar species: (1) Tree Lizard has several rows of enlarged scales down middle of the back, separated along the midline by small scales. (2) Long-tailed Brush Lizard has a much longer tail, usually over twice the length of the body, lacks blue on the throat, and has a well-defined band of enlarged scales down the middle of the back. (3) Side-blotched Lizard has a dark blotch behind the axilla and lacks blue belly patches.

Range: S. California from Borrego Palm Canyon on desert side and Cottonwood and Deerhorn Flat on coastal side of mts., south to near tip of Baja California.   Map 93

BANDED ROCK LIZARD *Streptosaurus mearnsi*   **Pl. 21**
   Identification: 3–4. A *flat-bodied lizard* with a *single black collar and banded tail;* restricted to rocks. Scales on dorsal surfaces granular, except on tail and limbs, where keeled and pointed. Above olive or gray, with numerous small spots of white or bluish. Wavy crossbars on back, sometimes faint. Ventral surfaces bluish; whitish or pinkish spots on throat. *Male:* Throat pattern and bluish color more pronounced than in female. In light phase, blue spots on back, tail, and hind limbs. *Female:* When gravid, orange on throat and above eye.

   This lizard can be identified by its movements, even at a great distance. It crawls over the sides and under surfaces of rocks with ease, limbs extended well out from its sides, body held low, and hindquarters swinging from side to side. Most abundant among massive rocks in the shady, narrower parts of canyons, on the desert slope of the mountains. Often wary. To catch rock lizards use a fine copper wire noose opened to diam. of 1½ or 2 in. When within a foot or so, sweep the noose over the lizard's head with a single quick stroke. Feeds on insects, spiders, blossoms, and buds.

Similar species: The Collared Lizard (p. 99) has 2 black collar marks, a non-spiny, unbanded tail and round body.

Range: S. California from San Gorgonio Pass south on desert slope of mts., through northern half of Baja California.   Map 94

Horned Lizards: Genus *Phrynosoma*

THESE ARE the "horny toads" cherished by small boys. Most are armed with daggerlike head spines ("horns") and sharp, projecting scales on the dorsal surfaces of the body. The horns, the flattened oval form, and pointed fringe scales on the sides of the body are distinctive. As with many iguanids, males have enlarged postanal scales and, when breeding, a swollen tail base.

Horned lizards are often difficult to find. They are usually solitary, and when approached often crouch low and "sit tight"; their markings and spiny skin blend with the ground. One may nearly step on them before they move.

To find them walk outward in a spiral from ant nests, near which they lie in wait for food, or search for their tracks. Ants and fine loose soil for burial seem to be essential. When picked up they may inflate themselves by gulping air, may jab with the horns, or — rarely — spurt blood from the eyes. The blood comes from a sinus at the base of the 3rd eyelid and is thought to repel predators.

Although favored as pets they ordinarily do not live long in captivity. It seems necessary for them to have large numbers of live ants, which seldom can be supplied.

There are some 14 species, ranging from B.C. to Guatemala and from w. Arkansas to the Pacific Coast.

TEXAS HORNED LIZARD *Phrynosoma cornutum* **Pl. 18**
  Identification: 2½–4¼. *Dark stripes on side of face radiate from eye region.* General coloration brown, yellowish, tan, reddish, or gray, varying with prevailing soil color. Beige or whitish vertebral stripe. Sooty or dark brown blotches on back and tail and a pair of large blotches on the neck. Rear margin of blotches edged with whitish or yellow. Skin of gular fold yellow. Two enlarged horns at back of the head. A row of enlarged scales on each side of the throat surrounded by small scales. Two rows of pointed fringe scales on each side of the body. Eardrums distinct. Scales of venter weakly keeled. *Young:* Hatchlings ⅘ in.
  Inhabits arid and semiarid open country with sparse plant growth — bunch grass, cactus, juniper, acacia, and mesquite. The ground may be of sand, loam, hardpan, or rock but some loose soil is usually present in which these lizards bury themselves. They also seek shelter under bushes, in burrows of other animals, or among rocks.
  Similar species: (1) Regal Horned Lizard has 4 large horns with bases in contact at back of the head. (2) Coast Horned Lizard has 2 or 3 rows of enlarged pointed scales on each side of the throat. (3) Desert Horned Lizard has a single rather than a double row of pointed fringe scales on sides of body.
  Range: Kansas to Durango, Tamaulipas, and Gulf Coast of Texas. Mississippi River to extreme se. Arizona. Old records for Santa Fe, Taos, and Abiquiu in n. New Mexico. To around 6000 ft. In West often coexists with Round-tailed Horned Lizard. **Map 100**

COAST HORNED LIZARD *Phrynosoma coronatum* **Pl. 18**
  Identification: 2½–4. Two horns at back of head, longer than the rest, their bases separated. *Two rows of pointed fringe scales on each side of the body. Two or 3 rows of enlarged pointed scales on each side of the throat.* General coloration yellowish, brown,

reddish, or gray, usually resembling the prevailing soil color. Wavy dark blotches on back and a pair of large dark blotches on the neck. No dark stripes on face. Below cream, beige, or yellow, usually with spots of dusky.

Frequents a variety of habitats — brushland, coniferous forests, and broadleaf woodland. Most common in the lowlands along sandy washes where there are scattered low bushes. Requirements seem to be open areas for sunning, warmth, bushes for cover, patches of fine loose soil for burial, and ants and other insect food.

Similar species: The Desert Horned Lizard has blunter snout, shorter horns, and body spines, only 1 row of well-developed fringe scales on each side of the body, and 1 row of enlarged scales on each side of the throat.

Range: Throughout most of California west of desert and Cascade-Sierran highlands; absent from humid Northwest; throughout Baja California. Single record for Grasshopper, south of Medicine Lake, Siskiyou Co., California. Sea level to around 6000 ft.

Subspecies: SAN DIEGO HORNED LIZARD, *P. c. blainvillei*. Scales enlarged toward center of head, convex and nearly smooth. CALIFORNIA HORNED LIZARD, *P. c. frontale*. Scales not enlarged toward center of head, flat or peaked and roughened; horns average smaller than in San Diego Horned Lizard.   Map 97

DESERT HORNED LIZARD *Phrynosoma platyrhinos*   **Pl. 18**
Identification: 2¾–3¾. The desert counterpart of the Coast Horned Lizard. Snout very blunt; horns and body spines relatively short. *One row of well-developed fringe scales on each side of body, and 1 row of slightly enlarged scales on each side of throat.* General coloration resembles the soil color of the habitat — beige, tan, reddish, gray, or black, the latter in individuals found on black lava flows. Wavy dark blotches on back and a pair of large dark neck blotches.

A lizard of arid lands, most common along washes and at the edges of dunes. Although this lizard is sometimes found on hardpan or among rocks, patches of sand are generally present. Associated with creosote bush, saltbush, cactus, and ocotillo in the desert and Basin sagebrush in the Great Basin. To find these lizards drive slowly along little-traveled roads in the morning or late afternoon. Watch for them on rocks or earthbanks where they bask. Usually easily caught by hand.

Similar species: See Coast Horned Lizard.

Range: S. Idaho and se. Oregon, south to ne. Baja California and nw. Sonora; western base central plateau of Utah to eastern base of Sierra Nevada and desert slope of mts. of s. California; San Jacinto River Wash, Riverside Co., California, on coastal side of mts. Reported in Ouray-Jensen area, Uintah Co., Utah. Old record, Fort Walla Walla, Walla Walla Co., Washington. Occasionally found in same habitat with the Flat-tailed Horned Lizard.

Subspecies: NORTHERN DESERT HORNED LIZARD, *P. p. platyrhinos.* Two longest horns at back of head usually less than 45 per cent of head length; space between their bases about equal to width of horn at its base. SOUTHERN DESERT HORNED LIZARD, *P. p. calidiarum.* Two longest horns at back of head usually 45 per cent or more of head length; space between their bases half width of horn at its base.   Map 96

SHORT-HORNED LIZARD   *Phrynosoma douglassi*   **Pl. 18**
   Identification: 2½–3¾. *The short stubby horns and single row of fringe scales* on each side of the body will distinguish it from other horned lizards. Throat scales all small. Above beige, gray, brown, reddish, or tan, blotched with dark brown and often speckled with whitish. A pair of large dark brown blotches on back of neck. Region of gular fold and chest usually buff or orange yellow. *Young:* About 1 in. at hatching.
   Ranges from semiarid plains high into the mountains. Frequents a variety of habitats — shortgrass prairie, sagebrush, and piñon-juniper, pine-spruce, and spruce-fir associations. The ground may be stony, sandy, or firm, but usually some fine loose soil is present. More cold-tolerant than other horned lizards. Live-bearing; as many as 3 dozen young in a litter.
   Range: Extreme s. Canada to s. Durango; w. Arizona and east of Cascade crest in Oregon and Washington to e. Kansas. Chiefly a mt. dweller in the southern part of its range. To above 10,000 ft. on San Francisco Peak, Arizona.
   Subspecies: PIGMY HORNED LIZARD, *P. d. douglassi.* Above dark brown or dark blue-gray; very small horns, projecting nearly vertically. EASTERN SHORT-HORNED LIZARD, *P. d. brevirostre.* Dorsal spots indistinctly bordered or bordered only along rear edge with light color; temporal horns shorter than width at base. SALT LAKE HORNED LIZARD, *P. d. ornatum.* Light borders generally confined to rear of dorsal spots; length of horns equal to or greater than width of base. DESERT SHORT-HORNED LIZARD, *P. d. ornatissimum.* Dorsal spots bordered along inner side and at rear with light color; tail longer than width of head; temporal horns shorter than width at base. MOUNTAIN SHORT-HORNED LIZARD, *P. d. hernandesi.* Dorsal spots bordered only at rear with light color; tail more than 1½ times head width; temporal horns as long as or longer than width at base.   Map 95

FLAT-TAILED HORNED LIZARD   *Phrynosoma m'calli*   **Pl. 18**
   Identification: 2¾–3¼. A pale gray, buff, or reddish-brown

lizard restricted to fine windblown sand. Closely matches the sand color. The only horned lizard with a *dark vertebral stripe*. *Tail* long, broad, and *very much flattened*. Long slender horns. Two rows of fringe scales on each side of the body. Below white, unmarked.

Lives only in areas of fine sand, sharing the habitat with fringe-toed lizards. Occupies extremely barren country, where vegetation is sparse or lacking. Often difficult to find. When approached, it flattens out against the ground and blends with the sand or quickly buries itself. Flat-tails run with great speed and when fleeing may be mistaken for a fringe-toe. They are active in the morning usually before the sand surface goes above 104° F.; in summer they may be 'abroad in the evening and occasionally are found on blacktop roads, where, although conspicuous, they can easily be mistaken for a rock.

Range: Dunes and sandy flats of low desert in s. California from Coachella Valley to head of Gulf of California.   Map 99

ROUND-TAILED HORNED LIZARD   Pl. 18
Phrynosoma modestum
Identification: 1½–2¾. A small horned lizard with relatively short, spikelike, well-separated horns of about equal length. Tail slender and round, broadening abruptly at its base. *No fringe scales on the sides of the body.* A pair of dark blotches on the neck, a dark patch on each side of the body, a pair of dark blotches on the lower back, and a barred tail; center of back usually unspotted. General color above ash-white, gray, light brown, or reddish, generally matching the predominant soil color. *Young:* Hatchlings ⅘ in.

Lives on sandy or gravelly soil of plains, desert flats, and washes, in arid and semiarid habitats. Rocks may or may not be present. Plants present may be cedar, ocotillo, oak, mesquite, creosote bush, or sumac. When on pebbly ground these lizards harmonize both in form and color with their background. In hot weather, most often abroad in the early morning on overcast days.

Range: N. New Mexico to San Luis Potosí; n. Texas to se. Arizona; Cimarron Co., Oklahoma. To around 6000 ft. Often found in same habitat with Texas Horned Lizard.   Map 101

REGAL HORNED LIZARD   *Phrynosoma solare*   Pl. 18
Identification: 3–4½. Our largest horned lizard, easily identified by its *4 large occipital horns, with bases in contact.* Large light-colored area on back — light gray, beige, or reddish, bordered on each side by broad dusky band. Sometimes a pale vertebral stripe. Single row of fringe scales on each side of body.

Frequents rocky and gravelly habitats of arid and semiarid plains, hills, and lower slopes of mountains. Seldom found on sandy flats. Vegetation may consist of cactus and other succulents, mesquite, and creosote bush. Search the vicinity of scrubby plant growth along washes, both in rocky canyons and on the plains. Usually not found in the same habitat with other species of Horned Lizards.

Range: S. Arizona to n. Sinaloa, west to Harquahala and Plomosa Mts., Arizona. Sea level to 4600 ft.   Map 98

Night Lizards: Family Xantusiidae

A SMALL FAMILY of New World lizards with representatives from sw. U.S. to Panama; a single species in Cuba. Four living genera; 12 species.

Small secretive lizards with lidless eyes and vertical pupils. The skin is soft; dorsal scales are granular; ventral scales are large and squarish. A gular fold and a fold of skin on each side of the body. Live-bearing.

GRANITE NIGHT LIZARD *Xantusia henshawi*   **Pl. 26**
  Identification: 2–2¾. *A flat-bodied lizard with soft, pliable skin. Dorsum marked with large dark brown or black spots* on a pale background. The light color between the spots becomes reduced to a network of whitish or pale yellow when the lizard is in the dark phase. Color change may occur rapidly. Scales smooth and granular on dorsum, large and squarish on venter. Eyes with fixed transparent covering and vertical pupils. Head broad and flat, with large symmetrically arranged plates. *Male:* Whitish oval-shaped patch along anterior border of femoral pore row.

  Inhabits rocky canyons and hillsides in arid and semiarid regions, where it seems to prefer massive outcrops in the shadier parts of canyons or near water. Avoids hot south-facing slopes. Secretive and crevice-dwelling, seldom venturing from its hiding place except at night. Live-bearing, 1 or 2 young per brood. Food includes insects, spiders, ticks, scorpions, centipedes, and some plant materials. In hunting these lizards remove cap rocks and flakes from the sides of boulders. Keep one hand free to seize the lizards while they are light-struck. Avoid the tail; it is easily lost. Because of lizard's small size and restriction to rocks, it is seldom found on roadways at night.
  Similar species: The Leaf-toed Gecko (p. 93), with which it coexists in some parts of its range, has broad, flat, toe tips.
  Range: From southern side of San Gorgonio Pass in s. California, southward on both desert and coastal sides of mts. into n. Baja California in Sierra Juárez and Sierra San Pedro Mártir. To 7600 ft.   Map 72

DESERT NIGHT LIZARD *Xantusia vigilis* **Pl. 26**
Identification: 1½–1¾. A slim, velvet-skinned lizard with *olive, gray, or dark brown dorsum, speckled with black.* Usually a beige stripe edged with black from eye to shoulder. No eyelids; *pupils vertical.* Dorsal scales smooth, granular, generally in 33 to 40 longitudinal rows at midbody; ventral ones large and squarish. Eighteen to 25 transverse rows of scales (lamellae) on underside of 4th toe. *Male:* Large femoral pores give thigh more angular contour in cross section than female's.

A secretive lizard of arid lands that lives chiefly beneath fallen branches of Joshua trees, dead clumps of various other species of yucca (Mojave yucca, Spanish bayonet, etc.), nolina, agave, and cardons (Sonora). Also found in rock crevices, beneath cow chips and other debris, and beneath logs and under the bark of Digger pines (inner Coast Ranges and s. Sierra Nevada, California). Ranges into the piñon-juniper belt in the Panamint Mts. Chiefly diurnal and crepuscular; may be nocturnal during warm summer months. Live-bearing, 1 to 3 young. At one time considered to be extremely rare but now regarded as one of the most abundant lizards. Feeds on insects, spiders, and other arthropods.

Similar species: Arizona Night Lizard averages larger and is flatter; usually has 42 or more longitudinal dorsal scale rows at midbody, whereas Desert Night Lizard has 40 or less.

Range: Mojave Desert and inner Coast Ranges of California, s. Nevada, s. Utah, and nw. Arizona, south to extreme nw. Sonora and throughout Baja California. Near sea level to 9300 ft. (Telescope Peak, California).

Subspecies: DESERT NIGHT LIZARD, *X. v. vigilis.* Olive to dark brown above; lamellae on 4th toe 18–21. Range as given for species except s. Utah. Scattered populations in California in inner Coast Ranges to Pinnacles Nat'l Monument and Panoche Pass; Kern River Canyon, Kern Co.; and San Gabriel wash, Los Angeles Co. Kofa and Castle Dome Mts., Arizona. UTAH NIGHT LIZARD, *X. v. utahensis.* Orange-buff above; lamellae on 4th toe 23–25. Henry Mts. east to Natural Bridges Nat'l Monument, south to San Juan River, Utah.   Map 70

ARIZONA NIGHT LIZARD *Xantusia arizonae* **Pl. 26**
Identification: 1¾–2⅜. A close relative of the Desert Night Lizard, resembling it in color and scalation. It differs, however, in reaching larger size, in having relatively longer limbs, a more flattened body and higher scale counts. Longitudinal dorsal scale rows at midbody usually 42 or more. Twenty-five to 28 lamellae (see above) on underside of 4th toe.

Frequents rocky areas in the chaparral-oak belt and mixed desert and woodland vegetation along the southern edge of the Colorado Plateau. Found under exfoliating flakes of massive granite boulders, in rock crevices, and occasionally under dead yuccas in the vicinity of rocks.

Similar species: See Desert Night Lizard.

Range: Arizona in the Weaver (near Yarnell), McCloud (3 mi. north of Hillside), and Superstition (5 mi. northeast of Apache Junction) Mts.; also at Tonto Nat'l Monument and Valentine.
Map 70

ISLAND NIGHT LIZARD *Klauberina riversiana*   Pl. 26

Identification: 2¾–3¾. A large night lizard confined to islands off the coast of s. California. Sixteen instead of 14 or 12 *longitudinal rows of squarish scales on belly. Two rows of supraoculars* (1 row in other species). Above, with soft granular scalation. Folds of skin on neck and along side of body. Dorsum mottled with pale ash-gray or beige and yellowish brown, darkened in varying amounts with black. Occasional individuals have a pale gray dorsolateral stripe on each side edged with brown and black; a brown vertebral stripe may be present. Below pale gray, sometimes with bluish cast, suffused on belly and often on tail with yellow. Underside of feet may be yellowish. *Male:* Slightly larger femoral pores than female's.

Inhabits grassland, clumps of cactus, cliffs, and rocky beaches. Found under rocks, driftwood, and fallen branches. Less secretive than other night lizards; may be seen abroad in the daytime. Live-bearing, 4 to 9 young. Feeds on insects, spiders, centipedes, scorpions, marine isopods, and the stems, leaves, blossoms, and seeds of plants.

Range: San Clemente, Santa Barbara, and San Nicholas Is. off coast of s. California.   Map 70

Skinks: Family Scincidae

A WIDELY distributed family with representatives in the Old World tropics, East Indies, Australia, Pacific islands, and the New World. The striped skinks (*Eumeces*), the only genus in the West, occur in Africa, Asia, and from s. Canada to Costa Rica.

Skinks are usually alert, agile, slim-bodied lizards with *shiny, cycloid scales*, reinforced with bone. The scales of the dorsal and ventral surfaces are similar in size, but those on top of the head are enlarged, symmetrically arranged, and of varied shape. Limbs are small, and in some burrowing species are absent. The tongue is forked and frequently protruded. Some skinks have a window in the lower eyelid permitting vision when the eyes are closed. All our species have limbs and lack the eyelid window.

These lizards often occur in habitats where there is some moisture nearby — damp soil or a spring or stream. As a group they seem to be more dependent on moisture than most lizards, yet some live in deserts.

It is almost impossible to noose skinks because of their wariness, slick scales, small head, and thick neck. Look for them under stones, boards, logs, and other objects and catch them by hand. Avoid the tail; it is easily shed.

Our species lay eggs but elsewhere many species are live-bearing.

GREAT PLAINS SKINK   *Eumeces obsoletus*   **Pl. 24**
Identification: 3–5. Our largest skink, unique in having *oblique* instead of horizontal *scale rows on the sides of the body.* Above light gray, olive-brown, or tan, *usually profusely spotted with black or dark brown*, the spots uniting here and there to form scattered longitudinal lines. Occasionally spotting is absent. Sides generally flecked with salmon. Ground color of tail and feet yellowish or pale orange. Below pale yellow, unmarked. *Young:* Black above, dark gray below; tail blue; orange and white spots on head. With growth the black pigment fades and becomes limited to the rear edge or sides of the scales.

Frequents both grassland and woodland from the plains into the mountains. In the eastern and central part of its range it is chiefly a prairie species, most abundant in open habitats with low vegetation. In the West it enters semiarid environments of canyons, mesas, and mountains, usually where there is grass and low shrubby growth. Rock outcrops near thickets along permanent or intermittent streams are especially favored. Found under rocks, logs, bark, and boards. A secretive, nervous species that usually attempts to bite when caught. Nests beneath sunken rocks and broods its eggs. Feeds on insects, spiders, and lizards.
Range: Nebraska to cent. Tamaulipas; extreme w. Missouri to cent. Arizona. To above 7000 ft.   Map 103

MANY-LINED SKINK   *Eumeces multivirgatus*   **Pl. 24**
Identification: 2¼–3. A slim long-bodied skink with very long tail. Proportions alone set it off from our other species. Dorsal coloration variable — many dark and light longitudinal stripes, a single light stripe on each side bordered below by a dark one, a broad pale stripe down middle of the back, or no striping at all. When light stripes are present, 1 on each side is confined to the 3rd scale row (counting from middle of back). Stripes vary in intensity and some dark ones may actually consist of rows of spots. *Young:* Generally fewer stripes than adult, or stripes absent. Tail blue, fading with age.

Lives in a variety of habitats from shortgrass prairie into the mountains. Also occurs near human habitation, in vacant lots, city dumps, and backyards. Local environments vary from creosote bush desert to dense streamside growth, and from arid to moist. The ground may be loamy, sandy, or rocky. Most abundant where there is water or moist subsoil. Look for this skink under rocks, logs, boards, and dried cow chips. Chiefly insectivorous.

Similar species: See Mountain Skink.

Range: S. Nebraska to w. Texas and cent. Chihuahua, west to extreme w. Arizona. Distribution spotty in southern part of range. Isolated population 15 mi. north of Topock, Mohave Co., Arizona. From 3000 to around 8200 ft.

Subspecies: NORTHERN MANY-LINED SKINK, *E. m. multivirgatus.* Little variation in color pattern. Body pale, with dorsolateral light stripes only slightly lighter than ground color and a broad, clearly defined dorsal dark line with uninterrupted margins on adjacent portions of 1st and 2nd scale rows (see Fig. 20, opposite Pl. 24). No plain-colored phase. Sandhill and prairie habitats below 5500 ft. SOUTHERN MANY-LINED SKINK, *E. m. epipleurotus.* Coloration highly variable. Both striped and plain-colored phases occur. Striped individuals are darker than Northern Many-lined Skink, have strongly contrasting dorsolateral light lines (see Fig. 20), a contrasting mid-dorsal light line in the young, and varied reduction of dark lines through invasion of ground color from the sides. Unstriped, dark, plain-colored individuals are of variable occurrence, but are particularly common at lower altitudes in the southernmost, drier parts of the range. These were formerly regarded as a distinct species, the Pecos Skink. Habitats vary — high mountains, plateaus, and lowlands, in pine and spruce forests, mesquite grassland, and creosote bush desert.   Map 105

MOUNTAIN SKINK *Eumeces callicephalus*   **Pl. 24**
Identification: 2–2½. Above olive or tan, with a pale dorsolateral stripe on each side extending from above the eye to the trunk, where *confined to the 4th scale row* (counting from the midline). Below the pale stripe is a broad dark brown band extending from the eye to the groin. Sometimes a whitish or pale orange *Y-shaped mark on the head* with its base on the neck. Tail bluish. *Young:* About 1 in. Blue tail and striping more vivid than in adult; Y mark distinct.

In the U.S. it frequents oak and pine habitats in rocky areas in the mountains but in Mexico it ranges to near sea level. Feeds on insects and spiders.

Similar species: (1) Many-lined Skink has the light stripes on 3rd scale row from the midline. Striped individuals of (2) Gilbert's and (3) Western Skinks have a broad light stripe on 3rd and 4th scale rows.

Range: Pajarito, Baboquivari, Santa Rita, and Huachuca Mts., Arizona; Guadalupe Mts. (Guadalupe Canyon), New Mexico; w. Mexico southeast to Querétaro. From coastal plain

in Sinaloa and Nayarit well up into Sierra Madre Occidental.
To above 6500 ft.   Map 106

WESTERN SKINK *Eumeces skiltonianus*   Pl. 24
Identification: 2¼–3¼. Aside from fading with age, color pattern varies little. There is a *broad brown stripe down the back edged with black and bordered on each side by a conspicuous whitish dorsolateral stripe* that originates on the nose, extends over the eye and back along the side of the body onto the tail. The white dorsolateral stripes are on joined halves of 2nd and 3rd scale rows (counting from middle of the back). A 2nd pale stripe, starting on the upper jaw, occurs low on each side and is separated from the first by a broad dark brown or black band originating on the side of the head and extending onto the tail. Tail dull blue or gray. In the breeding season orange color appears on side of head and chin and occasionally on tip and underside of tail. Usually 7 upper labials and 4 enlarged nuchals. *Young:* Hatchlings about 1 in. Striped pattern more vivid and tail brighter blue than in adult.

Frequents grassland, woodland, and forest. Seems to prefer rocky habitats near streams where there is abundant plant cover, but also is found on dry hillsides far from water. In forested areas search the sunnier parts of clearings. Turn rocks and logs, and look under the bark and in the interior of rotten logs. Active in the daytime but usually keeps out of sight. Feeds on insects, spiders, and sowbugs.

Similar species: The striped, blue-tailed subspecies of Gilbert's Skink (*gilberti* and *placerensis*) closely resemble the Western Skink, but the scales of the light lines on the back are usually edged with brown or gray and the blue tail color disappears in adults. Fortunately, where Western and Gilbert's Skinks coexist in s. California, they are easily distinguished (see Gilbert's Skink).

Range: Southern B.C. to tip of Baja California and in Great Basin to extreme n. Arizona; cent. Utah to Pacific Coast. Absent from floor of San Joaquin Valley, s. Sierra Nevada, and deserts of California. On Santa Catalina, Los Coronados, and Todos Santos Is. off coast of California and Baja California. Isolated montane populations in Great Basin. To over 8000 ft., North Rim Grand Canyon, Arizona.

Subspecies: WESTERN SKINK, *E. s. skiltonianus.* Dorsolateral stripe narrow, usually occupying no more than half of the 2nd scale row, at midbody less than half the width of the dark dorsal stripe. GREAT BASIN SKINK, *E. s. utahensis.* Dorsolateral stripe wider than in Western Skink, occupying more than half of the 2nd scale row, at midbody equal in width to half or more of the dark dorsal stripe. In rocky areas in habitats of scrub oak, sagebrush, juniper, and grass from 4500 to 7000 ft.

CORONADO ISLAND SKINK, *E. s. interparietalis*. Differs from Western and Great Basin Skinks in having the inter-parietal reduced in size and enclosed posteriorly by the parietals and the median and lateral dark stripes extending to or beyond the middle of the tail.   Map 104

GILBERT'S SKINK *Eumeces gilberti*   **Pl. 24**
Identification: 2½–4½. Adults are plain olive or brown above or have varied amounts of dark spotting, which may form an intricate pattern. Light and dark striping is more or less distinct in adults of some populations and varies with age and locality. The tail becomes brick-red or orange with age in both sexes and some individuals develop red on the head. At some localities this skink is difficult to distinguish from the Western Skink except when full-grown and striping has been lost. Commonly 8 upper labials and often 2 or 3 enlarged nuchals. *Young:* Pair of whitish stripes on each side, enclosing a broad black or dark brown stripe which narrows on the tail and stops abruptly near base of the tail; broad olive stripe down middle of the back. Tail blue in the northern and eastern part of the range, salmon or pink in the south (see *Subspecies*). *Male:* Tends to lose striping sooner than female.
    Lives in a variety of habitats — grassland, woodland, and forest, often in rocky areas in the vicinity of intermittent or permanent streams and springs, from the lowlands high into the mountains. Habits and habitat closely resemble the Western Skink's. Food includes insects and spiders.
Similar species: In the Western Skink the broad lateral stripes are uniformly brown (they are absent or variegated in Gilbert's Skink), blue or blue-gray tail color usually persists in adults, and all young have blue tails. In areas where the two species are known to coexist (mountains of s. California), young Gilbert's Skinks have pink or salmon tails and the dark lateral stripe stops near the base of the tail. Young Western Skinks have blue tails and stripe extends well out on the tail.
Range: Foothills and middle elevations in Sierra Nevada from Yuba River south; inner Coast Ranges opposite San Francisco Bay south into mts. of s. California and San Pedro Mártir Mts., Baja California. Isolated populations in mts. of se. California, s. Nevada, and w.-cent. Arizona. From near sea level to above 8000 ft.
Subspecies: GREATER BROWN SKINK, *E. g. gilberti*. Young with blue tail; females average smaller than males (not true of other subspecies); usually 2 pairs of nuchals; for dorsal pattern see Fig. 20, opposite Pl. 24. NORTHERN BROWN SKINK, *E. g. placerensis*. Young with blue tail; retains striping longer than Greater Brown Skink; usually 1 pair of nuchals. VARIEGATED SKINK, *E. g. cancellosus*. Young with pink

tail tinged with blue above; older young and adults with barring or latticework of dark markings (see Fig. 20). WESTERN RED-TAILED SKINK, *E. g. rubricaudatus.* Young with pink tail (blue in Panamint and other desert mountains), lacking blue tinge (see above); striping and barring lost earlier (especially in females) than in Variegated Skink. Many isolated populations. In California at Covington Flat, Riverside Co., Deep Springs and Saline Valleys, Inyo Co., and in Panamint, Kingston, Clark, and Providence Mts.; in Nevada in Sheep and Charleston Mts. and at Grapevine Peak; in Baja California in San Pedro Mártir and reported at San Antonio del Mar. ARIZONA SKINK, *E. g. arizonensis.* Tends to retain juvenile striping; young with pinkish on underside of tail. Isolated populations in Arizona in piñon-juniper woodland and yellow-pine forest in vicinity of Prescott, Bradshaw Mts.; chaparral-oak association at Yarnell; and in cottonwood, willow, and mesquite bottomlands of Hassayampa River near Wickenburg.   Map 102

Whiptails and Their Allies:
Family Teiidae

A LARGE New World family distributed throughout the Americas and the West Indies. S. America has greatest number and variety of species. Eleven species of whiptails (*Cnemidophorus*), the only genus reaching the U.S., occur in the West.

Many teiids, including the whiptails, are slim-bodied, long-tailed, alert, and active diurnal lizards. They move with jerky gait, rapidly turning the head from side to side, and frequently protrude the slender forked tongue. They may move the front feet as though walking on a hot surface. At the other extreme are secretive burrowers with the limbs and toes reduced, sometimes to mere stumps. They spend much time under stones, in leaf litter, or dense plant growth; none of these species occur in the U.S.

Whiptails have large squarish scales (ventrals) in regular longitudinal and transverse rows on the belly (*8 longitudinal rows* in our species), and small scales on the back, the "dorsal granules." The number of the granules (counted across the back at midbody) is probably the most important single character in the systematics of whiptails; hence, although of little use in field identification, counts of these scales have been given. Head plates are large and symmetrical and the snout is slender. Most species have a divided frontoparietal. There are several gular folds. The posteriormost one is referred to in the descriptive accounts. Supraorbital semicircles (Fig. 21, opposite Pl. 27) may extend only a short distance forward, failing to reach the frontal, a condition referred to in the accounts as "normal," or they may penetrate far forward, separating the supraoculars from the frontal. The tail is slender, covered with keeled scales, and is two or more times the length of the body, therefore the common name. Some species are striped, others are spotted or have a checkered pattern. Some combine both spotting and striping. Striped species have pale stripes alternating with broader darker ones, referred to as "dark fields" (see Fig. 21, opposite Pl. 27).

These lizards are among the most difficult to capture. Although they sometimes allow close approach, they usually manage to stay just out of reach and may suddenly dash to cover. When relentlessly pursued, they often seek shelter in rodent burrows. When they are cornered in a bush, press in any burrow openings with a stick before attempting capture. The broad neck, slender head, and great activity make them difficult to snare with a noose.

Whiptails are difficult to identify because of the subtle differences among some species in scale counts and coloration, and the color variation that occurs with sex, age, and geographic location. Characteristic color patterns in many instances are well developed only in large individuals, and females (in particular) may mature before the "adult" pattern is attained. Habitat differences and distribution must be relied upon to aid identification.

Reproductively they are of special interest because a number of species seem to consist only of females which reproduce by parthenogenesis. Clones have been recognized in both the Chihuahua and Checkered Whiptails. In some areas within the ranges of each, their clones overlap and behave as distinct species. Differences in color and scalation are subtle, however, and are not described in this *Field Guide* (see C. H. Lowe and J. H. Wright, *Journal* Ariz. Acad. Sci., Vol. 3 (1964), No. 2, and R. Zweifel, *Amer. Mus. Novitates*, No. 2235 [1965], for details).

Whiptails feed on insects, spiders, scorpions, and other small animals, some of which they dig out of the ground and evidently detect by odor.

ORANGE-THROATED WHIPTAIL   Pl. 27
Cnemidophorus hyperythrus

   Identification: 2–2½. A striped, unspotted whiptail with an orange throat. *Frontoparietal single.* Top of head olive-gray. Pair of beige stripes down back, sometimes more or less united. Dorsolateral stripe yellowish, side stripe whitish. Ground color between stripes dark brown to black. *Young:* Tail bluish.

   Inhabits washes and other sandy areas where there are rocks and patches of brush. An inhabitant of coastal chaparral in extreme s. California.

   Similar species: The Western Whiptail lacks or has vague striping, has a spotted pattern, and a divided frontoparietal.

   Range: Laguna Beach and vicinity of Riverside and San Jacinto

in s. California, west of crest of mts. to tip of Baja California.
Subspecies: The ORANGE-THROATED WHIPTAIL, *C. h. beldingi*, occurs in our area. Map 110

GIANT SPOTTED WHIPTAIL *Cnemidophorus burti* **Pl. 29**
Identification: 3½–5½. A large spotted whiptail with striping faint or absent in *large* adults. Stripes 6, sometimes 7; vertebral stripe present or absent. Dorsum more or less speckled with pale spots. Reddish color on head and neck, sometimes over entire back. Supraorbital semicircles normal, extending anteriorly to or near frontoparietal suture. Enlarged scales on posterior surface of forearm. *Young:* Striping distinct; spots in dark fields; orange tail.

Inhabits mountain canyons, arroyos, and mesas in arid and semiarid regions. Found in dense shrubby vegetation, often among rocks near permanent and intermittent streams and in desert grassland and evergreen woodland.
Similar species: See Chihuahua Whiptail (p. 130).
Range: Arizona in extreme southeastern part and in Santa Catalina, Ajo, Puerto Blanco, Baboquivari, and Pajarito Mts. and vicinity of Oracle and Mineral Hot Springs; extreme sw. New Mexico; Sonora. Near sea level to around 4500 ft.
Subspecies: RED-BACKED WHIPTAIL, *C. b. xanthonotus* (illus.). Back reddish brown to reddish orange, red color stopping abruptly along upper sides. Ground color of sides and upper surfaces of neck, legs, and feet, dark grayish green to bluish. Dorsal striping and spotting more or less obscured by reddish-brown back color, less so in young. Juniper-oak, desert-edge habitats in Ajo (Alamo Canyon, Bull Pastures), Dripping Springs, and Puerto Blanco Mts., Organ Pipe Cactus Nat'l Monument, Pima Co., Arizona. GIANT SPOTTED WHIP-TAIL, *C. b. stictogrammus* (illus.). Adults reach much larger size than Red-backed Whiptail. Red on dorsum less extensive, usually confined to head and neck; young with bright orange to reddish tail. The only whiptail in the West except Texas Spotted Whiptail with 100 or more dorsal granules; enlarged scales on the posterior surface of forearms and abruptly enlarged scales on the gular fold. Se. Arizona, extreme sw. New Mexico, and Sonora. Map 117

NEW MEXICAN WHIPTAIL Pl. 27
Cnemidophorus neomexicanus
Identification: 2½–3. A 7-striped whiptail with a *wavy vertebral stripe and supraorbital semicircles penetrating deeply anteriorly,* usually separating the 3rd and often the 2nd supraocular from the frontal. Small diffuse light spots on the sides between light stripes. Below often pale greenish to bluish. Tail grayish at base grading to greenish or greenish blue toward tip. Scales on

posterior surface of forearm granular; 71–85 dorsal granules. *Young:* Ground color of body black, stripes yellow, well-defined whitish spots in dark fields on sides; greenish to greenish-blue tail. Males unknown.

Primarily a bottomland dweller, found in areas of loose sand or packed sandy soil amid low grass, saltbush, desert tea, and scattered yucca and mesquite. Inhabits particularly sandy alluvia and the margins of desert playas.

Similar species: Distinguished from other striped whiptails by the anterior extension of the supraorbital semicircles, the well-defined stripes with light spots in the lateral dark fields, the wavy vertebral stripe, and greenish tail.

Range: Rio Grande Valley, New Mexico, from north of Santa Fe, into extreme w. Texas (known only from El Paso) and probably Mexico. In extreme southwestern part, ranges west to vicinity of Lordsburg.   Map 112

LITTLE STRIPED WHIPTAIL   Pl. 27
Cnemidophorus inornatus

Identification: 2–2¾. There are 6 to 7 (usually 7) pale stripes, the median stripe sometimes faint or absent; stripes yellowish to whitish, the ground color between them blackish to reddish brown, *without light spots*, becoming lighter with age. *Tail bluish toward tip.* Below usually bluish white to blue (in males). A pale form with faint stripes occurs at White Sands, New Mexico. Scales on the posterior surface of the forearm and anterior to the gular fold only slightly enlarged. Supraorbital semicircles normal; 52–72 dorsal granules. *Young:* Less blue ventrally than adult. *Male:* Chin and belly more bluish than in female. Both sexes have more vivid blue on the underside of the tail than on the remaining underparts.

Chiefly a prairie grassland species but ranges into grassy areas of the piñon-juniper zone. Frequents sandy or silty, sometimes gravelly, ground of elevated plains or alluvial flatlands; seldom found in rocky or very barren areas or in mesquite habitats commonly occupied by the Desert-Grassland Whiptail.

Similar species: (1) Plateau Whiptail larger, has relatively smaller scales, and occurs generally at higher elevations. (2) Chihuahua Whiptail has large scales on the rear of the forearm and spots in the dark fields. See also (3) Desert-Grassland Whiptail, with which it overlaps in range in the grassland of sw. New Mexico and se. Arizona, and (4) Checkered Whiptail. (5) Six-lined Racerunner has broad brownish stripe down middle of back and generally greenish foreparts.

Range: Throughout most of lowlands of New Mexico — Rio Grande Valley to northwest of Albuquerque, east to between Santa Rosa and Tucumcari, south to vicinity of Carlsbad; west into extreme sw. New Mexico; w. Texas to cent. San Luis Potosí. Isolated populations in San Juan River basin of extreme nw.

New Mexico and vicinity of Wilcox Playa, Cochise Co., Arizona. 1000 to 5500 ft., occasionally to 7000 ft. (3000 to 7000 ft. in our area). Map 113

DESERT-GRASSLAND WHIPTAIL   Pl. 28
Cnemidophorus uniparens

Identification: 2–2¾. A small 6- or 7-striped whiptail with dark brown to black fields, without spots. *Tail greenish olive to bluish green.* Scales on back of forearm slightly enlarged and angular. Supraorbital semicircles normal; 60–75 dorsal granules. Males unknown.

Chiefly a lowland species of desert and mesquite grassland, but follows rivers into the mountains, where it occurs in ever-green woodland, as at Oak Creek, Arizona. Generally found on plains and gentle foothill slopes, occasionally in areas with scant cover of grasses and herbs, but more commonly where mesquite and yucca are present and often where mesquite is dense.

Similar species: Adults differ from (1) Plateau and (2) Little Striped Whiptails in having a greenish-olive to bluish-green rather than a blue tail. Occurs generally at lower elevations than the Plateau Whiptail but coexists with the Little Striped Whip-tail in sw. New Mexico and se. Arizona. (3) See also Checkered Whiptail.

Range: Se. Arizona and sw. New Mexico, up Rio Grande Valley to vicinity of Socorro, south into Mexico; western outpost in Prescott-Cornville area in western part of cent. Arizona plateau. To around 5000 ft. Map 111

PLATEAU WHIPTAIL *Cnemidophorus velox*   Pl. 27

Identification: 2½–3⅛. Six or 7 dorsal stripes, the vertebral stripe variable; when present, less distinct than the others. No spots in black to blackish-brown dark fields in either young or adults. *Tail light blue.* Below whitish, unmarked or with tinge of bluish green, especially on the chin. Scales on back of forearm slightly enlarged; those bordering the gular fold conspicuously enlarged and abruptly differentiated from the adjacent granular scales. Supraorbital semicircles normal; 65–85 dorsal granules. *Young:* Bright blue tail. Males unknown.

Found chiefly in the mountains in piñon-juniper woodland, oak woodland, and lower edges of ponderosa pine forests. At lower elevations frequents broadleaf streamside woodland of permanent and semipermanent streams.

Similar species: (1) The Chihuahua Whiptail, with which its range is contiguous to the south, is larger, has greatly enlarged scales on the back of the forearm (to 4 or more times the size of the adjacent scales), is spotted dorsally in the lateral dark fields, and lacks blue color on the tail. (2) Little Striped Whiptail has fewer dorsal scales. See also (3) Desert-Grassland and (4) Checkered Whiptails.

Range: Central plateau of Arizona and New Mexico, north into s. Utah and w. Colorado; population in vicinity of Caballo Reservoir Dam, Sierra Co., New Mexico. Mostly from 5000 to 8000 ft.   Map 114

SIX-LINED RACERUNNER *Cnemidophorus sexlineatus* **Pl. 28**
Identification: 2½–3⅛. In our area a small 7-striped, unspotted whiptail with greenish forepart in adults. Light stripes usually yellowish anteriorly (western subspecies), fading to white posteriorly, or sometimes pale gray or pale blue. A broad brownish stripe down middle of the back and a dark brown to blackish stripe dorsolaterally between the 2 uppermost pale stripes. A lighter brown stripe on the sides. Below whitish or pale blue except on underside of limbs and tail. Scales on posterior surface of forearm not or slightly enlarged. Scales anterior to the gular fold conspicuously enlarged and usually not grading gradually into the smaller scales of the fold. Supraorbital semicircles normal; 68–110 granules. *Young:* Hatchlings 1¼ in. Distinct yellow stripes; light blue tail. *Male:* Belly bluish; striping sometimes vague.

Frequents open grassland with scattered bushes, often where the soil is sandy but also occurs on loam, gravel, and hardpan. Frequents both the lowlands and hills, occurring on the floodplains and banks of rivers and in the vicinity of rock outcrops. **Similar species:** (1) New Mexican Whiptail lacks greenish foreparts. (2) Little Striped Whiptail has no broad brownish stripe down middle of back, lacks green on foreparts. (3) Chihuahua and (4) Texas Spotted Whiptails have light spots in the dark fields and enlarged scales on posterior surface of forearms. (5) See also Checkered Whiptail.
Range: S. Nebraska to Gulf Coast of Texas; e. Colorado and e. New Mexico to Atlantic Coast. Locality in se. New Mexico is 11 mi. northeast of Elkins, Chaves Co.
Subspecies: The PRAIRIE LINED RACERUNNER, *C. s. viridis*, occurs in our area.   Map 108

CHIHUAHUA WHIPTAIL *Cnemidophorus exsanguis* **Pl. 27**
Identification: 3–3¾. A striped whiptail with light spots in the brown fields. Usually 6 light stripes, pale yellowish to gray on neck grading to whitish or beige posteriorly. Middorsal stripe may be narrow and broken into a series of spots or indistinct or absent. Tail greenish, brownish, or pinkish. Below whitish to cream, unmarked. Enlarged scales along the anterior margin of the gular fold and on the rear of the forearm, the latter 4 or more times the size of the adjacent scales. Supraorbital semicircles normal; 65–86 dorsal granules. Males unknown. *Young:* Tail orange or reddish.

Chiefly an upland form, ranging from desert and desert grassland into the oak-pine and ponderosa pine forests in the mountains, where it occurs on rocky hillsides, sandy alluvium of washes, and in canyons. Characteristic habitat consists of canyon bottoms in the oak and oak-pine belts.

Similar species: (1) Differs from Giant Spotted Whiptail (p. 127) — with which it was formerly confused and with which it co-exists in mt. areas in se. Arizona — in being smaller, having a smaller number of dorsal granules (fewer than 95 where ranges of the two species overlap), and persistent striping. See also (2) Plateau, (3) Little Striped, (4) Texas Spotted, and (5) Checkered Whiptails, and (6) Six-lined Racerunner.

Range: Trans-Pecos Texas to cent. Arizona; n. New Mexico into Sonora and Chihuahua.   Map 116

TEXAS SPOTTED WHIPTAIL *Cnemidophorus gularis*

Identification: 2½–3½. *A striped whiptail with a dark blue to blackish chest in adult males.* In dorsal coloration closely resembles the Chihuahua Whiptail (Plate 27). Seven or 8 stripes, the vertebral stripe broader and less distinct than the rest; yellow-brown spots in the dark fields. Tail brown or reddish. Scales on the anterior margin of the gular fold and posterior surfaces of the forearms enlarged. Supraorbital semicircles normal; 78–96 dorsal granules, 10 to 21 (average 15) between the paravertebral stripes. *Young:* Striped, but spotting faint or absent. With growth, paired vertebral wavy light lines tend to fuse into the broad light vertebral stripe of adults; rump and tail reddish, fading with age. In our area reddish cast to tail may persist even in some adults and is apparent at a considerable distance. *Male:* Throat and often underside of the tail orange or pinkish salmon; chest and belly purplish or bluish, often darkened with varying amounts of black.

Chiefly a species of prairie grassland in washes and river-bottoms grown to mesquite, acacia, cactus, and brush. The soil is usually sandy or gravelly. More deliberate in its movements than the Six-lined Racerunner and generally less wary.

Similar species: (1) Six-lined Racerunner has a short light stripe on the sides of its tail, extending backward from the hind leg and bordered below by a dark line, and lacks spotting in the dark fields. (2) In areas of overlap, the Chihuahua Whiptail has 3–7 (average 5) granules between the paravertebral stripes and prefers more rugged upland habitats. Its young lack the reddish tail (except for some western populations) and paired vertebral stripes of the juvenile Texas Spotted Whiptail. (3) See also Checkered Whiptail.

Range: S. Oklahoma to n. Veracruz and Hidalgo; e. Texas to extreme se. New Mexico. Coexists on lower mt. slopes with Chihuahua Whiptail.   Map 115

WESTERN WHIPTAIL *Cnemidophorus tigris*   Pl. 28

Identification: 3–3¾. *Back and sides with spots, bars, or network of dusky or black on background of gray, brown, yellowish, or tan.*

Stripes may be present but they often fade on the lower back and base of the tail. Head, shoulders, and tail often gray-brown or olive, tail becoming dark brown, dusky, or bluish toward tip. Below usually cream-colored or yellowish with scattered spots of blackish, especially on chest and throat. In extreme ventral darkening, the throat, chest, underside of front legs, and belly are black; orange or pink on throat may be reduced to a few tan flecks. Rust-colored patches often present on sides of belly. Scales anterior to gular fold only slightly enlarged and grading gradually into the small granules of the fold. Postantebrachials not enlarged. *Young:* Above spotted, marbled, or striped with black, black fields alternating with narrow orange-yellow ones. Tail bright blue.

An active lizard of arid and semiarid habitats usually where plants are sparse and there are open areas for running. Also found in woodland, streamside growth, and in the warmer, drier parts of forests. Avoids dense grassland and thick growth of shrubs. The ground may be firm soil, sandy, or rocky. Ranges from deserts to pine forests in the mountains.

Similar species: The Checkered Whiptail has enlarged scales anterior to the gular fold.

Range: N.-cent. Oregon and sw. Idaho, west of Rocky Mts., into Baja California, east to w. Texas. Localities in n. Oregon are Clarno and Kimberly on John Day River. Below sea level to above 5000 ft.

Subspecies: GREAT BASIN WHIPTAIL, *C. t. tigris.* Four light stripes on back which tend to become obscure with age, particularly in southern part of range. Usually has vertical dark barring on sides. Hind limbs with black or dusky flecks or broken black network. Much variation in ventral color, from nearly plain unmarked throughout to heavily dark-spotted, particularly on chest. Both dorsal and ventral dark spotting tends to be reduced in southern part of range, but there is much variation. CALIFORNIA WHIPTAIL, *C. t. mundus* (illus.). Typically 8 light stripes but lateral stripes often with irregular borders and sometimes indistinct; dorsal dark markings often large and vivid. Usually no distinct dark barring on sides. Throat pale, usually with distinct black spots. COASTAL WHIPTAIL, *C. t. multiscutatus.* Resembles the California Whiptail but stripes on sides usually less well defined. Perhaps a greater frequency of individuals with large dark spots on throat, but there is much variation. SOUTHERN WHIPTAIL, *C. t. gracilis.* Tendency toward retention in large individuals of distinct even-edged brown stripes; typically with 4 distinct stripes on back and an additional less distinct one on each side. Striping vague or absent in some adults. Hind limbs, sides, and dark fields commonly with rounded light spots giving overall spotted effect. Outstanding characteristic is strong tendency toward darkening of throat, chest, and underside of forelimbs. In large adults throat and chest may be uniformly black. NORTHERN WHIPTAIL, *C. t. septentrionalis.* Striped as in Southern Whiptail but stripes yellow. Dark stripes usually stop short of hind legs. Throat with small black spots. MARBLED WHIPTAIL, *C. t. marmoratus* (illus.). Adult with pronounced marbled pattern dorsally but usually with alternating vertical dark and light bars on sides and slight indication of dorsal striping. Throat plain white, pink, or orange, sometimes with a few black spots. Chest pink or orange often with some black spots. Young spotted.   Map 109

CHECKERED WHIPTAIL *Cnemidophorus tesselatus*   **Pl. 27**
Identification: 3¼–4⅛. Resembles the Western Whiptail. Above with conspicuous black spots and bars often arranged in a more or less checkered pattern. Dorsum with pale stripes. Dark bars on sides. A few scattered black spots on throat, chest, and belly, or unspotted. *Scales anterior to gular fold abruptly and conspicuously enlarged.* Males extremely rare.
   Ranges from creosote bush plains to the piñon zone in the mountains. Although soil conditions may vary from hardpan to sand, this lizard seems to prefer rocky habitats with scant vegetation and open areas for running.
Similar species: (1) Chihuahua and (2) Texas Spotted Whiptails have greater enlargement of scales on back of forearm. (3) Six-lined Racerunner, (4) Little Striped, (5) Desert-Grassland, and (6) Plateau Whiptails typically are smaller and have a striped pattern without spots or other marks in the dark fields. (7) See also Western Whiptail.
Range: Se. Colorado to s. Chihuahua; w. Texas to extreme se. Arizona, 22 mi. southwest of Rodeo, Cochise Co., and sw. New Mexico, at Antelope Pass and 5 mi. north of Animas, Hidalgo Co.   Map 107

Alligator Lizards and Their Allies: Family Anguidae

A SMALL but widely distributed family with representatives in the Americas, West Indies, Europe, North Africa, Asia, Sumatra, and Borneo. Only the alligator lizards (*Gerrhonotus*) reach our area. They have short limbs, a slim body, long tail, and a distinctive fold on the side of the body formed in a strip of granular scales that separates large squarish scales on the back and belly. Since the dorsal and ventral scales are reinforced with bone, and form a firm exterior, the fold may provide flexibility for breathing and accommodation of food, eggs, or developing young (some species are live-bearing). There is a tendency in the family toward reduction and loss of limbs, from dwarfing of the limbs and loss of toes in species in the Antilles and S. America to complete loss of the limbs in the "slow-worm" (*Anguis fragilis*) of Europe and the glass lizards (*Ophisaurus*) of the Old and New Worlds.

Alligator lizards generally frequent moist environments in foothills and mountains, but they may range into arid lowlands in the vicinity of springs and streams. They are secretive lizards and generally seek dense vegetation.

Look for them by turning logs, rocks, boards, and other objects in sunny glades where there is an abundance of plant or rock cover. When caught they often attempt to bite and may writhe about, smearing their captor with feces. Males may extrude the hemipenes. Avoid grabbing the tail — it is readily lost.

SOUTHERN ALLIGATOR LIZARD   Pl. 25
Gerrhonotus multicarinatus

Identification: 4–6½. Dark longitudinal stripes or dashed lines on belly *down the middle of the scale rows* but sometimes belly unmarked. *Fourteen longitudinal rows of large dorsal scales at midbody. Usually well-defined regular crossbands* on back and tail. Black or dusky vertical bars on sides, spotted with white. General coloration above brown, gray, reddish, or yellowish. *Eyes pale yellow.* Tail long, when not regenerated over twice the length of body; somewhat prehensile, sometimes wrapped around branches in climbing. *Young:* Back with broad stripe of tan, beige, or gray, brightening on tail; sides barred as in adult.

Frequents grassland, chaparral, oak woodland, and forests. In the drier parts of its range it is most likely to be found near streams or in the moist bottoms of canyons where there is abundant plant cover. Occasionally enters water to escape an enemy. Around houses, it may live in old woodpiles and trash heaps. It feeds on slugs, insects, centipedes, scorpions, and spiders, including the highly venomous black widow. May climb bushes and trees in search of insects and the eggs and young of birds.

Similar species: (1) Northern Alligator Lizard has longitudinal stripes *between* the scale rows on the belly, usually 16 dorsal scale rows, irregular markings on back, a shorter tail, and darker eyes. (2) See also Panamint Alligator Lizard.

Range: Chiefly west of Cascade-Sierran crest from s. Washington to tip of Baja California. Islands off coast of s. California (San Miguel, Santa Rosa, Santa Cruz, Anacapa, San Nicholas, and Catalina) and n. Baja California (Los Coronados and San Martín). Isolated populations east of Sierra Nevada at Walker Creek near Olancha and 5 mi. west and 1¼ mi. south of Independence. Occurs in desert along Mojave River.

Subspecies: CALIFORNIA ALLIGATOR LIZARD, *G. m. multicarinatus.* Red blotches on back; top of head often mottled;

Plates

Plate 1

NEWTS (*Taricha*) × ¾

Skin rough in terrestrial stage, smooth in breeding male; teeth in roof of mouth in diverging longitudinal rows (Fig. 9); costal grooves indistinct

	Map	Text
CALIFORNIA, *T. torosa*	8	38

Lower eyelids pale; eyes reach outline of head, viewed from above (Fig. 9); teeth in Y-shaped pattern. (Contra Costa Co., Calif.)

ROUGH-SKINNED, *T. granulosa*   6   38

Lower eyelids dark; eyes usually fail to reach outline of head, viewed from above; teeth in V-shaped pattern. See Fig. 9.

RED-BELLIED, *T. rivularis*   9   39

Eyes dark brown. (Sonoma Co., Calif.)

AMBYSTOMATIDS (× ¾)

Skin smooth; teeth in roof of mouth in transverse row; costal grooves distinct (Fig. 5, No. 4, p. 24).

PACIFIC GIANT SALAMANDER, *Dicamptodon ensatus*   1   36

Marbled pattern; to 6 in. (Mendocino Co., Calif.)

OLYMPIC SALAMANDER, *Rhyacotriton olympicus*   4   36

Large eyes; squarish vent lobes in male.

    Southern, *R. o. variegatus.* Above mottled; numerous dark   4   37
    blotches on yellowish-green venter. (Trinity Co., Calif.)

    Northern, *R. o. olympicus.* Above mostly plain brown; below   4   37
    yellow-orange, with scant blotching. (Mason Co., Wash.)

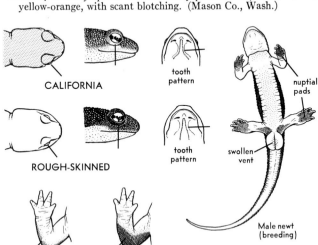

CALIFORNIA

tooth pattern

nuptial pads

ROUGH-SKINNED

tooth pattern

swollen vent

Male newt (breeding)

underside of forelimbs

CALIFORNIA   RED-BELLIED

Fig. 9. Characteristics of newts

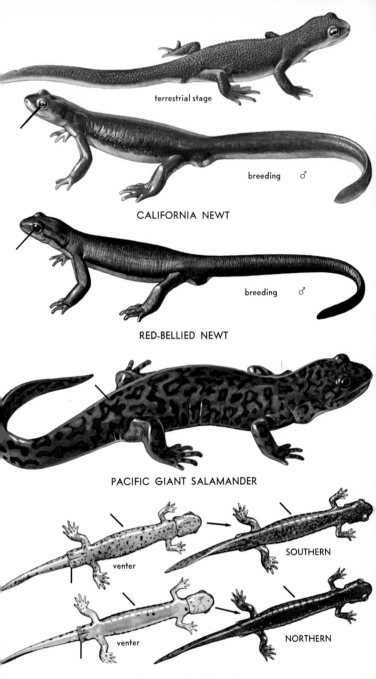

terrestrial stage

breeding ♂

CALIFORNIA NEWT

breeding ♂

RED-BELLIED NEWT

PACIFIC GIANT SALAMANDER

venter

SOUTHERN

venter

NORTHERN

OLYMPIC SALAMANDER

Plate 2

AMBYSTOMATIDS (*Ambystoma*) × ⅗

Costal grooves distinct; teeth in roof of mouth in transverse row (Fig. 5, No. 4, p. 24).

	Map	*Text*
TIGER SALAMANDER, *A. tigrinum*	5	33

Varied pattern (Fig. 10) but over much of its range spotted and/or barred with yellow or cream on dark ground color.

California, *A. t. californiense.* Yellow or cream spots on black ground color. Confined to California. (Contra Costa Co.) — 5, 34

Barred, *A. t. mavortium.* Large bars and blotches of yellow on dark ground color. (Socorro Co., New Mex.) — 5, 34

NORTHWESTERN SALAMANDER, *A. gracile* — 2, 34

Conspicuous parotoid glands and glandular ridge on tail. (Humboldt Co., Calif.)

LONG-TOED SALAMANDER, *A. macrodactylum* — 3, 35

Long slender toes; dorsal stripe or series of blotches.

Southern, *A. m. sigillatum.* Yellow dorsal stripe variously broken into series of blotches. (Amador Co., Calif.) — 3, 35

Santa Cruz, *A. m. croceum.* Yellow-orange blotches on back; ground color black. Found only near Aptos, Santa Cruz Co., Calif. — 3, 35

Western, *A. m. macrodactylum.* Greenish to yellowish dorsal stripe; sides seem whitewashed. (Benton Co., Ore.) — 3, 35

Northern, *A. m. krausei.* Well-defined yellow stripe originating on head. (Latah Co., Idaho) — 3, 35

GRAY   UTAH   BLOTCHED   CALIFORNIA   BARRED

Fig. 10. Dorsal pattern in Tiger Salamanders

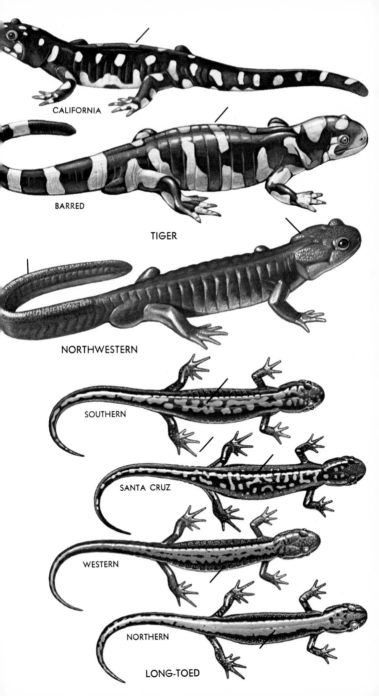

CALIFORNIA

BARRED

TIGER

NORTHWESTERN

SOUTHERN

SANTA CRUZ

WESTERN

NORTHERN

LONG-TOED

Plate 3

Tail constricted at base; nasolabial grooves (Fig. 5, No. 1, p. 24).

Blotched Subspecies

	Map	Text

Sierra Nevada Salamander, *E. e. platensis.* Orange spots 10 45
on brownish ground color. (Kern Co., Calif.)

Yellow-blotched Salamander, *E. e. croceater.* Greenish- 10 45
yellow to cream-colored blotches on blackish ground
color. Young with greenish-yellow blotches. (Kern
Co., Calif.)

Intergrade (between Yellow-blotched and Large-blotched 10
Salamanders). Like Yellow-blotched but markings less
irregular in outline. Blotch color changes from greenish
yellow to cream with age. (San Bernardino Co., Calif.)

Large-blotched Salamander, *E. e. klauberi.* Orange or 10 45
cream bars, bands, and blotches on blackish ground
color. Young with bright orange marks. (San Diego,
Calif.)

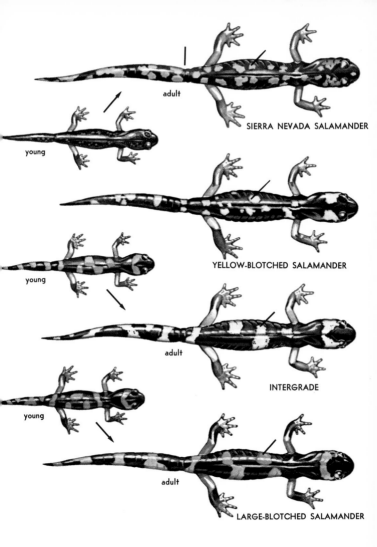

adult

SIERRA NEVADA SALAMANDER

young

YELLOW-BLOTCHED SALAMANDER

young

adult

INTERGRADE

young

adult

LARGE-BLOTCHED SALAMANDER

LARGE-BLOTCHED SALAMANDER
color variation

ENSATINA

Plate 4

Tail constricted at base; nasolabial grooves (Fig. 5, No. 1, p. 24).

Blotched and Plain-colored Subspecies

	Map	Text
Intergrade (between Oregon and Sierra Nevada subspecies). Diffuse orange spots on brownish ground color. Young black, with yellow limb bases. (Shasta Co., Calif.)	10	
Painted Salamander, *E. e. picta.* Variegated pattern of black and pale yellow or orange spots, especially on tail. (Del Norte Co., Calif.) $\times 1$	10	45
Oregon Salamander, *E. e. oregonensis.* Plain brown or nearly black above; belly pale, with minute black specks. (King Co., Wash.) Young dark-blotched. (Multnomah Co., Ore.)	10	44
Yellow-eyed Salamander, *E. e. xanthoptica.* Belly orange; conspicuous yellow eye patch. (Contra Costa Co., Calif.)	10	44
Monterey Salamander, *E. e. eschscholtzi.* Belly whitish; eyes black.	10	44

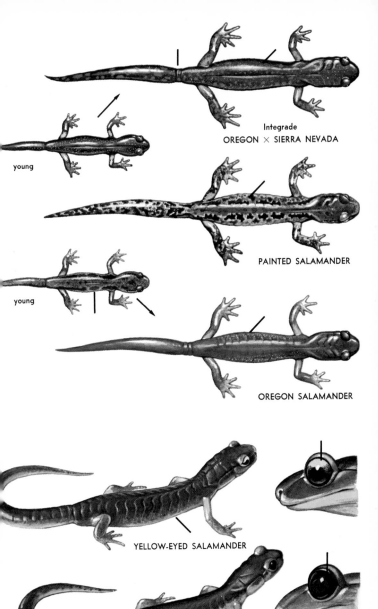

young

Integrade
OREGON × SIERRA NEVADA

PAINTED SALAMANDER

young

OREGON SALAMANDER

YELLOW-EYED SALAMANDER

MONTEREY SALAMANDER

ENSATINA

Plate 5

WOODLAND SALAMANDERS (*Plethodon*) × ⅔

Slim-bodied, short-legged; often with a dorsal stripe. Nasolabial grooves (Fig. 5, No. 1, p. 24).

	Map	*Text*
DUNN'S SALAMANDER, *P. dunni*	12	40

Mottled tan to greenish-yellow stripe failing to reach tip of tail; usually 15 costal grooves. (Benton Co., Ore.)

WESTERN RED-BACKED SALAMANDER, *P. vehiculum* 11 41
Tan, reddish-brown, orange, or yellow stripe, even-edged and extending to tip of tail; belly mottled (Fig. 11); usually 16 costal grooves. (Red phase, Benton Co., Ore.)

VAN DYKE'S SALAMANDER, *P. vandykei* 16 41
Stripe with even or scalloped margins; large pale throat patch (Fig. 12); usually 14 costal grooves.
  Coeur d'Alene Salamander, *P. v. idahoensis.* Dark pigmentation generally more intense than in Washington Salamander. (Kootenai Co., Idaho) 16 42
  Washington Salamander, *P. v. vandykei.* Plain-color phase. (w. Wash.) 16 41

LARCH MOUNTAIN SALAMANDER, *P. larselli* 14 42
Belly red to reddish orange or salmon-pink; usually 15 costal grooves. (Multnomah Co., Ore.)

JEMEZ MOUNTAINS SALAMANDER, *P. neomexicanus* 15 42
Fifth toe absent or reduced; usually 19 costal grooves. Known only from Jemez Mts., Sandoval Co., New Mex.

DEL NORTE SALAMANDER, *P. elongatus* 13 43
Toes short and partly webbed; usually 18 costal grooves. Dark phase along coast. Brown-striped phase at inland localities.

SISKIYOU MOUNTAIN SALAMANDER, *P. stormi* 13 43
Resembles Del Norte Salamander but dorsum sprinkled with small white flecks. (Jackson Co., Ore.)

throat

Fig. 11, left. Venters of Western Red-backed Salamander
Fig. 12, right. Van Dyke's Salamander

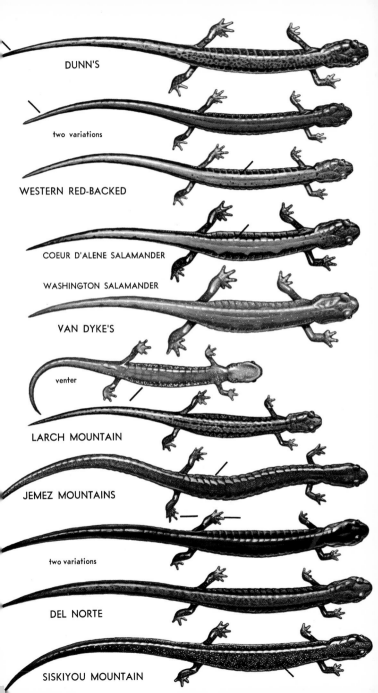

DUNN'S

two variations

WESTERN RED-BACKED

COEUR D'ALENE SALAMANDER

WASHINGTON SALAMANDER

VAN DYKE'S

venter

LARCH MOUNTAIN

JEMEZ MOUNTAINS

two variations

DEL NORTE

SISKIYOU MOUNTAIN

Plate 6

CLIMBING SALAMANDERS (*Aneides*) × ⅗
(see also Plate 7)

Triangular head; projecting upper jaw teeth (Fig. 5, No. 11, p. 24).

Map Text

ARBOREAL SALAMANDER, *A. lugubris*   20 50
Adult usually brown with yellow spots; squarish toe
tips. Young mottled; limb bases, tail, and shoulders
yellowish. (Contra Costa Co., Calif.)

BLACK SALAMANDER, *A. flavipunctatus*   23 49
Slim-bodied; short toes and limbs; belly black, some-
times with ash-gray markings.
Santa Cruz, *A. f. niger.* Adult black above and below. 23 49
Young, above black, with minute pale flecks.
Speckled, *A. f. flavipunctatus.* Above spotted with 23 49
white or pale yellow, or suffused with ash-gray to
greenish. Young, limb bases yellow.

SLENDER SALAMANDERS (*Batrachoseps*) × ⅗
(see also Plate 7)

Minute limbs; slender, wormlike body.

CALIFORNIA, *B. attenuatus*   17 47
Limbs very short; belly with fine black network.
(Contra Costa Co., Calif.)

WEB-TOED SALAMANDERS (*Hydromantes*) × ⅗

Toes short and webbed; tongue pediceled (Fig. 5, No. 9, p. 24).

LIMESTONE SALAMANDER, *H. brunus*   7 52
Adult plain brown above. Young apple-green to pale
yellow. (Merced Co., Calif.)

MOUNT LYELL SALAMANDER, *H. platycephalus*   7 51
Adult with granite-matching pattern. Young greenish.
(Tuolumne Co., Calif.)

SHASTA SALAMANDER, *H. shastae*   7 52
Adult gray-green to reddish, mottled; tail yellow to
yellow-orange. Young resembles adult. (Shasta Co.,
Calif.)

adult

ARBOREAL

BLACK young

young

ARBOREAL

SANTA CRUZ

SPECKLED

BLACK

two variations

CALIFORNIA SLENDER

LIMESTONE

young

MOUNT LYELL

adult

SHASTA

Plate 7

CLIMBING SALAMANDERS (*Aneides*) × ⅗
(see also Plate 6)

Triangular head; projecting upper jaw teeth (Fig. 5, No. 11, p. 24).

Map *Text*

ARBOREAL SALAMANDER, *A. lugubris*   20   50
Adult brown above, often with yellow spots; toes
square-tipped; curls tail. (Marin Co., Calif.) Young
resembles young of Clouded Salamander but proportions chunkier.

CLOUDED SALAMANDER, *A. ferreus*   19   50
Adult with mottled pattern of brown, ash-gray or
brassy; long square-tipped toes and long limbs. (Mendocino Co., Calif.) Young with yellowish to rust marks
on snout, shoulders, limb bases, and tail. (Mendocino
Co., Calif.)

BLACK SALAMANDER, *A. flavipunctatus*   23   49
Ground color of adult black, including belly; toes rela-
tively short and tips rounded. (Mendocino Co., Calif.)
Young speckled with whitish and variously suffused
with green; bases of limbs yellow. (Humboldt Co.,
Calif.)

SACRAMENTO MOUNTAIN SALAMANDER, *A. hardyi*   22   48
Limbs short; toe tips rounded; belly pale.

SLENDER SALAMANDERS (*Batrachoseps*) × ⅗
(see also Plate 6)

Wormlike; minute limbs.

OREGON, *B. wrighti*   18   45
Large white spots on black belly. (Clackamas Co., Ore.)

PACIFIC, *B. pacificus*   21   46
Belly usually pale, peppered with minute black specks;
head broad; limbs and toes relatively long. (Santa Rosa
I., Santa Barbara Co., Calif.)

CALIFORNIA, *B. attenuatus*   17   47
Belly dark, with fine network of black, speckled with
minute white flecks; head narrow; limbs and toes relatively short. (Contra Costa Co., Calif.)

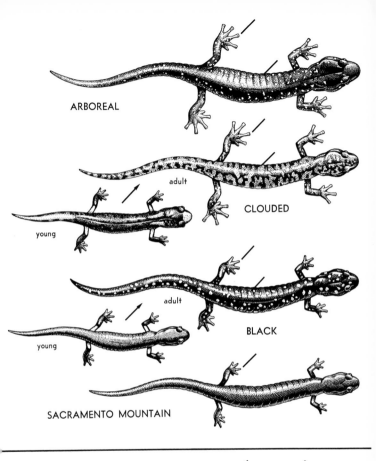

ARBOREAL

CLOUDED

young → adult

young → adult

BLACK

SACRAMENTO MOUNTAIN

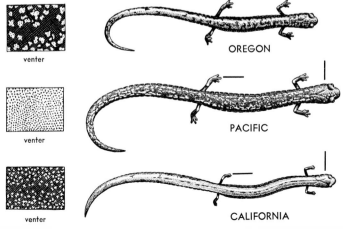

venter

OREGON

venter

PACIFIC

venter

CALIFORNIA

Plate 8

TRUE TOADS (*Bufo*) × ⅚
(see also Plates 9 and 10)

Stocky build; parotoid glands; warts.

| | Map | Text |

SONORAN GREEN TOAD, *B. retiformis*   38   65
Large, divergent parotoids; above with large oval greenish to yellowish spots set off by black network. (Pima Co., Ariz.)

GREEN TOAD, *B. debilis*   38   64
Resembles above but averages smaller and has less complete black network. (Socorro Co., New Mex.)

SPADEFOOT TOADS (*Scaphiopus*) × ⅚

Single black "spade" on hind foot; pupils vertical.

WESTERN SPADEFOOT, *S. hammondi*   26   57
No boss between eyes. (Madera Co., Calif.)

GREAT BASIN SPADEFOOT, *S. intermontanus*   24   57
Glandular boss between eyes. (Salt Lake Co., Utah)

PLAINS SPADEFOOT, *S. bombifrons*   25   58
Bony boss between eyes. (Phillips Co., Colo.)

COUCH'S SPADEFOOT, *S. couchi*   27   56
No boss; eyes widely separated; sickle-shaped spade (Fig. 13). (Maricopa Co., Ariz.)

COUCH'S
sickle-shaped

OTHER SPECIES
wedge-shaped

Fig. 13. "Spades" of spadefoot toads

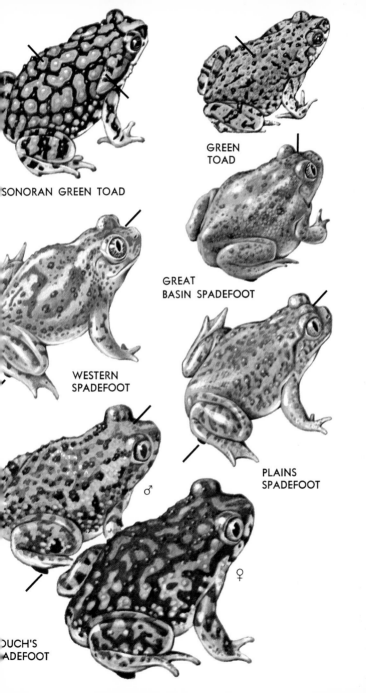

SONORAN GREEN TOAD

GREEN
TOAD

GREAT
BASIN SPADEFOOT

WESTERN
SPADEFOOT

PLAINS
SPADEFOOT

♂

♀

COUCH'S
SPADEFOOT

Plate 9

TRUE TOADS (*Bufo*) $\times \frac{3}{5}$
(see also Plates 8 and 10)

Stocky build; parotoid glands; warts.

Map Te

WESTERN TOAD, *B. boreas*   31   5
   Whitish dorsal stripe; weak cranial crests. (Contra
   Costa Co., Calif.)

YOSEMITE TOAD, *B. canorus*   32   6
   Large flat parotoids; female with black blotches, absent
   or reduced in male. Confined to California Sierra
   Nevada. (Tuolumne Co., Calif.)

GREAT PLAINS TOAD, *B. cognatus*   36   6
   Blotches on back often in pairs; prominent cranial
   crests. (Pima Co., Ariz.)

COLORADO RIVER TOAD, *B. alvarius*   39   5
   Skin relatively smooth; large warts on hind legs; adult
   to 6 in. (Dark phase, Santa Cruz Co., Ariz.)

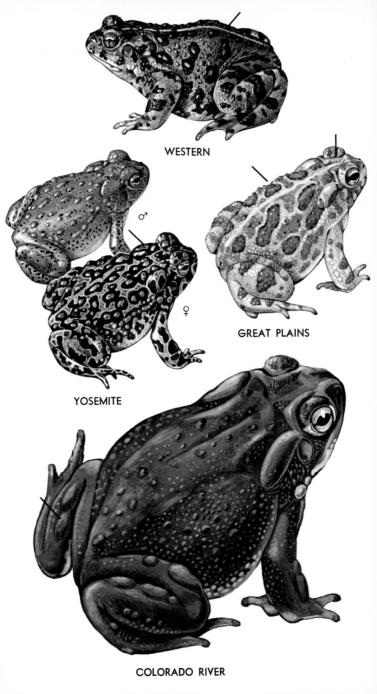

WESTERN

YOSEMITE

♂

♀

GREAT PLAINS

COLORADO RIVER

Plate 10

TRUE TOADS (*Bufo*) × ⅔
(see also Plates 8 and 9)

Stocky build; parotoid glands; warts.

	Map	Text

WOODHOUSE'S TOAD, *B. woodhousei* — Map 34, Text 61
Dorsal stripe; prominent cranial crests. (Benton Co., Wash.)

DAKOTA TOAD, *B. hemiophrys* — Map 35, Text 64
Boss on top of head. (Saskatchewan, Canada)

SOUTHWESTERN TOAD, *B. microscaphus* — Map 33, Text 61
Anterior portion of parotoids and eyelids usually pale-colored.
Arroyo Toad, *B. m. californicus.* Above dark-spotted. Map 33, Text 62
(San Bernardino Co., Calif.)
Arizona Toad, *B. m. microscaphus.* Dark spotting Map 33, Text 62
weak or absent. (Lincoln Co., Nev.)

RED-SPOTTED TOAD, *B. punctatus* — Map 40, Text 62
Small round parotoids. (Riverside Co., Calif.) × ⅚

TEXAS TOAD, *B. speciosus* — Map 37, Text 63
No stripe; cranial crests weak or absent. (Eddy Co., New Mex.)

LEPTODACTYLID FROGS (× ⅔)

BARKING FROG, *Eleutherodactylus augusti* — Map 30, Text 55
Fold of skin at back of head; semitransparent eardrum. (Sonora, Mex.) Young with broad white body band. (Mex.)

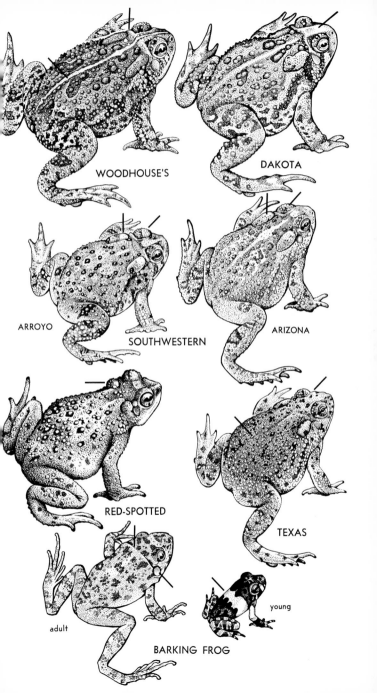

WOODHOUSE'S

DAKOTA

ARROYO

SOUTHWESTERN

ARIZONA

RED-SPOTTED

TEXAS

adult

young

BARKING FROG

Plate 11

TRUE FROGS (*Rana*) × ½
(see also Plate 12)

Most have dorsolateral folds and long hind legs.

	Map	Text
RED-LEGGED FROG, *R. aurora*	48	70

Light jaw stripe usually fails to reach shoulder (Fig. 14); adults usually red on underside of hind limbs. (Alameda Co., Calif.)

SPOTTED FROG, *R. pretiosa*   50   72
Light jaw stripe usually reaches shoulder; adults red, orange, or yellow on underside of hind limbs; eyes turned upward (Fig. 14). (Benton Co., Ore.)

MOUNTAIN YELLOW-LEGGED FROG, *R. muscosa*   54   74
Vague dorsolateral folds; toe tips usually dark. (Los Angeles Co., Calif.)

CASCADES FROG, *R. cascadae*   49   73
Ink-black spots on back, often with light centers. (Shasta Co., Calif.)

TARAHUMARA FROG, *R. tarahumarae*   56   75
No mask or light-colored jaw stripe; below often dusky, including throat. (Pima Co., Ariz.)

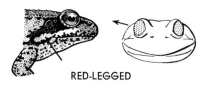

RED-LEGGED

SPOTTED

Fig. 14. Characteristics of frogs

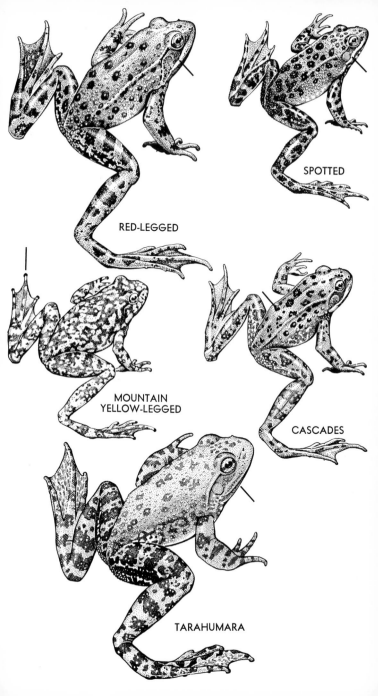

RED-LEGGED

SPOTTED

MOUNTAIN
YELLOW-LEGGED

CASCADES

TARAHUMARA

Plate 12

TRUE FROGS (*Rana*) × ¾
(see also Plate 11)

Most have dorsolateral folds and long hind limbs.

	Map	Text

RED-LEGGED FROG, *R. aurora* — Map 48, Text 70
Usually with coarse, black, yellow, and/or red mottling in groin; red on underside of hind limbs; well-developed dorsolateral folds. (Contra Costa Co., Calif.)

FOOTHILL YELLOW-LEGGED FROG, *R. boylei* — Map 55, Text 73
Pale triangle on snout; dorsolateral folds vague; underside of hind limbs yellow. (Contra Costa Co., Calif.)

LEOPARD FROG, *R. pipiens* — Map 51, Text 75
Dark rounded spots, usually with pale borders. (Maricopa Co., Ariz.)

MOUNTAIN YELLOW-LEGGED FROG, *R. muscosa* — Map 54, Text 74
Vague dorsolateral folds; dusky toe tips; yellow or orange on belly and underside of hind legs. (Mariposa Co., Calif.)

BULLFROG, *R. catesbeiana* — Map 53, Text 76
Fold around conspicuous eardrum; no dorsolateral folds.

WOOD FROG, *R. sylvatica* — Map 47, Text 71
Conspicuous dark mask contrasting with whitish jaw stripe; dorsal stripe present or absent. Light phase.

RED-LEGGED

FOOTHILL
YELLOW-LEGGED

venter

venter

LEOPARD

MOUNTAIN
YELLOW-LEGGED

BULLFROG

WOOD

Plate 13

GREAT PLAINS NARROW-MOUTHED TOAD, TREEFROGS, AND TAILED FROG

(first two species natural size, remainder × ⅚)

	Map	*Text*

GREAT PLAINS NARROW-MOUTHED TOAD
Gastrophryne olivacea   29   78
    Fold of skin at back of head; narrow, pointed head. To
    1⅜ inches. (Santa Cruz Co., Ariz.)

CRICKET FROG, *Acris crepitans*   43   66
    White bar on side of face; dark stripe on rear of thigh.
    To 1⅜ in.

CHORUS FROG, *Pseudacris triseriata*   41   66
    Back striped; stripe through eye, but no toe pads.
    Boreal, *P. t. maculata.* Short hind legs.   41   67
    Western, *P. t. triseriata.* Hind legs not notably short-   41   67
    ened.

PACIFIC TREEFROG, *Hyla regilla*   44   68
    Stripe through eye; toe pads; webbing moderately de-
    veloped (Fig. 15). (Contra Costa Co., Calif.)

ARIZONA TREEFROG, *Hyla wrightorum*   45   69
    Resembles preceding but stripe extends well back along
    side of body; webbing poorly developed (Fig. 15).
    (Cochise Co., Ariz.)

CANYON TREEFROG, *Hyla arenicolor*   46   67
    No eyestripe; toe pads prominent; webbing well de-
    veloped (Fig. 15); voice a hoarse trill. (Washington
    Co., Utah)

CALIFORNIA TREEFROG, *Hyla californiae*   46   68
    Resembles preceding but voice a quacking sound.

BURROWING TREEFROG, *Pternohyla fodiens*   42   67
    Fold of skin at back of head; single metatarsal tubercle.
    (Pima Co., Ariz.)

TAILED FROG, *Ascaphus truei*   28   54
    Outer hind toe broadest; tail-like copulatory organ in
    male. (Shoshone Co., Idaho)

Variation in webbing

Fig. 15. Hind feet of treefrogs

GREAT PLAINS
NARROW-MOUTHED TOAD

CRICKET
FROG

BOREAL

WESTERN

CHORUS FROG

two variations

PACIFIC TREEFROG

ARIZONA TREEFROG

CANYON TREEFROG

two
variations

CALIFORNIA TREEFROG

two variations

BURROWING TREEFROG

TAILED FROG

Plate 14

TURTLES (× ½)

	Map	Text
SONORA MUD, *Kinosternon sonoriense*	61	82

Nipple-like projections on throat; head mottled (Fig. 16); 9th marginal not higher than wide. (Mex.)

| **YELLOW MUD,** *Kinosternon flavescens* | 62 | 82 |

Like preceding but head not mottled (Fig. 16) and 9th marginal higher than wide.

| **SNAPPING,** *Chelydra serpentina* | 57 | 81 |

Prominent crest on tail; small plastron (Fig. 17). (Young, Kans.)

| **WESTERN POND,** *Clemmys marmorata* | 59 | 83 |

Dark flecks and lines radiating from center of shields. (Alameda Co., Calif.)

| **WESTERN BOX,** *Terrapene ornata* | 60 | 86 |

Shell with light and dark striping; plastron hinged in front. (Otero Co., New Mex.)

YELLOW

pale throat
dark dorsum

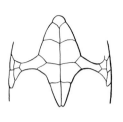 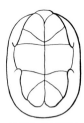

SONORA

mottled

Fig. 16. Head pattern in mud turtles

SNAPPING   TYPICAL FORM

Fig. 17. Plastrons of turtles

SONORA MUD

SNAPPING

TERN POND

WESTERN BOX

Plate 15

TURTLES (× ⅓)

DESERT TORTOISE

PAINTED TURTLE

POND SLIDER

SPINY SOFTSHELL

Plate 16

SEA TURTLES

Forelimbs modified as flippers; marine.

Text

LEATHERBACK, *Dermochelys coriacea*   89
  Carapace with longitudinal toothed ridges. To 8 ft.

GREEN TURTLE, *Chelonia mydas*   87
  Single pair of prefrontals; 4 costal shields on each side.
  To around 5 ft.

PACIFIC RIDLEY, *Lepidochelys olivacea*   89
  Two pairs of prefrontals; 5 to 9 costal shields possible
  on each side; bridge with 4 shields. To around 2 ft.

LOGGERHEAD, *Caretta caretta*   88
  Shell high in front; 5 or more costal shields, but bridge
  with 3 shields. To around 7 ft.

LEATHERBACK

GREEN TURTLE

PACIFIC RIDLEY

LOGGERHEAD

Plate 17

CHUCKWALLA AND GILA MONSTER (× ½)

	Map	Text
CHUCKWALLA, *Sauromalus obesus*	71	95

Loose folds of skin on sides of neck and body; no rostral. Young with yellow- and black-banded tail. (Riverside Co., Calif.)

GILA MONSTER, *Heloderma suspectum* 119 138

Venomous. Beadlike scales and contrasting pattern of orange or yellow and black. (Pima Co., Ariz.)

young

CHUCKWALLA

GILA MONSTER

Plate 18

HORNED LIZARDS (*Phrynosoma*) × ½

Horns at back of head; body flattened; tail short.

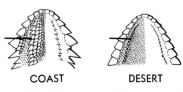

COAST   DESERT

Fig. 18. Throat scales of horned lizards

SHORT-HORNED

FLAT-TAILED

REGAL

ROUND-TAILED

TEXAS

DESERT

COAST

Plate 19

EARLESS, ZEBRA-TAILED, AND FRINGE-TOED LIZARDS
(× ½)

	Map	*Text*

LESSER EARLESS, *Holbrookia maculata*   74   96
Ear openings absent; underside of tail without markings. (Grant Co., New Mex.)

GREATER EARLESS, *Holbrookia texana*   75   96
Ear openings absent; underside of tail with black bars; belly markings behind midpoint of body. (El Paso Co., Texas)

ZEBRA-TAILED, *Callisaurus draconoides*   76   97
Ear openings present; underside of tail with black bars; belly markings at midpoint of body. (San Bernardino Co., Calif.)

FRINGE-TOED LIZARDS (*Uma*) × ½

Prominent fringe scales on hind toes.

MOJAVE, *U. scoparia*   77   99
Crescents on throat; black spots on sides of belly. (Riverside Co., Calif.)

COLORADO DESERT, *U. notata*   77   98
Streaks on throat; prominent black spots on sides of belly.

COACHELLA VALLEY, *U. inornata*   77   99
Streaks on throat; belly markings absent or small black dot(s) on each side.

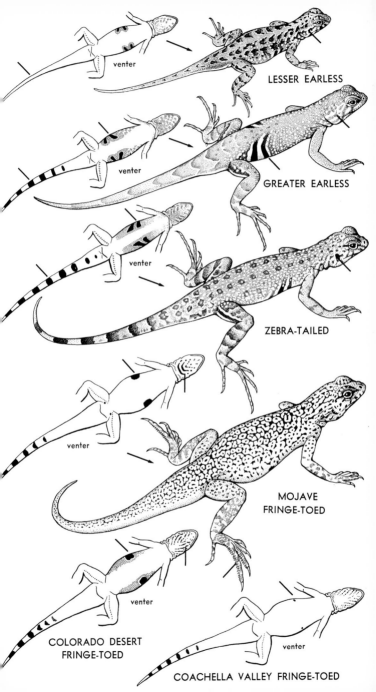

LESSER EARLESS

GREATER EARLESS

ZEBRA-TAILED

MOJAVE
FRINGE-TOED

COLORADO DESERT
FRINGE-TOED

COACHELLA VALLEY FRINGE-TOED

venter

Plate 20

DESERT IGUANA; LEOPARD AND
COLLARED LIZARDS (× ½)

DESERT IGUANA, *Dipsosaurus dorsalis* 73 94
Row of enlarged scales down middle of back. (San
Bernardino Co., Calif.)

LEOPARD LIZARD, *Crotaphytus wislizenii* 78 100
Pattern of spots and pale crossbars. (San Bernardino
Co., Calif.)

COLLARED LIZARD, *Crotaphytus collaris* 79 99
Prominent collar markings; spots on face. (San Bernardino Co., Calif.)

DESERT IGUANA

LEOPARD LIZARD

COLLARED LIZARD

Plate 21

SIDE-BLOTCHED, TREE, AND ROCK LIZARDS (× ⅔)

Complete gular fold (Fig. 7, No. 10, p. 27); large scales on top of head between eyes (Fig. 7, No. 13)

	Map	Text

SIDE-BLOTCHED, *Uta stansburiana*   92   110
    Dark blotch on side. (Fresno Co., Calif.)

SMALL-SCALED, *Urosaurus microscutatus*   93   112
    Resembles Tree Lizard. Dorsal scales enlarge gradually toward midline. (Baja Calif., Mex.)

TREE, *Urosaurus ornatus*   90   112
    Large scales on back interrupted along midline by small scales (Fig. 19). (Cochise Co., Ariz.)

LONG-TAILED BRUSH, *Urosaurus graciosus*   91   111
    Uninterrupted broad band of large scales down middle of back (Fig. 19); long tail. (San Bernardino Co., Calif.)

BANDED ROCK, *Streptosaurus mearnsi*   94   113
    Single black collar; banded tail; rock dweller. (Riverside Co., Calif.)

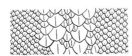 

       TREE   LONG-TAILED BRUSH

Fig. 19. Back scales in Tree and Long-tailed Brush Lizards

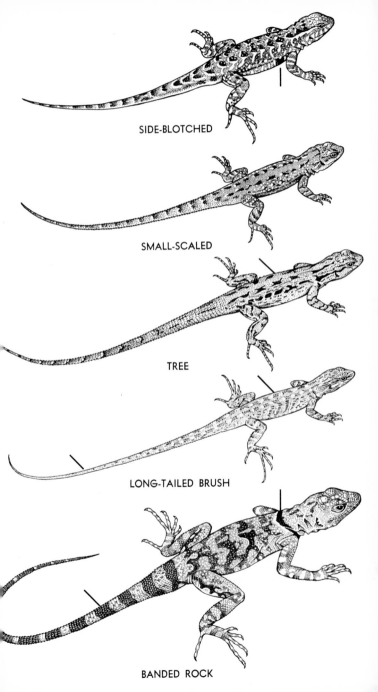

SIDE-BLOTCHED

SMALL-SCALED

TREE

LONG-TAILED BRUSH

BANDED ROCK

Plate 22

SPINY LIZARDS (*Sceloporus*) × ⅔

Dorsal scales keeled and pointed; incomplete gular fold (Fig. 7, No. 9, p. 27).

Map Text

BUNCH GRASS LIZARD *S. scalaris* 88 101
  Rows of scales on sides parallel dorsal rows; males have blue belly patches. (Cochise Co., Ariz.)

SAGEBRUSH LIZARD, *S. graciosus* 86 109
  Scales relatively small; no yellow on rear of limbs; axilla rust; males have blue throat and belly patches. (Contra Costa Co., Calif.)

WESTERN FENCE LIZARD, *S. occidentalis* 84 106
  Coarser scalation than in preceding; yellow on rear of limbs; males have blue on throat and sides of belly. (Contra Costa Co., Calif.)

STRIPED PLATEAU LIZARD, *S. virgatus* 87 108
  Striped pattern; small blue spot on each side of throat in male; no blue patches on belly; mts.

YARROW'S SPINY LIZARD, *S. jarrovi* 89 102
  Black lace-stocking pattern; black collar edged with white. (Cochise Co., Ariz.)

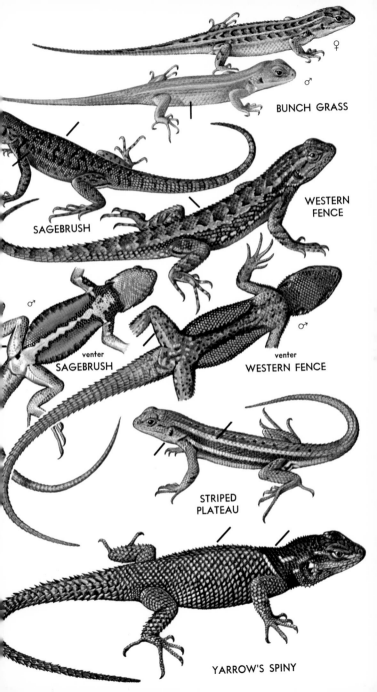

♀

♂

BUNCH GRASS

SAGEBRUSH

WESTERN
FENCE

♂

venter
SAGEBRUSH

♂

venter
WESTERN FENCE

STRIPED
PLATEAU

YARROW'S SPINY

Plate 23

SPINY LIZARDS (*Sceloporus*) $\times$ $\frac{1}{2}$

Dorsal scales keeled and pointed; incomplete gular fold (Fig. 7, No. 9, p. 27).

<table>
<tr><td></td><td>Map</td><td>Text</td></tr>
</table>

GRANITE, *S. orcutti*   83   105

Dark coloration; males with blue belly and throat and purple stripe on back in light phase; black wedge on shoulder inconspicuous. (Baja Calif., Mex.)

DESERT, *S. magister*   80   103

Paler than preceding; scales more pointed; conspicuous black wedge on shoulder; males with blue belly patches and throat; sometimes purple area on back. (Pima Co., Ariz.)

CLARK'S, *S. clarki*   81   104

Black wedge on shoulder and black bars on forelimbs; males with blue belly patches and throat. (Pima Co., Ariz.)

CREVICE, *S. poinsetti*   82   103

Conspicuous collar marking and banded tail; rock dweller. (New Mex.)

GRANITE

DESERT

CLARK'S

CREVICE

Plate 24

SKINKS (*Eumeces*) × ½

Smooth cycloid scales (Fig. 7, No. 2, p. 27).

Map *Text*

GREAT PLAINS, *E. obsoletus*   103 121
Network or heavy spotting of black or dark brown; scale rows on sides diagonal to dorsal rows. Young black, with white spots on labials. (Kans.)

GILBERT'S, *E. gilberti*   102 124
Adults plain olive or brown, with varied amounts of dark spotting. Young with blue or red tail; dark lateral stripe stops at base of tail.

WESTERN, *E. skiltonianus*   104 123
Adult striped. Young with blue tail; dark lateral stripe extends well out on tail. (Young, San Luis Obispo Co., Calif.; adult, Contra Costa Co., Calif.)

MOUNTAIN, *E. callicephalus*   106 122
Pale Y-shaped marking on head. (Santa Cruz Co., Ariz.)

MANY-LINED, *E. multivirgatus*   105 121
Short limbs; many dark and light lines on body; some individuals dark-colored, without striping. (Adams Co., Colo.)

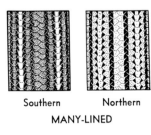

Southern   Northern

MANY-LINED

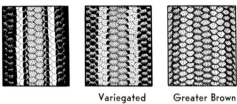

Variegated   Greater Brown

WESTERN   GILBERT'S

Fig. 20. Dorsal pattern of skinks

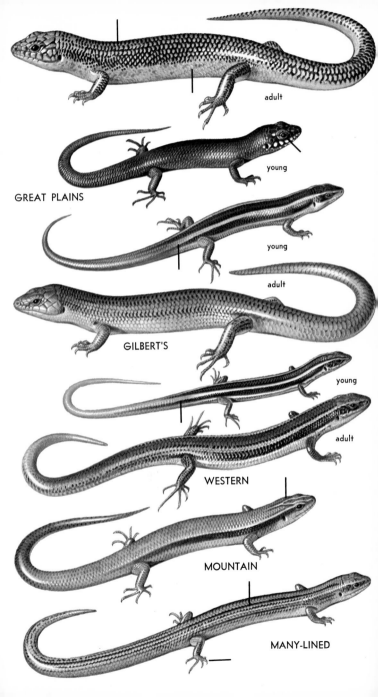

GREAT PLAINS

GILBERT'S

WESTERN

MOUNTAIN

MANY-LINED

adult

young

young

adult

young

adult

Plate 25

ALLIGATOR LIZARDS (*Gerrhonotus*) × ½

Conspicuous fold on side of body; short limbs.

	Map	*Text*

ARIZONA, *G. kingi*   118 135
    Black and white spots on upper jaw; prominent crossbands on body and tail. Young banded. (Ariz.)

PANAMINT, *G. panamintinus*   118 135
    Paler than preceding; lacks jaw markings. Young with contrasting dark and light crossbands. (Inyo Co., Calif.)

SOUTHERN, *G. multicarinatus*   118 134
    Dusky longitudinal stripes or dashed lines down middle of ventral scale rows; crossbands usually distinct. Young with broad longitudinal stripe.

NORTHERN, *G. coeruleus*   120 136
    Dusky longitudinal stripes between ventral scale rows; crossbands indistinct, often irregular. Young striped as in preceding.

ARIZONA

adult

young

PANAMINT

young

adult

SOUTHERN

NORTHERN

Plate 26

NIGHT LIZARDS ($\times$ $\frac{3}{5}$)

Vertical pupils; dorsal scales granular, ventrals squarish.

	Map	Text

ISLAND, *Klauberina riversiana*   70   120
    Large for night lizard; 2 rows of supraoculars. Confined
    to s. Calif. islands. (San Clemente I.)

ARIZONA, *Xantusia arizonae*   70   119
    Coarse dark spots. (Yavapai Co., Ariz.)

DESERT, *Xantusia vigilis*   70   119
    Averages smaller than preceding; finer dorsal spotting.
    (San Benito Co., Calif.)

GRANITE, *Xantusia henshawi*   72   118
    Large dark spots; flat head and body; rock dweller.
    (San Diego Co., Calif.)

ISLAND

ARIZONA

DESERT

GRANITE

Plate 27

WHIPTAILS (*Cnemidophorus*) × ½
(see also Plates 28 and 29)

Scales granular above, large and squarish below.

Wavy vertebral stripe; supraorbital semicircles penetrate far forward (Fig. 21); tail greenish or greenish blue toward tip. (Socorro Co., New Mex.)

Frontoparietal single rather than divided as in Fig. 21; throat orange. (San Bernardino Co., Calif.)

Tail bluish toward tip; venter bluish white to blue. (Otero Co., New Mex.)

Below whitish with tinge of bluish green. (Navajo Co., Ariz.)

Light spots in dark fields; enlarged postantebrachials (Fig. 21). (Grant Co., New Mex.)

Dorsum marked with conspicuous black spots and bars; scales anterior to gular fold abruptly and conspicuously enlarged. (El Paso Co., Texas)

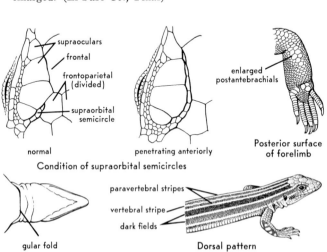

Fig. 21. Characteristics of whiptail lizards

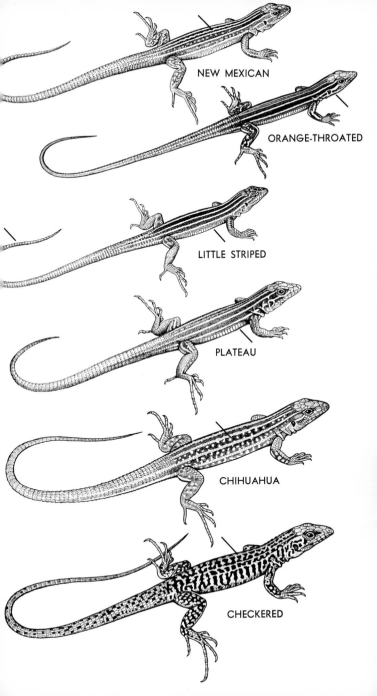

NEW MEXICAN

ORANGE-THROATED

LITTLE STRIPED

PLATEAU

CHIHUAHUA

CHECKERED

Plate 28

WHIPTAILS (*Cnemidophorous*) × ⅔
(see also Plates 27 and 29)

Scales granular above, large and squarish below.

	Map	Text
WESTERN WHIPTAIL, *C. tigris*	109	131

Dorsum spotted with black or dusky; pale stripes usually present; postantebrachials not enlarged as in Fig. 21, opposite Pl. 27.

California Whiptail, *C. t. mundus.* Usually 8 stripes but lateral ones often with irregular borders and sometimes indistinct. (Alameda Co., Calif.) 109 132

Marbled Whiptail, *C. t. marmoratus.* Marbled dorsal pattern. (Dona Ana Co., New Mex.) 109 133

DESERT-GRASSLAND WHIPTAIL, *C. uniparens* 111 129
Tail greenish olive to bluish green; dark fields (Fig. 21, opposite Pl. 27) unspotted. (Yavapai Co., Ariz.)

SIX-LINED RACERUNNER, *C. sexlineatus* 108 130
Foreparts greenish in adults; dark fields unspotted.

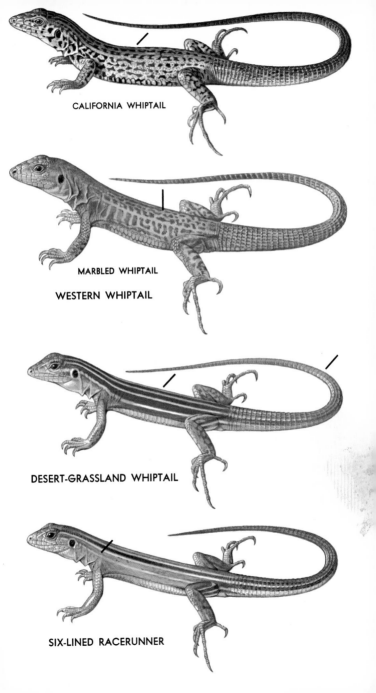

CALIFORNIA WHIPTAIL

MARBLED WHIPTAIL

WESTERN WHIPTAIL

DESERT-GRASSLAND WHIPTAIL

SIX-LINED RACERUNNER

Plate 29

WHIPTAILS (*Cnemidophorus*) × ⅗
(see also Plates 27 and 28)

Scales granular above, large and squarish below.

	Map	*Text*
GIANT SPOTTED, *C. burti*	117	127
Red-backed Whiptail, *C. b. xanthonotus*. Reddish color on back stops abruptly on sides. (Pima Co., Ariz.)	117	127
Giant Spotted Whiptail, *C. b. stictogrammus*. Adults with large spots; striping faint or absent.	117	127

GECKOS (× ⅗)

Pupils vertical; scalation granular.

LEAF-TOED, *Phyllodactylus xanti* Toe pads conspicuous; eyes without lids.	68	93
BANDED, *Coleonyx variegatus* No toe pads; eyes with prominent lids. Preanal pores generally in continuous row.	69	92

LEGLESS LIZARDS (*Anniella*) × ⅔

CALIFORNIA, *A. pulchra* Legless; eyelids movable; skin appears polished. Black form in Monterey area.	121	137

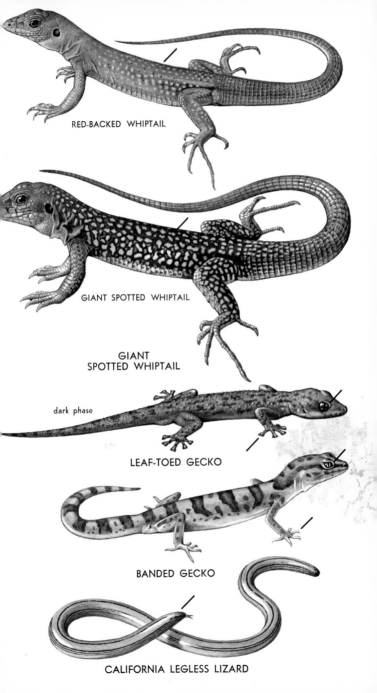

RED-BACKED WHIPTAIL

GIANT SPOTTED WHIPTAIL

GIANT
SPOTTED WHIPTAIL

dark phase

LEAF-TOED GECKO

BANDED GECKO

CALIFORNIA LEGLESS LIZARD

Plate 30

BLIND SNAKES, BOAS, AND RACERS (× ³⁄₅)

Smooth scales.

	Map	*Text*

WESTERN BLIND SNAKE, *Leptotyphlops humilis*   122   140
   Vestigial eyes; body covered with cycloid scales; single
   scale between oculars (Fig. 22). (San Diego Co., Calif.)

TEXAS BLIND SNAKE, *Leptotyphlops dulcis*   124   141
   As preceding but usually 3 scales between oculars
   (Fig. 22).

RUBBER BOA, *Charina bottae*   126   142
   Vertical pupils; large plates on top of head; above plain
   brown. (Contra Costa Co., Calif.)

ROSY BOA, *Lichanura trivirgata*   125   142
   Vertical pupils; broad stripes or variegated pattern;
   small scales on top of head. (San Diego Co., Calif.)

RACER, *Coluber constrictor*   135   148
   Plain olive or brown above. Young blotched. (Contra
   Costa Co., Calif.)

STRIPED RACER, *Masticophis lateralis*   131   150
   Single cream, yellow, or orange stripe on each side;
   underside of tail pink. (Contra Costa Co., Calif.)

SONORA WHIPSNAKE, *Masticophis bilineatus*   134   151
   Two or 3 light-colored stripes on each side; yellow on
   underside of tail. (Cochise Co., Ariz.)

STRIPED WHIPSNAKE, *Masticophis taeniatus*   133   151
   Cream or white stripe on side bisected by a continuous
   or dashed black line. (Inyo Co., Calif.)

COACHWHIP, *Masticophis flagellum*   132   149
   No stripes; general coloration often reddish, pink, or
   tan; dorsal scales in 17 rows at midbody. (Santa Cruz
   Co., Calif.)

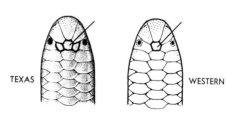

TEXAS   WESTERN

Fig. 22. Head scales of blind snakes

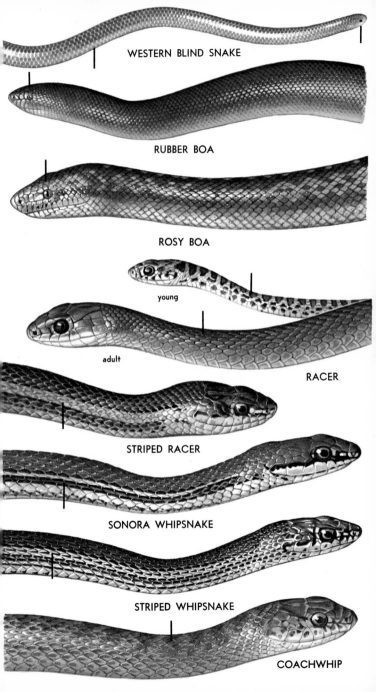

WESTERN BLIND SNAKE

RUBBER BOA

ROSY BOA

young

adult

RACER

STRIPED RACER

SONORA WHIPSNAKE

STRIPED WHIPSNAKE

COACHWHIP

Plate 31

CORAL AND LONG-NOSED SNAKES (× ½)

Smooth scales.

<table>
<tr><td></td><td align="right">Map</td><td align="right">Text</td></tr>
<tr><td>ARIZONA CORAL, Micruroides euryxanthus</td><td align="right">176</td><td align="right">185</td></tr>
</table>

ARIZONA CORAL, *Micruroides euryxanthus*   176 185
    Venomous. Red bands bordered by yellow or white (by black
    in kingsnakes). (Santa Cruz Co., Ariz.)
LONG-NOSED, *Rhinocheilus lecontei*   150 161
    White spots laterally in black bands. (San Joaquin Co.,
    Calif.)

KINGSNAKES (Lampropeltis) × ½

Smooth scales; usually a banded pattern.

SONORA MOUNTAIN KINGSNAKE, *L. pyromelana*   149 159
    Red bands bordered by black; snout whitish or flecked with
    white; white rings usually not widened ventrally. (Ariz.)
CALIFORNIA MOUNTAIN KINGSNAKE, *L. zonata*   146 158
    Red bands and white rings as in preceding; snout usually
    black, with or without red markings. (Santa Cruz Co., Calif.)
MILK SNAKE, *L. triangulum*   147 160
    White bands widen ventrally.
COMMON KINGSNAKE, *L. getulus*   148 157
    Broad dark and light banding or flecked with white or cream
    on dark background (Fig. 23). (Contra Costa Co., Calif.)

BLACK-HEADED AND RINGNECK SNAKES (× ½)

WESTERN BLACK-HEADED, *Tantilla planiceps*   173 180
    Blackish head; white neck ring; belly orange or reddish along
    midline. (Contra Costa Co., Calif.)
RINGNECK, *Diadophis punctatus*   127 143
    Entire belly yellow to orange red; orange neck ring, occa-
    sionally absent.

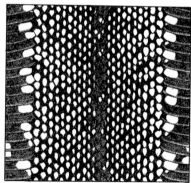

SONORA
KINGSNAKE

Fig. 23. Pattern of spotted subspecies of Common Kingsnake

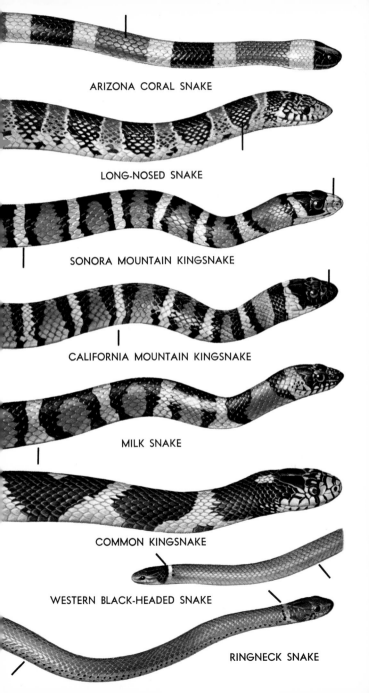

ARIZONA CORAL SNAKE

LONG-NOSED SNAKE

SONORA MOUNTAIN KINGSNAKE

CALIFORNIA MOUNTAIN KINGSNAKE

MILK SNAKE

COMMON KINGSNAKE

WESTERN BLACK-HEADED SNAKE

RINGNECK SNAKE

Plate 32

GROUND SNAKES AND RELATIVES ($\times 1\frac{1}{4}$)

Dorsal scales smooth; anal divided.

	Map	Tex

WESTERN SHOVEL-NOSED SNAKE, *Chionactis occipitalis* 168 17◦
Snout flat or only slightly convex; black body bands
usually 21 or more.

SONORA SHOVEL-NOSED SNAKE, *Chionactis palarostris* 167 17″
Snout convex; black body bands usually fewer than 21.

BANDED SAND SNAKE, *Chilomeniscus cinctus* 169 17◦
Rostral separates internasals.

WESTERN GROUND SNAKE, *Sonora semiannulata* 165 17◦
Dark blotch at base of scales; back with stripe, dark
crossbands, or plain. (Yuma Co., Ariz.)

GROUND SNAKE, *Sonora epsicopa* 166 17◦
Resembles Western Ground Snake but averages fewer
caudals (see text, p. 176).

RAT SNAKES (*Elaphe*) $\times \frac{3}{5}$

Dorsal scales weakly keeled, in 25 or more rows; anal divided.

CORN SNAKE, *E. guttata* 144 153
Spear point between eyes. (Travis Co., Texas)

TRANS-PECOS RAT SNAKE, *E. subocularis* 145 154
H-shaped markings on back; large eyes. (Young,
Brewster Co., Texas)

GREEN RAT SNAKE, *E. triaspis* 143 154
Plain green or olive above. (Cochise Co., Ariz.)

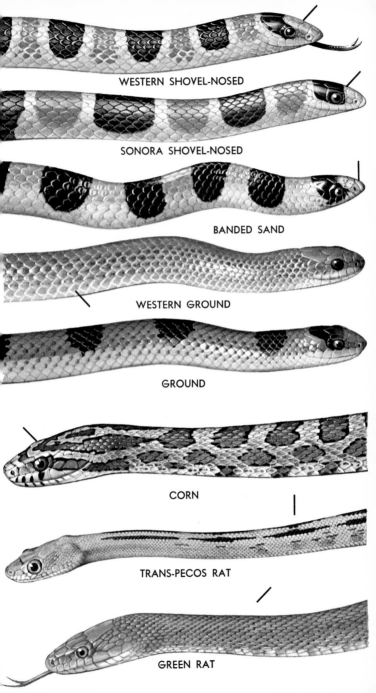

WESTERN SHOVEL-NOSED

SONORA SHOVEL-NOSED

BANDED SAND

WESTERN GROUND

GROUND

CORN

TRANS-PECOS RAT

GREEN RAT

Plate 33

GOPHER, GLOSSY, SHARP-TAILED, GREEN, LYRE, AND NIGHT SNAKES (× ⅔)

	Map	Text

GOPHER, *Pituophis melanoleucus* — Map 141, Text 156
Usually 4 prefrontals; dorsal scales keeled. (Contra Costa Co., Calif.)

GLOSSY, *Arizona elegans* — Map 142, Text 155
Faded coloration; scales smooth and glossy. (San Joaquin Co., Calif.)

SHARP-TAILED, *Contia tenuis* — Map 130, Text 144
Belly marked with regular black crossbars on pale gray ground color; tail ends in small sharp spine. (Contra Costa Co., Calif.)

SMOOTH GREEN, *Opheodrys vernalis* — Map 136, Text 147
Plain green above; dorsal scales smooth.

ROUGH GREEN, *Opheodrys aestivus* — Map 138, Text 147
Plain green above; dorsal scales keeled, in 17 or fewer rows. (Harris Co., Texas)

SONORA LYRE, *Trimorphodon lambda* — Map 178, Text 183
Lyre-shaped marking on head; pupils vertical. For two other similar species see text, pp. 182, 184. (Ariz.)

NIGHT, *Hypsiglena torquata* — Map 175, Text 184
Usually has large dark blotches on neck and spotted dorsal pattern; pupils vertical. (Contra Costa Co., Calif.)

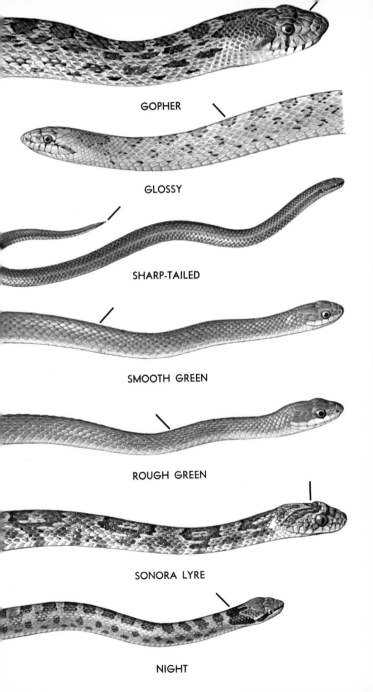

GOPHER

GLOSSY

SHARP-TAILED

SMOOTH GREEN

ROUGH GREEN

SONORA LYRE

NIGHT

Plate 34

HOGNOSE, LEAF-NOSED, PATCH-NOSED, HOOK-NOSED, AND VINE SNAKES (× 1)

All have modified rostrals.

WESTERN HOGNOSE, *Heterodon nasicus* Map 123 Text 145
Rostral keeled above and turned upward.

SPOTTED LEAF-NOSED, *Phyllorhynchus decurtatus* 129 146
Rostral patchlike, completely separating internasals;
spotted pattern; vertical pupils. × 1⅓

SADDLED LEAF-NOSED, *Phyllorhynchus browni* 128 146
Rostral and pupils as in preceding but pattern of large
dark brown saddles. (Pima Co., Ariz.) × 1⅓

MOUNTAIN PATCH-NOSED, *Salvadora grahamiae* 137 153
Rostral patchlike but not completely separating internasals; broad pale dorsal stripe bordered on each side
by dark stripe. See Fig. 24.

WESTERN PATCH-NOSED, *Salvadora hexalepis* 139 152
Similar to preceding but dorsal stripe bordered on each
side by several dark stripes (Fig. 24).

WESTERN HOOK-NOSED, *Ficimia cana* 170 178
Rostral turned up but flat or convex above and com-
pletely separating internasals; brown crossbands.
(Grant Co., New Mex.)

DESERT HOOK-NOSED, *Ficimia quadrangularis* 171 179
Rostral as in preceding; pattern of black saddles setting
off pale squarish areas on back. (Santa Cruz Co., Ariz.)
× 1⅓

VINE, *Oxybelis aeneus* 140 182
Extremely slender, vinelike; snout greatly elongate.

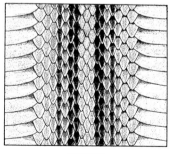 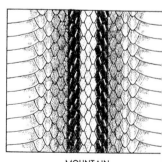

WESTERN   MOUNTAIN

Fig. 24. Patterns of patch-nosed snakes

WESTERN HOGNOSE

SPOTTED LEAF-NOSED

SADDLED LEAF-NOSED

WESTERN PATCH-NOSED

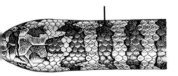

WESTERN HOOK-NOSED

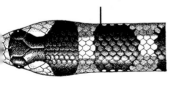

DESERT HOOK-NOSED

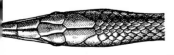

VINE

Plate 35

BLACK-HEADED SNAKES (*Tantilla*) × 2

Small snakes (usually under 16 in. total length) with dark caps; dorsum plain brown. Rely mainly on geographic distribution in identifying them.

Map *Text*

WESTERN BLACK-HEADED SNAKE, *T. planiceps* 173 180
Black cap with rounded or straight border behind, extending 0 to 3 scale rows behind parietals; a light collar marking; usually a faint dark vertebral line.

California Black-headed Snake, *T. p. eiseni.* Black cap 173 181
extends laterally on side of head to or below corner of mouth. Ventrals in males 163–175, in females 167–185.

Utah Black-headed Snake, *T. p. utahensis.* Lateral ex- 173 180
tension of black cap fails to reach corner of mouth. Ventrals in males 153–165, in females 162–174.

Mexican Black-headed Snake, *T. p. atriceps.* Similar to 173 181
utahensis but ventrals in males 135–151, in females 145–160.

Yaquia Black-headed Snake, *T. p. yaquia.* Cream- 173 181
colored spot on side of head; neck band usually prominent.

PLAINS BLACK-HEADED SNAKE, *T. nigriceps* 174 181
Cap often pointed behind, extending 3 to 5 scale rows behind parietals; usually no light collar marking.

HUACHUCA BLACK-HEADED SNAKE, *T. wilcoxi* 172 182
Broad white neck band crosses tips of parietals; cap extends to or below corner of mouth (Cochise Co., Ariz.)

LINED AND RED-BELLIED SNAKES (× 1¼)

LINED SNAKE, *Tropidoclonion lineatum* 163 174
Five or 6 upper labials; usually 2 rows of black spots on belly.

RED-BELLIED SNAKE, *Storeria occipitomaculata* 153 164
Blackish head; dorsal stripe; dorsal scales in 15 rows. Found in Black Hills, S. Dakota.

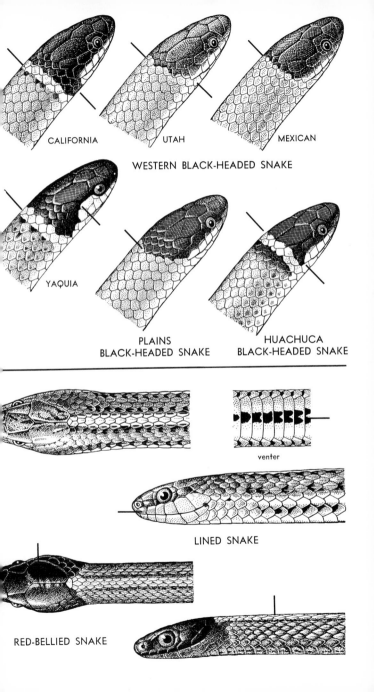

CALIFORNIA   UTAH   MEXICAN

WESTERN BLACK-HEADED SNAKE

YAQUIA

PLAINS
BLACK-HEADED SNAKE

HUACHUCA
BLACK-HEADED SNAKE

venter

LINED SNAKE

RED-BELLIED SNAKE

Plate 36

GARTER SNAKES (*Thamnophis*) × ⅔
(see also Plate 37)

Keeled scales lacking apical pits; anal single.

| | *Map* | *Text* |

MEXICAN GARTER SNAKE, *T. eques*   155   172
Paired black blotches on head; lateral stripe on 3rd and
4th scale rows anteriorly; upper labials 8 or 9. (Mex.)

BLACK-NECKED GARTER SNAKE, *T. cyrtopsis*   156   172
Paired black blotches on head; lateral stripe on 2nd
and 3rd scale rows. (Pima Co., Ariz.)

CHECKERED GARTER SNAKE, *T. marcianus*   154   173
Checkered pattern; lateral stripe usually confined to
3rd scale row. (Santa Cruz Co., Ariz.)

PLAINS GARTER SNAKE, *T. radix*   160   173
Lateral stripe on 3rd and 4th scale rows; upper labials
usually less than 8. (Boulder Co., Colo).

NORTHWESTERN GARTER SNAKE, *T. ordinoides*   164   170
Belly often flecked with red; usually 7 upper and 8 or 9
lower labials. (Benton Co., Ore.)

WESTERN RIBBON SNAKE, *T. proximus*   159   174
Pale unmarked upper labials contrast with dark head
color.

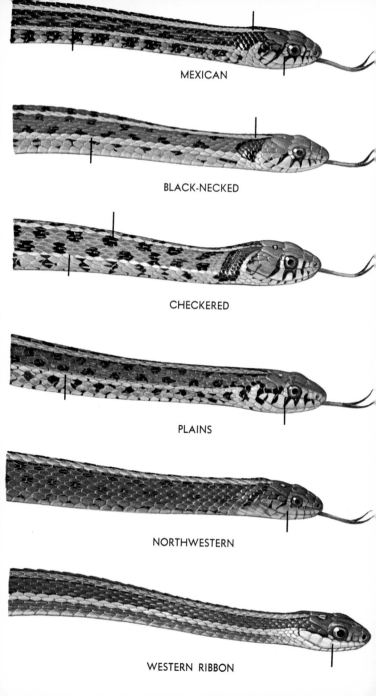

MEXICAN

BLACK-NECKED

CHECKERED

PLAINS

NORTHWESTERN

WESTERN RIBBON

Plate 37

GARTER SNAKES (*Thamnophis*) × ½
(see also Plate 36)

Keeled scales lacking apical pits; anal single.

Map *Text*

WESTERN AQUATIC, *T. couchi*   162 169
Usually 8 upper labials; belly color varies but seldom bluish; great variation in dorsal pattern (Fig. 29, p. 171).
Subspecies illustrated is **Santa Cruz Garter Snake,** *T. c.* 162 170 *atratus.* Throat usually lemon-yellow. (Santa Cruz. Co., Calif.)

WESTERN TERRESTRIAL, *T. elegans*   161 166
Usually 8 upper labials; belly color varies but seldom bluish; great variation in dorsal pattern (Fig. 28, p. 168).
Subspecies illustrated is **Coast Garter Snake,** *T. e. ter-* 161 169 *restris.* Red flecks usually present on belly and sides, including lateral stripe. (Contra Costa Co., Calif.)

COMMON, *T. sirtalis*   157 165
Eyes relatively large; usually 7 upper labials; belly often bluish.
San Francisco Garter Snake, *T. s. tetrataenia.* Red on 157 166 side usually forms continuous stripe; belly greenish blue. (San Mateo Co., Calif.)
California Red-sided Garter Snake, *T. s. infernalis.* Red 157 166 spots on sides; lateral stripe distinct. San Francisco Bay area)

NARROW-HEADED, *T. rufipunctatus*   158 165
Eyes high on head; olive or brown above, with spotted pattern. (Catron Co., New Mex.)

WATER SNAKES (*Natrix*) × ½

Keeled scales with apical pits; anal divided.

PLAIN-BELLIED, *N. erythrogaster*   151 162
Belly plain yellow, often tinged with orange and faintly spotted. (w. Texas)

COMMON, *N. sipedon*   152 163
Crossbands anteriorly; black or reddish half-moons on belly. (Kans.)

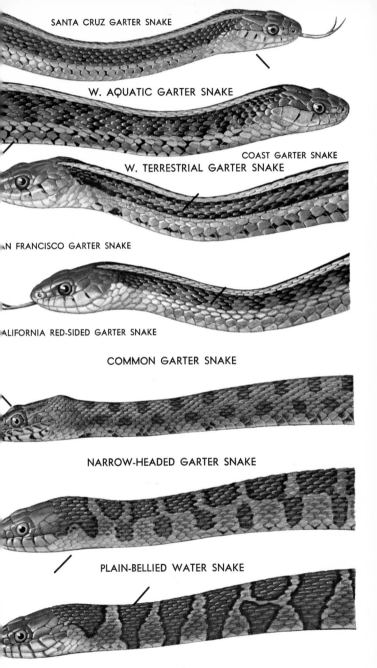

SANTA CRUZ GARTER SNAKE

W. AQUATIC GARTER SNAKE

COAST GARTER SNAKE

W. TERRESTRIAL GARTER SNAKE

N FRANCISCO GARTER SNAKE

ALIFORNIA RED-SIDED GARTER SNAKE

COMMON GARTER SNAKE

NARROW-HEADED GARTER SNAKE

PLAIN-BELLIED WATER SNAKE

COMMON WATER SNAKE

Plate 38

RATTLESNAKES (*Crotalus*) × ¾

Venomous. Horny button or rattle on tail; keeled scales.

	Map	Text

WESTERN RATTLESNAKE, *C. viridis* — 185 191
 Only rattler with usually more than 2 internasals in contact with rostral (Fig. 25). (Contra Costa Co., Calif.) Size and shape of dorsal blotches vary. See Fig. 26 for pattern of Prairie Rattlesnake, a subspecies.

MOJAVE RATTLESNAKE, *C. scutulatus* — 190 192
 Light scales of dorsal pattern usually unmarked; large scales on snout and between supraoculars (Fig. 25). (Santa Cruz Co., Ariz.)

WESTERN DIAMONDBACK RATTLESNAKE, *C. atrox* — 186 187
 Markings often indefinite and peppered with small dark spots; conspicuous black and white bands on tail. (Pima Co., Ariz.)

RED DIAMOND RATTLESNAKE, *C. ruber* — 188 188
 Reddish or tan coloration; tail as above; 1st pair of lower labials usually divided transversely. (Riverside Co., Calif.)

SPECKLED RATTLESNAKE, *C. mitchelli* — 189 189
 Dorsum often with salt-and-pepper speckling; supraoculars pitted or creased (Panamint subspecies, Fig. 25), or prenasals separated from rostral by small scales (Southwestern subspecies, Fig. 25). (Riverside Co., Calif.)

SIDEWINDER, *C. cerastes* — 187 190
 Supraoculars hornlike; crawls sideways. (Pima Co., Ariz.)

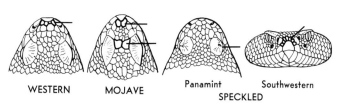

WESTERN   MOJAVE   Panamint   Southwestern
SPECKLED

Fig. 25. Head scales of rattlesnakes

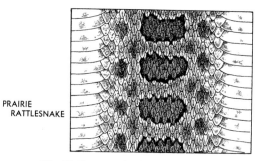

PRAIRIE
RATTLESNAKE

Fig. 26. Pattern of subspecies of Western Rattlesnake

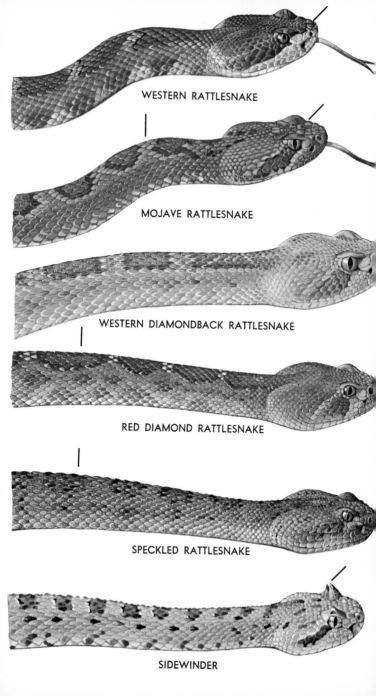

WESTERN RATTLESNAKE

MOJAVE RATTLESNAKE

WESTERN DIAMONDBACK RATTLESNAKE

RED DIAMOND RATTLESNAKE

SPECKLED RATTLESNAKE

SIDEWINDER

Plate 39

RATTLESNAKES (*Crotalus*) × ⅔

Venomous. Horny button or rattle on tail; keeled scales.

	Map	*Text*

TIGER RATTLESNAKE, *C. tigris* — Map 182, Text 191
Pattern of many, often faint, crossbands; small head and relatively large rattle (Pima Co., Ariz.)

ROCK RATTLESNAKE, *C. lepidus* — Map 183, Text 188
Pattern of distinct, widely spaced crossbands.

BLACK-TAILED RATTLESNAKE, *C. molossus* — Map 181, Text 190
Tail, and often snout, black; light-colored scales interrupt dark dorsal markings. (Cochise Co., Ariz.)

RIDGE-NOSED RATTLESNAKE, *C. willardi* — Map 184, Text 193
Ridge contours snout; dorsum with whitish crossbars edged with dusky.

TWIN-SPOTTED RATTLESNAKE, *C. pricei* — Map 180, Text 193
Two rows of brown spots on back.

MASSASAUGA, *Sistrurus catenatus* — Map 179, Text 187
Large plates on top of head; head markings extend onto neck. (Young, se. Colo.)

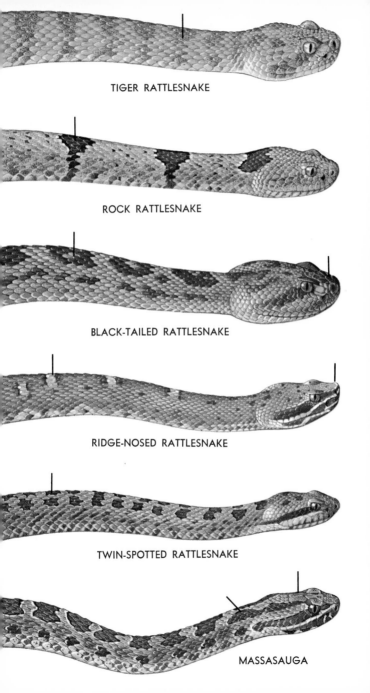

TIGER RATTLESNAKE

ROCK RATTLESNAKE

BLACK-TAILED RATTLESNAKE

RIDGE-NOSED RATTLESNAKE

TWIN-SPOTTED RATTLESNAKE

MASSASAUGA

1 to 3 rows of scales on upper arm weakly keeled in adult.
SAN DIEGO ALLIGATOR LIZARD, *G. m. webbi*. Larger
size and more prominent keeling than in other subspecies;
temporal scales keeled, upper ones strongly so. OREGON
ALLIGATOR LIZARD, *G. m. scincicauda*. Dorsal scales less
heavily keeled than in San Diego Alligator Lizard, temporals
smooth or only upper ones weakly keeled; scales of lateral fold
cinnamon; head usually not mottled.   Map 118

PANAMINT ALLIGATOR LIZARD   Pl. 25
Gerrhonotus panamintinus

   Identification: 4–6. Above light yellow or beige with *regular
broad brown crossbands, 7 or 8 between back of head (marked by
ear openings), and anterior border of thighs.* Eyes pale yellow.
Dorsal scales in 14 rows, smooth or weakly keeled. Long tail,
to twice length of body. *Young:* Above with contrasting dark
crossbars on pale ground color.
   Found beneath thickets of willow and wild grape near water
or in drier habitats grown to creosote bush and desert mint. A
secretive species that spends much of its time in rockslides and
dense plant growth. Search for it by turning rocks in damp
gullies and along streams.
   Similar species: (1) Arizona Alligator Lizard has orange or pink
eyes and 8 to 11 crossbands between back of the head and
anterior border of the thighs. (2) Southern Alligator Lizard has
9 to 13 crossbands and the young have a longitudinal stripe.
   Range: Known from Panamint (Surprise Canyon, 2800–4800
ft.), Nelson (Grapevine Canyon, 4850–5100 ft.), and Inyo (Daisy
Canyon, 4000 ft.) Mts., California.   Map 118

ARIZONA ALLIGATOR LIZARD   *Gerrhonotus kingi*   Pl. 25
   Identification: 3–5. Belly with scattered dusky spots and bars;
no longitudinal stripes. Above pale gray or brown with distinct
wavy crossbars, 8 to 11 between back of head (marked by ear
openings) and anterior border of thighs. Eyes orange or pink.
Conspicuous black and white spots on upper jaw. Scales smooth
or weakly keeled. Usually 14 rows of dorsal scales. *Young:*
Contrasting dark crossbars on back and tail.
   Chiefly a mountain form that frequents chaparral, oak woodland, and pine-fir forests in rocky places near permanent or
temporary streams. May also occur in broadleaf stream-border
habitats along major drainageways in desert and grassland.
Found under logs, rocks, and in woodrat nests and leaf litter in
and near dense plant growth. Sometimes abroad at dusk or
after dark. Chiefly ground-dwelling but occasionally climbs.
Feeds on insects and scorpions.
   Similar species: See Panamint Alligator Lizard.
   Range: Southern edge central plateau of Arizona south in Sierra

Madre to Jalisco. Huachuca, Santa Rita, Pajarito, and Chiricahua Mts., Arizona; sw. New Mexico. From 2400 to nearly
9000 ft.
Subspecies: The ARIZONA ALLIGATOR LIZARD, *G. k.
nobilis*, occurs in our area.   Map 118

NORTHERN ALLIGATOR LIZARD   Pl. 25
Gerrhonotus coeruleus
   Identification: 3½–5¼. Dark *longitudinal stripes on belly
between the scale rows*, but sometimes lacking. Dorsum with 14
or 16 scale rows at midbody, crossbands seldom regular enough
to count, and eyes completely dark or dark around the pupils.
Above olive, greenish, or bluish, heavily blotched or barred with
dusky. *Young:* Broad longitudinal dorsal stripe of beige or gray.
   Chiefly an inhabitant of woodland and forest; sparingly in
grassland and sagebrush habitats. Occurs under bark, inside
rotten logs, and under rocks and other objects on the ground.
Generally found in cooler, damper places than the Southern
Alligator Lizard, and is less inclined to climb. Feeds on insects,
spiders, millipedes, and snails. Live-bearing, 2 to 15 young.
   Similar species: See Southern Alligator Lizard.
   Range: Southern B.C. to cent. coast and Sierra Nevada of
California; Rocky Mts. of w. Montana and n. Idaho. Isolated
population in Warner Mts., California. To 10,500 ft.
   Subspecies: SAN FRANCISCO ALLIGATOR LIZARD,
G. c. coeruleus. Usually large dark blotches or irregular cross-
bands on back; scales of back and sides heavily keeled. Other-
wise resembles Northern Alligator Lizard (see below). SHASTA
ALLIGATOR LIZARD, *G. c. shastensis*. Dorsal scales in 16
rows; temporals smooth. In the north, head may be slate-gray
and body yellowish green. NORTHERN ALLIGATOR
LIZARD, *G. c. principis*. Size small, usually less than 4 in.
Usually has broad stripe of tan or golden brown down back,
with or without spots. Sides dusky, contrasting with back color.
Dorsal scales weakly keeled, in 14 rows. SIERRA ALLIGATOR
LIZARD, *G. c. palmeri*. Markings extend across back, are
confined to sides, or are absent. Dorsal scales in 16 rows;
temporals all keeled.   Map 120

California Legless Lizards:
Family Anniellidae

SNAKELIKE burrowing lizards confined to California and Baja
California. There are 2 species, about the size of a lead pencil,
covered with small, smooth cycloid scales, which make possible
easy movement through sand or loose soil. Eyes small, with mov-

able lids. Snout shovel-shaped, lower jaw inset, preventing sand getting in the mouth. No ear openings. Blunt tail permits reverse movements when burrowing. Although they are limbless and snakelike, their eyelids distinguish them from snakes. When taken in hand, they may probe with their snout with surprising force.

Legless lizards inhabit washes, beaches, and loamy soil from sea level to above 6000 ft. They are susceptible to drying and must live where they can reach damp soil. Food includes insects and spiders. Live-bearing, 1 to 4 young.

CALIFORNIA LEGLESS LIZARD *Anniella pulchra*   **Pl. 29**
  Identification: 4½–6½. Although the eyes are small, the lids can be seen. Watch an individual in good light to see it blink. Generally silver or beige above, yellow below. A black vertebral line runs the length of the body; other lines on sides where dorsal and ventral colors join. The skin looks polished. Dark brown or black individuals with contrasting yellow underparts are found along the coast from Monterey to Morro Bay. *Young:* Cream or silver above, light gray or pale yellow below.

  Requirements are loose soil for burrowing (sand, loam, or leaf mold), moisture, warmth, and plant cover. Frequents the sparse vegetation of beaches, chaparral, pine-oak woodland, and streamside growth of sycamores, cottonwoods, and oaks. Bush lupine is often an indicator of suitable conditions. Burrows in washes, the dune sand of beaches, and loose alluvium near permanent or intermittent streams. Usually remains concealed during the day, but may emerge on the surface at dusk or at night. Appears to be most active in May. Look under rocks, driftwood, logs, and boards. Drag a stick through the soil exposed under objects to uncover buried individuals. Rake through leaf litter beneath bushes.

  Range: From San Joaquin River near Antioch, California, to n. Baja California, chiefly west of Sierra Nevada. Desert outpost at Whitewater, Riverside Co., California. Los Coronados and Todos Santos Is. off Baja California. Occurrence spotty. Probably has been eliminated by agriculture in many parts of Great Valley, California. Sea level to 6400 ft. (Giant Forest, Sequoia Nat'l Park).

  Subspecies: SILVERY LEGLESS LIZARD, *A. p. pulchra.* Above silvery, gray, or beige with dark vertebral line; below yellow, with fine longitudinal lines between the scale rows. BLACK LEGLESS LIZARD, *A. p. nigra.* Above black or dark brown; below yellow, without longitudinal lines or lines very faint or confined to tail. Young resemble Silvery Legless Lizard but darken with age. Most typical form on Monterey Peninsula.
                                                        Map 121

Venomous Lizards:
Family Helodermatidae

THE Gila Monster (*Heloderma suspectum*) of sw. U.S. and Sonora and the Mexican Beaded Lizard (*H. horridum*) are the only known venomous lizards. They have a large, heavy body, massive head, sausage-shaped tail, and short limbs with strong curved claws. The dorsum is covered with small, round, closely set scales and patterned with contrasting markings of orange or yellow and black, suggesting Indian beadwork. The tail, a fat-storage organ, becomes slim in starved individuals.

These lizards live in deserts, wooded areas, and the vicinity of farms, often near washes and intermittent streams where they have access to water or damp soil. In captivity they sometimes completely immerse themselves. They are chiefly active at dusk and at night and crawl with an awkward lumbering gait but should be approached with care because they may lash out quickly with open mouth. Venom produced in glands in the lower jaw is expelled into the mouth along grooves in the teeth and injected by chewing. The venom seems to be used chiefly in defense rather than in killing prey.

Although formidable in appearance, these lizards are not dangerous unless molested or handled and should not be killed. In Arizona the Gila Monster is protected by law.

GILA MONSTER *Heloderma suspectum* **Pl. 17**
Identification: 12–16. A large heavy-bodied lizard with a short *swollen tail* and gaudy pattern of black and pink, orange, or yellow. *Dorsal surfaces with beadlike scales;* belly scales squarish. Loose folds of skin on neck; well-developed gular fold. *Fourth toe nearly the same length as 3rd toe.* Black forked tongue flicked out in snakelike fashion.

Inhabits the lower slopes of mountains and nearby outwash plains in arid or semiarid regions; ranges sparingly into oak woodland in Arizona and onto beaches in Sonora. Frequents canyon bottoms or arroyos with permanent or intermittent streams, where it digs burrows or uses those of other animals. Also seeks shelter in woodrat nests, dense thickets, and under rocks. Seems to prefer irrigated lands or rocky areas grown to scattered bushes. Often abroad at dusk or after dark following warm rains in summer. Diurnal during cold spring months. Chiefly ground-dwelling. The color pattern is concealing in dim light; on dark backgrounds the black markings blend and the light markings catch the eye and look like light-colored sticks and rocks. On pale backgrounds the reverse is true. Food includes small mammals, eggs of birds and reptiles, and, rarely, adult lizards.

Range: Extreme sw. Utah to s. Sonora; extreme sw. New Mexico to Colorado River. Recently reported in Charleston Mt. and Clark Mt. areas of s. Nevada and se. California. Old record for Kilbourne Hole, Dona Ana Co., New Mexico. Isolated record at El Dorado, Sinaloa. To 4100 ft.

Subspecies: RETICULATE GILA MONSTER, *H. s. suspectum*. Adults mottled and blotched with black and pink, with black predominating on dorsum of most individuals; a reticulate pattern with crossbands nearly or completely obscure. Dark tail bands mottled; and mottling in light interspaces. BANDED GILA MONSTER, *H. s. cinctum*. Adults retain juvenile pattern. Four black saddles or irregular double crossbands on body. Tail with 5 dark bands, little or not at all mottled; mottling slight or absent in the interspaces.   Map 119

X

Snakes

Slender Blind Snakes: Family Leptotyphlopidae

THESE snakes are sometimes called "worm snakes" because of their resemblance to earthworms. They are usually under 1½ ft. in length; brown, gray, or pink above, lighter below. The body is slender and cylindrical and there is no neck constriction. Scales are uniform in size, cycloid, smooth, and shiny and appear moist; there are no enlarged ventrals. Our species have a spine at the tip of the tail. The eyes are vestigial, appearing as dark spots beneath the oculars. Teeth are scarce and confined to the lower jaw. The slender form, uniform scalation, and degenerate eyes distinguish them from all our other snakes.

Blind snakes are crevice dwellers and burrowers. They live in loose soil — sand, loam, or humus, and emerge on the surface at night or on overcast days. In our species the track is distinctive. It consists of regular lateral undulations that show signs of skidding and in the latter respect differ from tracks of the ground snakes. A fine sinuous line is made by the tail spine. Blind snakes are susceptible to drying, and generally live where there is damp subsoil. They feed on ants, ant pupae, and termites; the solidly constructed skull, smooth, tough scales, and slender form permit them to enter ant nests and to resist the attacks of their prey. Our species are oviparous.

Only 1 genus (*Leptotyphlops*), with species ranging from s. U.S. to Argentina, the West Indies, tropical Africa, and s. Asia.

WESTERN BLIND SNAKE *Leptotyphlops humilis*   **Pl. 30**
  Identification: 9–16. A slim snake with no neck constriction and *blunt head and tail.* Eyes vestigial, appearing as dark spots under the head scales. A tiny terminal spine on the tail. Scales shiny and cycloid, not enlarged on the belly. *A single scale between the oculars.* Above purplish, brown, or pink, with a silvery sheen; below somewhat lighter — cream, pink, purplish, or light gray. *Young:* Around 4 in.

  Ranges from the desert to brush-covered mountain slopes where there is soil suitable for burrowing. Favors rocky hill-

sides with patches of loose soil, and canyon bottoms or washes
in the vicinity of permanent or intermittent streams. Seldom
found on sandy flats, dry lake bottoms, or alluvial fans. Burrows among the roots of bushes, beneath rocks, and in ant nests
in search of prey. Occasionally crawls exposed on the surface at
night, and sometimes can be found by night driving. By day,
search crevices and the soil under rock flakes that lie flat on the
ground or against boulders, especially where the soil is slightly
damp.

Similar species: The Texas Blind Snake usually has 3 scales
between the oculars and 2 rather than 1 labial between the
ocular and lower nasal.

Range: Extreme s. Nevada and sw. Utah south to Colima and
tip of Baja California; w. Texas to coast of s. California. Sea
level to above 5000 ft.   Map 122

TEXAS BLIND SNAKE *Leptotyphlops dulcis*   **Opp. Pl. 30**
  Identification: 6–13. A close relative of the Western Blind
  Snake. Brown, pink, to reddish brown above, often with a
  silvery sheen; pale gray or pink below. *Usually more than 1 scale
  between the oculars* and 1 or 2 labial scales between the ocular and
  lower nasal.

  Habits similar to the Western Blind Snake's. An inhabitant
  of prairies, canyon bottoms, and rocky or sandy deserts. Found
  in juniper-live-oak association in cent. Texas. Encountered in
  crevices, among roots of trees and shrubs, under stones and
  other objects, and on roadways at night. Most common after
  spring and summer rains.

  Similar species: See Western Blind Snake.

  Range: S. Kansas to n. Hidalgo; cent. Texas to se. Arizona.
  Sea level to 5200 ft.   Map 124

Boas: Family Boidae

A LARGE FAMILY containing the boas, pythons, and their relatives.
Throughout the tropics of both hemispheres (including Australia),
and extending well into temperate w. N. America. Generally
heavy-bodied snakes with smooth, glossy scales and vertical
pupils. Vestiges of the hind limbs are present, usually showing
externally, in male snakes especially, as a small spur on each side
of the vent. Some species have temperature-sensitive pits on the
labial scales. Prey killed by constriction. Pythons and their
relatives are found chiefly in the Old World tropics and subtropics
and are oviparous. Boas occur in both New and Old Worlds and
generally are live-bearing. Two species of boas occur in the West,
the only members of the family native to the U.S. They are thick-
bodied snakes, seldom more than 3 ft. long, with small head, small

eyes, blunt tail, and small, smooth scales; ventrals are reduced. When alarmed they may roll into a ball, concealing the head among the coils.

RUBBER BOA *Charina bottae*   **Pl. 30**
  Identification: 14–29. A stout-bodied snake that looks and feels like rubber. Sometimes called the "two-headed snake" because the *tail is shaped like the head*. Skin smooth and shiny, thrown into folds when the body is bent sharply; tail prehensile. Dorsal scales small and smooth; *top of head with large symmetrical plates;* no enlarged chin shields. Plain brown above, yellow below, without pattern or with a few dusky flecks on the lower sides. *Young:* 7–11. Pinkish to light brown above, belly light yellow. *Male:* Anal spurs usually present; small or absent in female.
  Frequents grassland, woodland, and forest, in and beneath rotting logs, under rocks, and under the bark of fallen and standing dead trees. A rocky stream having banks of sand or loam in a coniferous forest with meadows and numerous rotting logs is favorable habitat. A good swimmer, burrower, and climber. Feeds on small mammals and lizards. Live-bearing; 2 to 8 young.
  Range: Southern B.C. to s. Utah, cent. Nevada, and s. California; Pacific Coast to n.-cent. Wyoming (Bighorn Mts.). Distribution spotty. Near sea level to around 9000 ft.
  Subspecies: PACIFIC RUBBER BOA, *C. b. bottae.* Longitudinal scale rows at midbody (not counting ventrals) 45 or more; parietal usually divided. ROCKY MOUNTAIN RUBBER BOA, *C. b. utahensis.* Scale rows usually 44 or fewer; parietal usually not divided; ventrals more than 191. SOUTHERN RUBBER BOA, *C. b. umbratica.* Scale rows as in Rocky Mountain Boa but ventrals fewer than 192. Known only from Lake Arrowhead, San Bernardino Co., and Fern Valley near Idyllwild, Riverside Co., California. Reported from Mt. Pinos, Kern Co., California.   Map 126

ROSY BOA *Lichanura trivirgata*   **Pl. 30**
  Identification: 24–42. A heavy-bodied snake with head only a little wider than the neck. Scales smooth and shiny. Eyes small, pupils vertical. *No chin shields or large head plates,* except on snout. Ground color above slaty, beige, or rosy, marked with 3 broad brown longitudinal stripes or irregular brown patches; markings sometimes absent. Below cream, spotted or blotched with gray. *Young:* Generally lighter than adult and pattern more distinct. *Male:* Anal spurs usually well developed.
  Inhabits rocky brushlands and desert. Attracted to oases and permanent or intermittent streams but does not require permanent water. Chiefly nocturnal but may be active at dusk. A good climber. Search blacktop roads in rocky canyons or along lower mountain slopes. Feeds on small mammals and birds. Live-bearing.

Range: Death Valley region (Hanapauh Canyon), California, to tip of Baja California and Guaymas, Sonora; coastal s. California to s.-cent. Arizona. Absent from Coachella Valley southward, in extreme low desert. Distribution spotty. Sea level to around 4500 ft.

Subspecies: COASTAL ROSY BOA, *L. t. roseofusca*. Stripes of pink, reddish brown, or dull brown, with irregular borders, on a bluish-gray ground color. Stripe color may be present on scattered scales between the stripes or, occasionally, over all dorsal surfaces. DESERT ROSY BOA, *L. t. gracia*. Prominent stripes of rose, reddish brown or tan, even-edged and contrasting with the gray or beige of the ground color. Spotting of stripe color seldom present between the stripes. Below with brown flecking. Isolated populations in Harcuvar, Harquahala, Castle Dome, and Kofa Mts., Arizona. MEXICAN ROSY BOA, *L. t. trivirgata*. Contrasting longitudinal stripes of chocolate-brown on a light drab background. Below creamy white with only occasional black flecks. S. Arizona (Organ Pipe Cactus Nat'l Monument) to Guaymas, Sonora; tip of Baja California.   Map 125

Colubrids: Family Colubridae

WORLDWIDE except Arctic and Antarctic, some oceanic islands, Ireland, and s. and w. Australia. Includes most snakes in all continents except Australia, where elapids, relatives of the corals and cobras, are more numerous. Head plates are usually large and symmetrical and the teeth may be solid or grooved toward the back of the jaw. No hollow fangs. Some species are venomous but none in our area is dangerous to man. More than two thirds of the snakes in the West belong to this family.

RINGNECK SNAKE   *Diadophis punctatus*   **Pl. 31**
Identification: 12–30. Typically a slender olive, bluish, or nearly black snake with dark head and a conspicuous yellow or orange neck ring. The neck ring is absent in some populations in s. New Mexico and occasionally elsewhere. Rarely, melanistic individuals are found in California that lack both the neck ring and orange ventral color, and have dark crossbars on the belly. Below yellow-orange to red, the red intensifying on underside of tail; ventral surfaces usually spotted with black. When alarmed this snake coils its tail and turns the ventral surface of the tail uppermost, revealing the bright red color. Scales smooth, usually in 15 rows (sometimes 13) at midbody. Loreal present. *Young*: 4–6. Often dark above, sometimes nearly black. *Male*: Ridges may be present on scales above the vent.

A snake of moist habitats — woodland, forest, grassland,

chaparral, farms, and gardens. In the arid parts of the West it is restricted to mountains and water courses where it may descend in desert areas to 2400 ft. Seldom seen in the open. Usually found on the ground under bark, beneath and inside rotting logs, and under stones and boards. Feeds on slender and other salamanders, small frogs, lizards, small snakes, insects, and worms.

Similar species: (1) Black-headed snakes have a whitish or beige neck ring, and lack black spots on the ventral surfaces; the reddish color on the belly is bordered on each side by pale gray and there is no loreal. (2) See also Sharp-tailed Snake.

Range: S. Washington and Idaho to n. Baja California and southern part of the Mexican plateau. Atlantic to Pacific Coasts. Distribution spotty. Sea level to around 7000 ft.

Subspecies: PACIFIC RINGNECK SNAKE, *D. p. amabilis.* Scale rows usually 15, 15 or 15, 13 (counted on neck and at mid-body); neck ring 1–1½ scale lengths wide; ventral color on ½–1½ rows of lowermost dorsal scales. Many small black spots on belly. SAN BERNARDINO RINGNECK SNAKE, *D. p. modestus.* Scale rows usually 17, 15; ventral color confined to 1st row of dorsal scales. Conspicuous black spots on belly. NORTHWESTERN RINGNECK SNAKE, *D. p. occidentalis.* Ventral color on 1½–2 or more rows of dorsal scales; neck ring 1½–3 scales wide. A few small black dots on belly. CORAL-BELLIED RINGNECK SNAKE, *D. p. pulchellus.* Like Northwestern Ringneck but 1st 2 rows of dorsal scales not flecked with black; belly lightly or not at all spotted. SAN DIEGO RINGNECK SNAKE, *D. p. similis.* Scale rows usually 15, 15 or 15, 13; ventral color on ½ to ⅔ of each scale of 1st row of dorsals. MONTEREY RINGNECK SNAKE, *D. p. vandenburghi.* Scale rows usually 17, 15; ventral color on 1½–2 rows of dorsal scales; black spots on belly few and small. PRAIRIE RINGNECK SNAKE, *D. p. arnyi.* Belly color confined to ventrals except occasionally at extreme anterior end. Low ventral scale count. REGAL RINGNECK SNAKE, *D. p. regalis.* Averages larger and paler than preceding subspecies — gray with bluish, greenish, or slaty cast. Neck band sometimes faint or absent. Ranges into the aspen-fir belt.   Map 127

SHARP-TAILED SNAKE *Contia tenuis*   Pl. 33

Identification: 8–18. Above reddish brown or gray tending toward reddish on the tail; often with an indistinct yellowish or reddish line on each side. *Below distinctively marked with regular, alternating crossbars of black and cream.* Scales smooth; single preocular; tail with sharp terminal spine. *Young:* Around 3 in. Red above, fine dark lines on sides.

Frequents woodland, grassland and forest, usually near streams. Often found in pastures or open meadows on the edge of coniferous forests or among oaks in the lower foothills. Occasionally gregarious. A secretive snake of moist environments, abroad when the ground is damp but keeping out of sight under logs, bark of standing and fallen trees, rocks and other objects. Most likely to be found on warm days following rains. Peak activity, March to June. Retreats underground when the surface dries. Apparently feeds strictly on slugs, for which its long teeth are especially suited.

Similar species: Melanistic Ringneck Snakes resemble the Sharptail, including the dark and light crossbars on the ventral surface, but Ringnecks usually have 2 or 3 preoculars and dark flecks on the belly.

Range: B.C. (North Pender I.) to s. Sierra Nevada and central coast (Pine Mt., San Luis Obispo Co.), California. Isolated populations in Washington at northern end of Gravelly Lake, Pierce Co., and at Lyle, Klickitat Co. Distribution spotty. Sea level to 6300 ft.   Map 130

WESTERN HOGNOSE SNAKE *Heterodon nasicus*   **Pl. 34**
Identification: 16–32. A heavy-bodied blotched snake with broad neck and upturned snout. *Rostral much enlarged, spadelike and keeled above.* Prefrontals separated by small scales. Dorsal scales keeled. Anal divided. Enlarged teeth toward back of mouth. Much black pigment on underside of body and tail. *Young:* About 7 in.

Frequents sandy or gravelly prairies, farmlands, and floodplains of rivers. In the extreme western part of its range it occurs in semidesert habitats and occasionally in mountain canyon bottoms or on the floodplains of streams where there are alluvial deposits suitable for burrowing. Stream courses may be canopied by deciduous broadleaf trees. The Hognose uses its shovel-shaped snout in digging and its enlarged teeth in holding and perhaps deflating toads, a staple food. In addition it feeds on frogs, salamanders, and lizards.

When disturbed it often spreads its head and neck and strikes with open mouth, hissing, but seldom biting. This behavior has earned it the names "puff adder," "blow viper," and "hissing adder." May "play possum," suddenly turning belly up, writhing violently for a few moments, then lying still with mouth open and tongue lolling.

Similar species: (1) Hook-nosed snakes (pp. 178–79) have smooth dorsal scales and the rostral is concave rather than keeled above. (2) Leaf-nosed and (3) patch-nosed snakes have the tip of the rostral turned back between the internasals instead of extending free anteriorly. (4) The Eastern Hognose Snake (*H. platyrhinos*), expected in eastern Colorado, lacks black pigment on the underside of the tail and the prefrontals are in contact.

Range: S. Canada to n. Mexico; se. Arizona to cent. Illinois. From near sea level to 8000 ft.

Subspecies: PLAINS HOGNOSE SNAKE, *H. n. nasicus.* Dark middorsal blotches from head to above vent, more than 35 in males and more than 40 in females. Nine to 28 small scales in a group on top the head, directly behind the rostral. DUSTY HOGNOSE SNAKE, *H. n. gloydi.* Dark middorsal blotches, 23–32 in males and 28–37 in females. MEXICAN HOGNOSE SNAKE, *H. n. kennerlyi.* Two to 6 small scales in a group on top the head.   Map 123

SPOTTED LEAF-NOSED SNAKE   Pl. 34
Phyllorhynchus decurtatus

Identification: 12–20. A pale, blotched snake with a blunt snout formed by a *much enlarged rostral scale with free edges.* Above pink, tan, yellowish, or pale gray, with more than 17 middorsal brown blotches between the back of the head and the region above the vent. Below white, unmarked. *Pupils vertical.* Dorsal scales smooth except occasionally in males. Suboculars present. Rostral completely separates internasals. Anal single.

A secretive, nocturnal snake of sandy or gravelly desert; most of its range in the U.S. corresponds closely with the distribution of the creosote bush. Common on open desert plains. The modified rostral is used in burrowing. Feeds on small lizards, including banded geckos and their eggs. Search roads at night; otherwise it is rarely encountered.

Similar species: (1) Saddled Leaf-nosed Snake has fewer than 17 dorsal blotches (excluding the tail). (2) Patch-nosed snakes have the internasals only partly separated by the rostral. (3) In the Western Hognose Snake the anterior end of the rostral extends forward and is free.

Range: S. Nevada to tip of Baja California and s. Sonora; s. Arizona to desert base of mts. in s. California. To 3000 ft. Occasionally coexists in rocky, gravelly, desert foothills with the Saddled Leaf-nosed Snake.

Subspecies: CLOUDED LEAF-NOSED SNAKE, *P. d. nubilis.* Middorsal blotches (excluding tail), 42–60. Ventrals 167 or fewer in males, 178 or fewer in females. WESTERN LEAF-NOSED SNAKE, *P. d. perkinsi.* Middorsal blotches (excluding tail), 24–48. Ventrals 168 or more in males, 179 or more in females.   Map 129

SADDLED LEAF-NOSED SNAKE   Pl. 34
Phyllorhynchus browni

Identification: 12–20. Resembles the Spotted Leaf-nosed Snake in form and scalation but differs greatly in color. Large brown dark-edged dorsal blotches (saddles), *fewer than 17,* excluding the tail. Light color on the head and between the blotches, pink or cream. Below white, without markings.

A snake of upland desert grown to mesquite, saltbush, creosote bush, paloverde and saguaro cactus. A burrower in relatively coarse, rocky soils as well as in sand. Nocturnal. Usually found only by patrolling highways at night. Most active after the summer rains begin, especially on humid nights.

Similar species: See Spotted Leaf-nosed Snake.

Range: Vicinity of Tucson west to Organ Pipe Cactus Nat'l Monument, Arizona; southern base of Arizona plateau (Phoenix-Superior region) to cent. Sinaloa.

Subspecies: PIMA LEAF-NOSED SNAKE, *P. b. browni.* Blotches considerably wider than interspaces. Ventrals 166 or fewer in males, 179 or fewer in females. MARICOPA LEAF-NOSED SNAKE, *P. b. lucidus.* Blotches little, if any, wider than interspaces. Ventrals 167 or more in males, 180 or more in females.   Map 128

SMOOTH GREEN SNAKE *Opheodrys vernalis*   Pl. 33
Identification: 11–26. A slender snake, *plain green above* and white or yellowish below. The dorsal color changes to dull blue or gray upon death. *Dorsal scales smooth*, in 15 rows at midbody; a single anterior temporal. Anal divided. *Young:* 4–6. Dark olive-gray above.

Ranges from the lowlands well up into the mountains in damp grassy environments. In the West it inhabits meadows, stream borders, and rocky habitats interspersed with grass. Secretive and chiefly ground-dwelling but occasionally ascends bushes. Well camouflaged in green plant growth. Feeds on insects and spiders.

Similar species: (1) Rough Green Snake is more arboreal and has keeled dorsal scales. (2) Greenish examples of the Racer have 2 anterior temporals and the lower preocular wedged between the upper labials. (3) Green Rat Snake (p. 154) has 25 or more rows of dorsal scales, weakly keeled along the middle of the back.

Range: S. Canada to s. Texas; New Jersey to Utah. Isolated populations mostly in mts. in southern and western parts of range from Wyoming and se. Idaho to s. New Mexico and e. Texas. Sea level to 9500 ft.

Subspecies: The WESTERN SMOOTH GREEN SNAKE, *O. v. blanchardi*, occurs in our area. The Black Hills population (e. Wyoming and w. South Dakota) may belong to the eastern subspecies, the EASTERN SMOOTH GREEN SNAKE, *O. v. vernalis.*   Map 136

ROUGH GREEN SNAKE *Opheodrys aestivus*   Pl. 33
Identification: 15–47. A slender climbing snake, *plain green*

above, unmarked white, pale green, or yellowish below. Upon death the dorsal color turns dull blue or gray. *Dorsal scales keeled*, in 17 rows at midbody. Anal divided. *Young:* 6–8. Grayish green above.

Typically a snake of moist wooded habitats where there is abundant plant cover. Frequents bushes and trees usually near water, gliding smoothly among the branches. Camouflaged when in green plant growth. Freely enters shallow bodies of water. Feeds on grasshoppers, crickets, caterpillars, and spiders.
Similar species: The Smooth Green Snake has smooth scales.
Range: S. New Jersey and s. Illinois to Florida Keys, Gulf Coast, and Tamaulipas; Atlantic Coast to e. Kansas and w. Texas. Scattered localities in se. Iowa, ne. New Mexico, and w. Texas. In our area known only from Cimarron, Colfax Co., New Mexico. Sea level to 5000 ft.   Map 138

Racers and Whipsnakes:
Genera *Coluber* and *Masticophis*

SLENDER fast-moving, diurnal snakes with broad head, large eyes, and slender neck. Lower preocular wedged between the upper labials (Fig. 8, No. 7, p. 29). Adult racers (genus *Coluber*) are usually plain-colored above and the young are blotched. There are 2 species, one ranging from s. Canada to Guatemala, the other in ne. Asia. Whipsnakes (genus *Masticophis*) are striped or more or less crossbarred and the young generally resemble the adults. They range from the U.S. to n. S. America; 4 species occur in the West.

When hunting, these snakes commonly crawl with head held high and occasionally moved from side to side, perhaps to aid depth perception. Prey is seized with great speed, pinioned under loops of the body, and engulfed without constriction. Some individuals are aggressive, striking vigorously when cornered and biting when handled. When held by the neck, with body dangling, they may thrash with such force as to nearly jerk free. Most are good climbers and when pursued may escape by ascending bushes or trees.

RACER   *Coluber constrictor*   **Pl. 30**
   Identification: 22–78. A slim snake with large eyes and smooth scales in 15 to 17 rows at midbody (15 rows just anterior to vent). Lower preocular wedged between the upper labials. Anal divided. In the West this snake is plain brown or olive above and unmarked pale yellow below. Bluish dorsal coloration predominates in the region south of the Great Lakes, black (including the venter) in the East and Southeast, and mottling in e. Texas and Louisiana. *Young:* 9–14. Brown saddles on back,

smaller blotches on sides, fading on tail. Faint blotching sometimes evident in individuals 1½ to 2 ft. long.

In the West this snake favors open habitats — meadows, prairies, thin brush, and forest glades. Found in both semiarid and moist environments but is absent from extremely dry areas and high mountains. Often found in grassy places near rocks, logs, and other basking sites sought by lizards, upon which it feeds, or in the grass of streambanks, where it hunts frogs, small mammals, and especially insects. Chiefly ground-dwelling but may ascend bushes and trees.

Similar species: (1) The young resemble young Gopher Snakes (p. 156), from which they can be distinguished by their smooth scales and wedged preocular (Fig. 8, No. 7, p. 29). (2) Night Snake (p. 184) has vertical pupils. (3) See also Smooth Green Snake.

Range: From s. B. C. to Guatemala; Pacific to Atlantic Coasts. Absent from deserts. Isolated populations in mts. and river valleys in arid Southwest. Sea level to 6700 ft.

Subspecies: WESTERN YELLOW-BELLIED RACER, *C. c. mormon.* Upper labials usually 8; caudals more than 85. Young with 70–85 dorsal blotches. EASTERN YELLOW-BELLIED RACER, *C. c. flaviventris.* Upper labials usually 7; caudals usually fewer than 85. In some parts of range belly bright lemon-yellow. Young with 65–80 dorsal blotches.   Map 135

COACHWHIP *Masticophis flagellum*   **Pl. 30**
Identification: 36–102. The *wedged lower preocular* (Fig. 8, No. 7, p. 29), *smooth scales in 17 rows at midbody (13 or fewer just anterior to vent), and lack of longitudinal stripes* are diagnostic. Coloration highly variable (see *Subspecies*). Throughout most of our area the general tone above is tan, gray, or pink with black crossbars on the neck. Occasional individuals are black. The slender body and tail, and scalation suggesting a braided whip, have earned it its common name. Anterior temporals usually 2 or 3. Anal divided. *Young:* Blotched or crossbanded with dark brown or black on a light brown background; neck markings often faint or absent.

Frequents a variety of habitats — desert, prairie, brushland, woodland, and farmland. Generally avoids dense vegetation. The ground surface may be flat or hilly, sandy or rocky. More tolerant than most snakes of dry, warm environments, hence abroad by day in hot weather even in deserts. Crawls with great speed, often taking refuge in a rodent burrow, among rocks, or the branches of a bush where it may defend itself with spirit, hissing and striking repeatedly, and sometimes approaching aggressively. When caught it usually attempts to bite and large individuals can lacerate the skin. Feeds on small mammals, birds and their eggs, lizards, snakes, insects, and carrion.

Range: Southern half of U.S. from coast to coast, south to Guerrero. Sea level to around 6000 ft.

Subspecies: RED RACER, *M. f. piceus*; black phase called WESTERN BLACK RACER. *Red phase:* Generally reddish or pinkish above; black or dark brown crossbands on neck, sometimes more or less united; loreal with white bar bordered by black; young blotched. *Black phase:* All or nearly all dorsal surface black; belly pale or more or less blackened. Occurs at scattered localities in s. California, s. Arizona, throughout Baja California, and Sonora (see Map 132, black dots). LINED WHIPSNAKE, *M. f. lineatulus.* Neck markings and loreal bar absent; anterior dorsal scales each with longitudinal dark line or a posterior dark spot. Young with crossbands 2 or 3 scales long, not extending across venter. WESTERN COACHWHIP, *M. f. testaceus.* Above, essentially uniformly colored light yellow-brown to dark brown but occasional individuals may retain faint indications of the dark juvenile crossbands. Some populations are reddish as, for example, in cent. and se. Colorado. In this area red color is superimposed on a distinct dorsal pattern of brown, and a series of light lateral stripes runs between the scale rows of neck region. SAN JOAQUIN WHIPSNAKE, *M. f. ruddocki.* Light yellowish brown above, without dark head color and neck bands. SONORA COACHWHIP, *M. f. cingulum.* Above reddish brown with widely separated narrow pink crossbands, tending to be paired posteriorly. A single conspicuous light band at back of head.   Map 132

STRIPED RACER   *Masticophis lateralis*   **Pl. 30**

Identification: 30–60. Plain black or dark brown above, lightening on the tail. *A conspicuous pale yellow stripe on each side* (often orange in San Francisco Bay area) extending from the back of the head to or beyond the vent. Ventral surface cream, becoming coral pink on underside of tail. Scales smooth, in 17 rows at midbody. Wedged lower preocular. Anal divided.

The "chaparral snake" of California. Favorite haunts are brushlands broken by scattered grassy patches, and rocky gullies or stream courses. Chiefly a snake of the foothills but ranges in the mountains into mixed deciduous and pine forests. An active diurnal species that may be seen foraging with head held high. Sometimes climbs or seeks shelter among rocks or in a burrow. Feeds on frogs, lizards, snakes, small mammals, birds, and probably insects.

Similar species: (1) Striped Whipsnake has 15 scale rows at midbody and the lateral light stripes are bisected with a black line. (2) Sonora Whipsnake has 2 or 3 light stripes anteriorly, which fade out before reaching the tail and the venter is pale yellow posteriorly.

Range: From n. California, west of Sierran crest and desert, to

cent. Baja California. Apparently absent from floor of Great Valley except northern part. In s. California ranges to desert foothills. From near sea level to 6000 ft. Its distribution in California coincides closely with that of chaparral.
Subspecies: CALIFORNIA STRIPED RACER, *M. l. lateralis.* Stripes cream or yellow, 2 half-scale rows wide. ALAMEDA STRIPED RACER, *M. l. euryxanthus.* Stripes and anterior ventral surface orange. Stripes broad, 1 and 2 half-scale rows wide. Map 131

STRIPED WHIPSNAKE *Masticophis taeniatus* Pl. 30
Identification: 30–72. A close relative of the Striped Racer. In our area black, dark brown, or gray above, often with an olive or bluish cast. *A cream or white lateral stripe on each side, bisected by a black line.* Additional longitudinal black lines on the lower sides. The venter is yellowish, grading to white anteriorly and coral pink posteriorly. Dorsal scales smooth, *in 15 rows at midbody.* Wedged lower preocular. Anal divided.

A snake of brushlands, grasslands, sagebrush flats, piñon-juniper woodland, and open pine-oak forests. Often attracted to rocky stream courses, both permanent and intermittent. Frequents both flatlands and mountains. An alert, fast-moving, diurnal snake that forages and seeks shelter in rock outcrops, rodent burrows, and in trees and shrubs. Feeds on lizards, snakes, and small mammals.
Similar species: See (1) Striped Racer and (2) Sonora Whipsnake.
Range: S.-cent. Washington south in Great Basin between Cascade-Sierran crest and Continental Divide, thence southeast across Divide in New Mexico into w. and cent. Texas; south to Michoacán. Old records for west side of Cascade Mts., Jackson Co., Oregon — Blackwell Hill, 3 mi. east of Gold Hill; Van Dyke Cliffs, 5 mi. east of Talent; and near mouth of Little Applegate River. Sea level to around 9400 ft. (Panamint Mts., California).
Subspecies: The DESERT STRIPED WHIPSNAKE, *M. t. taeniatus,* occurs in our area. Map 133

SONORA WHIPSNAKE *Masticophis bilineatus* Pl. 30
Identification: 30–67. Olive, bluish gray, or light gray-brown above, lightening on posterior ⅔ of body. *Usually 2 or 3 light-colored stripes on each side fading rapidly posteriorly.* Below cream, becoming *pale yellow posteriorly.* Dorsal scales smooth, usually in 17 rows at midbody. Wedged lower preocular. Anal divided.

Ranges from semiarid lower mountain slopes, with growth of grass, saguaro cactus, paloverde, and ocotillo, through brushlands into the pine-oak belt in the mountains. Attracted to rocky stream courses. Both terrestrial and arboreal, climbing

gracefully in bushes and trees. Feeds on young birds and lizards.
Similar species: The Striped Whipsnake usually has 15 scale rows at midbody and 4 conspicuous dark longitudinal lines on the sides.

Range: Cent. Arizona and extreme sw. New Mexico, south to Oaxaca. To 6100 ft.

Subspecies: SONORA WHIPSNAKE, *M. b. bilineatus.* Above olive to light bluish gray; dorsolateral light stripe 2 half-scale rows wide, beginning usually on 4th scale behind the last upper labial. AJO MOUNTAIN WHIPSNAKE, *M. b. lineolatus.* Dorsum darker than above; dorsolateral light stripe narrow, half-scale row wide, including inner portion of 2 adjacent scale rows, beginning usually on 8th scale behind last upper labial. Northern branch of Alamo Canyon, Ajo Mts., Organ Pipe Cactus Nat'l Monument, Pima Co., Arizona. Most specimens have been found trapped in a steep-sided pit in the canyon floor.   Map 134

WESTERN PATCH-NOSED SNAKE   Pl. 34
Salvadora hexalepis

Identification: 20–45. A slender snake, with a broad yellow or beige dark-bordered stripe down the back and a large patchlike rostral. Stripe occasionally faint or obscured by crossbands. Below plain white, sometimes washed with dull orange, especially posteriorly. *Two or 3 small scales between the posterior chin shields; 9 upper labials.* Dorsal scales smooth. Anal divided. *Male:* Keeled scales above vent and at base of tail; keeling absent or weak in female.

An active diurnal resident of grasslands, chaparral, sagebrush plains, and desert scrub. Found in both sandy and rocky areas on the lower slopes of mountains and on low, dry creosote bush plains in the most extreme parts of the desert. Racer-like in speed, but sometimes can be caught with a noose when basking and not yet fully warm. Chiefly ground-dwelling. Feeds on small mammals, lizards, and probably lizard eggs.

Similar species: (1) Mountain Patch-nosed Snake usually has 8 upper labials and the posterior chin shields are in contact or separated by a single small scale. (2) The rostral in the leaf-nosed snakes completely separates the internasals, and the anal is single.

Range: W.-cent. Nevada south to tip of Baja California, n. Sinaloa, Chihuahua, and Coahuila. Coastal s. California to cent. Arizona, s. New Mexico, and w. Texas. From below sea level to 7000 ft.

Subspecies: DESERT PATCH-NOSED SNAKE, *S. h. hexalepis.* One upper labial reaches the eye; loreal divided; top of head gray; median stripe includes 3 scale rows. COAST PATCH-NOSED SNAKE, *S. h. virgultea.* Like above but top of head brown, and dorsal stripe narrower, including middorsal row of scales and median half of adjacent rows. BIG BEND PATCH-NOSED SNAKE, *S. h. deserticola*. Two upper labials reach the eye; loreal single. MOJAVE PATCH-NOSED SNAKE, *S. h. mojavensis*. Upper labials fail to reach the eye. Dorsal pattern sometimes vague and, in eastern part of range, crossbars obscure the stripe.   Map 139

MOUNTAIN PATCH-NOSED SNAKE   Pl. 34
Salvadora grahamiae
Identification: 20–30. Above with a white, gray, or yellow median stripe, 3 (or nearly so) scale rows wide, lighter than the sides. Stripe bordered on each side with a brown to nearly black stripe 2 or more scale rows wide.· Below plain white or yellowish. *Posterior chin shields in contact or separated by a single small scale; 8 upper labials.* Dorsal scales smooth. Anal divided. *Young:* 6¾.

A snake of roughlands — rocky canyons, plateaus, and mountain slopes. In the West, it lives chiefly in open woodland and forests in the mountains above 4000 ft., within the range of the Western Patch-nosed Snake but at higher elevation. In the more humid eastern part of its range it inhabits prairies and lowlands to sea level (s. Texas). Food includes lizards and probably small mammals.

Similar species: See Western Patch-nosed Snake.
Range: Se. Arizona, n.-cent. New Mexico, and cent. Texas south to n. Zacatecas. Sea level to over 6500 ft. but in West seldom below 4500 ft. Distribution spotty.
Subspecies: The MOUNTAIN PATCH-NOSED SNAKE, *S. g. grahamiae*, occurs in our area.   Map 137

CORN SNAKE   *Elaphe guttata*   Pl. 32
Identification: 18–72. Long, slender snake, varying greatly in color over its wide range. In the West it is usually light gray with dark-edged brown or dark gray blotches on back and a pair of dark neck lines that usually unite to form a *spear point between the eyes.* In the north the blotches are especially numerous and narrow. There is usually a distinct eyestripe and longitudinal dark and light stripes on the underside of the tail. *Dorsal scales in 25 to 35 rows at midbody* mostly smooth but weakly keeled on the back. *Anal divided.*

Occurs in a variety of habitats — along stream courses and river bottoms, on rocky wooded hillsides, and in coniferous forests. Often attracted to farmlands. Although it climbs well it is usually found on the ground. It is a secretive snake that spends much time in rodent burrows. Nocturnal during warm weather. Look for it beneath logs, rocks, and other objects and on highways at night. When caught it often voids feces and the contents of its anal scent glands. Food consists of small mammals and birds which it constricts in its strong coils. Young corn snakes feed also on lizards and frogs.

Similar species: (1) Trans-Pecos Rat Snake has suboculars and H-shaped dorsal blotches. (2) Green Rat Snake is greenish above, with or without faint pattern, and plain whitish below. Spotted young lack spear point on head. See also (3) Glossy, (4) Gopher, and (5) Common Water Snakes (p. 163).

Range: E. Utah and cent. New Mexico to Atlantic and Gulf Coasts; s. Nebraska to s. Coahuila and cent. Tamaulipas. In w. Colorado and e. Utah in major valleys of the Colorado River. Sea level to over 6000 ft.

Subspecies: The GREAT PLAINS RAT SNAKE, *E. guttata emoryi*, occurs in our area.   Map 144

GREEN RAT SNAKE   *Elaphe triaspis*   **Pl. 32**
  Identification: 24–50. A sleek, *plain green or olive* snake with *unmarked whitish or cream underparts* tinged with yellow. *Dorsal scale rows 25 or more*, weakly keeled along the middle of the back. Anal divided. *Young:* In Mexico dorsal blotches present, but sometimes faint. Color of young in the U.S. unknown.

In our area it is primarily a mountain snake that frequents wooded, rocky, canyon bottoms near streams. Vegetation may include pine, oak, sycamore, walnut, cottonwood, wild grape, and willow. Its habits are little known. In Arizona it is presumed to be chiefly crepuscular, spending much time during the day in trees or bushes and retiring at night into rock crevices and other underground retreats. The slender form and color help conceal it in vegetation. It has been found on the ground in the morning before 9:00 and in the afternoon after 5:00 into the early evening. In Mexico it has been found on roadways at night. Feeds on rodents (woodrats) and birds.

Similar species: (1) Smooth Green Snake (p. 147) has smooth scales in 15 to 17 rows at midbody. See also (2) Corn and (3) lyre (pp. 182–84) snakes.

Range: Se. Arizona and s. Tamaulipas south along slopes of Mexican highlands to Costa Rica. In Arizona in Baboquivari, Pajarito, Santa Rita, and Chiricahua Mts. To above 7000 ft.

Subspecies: The GREEN RAT SNAKE, *E. t. intermedia*, occurs in our area.   Map 143

TRANS-PECOS RAT SNAKE   *Elaphe subocularis*   **Pl. 32**
  Identification: The "H-snake." Dorsal pattern of H-shaped black or dark brown blotches with pale centers on a yellowish background. Lateral arms of H's may join to form longitudinal stripes, especially anteriorly. Venter olive-buff, becoming white on the neck and throat. Dorsal scales in 31 to 35 rows at mid-

body, weakly keeled along middle of the back. Head broad, body slender, eyes large. A row of small scales (suboculars) below the eye and preocular. Anal divided.

A snake of arid and semiarid habitats, found in the following plant associations — agave, creosote bush, and ocotillo; persimmon, shin oak, and cedar; yucca, mesquite, and cactus. Seems to prefer rocky areas.

Similar species: See (1) Corn and (2) Texas Lyre (p. 184) Snakes.
Range: S. New Mexico to s. Coahuila. In w. Texas in Apache, Guadalupe, Davis, and Chisos Mts. 1500 to 5000 ft. Map 145

GLOSSY SNAKE *Arizona elegans*   Pl. 33

Identification: 27–56. Its coloration suggests a faded Gopher Snake. The ground color above is light brown, cream, pinkish, or yellowish gray; blotches are tan or gray, edged with blackish. Sometimes called the "faded snake" because of its bleached appearance. *Ventral surface unmarked* white or pale buff (except for the California Glossy Snake, in which the edges of the ventrals have dark markings). *Scales smooth and glossy*, in 27–31 rows at midbody. Two prefrontals. *Lower jaw inset.* Pupils slightly vertical in life. *Anal single. Young:* 8½–11.

Occurs in a variety of habitats — chaparral-covered slopes, grassland, light brushy to barren desert, sagebrush flats, and woodland; in general prefers open areas. The ground is often sandy or loamy but some rocks are usually present. An excellent burrower. In the West it remains by day underground and is rarely encountered beneath objects on the surface. Active mostly at night except in the eastern part of its range, where it is often diurnal. Food consists of lizards, snakes, and small mammals.

Similar species: (1) Gopher Snake has keeled scales, (2) rat snakes have keeled scales and a divided anal, (3) Night Snake (p. 184) has a flattened head, distinctly vertical pupils, and divided anal. (4) Corn Snake lacks inset lower jaw and has divided anal. (5) See also California Lyre Snake (p. 182).
Range: Sw. U.S. from extreme sw. Nebraska and cent. Texas to cent. California; s. Utah to s. Sinaloa, Zacatecas, and San Luis Potosí. Below sea level to 6000 ft.
Subspecies: KANSAS GLOSSY SNAKE, *A. e. blanchardi.* Dorsal scale rows at midbody 31 or 29; ventrals usually 210 or fewer in males and 221 or fewer in females; body blotches usually 54 or more. A large-blotched, dark-colored, long-tailed form. PAINTED DESERT GLOSSY SNAKE, *A. e. philipi.* Dorsal scales at midbody usually in 27 rows (not over 29 rows); also a long-tailed form. CALIFORNIA GLOSSY SNAKE, *A. e. occidentalis.* Usually 27 rows of dorsal scales. Marks on edges of ventrals. Lower labials often spotted. The darkest western subspecies. This and the remaining subspecies are short-tailed

forms. ARIZONA GLOSSY SNAKE, *A. e. noctivaga*. Usually
27 scale rows. No marks on ventrals or spots on labials except
occasionally on last lower labial. Body blotches equal in width
to spaces between them. DESERT GLOSSY SNAKE, *A. e.
eburnata*. One preocular. A pale subspecies with small narrow
dorsal blotches, narrower than the spaces between them, rarely
more than 7 scale rows wide at the midline. MOJAVE GLOSSY
SNAKE, *A. e. candida*. Usually 2 preoculars. Narrow body
blotches, 9 scale rows wide at midline. Blotches shorter along
the body than the interspaces between them. A light-colored
form.   Map 142

GOPHER SNAKE *Pituophis melanoleucus*   Pl. 33

Identification: 36–100. A large yellow or cream-colored snake
with black, brown, or reddish-brown dorsal blotches, usually
more widely spaced on the tail than on the body. Smaller
blotches on the sides. Usually a dark line across the head in
front of the eyes and from behind the eye to the angle of the jaw.
Below white to yellowish, often spotted with black. Striped,
unblotched individuals are found occasionally in the Sacramento
Valley and in the vicinity of San Francisco and Monterey Bays,
California. *Dorsal scales keeled, in 27 or more rows* at midbody
Usually 4 prefrontals. Anal single. *Young:* Around 8 to 12 in.

Lives in a variety of habitats from the lowlands high into the
mountains and from coast to coast. Frequents desert, prairie,
brushland, woodland, coniferous forest, and farmland. In the
West it is especially common in grassland and open brushland.
Soil conditions vary — sand, loam, rock, or hardpan. This
snake is a good climber and burrower, active chiefly by day
except in hot weather. When aroused it hisses loudly and sometimes flattens its head and vibrates its tail. This behavior, along
with the diamond-shaped markings, causes these snakes to be
mistaken for rattlesnakes and killed. Feeds on rodents, rabbits,
birds and their eggs, and occasionally lizards. Kills by constriction.

Similar species: (1) The blotched young of the Racer (p. 148),
resemble Gopher Snakes but can be distinguished by their
smooth scales and large eyes. (2) Glossy Snake has smooth
scales. (3) Rat snakes have a divided anal. See also (4) Corn
and (5) California Lyre (p. 182) Snakes.

Range: New Jersey and Virginia to Pacific Coast; sw. Canada
to Florida and Gulf Coast; in Mexico to cent. Veracruz and s.
Sinaloa. Sea level to above 9000 ft.

Subspecies: BULLSNAKE, *P. m. sayi*. Rostral narrow, much
higher than wide, raised well above nearby scales. SONORA
GOPHER SNAKE, *P. m. affinis*. Rostral broad, little or not at
all raised above nearby scales. Ground color of the sides without
a gray wash. Anterior dorsal blotches brown, unconnected to

other blotches. GREAT BASIN GOPHER SNAKE, *P. m. deserticola*. Resembles the Sonora Gopher Snake but anterior dorsal blotches usually black (gray but black-edged in young) and connected to one another and the secondary blotches on sides of neck to form a lateral dark band, leaving interspaces as isolated pale dorsal blotches. PACIFIC GOPHER SNAKE, *P. m. catenifer*. Suffusion of grayish punctations on sides of body and on underside of the tail. Anterior dorsal blotches brown or black, separated from one another and the secondary blotches. SAN DIEGO GOPHER SNAKE, *P. m. annectens*. Resembles the Pacific Gopher Snake but anterior dorsal blotches black, more or less joined to each other and the secondary blotches. SANTA CRUZ ISLAND GOPHER SNAKE, *P. m. pumilis*. Dorsal scale rows at midbody usually 29 or fewer (other subspecies usually have over 29); no black-streaked scales in the anterior light spaces between the dorsal blotches.   Map 141

Kingsnakes: Genus *Lampropeltis*

THE GENERIC NAME means "shiny skin." Snakes of moderate size with smooth scales and a single anal; head little wider than the neck. The dorsal pattern is highly variable but frequently consists of dark and light rings; venter with dark markings.

Kingsnakes are found in a variety of habitats — woodland, coniferous forests, grassland, cultivated fields, tropical scrub, and desert, from se. Canada to Ecuador. Although some species are excitable when first encountered, and vibrate the tail, hiss, and strike, many quickly become tame and make good pets. Because of their snake-eating habits they should not be caged with other snakes. Prey is killed by constriction.

COMMON KINGSNAKE *Lampropeltis getulus*   Pl. 31
   Identification: 30–82. Over most of this snake's range in the West its pattern consists of alternating *rings of plain black or dark brown* and white or pale yellow, the pale bands broadening on the belly. Pattern alone will distinguish most individuals. In se. Arizona and New Mexico, however, light bands give way to varying amounts of *light speckling on a dark background*, and some individuals are entirely speckled (Fig. 23, opposite Pl. 31). Other pattern types are found farther east. A black form without bands occurs in s. Arizona and a striped phase with a more or less continuous pale yellow vertebral stripe occurs at scattered localities in sw. California (see Map 148, black dots). Black-bellied individuals with the pale crossbands broadening on the lower sides to form a lateral stripe are found in the northern part of the San Joaquin Valley, California (see Map 148, black triangles). Scales smooth and polished-looking; caudals divided;

anal single. *Young:* 9 to 12 in., usually patterned like the adult but in s. Arizona blotched at first, becoming spotted with age.

Frequents a great variety of habitats — coniferous forest, woodland, swampland, river bottoms, farmland, prairie, chaparral, and desert. Found in the vicinity of rock outcrops and clumps of vegetation and under rotting logs, old lumber, and rocks. Chiefly terrestrial but sometimes climbs. Active mostly in the morning and late afternoon but in hot weather abroad at night. Usually gentle but occasionally strikes, hisses, and vibrates its tail. Sometimes rolls into a ball with its head at the center and everts the lining of its cloaca. Food consists of snakes, including rattlers, lizards, frogs, birds and their eggs, and small mammals.

Similar species: (1) In the Sierra Nevada the California Mountain Kingsnake sometimes lacks red markings and resembles the Common Kingsnake, but the white rings usually are not broadened on the lowermost rows of dorsal scales. (2) Long-nosed Snake has some or all of the caudals undivided. (3) Ground (pp. 175–76), (4) Western Shovel-nosed (p. 176), and (5) Banded Sand (p. 178) Snakes have a divided anal. In addition shovel-nosed and Banded Sand Snakes have an inset lower jaw and latter has no loreal.

Range: Coast to coast, from s. New Jersey to Florida in the East and sw. Oregon to tip of Baja California in the West. On Mexican mainland to n. Sinaloa, San Luis Postosí, and n. Tamaulipas. Sea level to 7000 ft.

Subspecies: CALIFORNIA KINGSNAKE, *L. g. californiae.* No brown pigment on the white scales of the crossbands; broad white bars on the prefrontals. YUMA KINGSNAKE, *L. g. yumensis.* Brown pigment on the bases of the white scales of the crossbands; narrow white bars on the prefrontals. In se. Arizona, where it meets the Sonora Kingsnake, it occurs in the San Pedro and San Simon Valleys in creosote bush desert. SONORA KINGSNAKE, *L. g. splendida* (Fig. 23, opposite Pl. 31). Scales on side of body to row 5 or 10 light-spotted; belly black, with large yellow or whitish spots in a row on each side at ends of ventrals. In se. Arizona, where it meets the Yuma Kingsnake, it occurs in elevated grassland. BLACK KINGSNAKE, *L. g. nigritus.* Above uniformly dark brown or slaty black, usually without traces of rings or stripes.   Map 148

CALIFORNIA MOUNTAIN KINGSNAKE   Pl. 31
Lampropeltis zonata

Identification: 20–40. A beautiful serpent with smooth, glistening scales and black, white, and red rings, the red bordered on each side with black. The red rings may be interrupted on the back, appearing as a wedge on each side within a broad black band, may be wider than either the black or white bands, and occasionally, as in the central Sierra Nevada, may be completely lacking. The combination of red and black markings, a black ring more or less split by red, is called a triad. Head black in front of the 1st white ring on back of head. Snout generally black with or without red markings. Usually the *white rings do not broaden conspicuously on the lower scale rows.* Dorsal pattern imperfectly but variously carried onto the ventral surface. Scales smooth; anal single.

This harmless snake is sometimes called the Coral Kingsnake because of its fancied resemblance to the venomous coral snakes. It is an inhabitant of moist woods — coniferous forest, woodland, and chaparral, ranging from sea level high into the mountains. Search for it in the vicinity of well-illuminated rocky streams in wooded areas where there are rotting logs. Chiefly diurnal but nocturnal in warm weather. Food consists of lizards, snakes, birds (nestlings), and small mammals.

Similar species: (1) In the Sonora Mountain Kingsnake the black bands become narrow or disappear on the sides, and the snout is white or pale yellow. (2) In the Milk Snake the white bands usually become wider on the lowermost scale rows. (3) Long-nosed Snake has single caudals. (4) Arizona Coral Snake (p. 185) has the red markings bordered with white or yellow rather than black.

Range: S. Washington to n. Baja California; mts. of coastal and interior California except deserts. Old record for Maupin, Wasco Co., Oregon. Distribution spotty. Sea level to 8000 ft.

Subspecies: SIERRA MOUNTAIN KINGSNAKE, *L. z. multicincta.* Rear margin of the 1st white ring on the head located behind the angle of the mouth. Fewer than 60 per cent of the black bands completely split by red across the back. SAINT HELENA MOUNTAIN KINGSNAKE, *L. z. zonata.* First white ring as above but 60 per cent or more of the black bands completely split by red; snout dark; black pigment, bordering the red on the sides, usually more than 1 scale wide. COAST MOUNTAIN KINGSNAKE, *L. z. multifasciata.* Rear margin of the 1st white ring on the head behind or in front of the angle of the mouth: 60 per cent or more of the black bands completely split by red. Snout with red markings. SAN BERNARDINO MOUNTAIN KINGSNAKE, *L. z. parvirubra.* Rear margin of the 1st white ring on or in front of the last upper labial; snout dark; 37 or more triads on the body, exclusive of the tail. SAN DIEGO MOUNTAIN KINGSNAKE, *L. z. pulchra.* Like the San Bernardino Mountain Kingsnake but 36 or fewer triads. Map 146

SONORA MOUNTAIN KINGSNAKE   Pl. 31
Lampropeltis pyromelana

Identification: 18–41. A red-, black-, and white-banded kingsnake with a rather wide flat head. The amount of red in the black bands varies greatly, forming a wedge on each side or completely splitting the black bands. In some individuals the red forms broad bands and the black pigment is confined to a narrow border on each side of the red bands. *Black bands become narrow or disappear on the sides.* Dorsal pattern imperfectly but variously carried onto the ventral surfaces. *Snout white, pale yellow, or black flecked with white.* Ventrals more than 210 in area covered by *Field Guide.* Scales smooth; anal single. *Young:* Around 8 in.

A mountain dweller, ranging from piñon-juniper woodland and chaparral to the pine-fir belt. Frequents both brushland and coniferous forest, often near water. Usually found where there are rocks, logs, and dense clumps of vegetation — under objects or occasionally exposed. Food consists of lizards and probably snakes and small mammals.

Similar species: (1) The snout of the California Mountain Kingsnake is solid black or black with red markings and the black bands usually do not become narrow on the sides of the body. (2) Milk Snake in the West has fewer than 210 ventrals (fewer than 200 in areas of overlap with the Sonora Mountain Kingsnake), and the pale bands become wider on the lower sides. (3) Venomous Arizona Coral Snake (p. 185) has broad red bands bordered with white or yellow rather than black.

Range: Cent. Utah and e. Nevada south in mts. of Arizona and extreme sw. New Mexico into Sierra Madre Occidental to w.-cent. Chihuahua. Isolated in Egan Range (Water and Sawmill Canyons), White Pine Co., Nevada, and Hualpai Mts., Mohave Co., Arizona. Distribution spotty. From 2800 to 9100 ft.

Subspecies: UTAH MOUNTAIN KINGSNAKE, *L. p. infralabialis.* Nine lower labials. Fifty per cent or more of the white body rings extend unbroken across the belly. ARIZONA MOUNTAIN KINGSNAKE, *L. p. pyromelana.* Ten lower labials. Less than 50 per cent of the white body rings are complete across the belly, white rings usually more than 43. HUACHUCA MOUNTAIN KINGSNAKE, *L. p. woodini.* Like the Arizona Mountain Kingsnake but white body rings usually less than 43. Map 149

MILK SNAKE *Lampropeltis triangulum* **Pl. 31**
Identification: 14–54. Above with rings or saddles of red, orange, or reddish brown bordered by black and separated by white or yellow rings. *The white rings tend to widen on the lowermost scales.* Over its great range, which includes most of the U.S., there is much variation in the width of the rings. The red rings are very wide in se. and s. U.S., in the range of the venomous coral snakes, which also have wide red rings. Dorsal pattern

usually imperfectly but variously carried onto the ventral surfaces. Scales smooth; anal single. *Young:* 6–10.

Frequents a variety of habitats — coniferous forest, broad-leaf woodland, river bottoms, rocky hillsides, prairies, sand dunes, and farmland, from the lowlands well up into the mountains. Secretive; found inside rotten logs and stumps and under rocks, logs, bark, and boards. Occasionally encountered in the open. Often nocturnal, especially in warm weather. Foods include snakes, lizards, mice, and occasionally birds and their eggs. Because these snakes are often found in barnyards where they hunt mice, they have been erroneously accused of milking cows; hence the common name.

Similar species: See (1) California and (2) Sonora Mountain Kingsnakes. (3) Long-nosed Snake has single caudals. (4) Arizona Coral Snake (p. 185) has the red rings bordered with white or pale yellow instead of black.

Range: Se. Canada to S. America; Atlantic Coast to cent. Montana and cent. Utah. Old records for Fort Benton, Chouteau Co., Montana, and Fort Apache, Navajo Co., Arizona. Recently found near Sun Prairie, Phillips Co., Montana. Sea level to 8000 ft.

Subspecies: CENTRAL PLAINS MILK SNAKE, *L. t. gentilis.* Triads united across the belly, with the black bands often constricting or completely separating the red color at the middorsal line; head black. Ventrals 189 or more. White rings total 26 to 38; ventrals minus the white rings usually more than 160 (average 165). No black flecks on the anterior chin shields. PALE MILK SNAKE, *L. t. multistrata.* Triads not completely united across the belly; red replaced by orange. Belly light with a few black spots, frequently unmarked. Head with small black cap; snout light orange or whitish. NEW MEXICO MILK SNAKE, *L. t. celaenops.* First white ring 3 to 5 scales wide at the middorsal line; other white rings expanded at the middorsal line. The black bands of the triads united ventrally and laterally. Ventrals usually 190 or less. White rings total 30 to 48; ventrals minus white rings less than 160, usually 140–155. Anterior chin shields frequently flecked with black. UTAH MILK SNAKE, *L. t. taylori.* Ventrals and chin markings as in the New Mexico Milk Snake. First white ring 1 to 4 (usually less than 3) scales wide at the middorsal line; body rings not expanded middorsally. Triads with black bands frequently incomplete ventrally. In Arizona known only from the vicinity of Wupatki Nat'l Monument.   Map 147

LONG-NOSED SNAKE *Rhinocheilus lecontei*   **Pl. 31**
Identification: 20–41. Typically a slim speckled snake with black saddles that are flecked with whitish on the sides. Interspaces between the saddles pink or reddish dorsally or all red

except for a pale border next to the saddles. Interspaces usually marked with dark flecks on the sides. Belly whitish or pale yellow, with a few dark spots. Snout pointed and head only slightly wider than neck. *Most scales on the underside of the tail in a single row; scales smooth; anal single. Young:* Hatchlings 6½–8. Speckling on sides faint.

An inhabitant of deserts, prairies, and brushland. In the Southwest it is crepuscular and nocturnal and likely to be found on roadways at night in irrigated parts of the desert. Because it spends the daylight hours underground, it is seldom found under objects in the daytime. A good burrower. Feeds on lizards and their eggs, small mammals and insects.

Similar species: (1) Differs from the kingsnakes in having most of the caudal scales in a single rather than double row. (2) See also Desert Hook-nosed Snake (p. 179).

Range: Sw. Idaho and se. Colorado to cent. Durango, s. San Luis Potosí, and s. Tamaulipas; cent Texas to cent. California. Recently found near Page, San Juan Co., Utah. Sea level to 5400 ft.

Subspecies: TEXAS LONG-NOSED SNAKE, *R. l. tessellatus.* Snout sharp; rostral raised above nearby scales, giving snout upward tilt. WESTERN LONG-NOSED SNAKE, *R. l. lecontei.* Snout blunter than above; rostral only slightly raised and snout without upward tilt. In the more arid parts of its range occurs a contrastingly banded color phase (formerly regarded as a distinct subspecies, *clarus*) that usually lacks red in the interspaces and has scant black spotting on the sides; the black saddles are longer and fewer than in the typical form.

Map 150

PLAIN-BELLIED WATER SNAKE *Natrix erythrogaster* **Pl. 37**
Identification: 18–67. In our area known only from the valley of the Pecos River in extreme se. New Mexico. A moderately heavy-bodied snake with *blotched pattern and strongly keeled scales with apical pits.* The blotches are dark brown, edged with black on an olive, gray, or brown background. Most of the smaller blotches on the sides alternate with the dorsal ones. Sometimes the dorsal pattern is represented only by pale cross-bars edged with black. *Belly plain yellow, often tinged with orange and faintly spotted.* Underside of tail usually orange or reddish. Elsewhere in its range adults may be plain-colored above, and in the eastern and extreme northern part of its range the belly is reddish, hence the name "Copperbelly." Anal divided. *Young:* About 8½ to 12 in. Strongly blotched above on a ground color of pinkish; belly whitish. *Male:* Knobs on scale keels above the anal region.

In the western part of its range it follows river courses into arid country, seeking the permanent or semipermanent water of streams, ditches, and cattle tanks, which it enters freely, swimming and diving with ease. Although highly aquatic, it may wander from water in wet weather. When first caught it often discharges foul-smelling musk from its anal scent glands. Feeds on crayfish, fish, frogs, tadpoles, and salamander larvae. Live-bearing.

Similar species: (1) Garter snakes have a single anal. (2) Rat snakes (pp. 153–54) have weakly keeled scales confined to the upper part of the back. (3) See also Common Water Snake.

Range: S. Michigan to Gulf Coast, cent. Nuevo León, and e. Durango; Atlantic Coast to extreme w. Oklahoma and se. New Mexico. Sea level to 6700 ft. (Mexico).

Subspecies: The BLOTCHED WATER SNAKE, *N. e. transversa*, occurs in our area.   Map 151

COMMON WATER SNAKE *Natrix sipedon*   **Pl. 37**
Identification: 18–54. In our area, known only from e. Colorado. A moderately heavy-bodied serpent with *prominently keeled scales with apical pits*. The pits may be represented by oval discolored spots that are not indented. Crossbands on the anterior part of the body give way about midbody to large dorsal blotches which continue onto the tail and which alternate with smaller ones on the sides. Ground color varies from pale gray to dark brown and markings from bright reddish-brown to black. Some individuals are uniformly dark, virtually without pattern. *Black or reddish half-moons on the belly in regular or irregular arrangement*, or belly yellow or orange along the midline and uniformly stippled with gray at the sides. Anal divided. *Young:* About 6½ to 10 in. More contrastingly marked than adult. Pattern black or dark brown on a pale gray or light brown background. *Male:* Knobbed keels on the dorsal scales in the anal region.

Found in or near swamps, marshes, streams, rivers, and lakes. Individuals may be seen basking on shore or on logs or piles of rotting vegetation in the water, and when alarmed swim to the bottom or to the cover of emergent vegetation. A highly aquatic snake, seldom venturing far from water. When caught it may expel a foul-smelling secretion from its anal scent glands. Food consists of crayfish, insects, fish, salamanders, frogs, toads, tadpoles, and occasionally small mammals. Live-bearing. Large broods, to 70 or more young.

Similar species: (1) Plain-bellied Water Snake usually has an unmarked belly and the crossbands are largely confined to the neck. (2) Garter snakes lack apical pits on the dorsal scales and have a single anal. (3) Corn Snake (p. 153) has smooth scales on the sides and a spear-shaped mark on the head.

Range: E. Colorado to Atlantic Coast; s. Canada to Gulf Coast from e. Louisiana to w. Florida. Sea level to around 4500 ft.

Subspecies: The NORTHERN WATER SNAKE, *N. s. sipedon*, occurs in our area.   Map 152

RED-BELLIED SNAKE   *Storeria occipitomaculata*   **Pl. 35**
Identification: 8–16. Typically a red-bellied snake with dorsal stripes and *large light-colored blotches at the back of the head;* top of head blackish. Blotches may be small or absent in Black Hills population in our area (see below). *Usually 4 narrow dark stripes* and sometimes a broad light-colored median stripe. Ground color above varies — plain brown or occasionally black. Melanistic individuals usually have a dark belly. The belly, usually bright red, varies through orange to pale yellow. Dorsal scales keeled, in 15 rows. Anal divided. *Young:* 2–4.

Over much of its range it is primarily a snake of wooded hilly regions. It occurs under stones, logs, and boards, and inside rotten stumps, often at the edge of clearings and in or near sphagnum bogs. Found about human habitation. Feeds on slugs, earthworms, and soft-bodied insects. Live-bearing.
Range: Widespread over e. U.S. but distribution spotty. Extreme s. Canada to Gulf Coast. Atlantic Coast to e. North Dakota in north and Louisiana in south. Isolated population in Black Hills of sw. South Dakota and ne. Wyoming. Old record for Animas Co., Colorado. Sea level to 5000 ft.
Subspecies: The BLACK HILLS RED-BELLIED SNAKE, *S. o. pahasapae*, occurs in our area.   Map 153

Garter Snakes: Genus *Thamnophis*

MODERATELY slender serpents with head slightly wider than the neck. Dorsal scales keeled and without apical pits; anal usually single. The scales of water snakes (genus *Natrix*) have apical pits (see back endpaper) and the anal is divided. Dorsal scale counts are important in identification. A count of 17, 17, 15 means 17 rows at the neck, 17 at midbody, and 15 in front of the vent. Most species have a conspicuous pale yellow or orange vertebral stripe and a pale stripe low on each side. The fancied resemblance of this pattern to an old-fashioned garter has earned these snakes their common name. The position of the lateral stripe varies. It may be on scale rows 2 and 3, 3 and 4, or confined to row 3. Count upward from the ends of the ventrals about ¼ the body length behind the head. Some species are unstriped or have only the lateral stripes and a spotted or checkered pattern.

Garter snakes occupy a great variety of habitats from sea level to high in the mountains. Many are aquatic or semiaquatic but some are completely terrestrial. Like the water snakes, when caught they often void feces and expel musk from their anal scent glands. Live-bearing. About 20 species occur in the region from

Canada to Costa Rica and the Pacific to the Atlantic Coasts. The Common Garter Snake ranges farther north than any other reptile in the Western Hemisphere.

NARROW-HEADED GARTER SNAKE Pl. 37
Thamnophis rufipunctatus

Identification: 20–34. Dorsum olive or brown marked with *conspicuous dark brown spots* that fade on the tail. No well-developed stripes or pale crescent behind the corner of the mouth. Vestiges of the dorsal and lateral stripes are sometimes present on the neck. Below brownish gray, paling on the throat. Often a row of black wedge-shaped marks on each side of the belly. Head long; snout blunt; *8 upper labials.* Scales keeled, in 21 rows at midbody. Anal usually single.

Ranges from the piñon-juniper and oak-pine belts into forests of ponderosa pine along clear, permanent, or semipermanent rocky streams, where it seems to prefer the quieter well-illuminated sections. Highly aquatic. When frightened, usually dives to the bottom and takes refuge under a stone. Feeds on fish, frogs, tadpoles, and salamanders. Live-bearing.

Range: Mts. of cent. and e. Arizona and sw. New Mexico, south in Sierra Madre Occidental to cent. Durango.　　　Map 158

COMMON GARTER SNAKE *Thamnophis sirtalis* Pl. 37

Identification: 18–51. Coloration highly variable but the dorsal and lateral stripes are usually well defined and frequently there are *red blotches on the sides* between the stripes. Lateral stripe on 2nd and 3rd scale rows. Top of head brown, gray, red, or black. Venter bluish gray or dusky posteriorly, becoming pale on the throat. Eyes relatively large. *Usually 7 upper and 10 lower labials.* Scales keeled; anal single. *Young:* 6–9. *Male:* Knobbed keels on scales above vent.

The most widely distributed North American reptile, capable of living in many environments, from the Everglades of Florida to the cold prairies of w. Canada. Frequents ponds, marshes, prairie swales, roadside ditches, streams, sloughs, damp meadows, woods, farms and city lots. Tends to stay near water, entering it freely and retreating to it when frightened. A spirited snake that defends itself energetically when cornered. When caught, it often bites and smears its captor with excrement and the odorous contents of its anal scent glands. Food consists of fish, toads, frogs, tadpoles, salamanders, birds, small mammals, earthworms, slugs, and leeches. Live-bearing. Broods of 3 to 85 young; average one to two dozen, depending upon locality.

Similar species: (1) The usual presence of red markings between the stripes, the 7 (occasionally 8) upper labials, and the relatively large eyes (see Plate 37) generally will distinguish this species from other garter snakes with which it coexists. See also (2)

Northwestern (p. 170), and (3) Western Terrestrial, and (4) Western Aquatic Garter Snakes.

Range: From Pacific to Atlantic Coasts; Canada to Gulf Coast and Chihuahua. Absent from most of arid Southwest. Sea level to 8000 ft.

Subspecies: RED-SPOTTED GARTER SNAKE, *T. s. concinnus*. Ground color of dorsum black, extending onto the ventral surface. Dorsal stripe well defined, including the mid-dorsal row of scales and half of each adjacent scale row; lateral stripes sometimes hidden by black pigment. Top of head usually red. PUGET SOUND RED-SIDED GARTER SNAKE, *T. s. pickeringi*. Dark-colored like the Red-spotted Garter Snake but top of head dark and dorsal stripe largely confined to the middorsal scale row. VALLEY GARTER SNAKE, *T. s. fitchi*. Ground color slaty or brownish. Dorsal stripe broad, with regular, well-defined borders. Top of head black. Black of venter usually confined to tips of the ventrals. Slate-gray individuals that match their rock background occur within the caldera of Crater Lake (along the lakeshore and on Wizard I.). SAN FRANCISCO GARTER SNAKE, *T. s. tetrataenia* (illus.). One of the most beautiful serpents in N. America. Wide dorsal stripe of greenish yellow edged with black, bordered on each side by a broad red stripe followed by a black one. Belly greenish blue. Top of head red. Western portion of San Francisco Peninsula from about San Francisco Co. line south along crest of hills at least to Crystal Lake and along coast to point Año Nuevo, San Mateo Co., California. RED-SIDED GARTER SNAKE, *T. s. parietalis*. Dorsum with dark spots; red bars on sides; top of head mostly olive; stripes relatively broad and dull. CALIFORNIA RED-SIDED GARTER SNAKE, *T. s. infernalis* (illus.). Resembles the Red-sided Garter Snake but has generally darker ground color; dark spots of dorsum less distinct; stripes usually narrower and bright greenish yellow, lateral ones often merging with the ventral color. NEW MEXICO GARTER SNAKE, *T. s. ornata*. Resembles Red-sided Garter Snake but has a dull, dusky, or muddy appearance, pattern less sharply defined and duller. Dorsolateral areas olive, marked with red flecks and alternating rows of black spots. Upper black blotches tend to fuse with each other along their upper edges to form a black border to the dorsal stripe.   Map 157

WESTERN TERRESTRIAL GARTER SNAKE   Pl. 37
Thamnophis elegans

Identification: 18–42. Usually a well-defined middorsal stripe extends the length of the body, and a lateral stripe is present on each side on the 2nd and 3rd scale rows. The pale ground color between the stripes is checkered with dark spots, or is generally dark with scattered white flecks. *Internasals usually broader than long and not pointed anteriorly.* Usually 8 upper labials, the *6th and 7th enlarged, often higher than wide;* usually 10 lower labials. Chin shields of about equal length. Dorsal scales keeled; anal single. *Young:* 6¾–9.

Occurs in a great variety of habitats — grassland, brushland, woodland, and forest, from sea level to high in the mountains. Often found in damp environments near water; occasionally far from water. *Habits chiefly terrestrial but also aquatic,* depending upon the subspecies. When frightened, terrestrial forms tend to seek shelter in dense plant growth or other cover on land, and aquatic forms usually enter water. Food consists of slugs, leeches, earthworms, fish, salamanders, frogs, toads, tadpoles, lizards, snakes, small mammals, and occasionally birds. Live-bearing.

Similar species: (1) The distinct dorsal stripe usually will distinguish members of this group in areas of overlap with the Oregon, Sierra, and Two-striped Garter Snakes, subspecies of the Western Aquatic Garter Snake. East of the Sierra Nevada crest, however, some difficulty may be encountered in distinguishing the Wandering Garter Snake from the Western Aquatic subspecies, the Sierra Garter Snake. The latter has a narrow, dull dorsal stripe, ordinarily confined to the anterior third of the body and a checkered pattern of large squarish spots. The Wandering Garter Snake usually has a wider, more fully developed stripe and pattern of rounded, well-separated spots. Along the California coast where striped members of the Western Aquatic Garter Snake (Santa Cruz and Aquatic Garter Snakes) overlap in range the Coast Garter Snake, the former differ in lacking red markings, in usually having an orange (rather than yellow) dorsal stripe, a cream (rather than yellow) chin and throat, and generally a golden orange suffusion or blotches on the ventrals. In addition to the foregoing differences, the Western Aquatic subspecies usually have narrow, pointed internasals and the 6th and 7th upper labials are no higher than wide. (2) Northwestern Garter Snake has 17, 17, 15 scale rows, 7 upper labials, 8 or 9 lower labials, and a bright yellow, red, or orange dorsal stripe; whereas in the area of overlap with the Western Terrestrial Garter Snake the latter has 19, 19, 17 or more scale rows, 8 upper labials, 10 lower labials, and usually a dull yellow, brown, or gray dorsal stripe. (3) Common Garter Snake has relatively larger eyes, generally 7 upper labials, and a plain bluish-gray belly; where it coexists with the Coast Garter Snake (subspecies of the Western Terrestrial), it usually has a greenish-yellow dorsal stripe.

Range: Cent. B.C. to n. Baja California and s. Durango; w. South Dakota and extreme w. Oklahoma to Pacific Coast. Sea level to 10,500 ft.

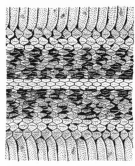

Coast (*terrestris*)

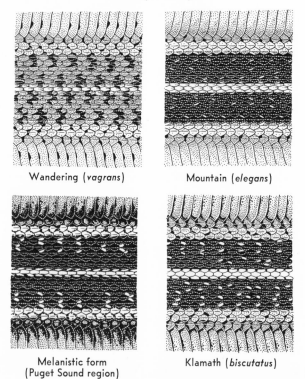

Wandering (*vagrans*)　　　　Mountain (*elegans*)

Melanistic form
(Puget Sound region)　　　　Klamath (*biscutatus*)

Fig. 28. Pattern variation in Western Terrestrial Garter Snake

Subspecies: MOUNTAIN GARTER SNAKE, *T. e. elegans* (Fig. 28, opposite). Well-defined dorsal and lateral stripes are separated by blackish ground color. Dorsal stripe yellow or orange-yellow. No red markings. Belly pale, unmarked, or with light spotting of dusky. COAST GARTER SNAKE, *T. e. terrestris* (Plate 37 and Fig. 28). Dorsal stripe typically bright yellow. Bright red or orange flecks usually present on belly and sides, including lateral stripes. Seeks shelter on land. WANDERING GARTER SNAKE, *T. e. vagrans* (Fig. 28). Dorsal stripe dull yellow or brown, fading on tail. Dark spots on body usually small and well separated but sometimes absent or variously enlarged, occasionally forming a completely black area between the stripes. Melanistic individuals (Fig. 28) occur in the vicinity of Puget Sound. KLAMATH GARTER SNAKE, *T. e. biscutatus* (Fig. 28). Well-defined dorsal and lateral stripes separated by dark ground color. Below light gray, often suffused with black or slate, especially on posterior half of body. Prefers rocky streams.   Map 161

WESTERN AQUATIC GARTER SNAKE   Pl. 37
Thamnophis couchi
Identification: 18–57. Coloration varies greatly depending upon the subspecies (see below). Over most of its range this snake is blotched and lacks or has only a weak dorsal stripe. The stripe is well defined, however, in subspecies in coastal California. Lateral stripe when present, on 2nd and 3rd scale rows. *Internasals tend to be narrower than long and pointed anteriorly.* Usually 8 upper labials, 6th and 7th not enlarged. Chin shields of about equal length. Scales keeled; anal single.

Primarily a snake of rivers and streams, but occurs in a great variety of aquatic environments from brackish marshes at sea level to high mountain streams, the habitat varying with the subspecies. Usually retreats to water when frightened. Primarily diurnal but the Two-striped Garter Snake often is active at dusk. Feeds on fish, fish eggs, frogs, toads, tadpoles, salamanders, earthworms, and leeches. Live-bearing.

Similar species: (1) Lack of a well-defined dorsal stripe in the blotched subspecies will distinguish them from the Western Terrestrial Garter Snake. The striped subspecies (Santa Cruz and Aquatic Garter Snakes), however, must be distinguished by other pattern characteristics (see below) and by their pointed internasals and unenlarged posterior upper labials. (2) The Common Garter Snake usually has 7 upper labials, larger eyes, well-defined dorsal stripe, and distinct red blotches on the sides.

Range: Sw. Oregon to n. Baja California; extreme w. Nevada to Pacific Coast. Throughout California except desert and extreme northeastern part. Sea level to 8000 ft.

Subspecies: OREGON GARTER SNAKE, *T. c. hydrophila*

(Fig. 29, opposite). Conspicuous dark markings in checkered arrangement on a pale gray ground color. Dorsal stripe
narrow and dull. Below light-colored, unmarked, with flesh or
purplish tinge toward tail. Usually 10 lower labials. Permanent
streams with rocky beds and swift, clear water. SIERRA
GARTER SNAKE, *T. c. couchi* (Fig. 29). Similar to Oregon
Garter Snake but usually has 11 lower labials. Dorsal stripe
narrow and faint, confined to the anterior part of the body.
Rocky streams with protected pools near shore. GIANT GAR-
TER SNAKE, *T. c. gigas* (Fig. 29). To over 4 ft. Dorsal
markings of small, well-separated spots in checkered arrangement. Dorsal stripe dull yellow, often with irregular margins.
Streams and sloughs with mud bottoms. AQUATIC GARTER
SNAKE, *T. c. aquaticus* (Fig. 29). Yellow to orange dorsal
stripe; ground color between the dorsal and lateral stripes dark
olive to black. Belly blotched with golden or
pale salmon. Iris gray. Ponds, small lakes, and sluggish streams.
SANTA CRUZ GARTER SNAKE, *T. c. atratus* (Plate 37 and
Fig. 29). Resembles Aquatic Garter Snake in appearance and
habitat, but averages slightly narrower dorsal stripe, throat
more often bright lemon-yellow, and iris nearly black. TWO-
STRIPED GARTER SNAKE, *T. c. hammondi* (Fig. 29). No
dorsal stripe, or only a remnant on the neck. Lateral stripes
usually present. Plain olive, gray, or brownish above, with dark
spots on the lower sides. Habitat resembles that of the Sierra
Garter Snake. Overlaps the range of the Santa Cruz Garter
Snake along the central coast of California. Since the Coast
Garter Snake, a subspecies of the Western Terrestrial Garter
Snake, also occurs there, 3 subspecies of Western Terrestrial and
Western Aquatic Garter Snakes coexist in this part of Cali-
fornia.   Map 162

NORTHWESTERN GARTER SNAKE   Pl. 36
Thamnophis ordinoides

Identification: 14–26. A small garter snake usually with a well-
defined dorsal stripe of yellow, orange, or red, but the stripe may
be faint or lacking. Lateral stripes distinct or faint. Dorsal
ground color black, brown, greenish, or bluish. *Belly* yellowish,
olive, or slate, *often with red blotches* and sometimes marked with
black, especially in the northern part of the range. Dorsal scales
keeled, typically in 17, 17, 15 rows (see p. 164). *Usually 7 upper
and 8 or 9 lower labials.* Anal single.

Chiefly terrestrial, frequenting meadows and clearings in
forested areas where there is abundant low-growing vegetation.
Active on warm sunny days. When frightened may retreat to
cover of dense vegetation rather than water. Feeds on slugs,
earthworms, salamanders, and frogs. Live-bearing.

Similar species: (1) Western Terrestrial Garter Snake usually

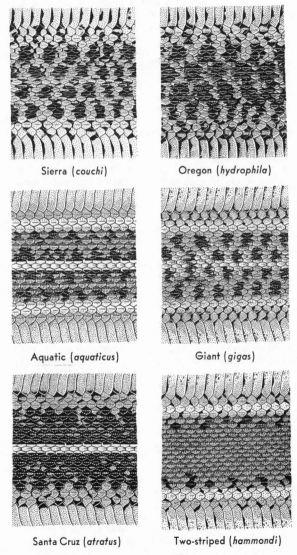

Sierra (*couchi*)   Oregon (*hydrophila*)

Aquatic (*aquaticus*)   Giant (*gigas*)

Santa Cruz (*atratus*)   Two-striped (*hammondi*)

Fig. 29. Pattern variation in Western Aquatic Garter Snake

has 8 upper labials and a higher dorsal scale row count. (2) Oregon Garter Snake, a subspecies of the Western Aquatic Garter Snake, with which it overlaps in range, generally has a narrow, dull yellow, brown, or gray dorsal stripe and 8 upper labials. (3) Common Garter Snake (p. 165) lacks red markings on the belly, has a longer, more triangular head, larger eyes, and usually 19 scale rows at midbody.

Range: Southwestern B.C. and Vancouver I. to extreme nw. California, chiefly west of crest of Cascade Mts. but crosses crest at several points in Washington. Sea level to 4000 ft.   Map 164

BLACK-NECKED GARTER SNAKE   Pl. 36
Thamnophis cyrtopsis

Identification: 16–37. A whitish or pale yellow vertebral stripe separates 2 *large black blotches at the back of the head*. A white crescent occurs between each blotch and the corner of the mouth. *Lateral stripe on the 2nd and 3rd scale rows*, often wavy because it may be partly invaded above and below by black spots. Dorsal ground color olive-brown with 2 alternating rows of elongate spots between the stripes which may appear as a zigzag line. The spots fade on the tail. Belly greenish white. Scales keeled, *usually in 19 rows at midbody*. Anal single.

Habitats vary — desert, grassland, mesquite flats, chaparral-covered hillsides, and forests of pine and fir. Frequents permanent and intermittent streams, but in wet weather may wander far from water. Feeds on frogs, toads, and tadpoles. Live-bearing.

Similar species: (1) Checkered Garter Snake usually has 21 scale rows at midbody and the lateral stripe is confined anteriorly to 3rd scale row; the checker pattern extends well out onto the tail. (2) Mexican Garter Snake has 19 or 21 scale rows at midbody and the lateral stripe is on 3rd and 4th scale rows.

Range: Se. Utah to El Salvador; cent. Texas to cent. and s. Arizona. Desert outpost in Ajo Mts., Pima Co., Arizona. Distribution spotty. Sea level to above 8000 ft.

Subspecies: The WESTERN BLACK-NECKED GARTER SNAKE, *T. c. cyrtopsis*, occurs in our area.   Map 156

MEXICAN GARTER SNAKE *Thamnophis eques*   Pl. 36
Identification: 18–40. A striped garter snake with a whitish to greenish crescent behind the corner of the mouth, *paired black blotches at back of head*, and the *lateral stripe on 3rd and 4th scale rows anteriorly*. Sides checkered with dark spots on an olive or brown ground color. Dorsal scales keeled, in 19 or 21 rows at midbody. Anal single. *Young:* Around 9½ in.

Primarily a highland snake of pine-oak forest, mesquite grassland, and desert, but in se. Arizona it occurs in the lowlands (Rillito Wash near Tucson, San Pedro Valley, and vicinity of

Douglas). Usually found in or near water, where it feeds on frogs. Live-bearing.

Similar species: (1) Checkered Garter Snake typically has the lateral stripe confined to the 3rd scale row anteriorly and more prominent paired dark blotches at the back of the head. See also (2) Black-necked and (3) Plains Garter Snakes.

Range: Cent. Arizona and extreme w. New Mexico, south in highlands of w. and s. Mexico, to Oaxaca. To 8500 ft.

Subspecies: The MEXICAN GARTER SNAKE, *T. e. megalops*, occurs in our area.   Map 155

CHECKERED GARTER SNAKE   Pl. 36
Thamnophis marcianus

Identification: 18–42. A rather pale snake with *checkered pattern of large squarish blotches on a brownish-yellow, brown, or olive ground color.* A pale yellow vertebral stripe. Paired black blotches at back of head. A whitish crescent between the dark blotches and corner of the mouth. *Lateral stripe usually confined to 3rd scale row* anteriorly and on 2nd and 3rd scale rows posteriorly. Scales keeled, usually in 21 rows at midbody. Anal single. *Young:* Around 8 in.

Chiefly a snake of the lowlands, frequenting ponds, springs, streams, and rivers in arid and semiarid regions, but ranges sparingly into the pine-oak belt in the mountains. A grassland species that is able to exist along streams in the desert and appears to be expanding its range with the irrigation of arid lands. Food includes fish, toads, frogs, tadpoles, lizards, and invertebrates. In the warmer, more arid parts of its range, it feeds chiefly at night. Live-bearing.

Similar-species: (1) Black-necked Garter Snake usually has 19 scale rows at midbody and the lateral stripe on 2nd and 3rd scale rows anteriorly. (2) Plains and (3) Mexican Garter Snakes have the lateral stripe on 3rd and 4th scale rows. (4) Coexists in Arizona and New Mexico with Wandering Garter Snake (a subspecies of the Western Terrestrial Garter Snake), which has lateral stripe on 2nd and 3rd scale rows.

Range: Sw. Kansas and s. Arizona to Tehuantepec; extreme se. California to e. Texas. Sea level to 5000 ft.   Map 154

PLAINS GARTER SNAKE *Thamnophis radix*   Pl. 36

Identification: 20–42. Well-defined dorsal stripe, orange or yellow anteriorly, becoming paler posteriorly. *Lateral stripe on 3rd and 4th scale rows*, cream, greenish, or bluish anteriorly, whitish posteriorly. A row of black spots set in a brownish border below the lateral stripe. Squarish dark blotches between the stripes on a greenish-gray, olive, reddish, or brownish ground color. Occasional dark individuals with obscure blotches. Prominent black bars on whitish upper labials. *Upper labials*

typically 7. Dorsal scales keeled, usually in 21 rows at midbody.
Anal single. *Young:* About 6 to 7 in.

Chiefly an inhabitant of wet prairies and farmland, but ranges
into the piñon-juniper belt. Found about ponds, sloughs,
swamps, lakes, streams, and rivers. May attempt to bite when
first caught. Feeds on frogs, toads, tadpoles, fish, earthworms,
insects, and carrion. Live-bearing. Broods of over 90 young.
Similar species: The (1) Common, (2) Western Terrestrial, (3)
Western Aquatic, and (4) Black-necked Garter Snakes have the
lateral stripe anteriorly on the 3rd and 4th scale rows. (4)
Checkered Garter Snake usually has stripe on 3rd scale row
only. (5) Mexican Garter Snake has 8 or 9 upper labials. (6)
See also Western Ribbon Snake.
Range: S. Canada to ne. New Mexico; cent. Montana to cent.
Ohio. From 500 to 6500 ft.
Subspecies: The WESTERN PLAINS GARTER SNAKE,
T. r. haydeni, occurs in our area.   Map 160

WESTERN RIBBON SNAKE *Thamnophis proximus*   **Pl. 36**
Identification: 18–51. An extremely slender snake with *pale
unmarked upper labials contrasting with darker color of top of the
head.* Dorsal stripe usually orange in area of this book but
yellow, orange, reddish, brown, or greenish elsewhere. *Lateral
stripe on 3rd and 4th scale rows* anteriorly. Ground color between
the stripes olive-brown, brown, gray, or black. *A very long tail,*
¼ *to* ⅓ *total length of the snake.* Upper labials 7 or 8. Dorsal
scales keeled. Anal single. *Young:* 5¾–10.

A highly adaptable species that occurs in a great variety of
habitats from temperate woodland and grassland to the tropics.
Agile and alert, frequenting the vegetation bordering streams,
lakes, ponds, sloughs, and marshes. When frightened it often
retreats to water and swims with speed and grace, usually staying among emergent plant growth near shore. It is an efficient
climber and may first be seen as it drops from a basking site in
overhanging vegetation into the water. Feeds on frogs, fish,
insects, and earthworms. Live-bearing.
Similar species: The long tail and the contrasting, pale, unmarked upper labials distinguish this snake from other species
with which it coexists.
Range: S. Wisconsin to Gulf Coast, thence through ne. Mexico
to Costa Rica; e. New Mexico to Mississippi Valley. Old
records for Rio Grande Valley, New Mexico. Sea level to 8000
ft. (Sierra Madre Oriental).
Subspecies: The PECOS RIBBON SNAKE, *T. p. diabolicus,*
occurs in our area.   Map 159

LINED SNAKE *Tropidoclonion lineatum*   **Pl. 35**
Identification: 9–21. Striped like a garter snake. Dorsal and
lateral stripes well defined and bordered by dark spots set in a

dark or light olive-gray ground color. Dorsal stripe whitish, pale gray, yellow, or orange. Belly whitish or yellow, marked with *2 rows of black spots along the midline.* Head about the same width as the neck. *Five or 6 upper labials.* Scales keeled. Anal single. *Young:* 3–5.

A locally abundant but secretive snake of prairies, open woods, floodplains, city dumps, and parks, secluding itself under objects in the daytime, and venturing forth at dusk and at night in search of earthworms. Activity is stimulated by wet weather. When first caught this snake often voids the contents of its anal scent glands. Live-bearing.

Range: Se. South Dakota to s. Texas; ne. New Mexico and e. Colorado (Boulder-Denver region and southeastern part) to cent. Illinois. Isolated population in Capitan Mts., Lincoln Co., New Mexico. Near sea level to around 5300 ft.

Subspecies: The NORTHERN LINED SNAKE, *T. l. lineatum,* occurs in our area. Map 163

WESTERN GROUND SNAKE *Sonora semiannulata* **Pl. 32**
Identification: 8–19. A small, crossbanded, longitudinally striped, or plain-colored snake with head only slightly wider than the neck. There is great variation in the dorsal pattern — dark crossbands may encircle the body, form saddles, be reduced to a single neck band, or be entirely lacking. Some populations have a distinct, broad flesh-colored, red, or orange vertebral stripe and greenish-gray or bluish gray sides (lower Colorado River). Plain, crossbanded, and striped individuals may all occur at the same locality. All pattern types have a dark blotch anteriorly on each scale, particularly evident on sides. Belly unmarked or with dark crossbands. Scales smooth and glossy; *53 or more caudals in males* (counting only one row), *45 or more in females.* Anal divided. *Young:* 4–5.

A secretive nocturnal snake of arid and semiarid regions, usually where there is sand and some subsurface moisture. Frequents river bottoms, desert flats, sand hummocks, and rocky hillsides where there are pockets of loose soil. Vegetation may be scant, as on the sagebrush plains of the Great Basin and in creosote bush desert, but along the lower Colorado River this snake occurs among thickets of mesquite, arrowweed, and willows. Feeds on spiders, centipedes, crickets, grasshoppers, and insect larvae.

Similar species: (1) Ground Snake usually has 52 or fewer caudals in males and 44 or fewer in females. (2) Shovel-nosed and (3) Banded Sand Snakes regularly have dark crossbands, a flatter snout, and deeply inset lower jaw.

Range: Snake River region of sw. Idaho south to cent. Chihuahua and Santa Rosalía, Baja California; se. California to sw. New Mexico and w. Texas. Sea level to 6000 ft. Map 165

GROUND SNAKE   *Sonora episcopa*   **Pl. 32**
    Identification: 9–16. Like the Western Ground Snake, it may
    be plain-colored, crossbanded, or longitudinally striped and
    some individuals may have a single dark collar band. All pattern
    types, including mixed patterns, may occur at the same locality.
    Usually each dorsal scale is marked with a dark blotch at its base.
    The blotches are sometimes bar-shaped and form dashed lines.
    Dorsal scales smooth and glossy, usually in 15 rows; *52 or fewer
    caudals in males and 42 or fewer in females* (counting single row).
    Anal divided.
        Chiefly a snake of prairies and open arid woodland, where
    there are rocks and loose sandy soil. A secretive burrowing
    species, usually found under stones, boards, and other objects.
    Feeds on spiders, centipedes, scorpions, and insects.
    Similar species: (1) Shovel-nosed and (2) Banded Sand Snakes
    are always banded, have a much flatter snout, and deeply inset
    lower jaw. (3) See also Western Ground Snake.
    Range: Cent. Kansas to ne. Mexico; sw. Missouri to extreme
    se. Colorado and e. New Mexico. Sea level to 5200 ft.
    Subspecies: The GREAT PLAINS GROUND SNAKE, *S. e.
    episcopa*, occurs in our area.   Map 166

WESTERN SHOVEL-NOSED SNAKE   **Pl. 32**
Chionactis occipitalis
    Identification: 10–17. *A dark- and light-banded snake* with a
    shovel-shaped snout, flatter than in most other snakes; *lower jaw
    deeply inset*. Head little wider than the neck. The *dark brown
    or black crossbands, usually 21 or more on the body*, are saddle-like
    or encircle the body. The ground color is whitish or yellow.
    Orange or red saddles are sometimes present between the black
    ones. *Dorsal scales smooth, usually in 15 rows at midbody;
    internasals not separated by rostral.* Anal divided.
        Restricted to the desert, occurring even in its driest parts.
    Frequents washes, dunes, sandy flats, alluvium, and rocky hill-
    sides where there are sandy gullies or pockets of sand among
    rocks. Vegetation usually scant — creosote bush, desert grasses,
    cactus, or mesquite. A burrowing nocturnal species capable of
    moving rapidly through loose sand. The smooth scales, inset
    lower jaw, nasal valves, and angular abdomen are adaptations
    for "sand swimming," which consists of wriggling through sand
    rather than tunneling in it. Usually stays underground in the
    daytime but roams on the surface at night, leaving smoothly
    undulating tracks on the bare sand between bushes. When
    hunting these snakes on foot, move quickly from bush to bush
    with light in hand in order to catch them on the surface before
    they have time to submerge or climb into the lower branches of
    bushes. Food consists of insects, spiders, scorpions, centipedes,
    and buried chrysalids of moths.

Similar species: (1) Banded Sand Snake has 13 scale rows at midbody and the rostral separates the internasals. (2) Ground snakes have dark pigment at the base of most of the dorsal scales and less extreme flattening of the snout. (3) See also Sonora Shovel-nosed Snake.

Range: Sw. Nevada to upper end of Gulf of California; s. Arizona to desert base of mts. of s. California. Below sea level to nearly 4700 ft.

Subspecies: MOJAVE SHOVEL-NOSED SNAKE, *C. o. occipitalis*. Bands brown, no black or brown secondary bands between the primary ones. Bands on body plus the unmarked anterior band positions on the ventral surface (indicated by the ends of dorsal bands) usually 45 or more. COLORADO DESERT SHOVEL-NOSED SNAKE, *C. o. annulata*. Bands usually black. Bands on body plus the unmarked anterior band positions on the ventral surface usually fewer than 45. TUCSON SHOVEL-NOSED SNAKE, *C. o. klauberi*. Black or brown secondary bands between the primary bands. Ventrals usually fewer than 152 in males and fewer than 160 in females. NEVADA SHOVEL-NOSED SNAKE, *C. o. talpina*. Dark scales in interspaces between brown bands may form secondary bands. Ventrals usually 152 or more in males and 160 or more in females.
                                                              Map 168

SONORA SHOVEL-NOSED SNAKE   Pl. 32
Chionactis palarostris

Identification: 10–16. Resembles the Arizona Coral Snake but is harmless. Crossbanded with black, yellow (or whitish), and red, most of the black bands encircling the body. The red saddles vary in width. In individuals from s. Arizona they are about the same width as the black bands but in Sonora they may be 2 or nearly 3 times wider. *Black bands on the body usually fewer than 21*, bordered in front and in back by a narrow or wide (Sonora) yellow band. Snout yellow, slightly convex in profile; back of head black. Scales smooth, usually in 15 rows. Anal divided.

A snake of arid lands. Vegetation includes cactus, creosote bush, and mesquite. In Arizona it occurs in upland desert in the paloverde-saguaro association. The ground surface may be rocky or sandy, but generally is coarser (rockier) and more irregular than that occupied by the Western Shovel-nosed Snake.

Similar species: (1) Western Shovel-nosed Snake lacks broad red saddles, usually has more than 21 body bands, and has a flatter, more pointed snout. (2) Arizona Coral Snake has a black snout, broader black bands, and the red bands encircle the body.

Range: In our area known only from extreme s. Arizona along the Sonoyta-Ajo road to about 25 miles north of the Mexican line; in Sonora to south of Hermosillo.

Subspecies: The ORGAN PIPE SHOVEL-NOSED SNAKE,
C. p. organica, occurs in our area.   Map 167

BANDED SAND SNAKE *Chilomeniscus cinctus*   **Pl. 32**
Identification: 7–10. Our most efficient "sand-swimmer."
Adaptations for burrowing life even more extreme than those
of the Western Shovel-nosed Snake. Head no wider than neck,
lower jaw deeply inset, snout flat, nasal valves present, eyes
small and turned upward, and belly angular on each side. The
skin appears varnished. The total number of black crossbands
on the dorsum varies from 19 to 49, those on the tail usually
completely encircling it. Ground color whitish, pale yellow to
reddish orange, sometimes with orange saddles or a continuous
area dorsally of orange between the black bands. *Rostral separates the internasals. Scales smooth, in 13 rows at midbody.* Anal
divided.
   A desert species that inhabits loamy, gravelly, or sandy soil
in which it "swims." It seldom emerges on the surface except
at night. It frequents both open desert (creosote bush association) and sandy-gravelly washes and arroyos in rocky uplands
(paloverde-saguaro association). When Sand Snakes burrow, the
soil collapses behind them to form serpentine furrows which are
usually found in sandy areas among bushes. Use a stick, hoe,
or rake to uncover buried individuals. Food consists of centipedes, sand-burrowing cockroaches, and probably ant pupae and
other insects.
Similar species: See Western Shovel-nosed Snake.
Range: Cent. and sw. Arizona to extreme s. Sonora; throughout
most of Baja California. Sea level to 3000 ft.   Map 169

WESTERN HOOK-NOSED SNAKE *Ficimia cana*   **Pl. 34**
Identification: 7–14. A smooth scaled, crossbanded snake with
rather stout, cylindrical body and upturned snout. The *rostral
scale is flat or concave above and widely separates the internasals.*
Crossbands are brown or yellowish brown, edged with black on
a grayish brown or yellowish gray ground color. Usually 17
scale rows at midbody. Anal divided.
   Seldom encountered, perhaps because of its burrowing and
nocturnal habits. Most individuals have been found roaming
on the surface on warm nights following rains. In the U.S., it
inhabits semiarid environments of grass, piñon-juniper woodland, and other scrubby plant growth. It has been found in
rocky areas, alluvial deposits, and on grassy desert flats. When
first disturbed, it writhes and contorts its body, swings its tail
forward, and everts the lining of the vent with a bubbling,
popping sound. Apparently feeds chiefly on spiders.
Similar species: Western Hognose Snake (p. 145) has keeled
scales and the rostral has a median ridge.

Range : Se. Arizona, cent. and s. New Mexico, to cent. Texas, south to El Calabazal, Zacatecas, and south of Matehuala, San Luis Potosí. Recent collections in King and Dickens Cos. confirm its occurrence in n. Texas. From 1000 to 6500 ft.   Map 170

DESERT HOOK-NOSED SNAKE   Pl. 34
Ficimia quadrangularis

Identification : 6–12. The *upturned* snout and the *dorsal black saddles* will distinguish this rarely found snake. A *red or rust-colored band*, broken by the black saddles, runs the length of the body on each side. The ground color between the saddles and red bands is ash-white and from above forms pale rectangular patches along middle of the back. Belly pale greenish yellow, without pattern. Usually 17 scale rows at midbody. Anal single. *Young:* Red usually darker than in adult.

A secretive burrowing snake of alluvial deposits of canyon bottoms and outwash plains of the western slope of the Sierra Madre Occidental of Mexico and southern headwaters of the Gila River drainage in Arizona. In Arizona it occurs in rolling foothills of mesquite grassland, including partly cultivated sections. It is evidently strictly nocturnal and abroad on the surface chiefly during and after rains. All specimens so far taken in Arizona have been collected in summer and fall.

Similar species : (1) Long-nosed Snake (p. 161) lacks the upturned snout. (2) See also Western Hognose Snake (p. 145).

Range : Extreme s. Arizona in the Patagonia-Pajarito Mts. area, Santa Cruz Co., south to Nayarit. In Arizona has been found at mouth of Temporal Canyon, Alum Canyon near Patagonia, and Ruby Road, 7 mi. south of Tumacacori, Santa Cruz Co. From near sea level to over 4400 ft.

Subspecies : The DESERT HOOK-NOSED SNAKE, *F q. desertorum*, occurs in our area.   Map 171

Black-headed Snakes: Genus *Tantilla*

SMALL, slender, smooth-scaled, flatheaded snakes, with the top of the head black or dark brown and back plain brown. Most species have a white collar, usually followed by a black band or row of black dots. Belly salmon or coral-red, without dark spotting, the red not extending to ends of the ventrals. Slightly enlarged and grooved teeth at back of upper jaw. Scales in 15 rows; no loreal; anal divided. Absence of the loreal and lack of red color on the ends of the ventrals distinguish these snakes from the Ringneck Snake (p. 143).

Secretive and ground-dwelling, spending much time under stones and in crevices. Food includes millipedes, centipedes, spiders, and probably insects. Cent. U.S. to S. America.

WESTERN BLACK-HEADED SNAKE   Pls. 31, 35
Tantilla planiceps

Identification: 7–15. The blackish cap extends 0 to 3 scale rows behind the parietals at the midline, and is usually not pointed behind. Often a narrow white collar, which may or may not be bordered by black dots. Cap color may or may not extend on side of head to or below corner of mouth. Above plain brown to olive-gray, usually faintly *marked with a narrow vertebral stripe*. Broad orange or reddish stripe down middle of the belly, not extending to tips of the ventrals; remainder of belly whitish, unmarked. Scales smooth. Anal divided.

In the more arid parts of its range (desert side of the mountains in s. California and to the east), the dorsal color is pale, the dark cap usually does not extend below the corner of the mouth, the white collar is faint or absent and seldom has a dark border (see Plate 35).

Little is known of the habits of this snake. It has been found in grassland, woodland, chaparral, and desert, under stones on both level ground and hillsides. In arid lands to the east and south, it has been found in association with mesquite, sotol, agave, yucca, creosote bush, ocotillo, cedar, and oak; locally abundant along rocky edges of washes, arroyos, and streams in desert valleys and on rocky hillsides. Apparently spends most of its time underground in crevices and in burrows of other animals. Seldom encountered abroad on the surface except on warm nights, when it may be found on roadways. Look under flat rocks, logs, boards, dead sotols, agaves, yuccas, and other objects.

Similar species: Plains Black-headed Snake averages larger, has the black cap extending 3 to 5 scales behind parietals, and lacks a light collar. The rear margin of the cap is usually somewhat pointed.

Range: Coastal mts. and parts of San Joaquin Valley, California, from south of San Francisco Bay to tip of Baja California; scattered localities east to extreme w. Colorado, thence south through Arizona and s. New Mexico to Nayarit and San Luis Potosí. To 6000 ft.

Subspecies: UTAH BLACK-HEADED SNAKE, *T. p. utahensis* (Plate 35). Black cap extends usually less than 2 scales posterior to parietals and on side of head fails to reach corner of mouth; light collar rare. Ventrals in males 153–165, in females 162–174; combined ventral and caudal counts usually more than 220, average approximately 225. Distribution spotty. Some localities are Saline Valley and Panamint Mts., Inyo Co., and Kingston Range (Horse Spring), San Bernardino Co., California; western edge of Yucca Flat, Nye Co., and Charleston Mts., Clark Co., Nevada; Topeats Creek, North Rim of Grand Canyon, Coconino Co., Arizona; a number of localities in s. Utah; Colorado Nat'l Monument, Mesa Co., Colorado. Individuals from in and near Sequoia Nat'l Park, California, may have reached the western slope of s. Sierra Nevada via mountain passes. Some of these localities are Flume Truck Trail and middle Fork of the Kaweah River, ½ mi. above Ash Mt. Headquarters, Sequoia Nat'l Park and Springville, Tulare Co. MEXICAN BLACK-HEADED SNAKE, *T. p. atriceps* (Plate 35). Similar to preceding but ventrals in males 135–151, in females 145–160; ventral-caudal counts usually less than 220, average approximately 207. Isolated population in vicinity of Organ Pipe Cactus Nat'l Monument — Estes Canyon, east base of Ajo Mts. on Ajo Mt. Drive, Pima Co., Arizona. CALIFORNIA BLACK-HEADED SNAKE, *T. p. eiseni* (Plate 35). Black cap extends posterior to parietals and laterally on side of head to or below corner of mouth; light collar usually present. Ventrals in males 163–175, in females 167–185; ventral-caudal counts usually less than 245; cap 1½ to 2½ scales posterior to parietal. Individuals from 10 mi. east and 1 mi. south of McFarland, Fresno Co., and Tehachapi Pass, 5 mi. west of Mojave, Kern Co., appear to be intergrades with *utahensis*. DESERT BLACK-HEADED SNAKE, *T. p. transmontana*. Black cap and collar as in California Black-headed Snake. Largest number of ventrals in species — males 175–185, females 187–198; ventral-caudal counts usually 245 or more; head cap extends 1½ to 2¼ scales posterior to parietals. Distribution very spotty. Some localities are: (in Riverside Co.) Palm Springs, $2\frac{3}{10}$ mi. north of Whitewater, 1½ mi. west of Cabazon, Snow Creek, Long Canyon in Joshua Tree Nat'l Monument; and (in San Diego Co.) La Puerta in Mason Valley, ½ mi. east of Borrego Junction, Sentenac Canyon, The Narrows, Yaqui Well. YAQUIA BLACK-HEADED SNAKE *T. p. yaquia* (Plate 35). Black cap and collar as in California Black-headed Snake. Ventrals less than 160; ventral-caudal counts less than 225; cap extends 2½ to 3 scales posterior to parietals. Arizona localities are 2½ mi. southeast of Pena Blanca Springs, Santa Cruz Co., and Tombstone and vicinity of Bisbee, Cochise Co.   Map 173

PLAINS BLACK-HEADED SNAKE *Tantilla nigriceps* **Pl. 35**
Identification: 7–18. *Black or gray-brown cap usually pointed behind, extending 3 to 5 scale lengths behind parietals. Usually without a white collar.* Dorsum brown with yellowish or grayish cast. Below whitish with pink or orange longitudinal stripe on the belly, fading on the throat. Scales smooth. Anal divided.

A secretive snake of shortgrass prairie, brushland, and woodland, where it is found under rocks, boards, and other objects by day and occasionally in the open at night. Look under flat rocks on hillsides, especially when the soil is damp.
Similar species: See Western Black-headed Snake.

Range: Sw. Nebraska south into Mexico; se. Arizona (Thatcher, Graham Co.) to cent. Texas. To 5000 ft.

Subspecies: The PLAINS BLACK-HEADED SNAKE, *T. n. nigriceps*, occurs in our area.   Map 174

HUACHUCA BLACK-HEADED SNAKE   Pl. 35
Tantilla wilcoxi

Identification: 7–14. The black cap is bordered by a *broad white collar that crosses the tips of the parietals* and contrasts with the head color. Collar bordered with black. Cap extends on side of head to corner of mouth. Above brown, with spots on the sides. Scales smooth. Anal divided.

Found under rocks, logs, dead plants (agave, yucca, and sotol) in shaded rocky canyons and on relatively open, sunny, rocky slopes in desert-grassland and evergreen woodland. In our area it is an extremely rare snake.

Similar species: The broad white collar crossing the tips of the parietals will distinguish it from all our other *Tantilla* species.

Range: Huachuca (Ramsey Canyon) and Patagonia Mts., Arizona, south to San Luis Potosí. From 3000 to 5000 ft.

Subspecies: The HUACHUCA BLACK-HEADED SNAKE, *T. w. wilcoxi*, occurs in our area.   Map 172

VINE SNAKE *Oxybelis aeneus*   Pl. 34

Identification: 40–60. An extremely slender snake, *vinelike in shape and color*. Head long, snout elongate and pointed. Above ash-gray to grayish brown, grading to yellowish brown anteriorly. Venter gray grading through whitish to yellow on underside of head. Lips yellowish, unmarked. A black eye-stripe. Scales smooth, in 17 rows at midbody. Anal divided.

In our area, a rare snake. Chiefly an inhabitant of brush-covered hillsides and stream bottoms grown to sycamore, oak, walnut, and wild grape. A well-camouflaged climber that feeds on lizards, which it catches among vegetation and on the ground, subduing them by injecting venom with enlarged grooved teeth toward back of the upper jaw. Look closely at vinelike objects in brush tangles and treetops. Hunt for these snakes in the morning or late afternoon when lizards are basking.

Range: Pajarito Mts. of extreme s. Arizona (known only from within 5 mi. of Mexican boundary) to Brazil. To at least 4000 ft.

Subspecies: The MEXICAN VINE SNAKE, *O. a. auratus*, occurs in our area.   Map 140

CALIFORNIA LYRE SNAKE *Trimorphodon vandenburghi*

Identification: 24–43. Resembles the Sonora Lyre Snake (Plate 33). A "cat-eyed" snake; *pupils vertical.* The head is broad and the neck slender. The common name comes from a lyre-shaped mark on top of the head. Twenty-eight to 43 (average 35) brown blotches on the back, excluding the tail, roughly hexagonal in shape and split by a pale crossbar. Ground color above light brown to pale gray. Belly cream or pale yellow, often with scattered brown dots. Scales smooth, in 21 to 24 rows at midbody. Anal single or divided. *Young:* Around 8 or 9 in.

A rock-dwelling snake of mesas and lower mountain slopes. Occurs at scattered localities in the desert and on both the coastal and desert side of the mountains of s. California. Usually frequents massive rocks, hiding by day in deep crevices and emerging at night. Feeds on lizards (Granite Night Lizard, Granite Spiny Lizard, and others) and small mammals, including bats, which are caught at their roosts and immobilized with venom injected by enlarged grooved teeth toward back of upper jaw. Little is known about the effect of the venom on man. To find this snake, remove large cap rocks and search roads in rocky areas at night.

Similar species: (1) Sonora and (2) Texas Lyre Snakes usually have fewer blotches, and the anal is usually divided. (3) Gopher (p. 156) and (4) Glossy (p. 155) Snakes have round pupils and a broad neck. (5) See also Night Snake.

Range: Desert slope of mts. of s. California to coast from Tehachapi Mts. into nw. Baja California. Desert outpost in Funeral Mts., Inyo Co., California. Sea level to around 3000 ft. Map 177

SONORA LYRE SNAKE *Trimorphodon lambda* Pl. 33

Identification: 24–41. A close relative of the California Lyre Snake but with fewer dorsal blotches (34 or less, averaging around 28), usually a divided anal, and a proportionately longer tail. Usually 24 or fewer dorsal scale rows.

Frequents desert, desert-grassland, evergreen woodland, and ponderosa-pine forest, chiefly in rocky canyons and on rocky hillsides. Seldom encountered in open, rockless, or treeless terrain. A good climber, ascending trees and entering rock crevices. Feeds on small mammals and lizards.

Similar species: (1) See California Lyre Snake. (2) Blotched young of Green Rat Snake (p. 154) distinguished by round pupils and 25 or more dorsal scale rows at midbody.

Range: Sw. Utah and s. Nevada south to Nayarit and cent. and s. Baja California; se. California to extreme sw. New Mexico. To 7400 ft. May hybridize with the Texas Lyre Snake in sw. New Mexico. Thus assignment of specimens to species in this region is uncertain. Localities for lyre snakes in sw. New Mexico are 2 mi. southeast of Glenwood, Catron Co., 9½ mi. west and 42 mi. south of Animas, Hidalgo Co., and east side of Tres Hermanas Mts., 26 mi. south and 4 mi. east of Deming, Luna Co.

Subspecies: The SONORA LYRE SNAKE, *T. l. lambda*, occurs in our area. Map 178

TEXAS LYRE SNAKE   *Trimorphodon vilkinsoni*
Identification: 24–40. Resembles the California and Sonora
(Plate 33) Lyre Snakes, but the lyre mark is faint, the body
blotches are widely spaced, fewer, narrower, and with faint
crossbars. Blotches, excluding those on the tail, usually fewer
than 23 (usually more than 22 in the other species). Usually 24
or fewer dorsal scale rows.
Similar species: (1) Trans-Pecos Rat Snake (p. 154) has round
pupils, 31 or more dorsal scale rows at midbody, and H-shaped
markings on its back. See also (2) California and (3) Sonora
Lyre Snakes.
Range: S. New Mexico and extreme w. Texas into Mexico. In
New Mexico it has been found chiefly in mts. on east side of the
Rio Grande north to Elephant Butte.   Map 178

NIGHT SNAKE   *Hypsiglena torquata*   **Pl. 33**
Identification: 12–26. A gray or beige snake with dark gray or
brown spots and usually a pair of *large dark brown blotches on the
neck.* There is considerable variation in the neck markings (see
Subspecies). The blotches may be connected, occasionally
absent, and sometimes in a group of 3. A black or dark brown
bar behind the eye contrasts with whitish upper labials. Belly
yellowish or white, without pattern. Head flat; *pupils vertical.*
Scales smooth. Anal divided. *Young:* About 5 to 6 in.
     Frequents a variety of habitats — plains, chaparral, sage-
brush flats, deserts, and woodland from near sea level to the
lower slopes of mountains. Occurs in both rocky and sandy
areas. A nocturnal prowler that feeds largely on frogs and
lizards, which it subdues by injecting venom with enlarged
grooved teeth toward the back of the upper jaw. Look in
crevices and under rocks, boards, dead branches of Joshua trees,
mesquite, saguaro, and other surface litter. Sometimes found
on highways at night.
Similar species: (1) Lyre snakes have pale crossbars within
hexagonal blotches on the body and a lyre-shaped mark on the
head. (2) Glossy Snake (p. 155) has a single anal and rounded
pupils. (3) Young Racers, which are blotched, have round
pupils and wedged lower preocular (p. 148).
Range: N. California, s.-cent. Washington, n. Utah, sw. Kansas
to tip of Baja California and Costa Rica; east to e. Texas.
Old record for Pueblo, Pueblo Co., Colorado. Sea level to
around 7000 ft.
Subspecies: CALIFORNIA NIGHT SNAKE, *H. t. nuchalata.*
Usually 19 scale rows at 100th ventral; upper labials usually 7.
MESA VERDE NIGHT SNAKE, *H. t. loreala.* This and fol-
lowing subspecies usually have 21 scale rows and 8 upper labials.
Two loreals. SPOTTED NIGHT SNAKE, *H. t. ochrorhyncha.*
One loreal; 2 spots or narrow band on neck. SAN DIEGO

NIGHT SNAKE, *H. t. klauberi.* Loreal as above but usually 3 large spots on neck, the median spot not contacting the parietals. TEXAS NIGHT SNAKE, *H. t. texana.* One loreal and 3 spots on neck but median spot elongate, contacting parietals, and nearly same width throughout. DESERT NIGHT SNAKE, *H. t. deserticola.* Resembles Texas Night Snake but median neck spot greatly expanded posteriorly.

Map 175

Coral Snakes: Family Elapidae

VENOMOUS serpents with immovable, hollow fangs in the front of the mouth. Old World representatives of the family occur in Africa, Asia, Malay Archipelago, and Australia and include the cobras, kraits, mambas, and most of the snakes of Australia, notably the deadly Taipan and Tiger Snake. New World representatives, the coral snakes, are usually gaudily ringed with red, black, and yellow, and are particularly abundant in Cent. and S. America. Only 2 coral snakes reach the U.S. Although they seldom bite, their venom is highly dangerous, and they should not be handled. Among our harmless snakes the red-banded kingsnakes and shovel-nosed and Banded Sand Snakes have a color pattern resembling that of the coral snakes. Differences between these western "mimics" and the Arizona Coral Snake are pointed out in the accounts of these species.

ARIZONA CORAL SNAKE *Micruroides euryxanthus* **Pl. 31**
   Identification: 15–21. A strikingly colored snake with broad, *alternating rings of red and black separated by narrower rings of white or yellow.* The markings encircle the body, becoming paler on the belly. Head black to behind the eyes. A broad white or yellow band at the back of the head extends across the tips of the parietals. Snout blunt; head and body somewhat flattened. Scales smooth and glossy, in 15 rows at midbody; no loreal; anal divided.
   An inhabitant of arid and semiarid regions in a variety of habitats, including thorn scrub, brushland, woodland, grassland, and farmland. Occurs both on the plains and lower mountain slopes, often among rocks. In Arizona it is most abundant in rocky upland desert where there is a variety of soil types, including loose sand and rocks. A secretive species abroad chiefly at night but sometimes encountered in the daytime on overcast days or after rains. Spends much time underground. The flattened shape suggests crevice-dwelling habits. When disturbed the head may be hidden under coils, the tail elevated and waved with the tip in a tight coil, and the vent lining everted with a popping sound. Venom highly dangerous.

Similar species: (1) Red-banded kingsnakes (pp. 158–61) have the red bands bordered by black. (2) Shovel-nosed (pp. 176–78) and (3) Banded Sand Snakes (p. 178) have pale snouts.

Range: Cent. Arizona and sw. New Mexico to s. Sinaloa. Sea level to 5800 ft.

Subspecies: The ARIZONA CORAL SNAKE, *M. e. euryxanthus*, occurs in our area.   Map 176

Vipers: Family Viperidae

Pit Vipers: Subfamily Crotalinae

RATTLESNAKES, cottonmouths, and the Copperhead — all venomous serpents — are members of this subfamily, but only the rattlesnakes reach our area. The family has the most highly developed venom injection mechanism among snakes. Large, hollow, movable fangs are located at the front of the upper jaw. In biting, they are swung forward from their folded position of rest and the victim is stabbed and poisoned in a rapid thrust. Pit vipers range from s. Canada to Argentina and in the Old World in e. Europe and Asia. They are closely related to the Old World "true vipers" (Subfamily Viperinae) and probably were derived from them; hence their inclusion in the same family. True vipers occur in Eurasia and Africa. Among pit vipers the loreal pit is distinctive, a temperature-sensitive structure on each side of the face between the eye and the nostril, by means of which they can sense the location of their prey.

Rattlesnakes: Genera *Sistrurus* and *Crotalus*

SOME 30 species from s. Canada to n. Argentina, the greatest number in sw. U.S. and n. Mexico. Twelve species in our area, one of which is a Ground Rattlesnake (*Sistrurus*), readily distinguished by its enlarged head scales. Rattlesnakes frequent a great variety of habitats from sea level to around 11,000 ft.

These are heavy-bodied, dangerously venomous snakes with a slender neck, broad triangular head, keeled scales, and single caudals at the base of the tail. The rattle, a series of loosely interlocking horny segments at the end of the tail, is found in no other serpents. A segment is added at the base each time the snake sheds. A young snake may add 3 or 4 segments a year, but an old snake only 1 or none. Recently born young have a blunt horny button at the tip of the tail that persists until broken off. All other western snakes except the boas have a slender tapered tail. Boas have no button and the neck is nearly as broad as the head.

Rattlers are often heard before they are seen. When alarmed

they may make a sound resembling a sudden burst of steam, but when only slightly disturbed may merely click the rattle. Volume and quality of the sound vary with age, size, and species. The rattling of the little Twin-spotted Rattler resembles the sound made by some kinds of cicadas. Occasionally a harmless snake vibrates its tail among dry leaves and produces a sound resembling that of a rattler and may broaden its head, hiss, and strike in a threatening manner. If a rattlesnake is heard, stand still until it is located; avoid jumping and running blindly. Treat a dead one with care. People have been bitten by reflex action of the jaws, even of badly mangled specimens.

Small mammals and birds are the chief foods but lizards and frogs are also eaten. Live-bearing.

MASSASAUGA *Sistrurus catenatus*   **Pl. 39**

Identification: 18–40. A row of large rounded dark brown spots down middle of back; 3 rows of smaller, usually fainter, alternating spots on the sides. *Elongate dark brown markings on the head extend onto the neck,* sometimes forming a lyre mark. Ground color of dorsum gray or grayish brown. Belly pale, in the West largely unmarked. Occasional melanistic individuals may be generally dark above and below. *Large plates on top of the head. Young:* 6–10. Ground color paler and pattern more conspicuous than in the adult. Yellowish-white tail.

The "swamp rattler" of e. U.S., an inhabitant of river bottoms, wet prairies, swamps, and bogs, but also enters dry woodland. In the West it occurs in desert grassland, particularly in low areas of rank growth — in the Rio Grande Valley in low plains of mesquite, juniper, and grassland and in se. Arizona in yucca grassland. Live-bearing.

Similar species: The enlarged head scales and elongate head markings will distinguish it from our other rattlers.

Range: Cent. New York and s. Ontario to extreme se. Arizona and Gulf Coast of Texas. The population in Kiowa and adjacent counties in Colorado is apparently isolated and intermediate in characteristics between *S. c. edwardsi* and the subspecies to the east. Sea level to 5000 ft.

Subspecies: The DESERT MASSASAUGA, *S. c. edwardsi,* occurs in our area.   Map 179

WESTERN DIAMONDBACK RATTLESNAKE   **Pl. 38**
Crotalus atrox

Identification: 30–89. The largest western rattlesnake. Above gray, brown, or pink with brown diamond or hexagonal blotches on the back and fainter smaller blotches on the sides. *Markings often indefinite and peppered with small dark spots,* giving an overall speckled or dusty appearance. Tail set off from the rest of the body by broad black and white rings, about equal in width; hence sometimes called the "coontail" rattler. A light diagonal stripe behind the eye intersects the upper lip well in front of the corner of the mouth. *Young:* 9–14. Markings more distinct than in adult.

Frequents a variety of habitats in arid and semiarid regions from the plains into the mountains — desert, grassland, brushland, woodland, rank growth of river bottoms, rocky canyons, and lower mountain slopes. Crepuscular and nocturnal, but also abroad in daytime. Perhaps the most dangerous North American serpent, often holding ground and boldly defending itself when disturbed. Live-bearing.

Similar species: (1) Red Diamond Rattlesnake is reddish, has a less definite pattern, and the 1st lower labial is divided transversely. (2) Mojave Rattlesnake has narrow black tail rings and the white stripe behind the eye extends behind the corner of the mouth. (3) Speckled Rattlesnake has salt-and-pepper markings, the prenasals are usually separated from the rostral by small scales or the supraoculars are pitted, deeply furrowed, or have broken outer edges.

Range: Se. California to e. Oklahoma and e. Texas, south to Isthmus of Tehauantepec. Old records for cent. Arkansas and Trinidad, Las Animas Co., Colorado. Sea level to 7000 ft.

Map 186

RED DIAMOND RATTLESNAKE *Crotalus ruber*   **Pl. 38**
Identification: 30–65. A tan, pink, or reddish relative of the Western Diamondback. Dorsal diamonds usually less well defined and without or with only faint pepper marks. Conspicuous "coontail," the broad black and white rings contrasting with the rest of the body color. *First pair of lower labials usually divided transversely. Young:* About 9 to 13 in. at birth, dark gray at first but changing to reddish brown.

In our area, found only in extreme sw. California, where it frequents rocky brushlands on both the coastal and desert sides of the mountains. Also occasionally found in grassland and cultivated areas. Absent from higher elevations. On the desert slope, occurs in areas of mesquite and cactus on the rocky alluvial fans near the base of the mountains. A milder snake than the Western Diamondback, less prone to stand ground, and with a weaker, but still dangerous venom. Live-bearing.

Similar species: See Western Diamondback Rattlesnake.

Range: Sw. California from Morongo Pass, San Bernardino Co., to tip of Baja California. Sea level to 5000 ft.

Subspecies: The RED DIAMOND RATTLESNAKE, *C. r. ruber*, occurs in our area.   Map 188

ROCK RATTLESNAKE *Crotalus lepidus*   **Pl. 39**
Identification: 15–30. *Dorsum marked with widely and regularly*

spaced narrow black or dark brown crossbands, which sometimes become faint anteriorly. The bands are bordered with light color and are irregular in outline. The general tone of the dorsum varies greatly — pale gray, bluish gray, greenish gray, or tan, sometimes heavily speckled with dusky. Tail yellowish brown or salmon, with dark crossbands. Upper preocular split vertically. *Young:* 7–9. In the Banded Rock Rattlesnake the tail is bright yellow at the tip.

Chiefly a mountain rock dweller that frequents rocky ridges, hillsides, and gorges in arid and semiarid habitats but may occur in the lowlands. Ranges from desert grassland to the lower edge of the ponderosa pine forest. Often found in the vicinity of permanent or intermittent streams. Basks among rocks on rather barren ridges or in open areas in woods. Live-bearing.

Range: Se. Arizona, s. New Mexico, and w. Texas, south to Jalisco. From around 1000 to 9600 ft.

Subspecies: MOTTLED ROCK RATTLESNAKE, *C. l. lepidus.* Overall dusky appearance. Considerable dark spotting between the dark body bands, sometimes forming additional bands between the primary ones. In our area known only from Guadalupe Mts. of s. New Mexico. BANDED ROCK RATTLESNAKE, *C. l. klauberi.* Dark body bands conspicuous, contrasting strongly with the ground color. Interspaces moderately dark-spotted. Mts. of sw. New Mexico and se. Arizona (Santa Rita, Dragoon, Huachuca, and Chiricahua). Map 183

SPECKLED RATTLESNAKE *Crotalus mitchelli* **Pl. 38**
Identification: 24–52. The color of the dorsum varies — cream, gray, yellowish, tan, pink, or brown, and usually harmonizes with background. The rough scales and salt-and-pepper speckling suggest decomposed granite. The markings, which are sometimes vague, usually consist of bands, but may be hexagonal, hourglass- or diamond-shaped. Dark rings on the tail. *Prenasals usually separated from rostral by small scales or supraoculars pitted, creased, or with rough outer edges. Young:* 8–12.

Over much of its range it dwells among rocks in the mountains, but in coastal s. California and Baja California it ranges to sea level. Found on barren rocky buttes, in open brushland, piñon-juniper woodland, and occasionally in sandy areas. An alert, nervous snake often holding its ground when cornered. Live-bearing.

Similar species: (1) Western Diamondback Rattlesnake has "coontail" markings, lacks pitted and creased supraoculars and small scales between the prenasals and rostral. (2) Mojave Rattlesnake has enlarged scales between the supraoculars and a well-defined dorsal pattern (3) See also Tiger Rattlesnake.

Range: S. Nevada to tip of Baja California; s. California to cent. Arizona. Sea level to 8000 ft.

Subspecies: SOUTHWESTERN SPECKLED RATTLE-SNAKE, *C. m. pyrrhus* (Fig. 25, opposite Pl. 38). Small scales usually separate the prenasals from the rostral. Supraoculars unmodified. PANAMINT RATTLESNAKE, *C. m. stephensi* (Fig. 25). No small scales between the prenasals and rostral. Supraoculars often pitted, furrowed, or the outer edges irregular.
Map 189

SIDEWINDER *Crotalus cerastes*   **Pl. 38**
   Identification: 17–31. The sidewise locomotion, with the body moving in an S-shaped curve, is characteristic. Dorsum generally pale, harmonizing with background — cream, tan, pink, or gray, without conspicuous pattern. *Supraoculars hornlike*, pointed, and turned upward, hence sometimes called the "horned rattler." *Male:* Averages smaller than female. *Young:* 6½–8.
   A desert species, usually found in areas of fine windblown sand in the vicinity of rodent burrows (kangaroo rats, etc.). Most common where there are sand hummocks topped with creosote bushes, mesquite, or other desert plants, but it may also occur on windswept flats, barren dunes, hardpan, and rocky hillsides. Sidewinding is a rapid form of locomotion and appears to be best suited to openness of terrain where broadside movements are unobstructed by rocks and vegetation. It also minimizes slippage on loose soil and permits crawling over warm surfaces with little danger of overheating because of the greatly reduced contact between the snake's body and the ground. Most easily found by tracking or night driving in sandy areas. The track often shows impressions of the belly scutes and consists of a series of parallel J-shaped marks with the hook of the *J* pointing in the direction of travel. Chiefly nocturnal, hiding by day in animal burrows or coiled in a shallow pit at the base of a bush. A quick, agile snake that moves with surprising speed. Live-bearing.
   Range: S. Nevada and extreme sw. Utah into ne. Baja California and w.-cent. Sonora; desert base of mts. of s. California to s.-cent. Arizona. Below sea level to 6000 ft., but mostly below 4000 ft. **Subspecies:** MOJAVE DESERT SIDEWINDER, *C. c. cerastes*. Basal segment of rattle brown in adult; dorsal scale rows at midbody usually 21. SONORA SIDEWINDER, *C. c. cercobombus*. Similar to Mojave Desert Sidewinder but basal segment of rattle black in adult. COLORADO DESERT SIDEWINDER, *C. c. laterorepens*. Basal segment of rattle black in adult; scales at midbody usually 23.   Map 187

BLACK-TAILED RATTLESNAKE *Crotalus molossus*   **Pl. 39**
   Identification: 28–51. *Tail and sometimes the snout black*, contrasting with the rest of the body. Dorsum with black or brown crossbands of irregular outline, edged with whitish and with

central patches of light scales. Anterior dark markings sometimes diamond-shaped. Scales in pattern areas usually one color
or another, not partly dark and light. Ground color above
yellow, grayish, olive, or greenish. Enlarged scales on the upper
surface of snout. *Young:* 10–12.

Over much of its range it is a mountain snake inhabiting
rockslides, outcrops, the vicinity of cliffs, and rocky stream
courses. Avoids barren desert. Ranges from the paloverde,
cactus, thornbush association into the pine-oak belt. Abroad
both day and night; especially active following warm rains.
Usually unaggressive. Live-bearing.

Range: N. Arizona to southern edge of Mexican plateau; w.
Arizona (Castle Dome Mts.) to Edwards Plateau of cent. Texas.
Sea level to 9500 ft.

Subspecies: The NORTHERN BLACK-TAILED RATTLE-
SNAKE, *C. m. molossus*, occurs in our area.   Map 181

TIGER RATTLESNAKE *Crotalus tigris*   **Pl. 39**
Identification: 18–36. Dorsum with irregular crossbands ("tiger"
markings) of dark gray or brown, composed of dark dots and
often with vague borders. In general *more distinctly crossbanded
than other western rattlesnakes*. Head small, rattle large. Ground
color gray, bluish gray, pink, lavender, or buff, becoming pale
orange or cream on the sides. Tail rings usually indistinct
because of darkening of the light rings. *Young:* Around 9 in.

Largely restricted to rocky canyons and foothills of desert
mountain ranges, where it occurs in arid environments of cactus,
mesquite, and creosote bush on the lower slopes up into the oak
belt. Active both day and night; often abroad after warm rains.
Live-bearing.

Similar species: (1) Speckled Rattlesnake, with which it overlaps in range, has small scales between the rostral and prenasals.
(2) Western Rattlesnake has dark dorsal blotches anteriorly
rather than crossbands.

Range: Cent. and s. Arizona to s. Sonora. Sea level to 4800 ft.
                                                    Map 182

WESTERN RATTLESNAKE *Crotalus viridis*   **Pl. 38**
Identification: 15–62. A blotched rattlesnake with a light stripe
behind the eye extending behind the corner of the mouth.
Blotches brown or black, usually with light-colored edges,
giving way posteriorly to crossbands. The general coloration
varies greatly over the wide range of this snake — cream, yellowish, gray, pink, greenish, brown, or black, often harmonizing
with the surroundings. Tail with dark and light rings but not
sharply contrasting with the body color. *Our only rattlesnake
with usually more than 2 internasals in contact with the rostral.*
Young: 6–12.

Frequents a great variety of habitats, from brush-covered coastal sand dunes to timberline and from midwestern prairies to mountain forests of the Pacific Coast. Inhabits grassland, brushland, woodland, and forest, but avoids the desert. Rock outcrops, talus, rocky stream courses, and ledges are favorite haunts and in more northerly areas and at high altitudes it may den in rock crevices or caves in large numbers. Live-bearing.

Similar species: The presence of more than 2 internasals in contact with the rostral generally will distinguish this rattler from all others.

Range: Extreme sw. Canada to cent. Baja California and n. Coahuila; Pacific Coast to w. Iowa and cent. Kansas. Absent from deserts and habitats above 11,000 ft. Sea level to around 11,000 ft.

Subspecies: PRAIRIE RATTLESNAKE, *C. v. viridis*. Above usually with greenish cast, occasionally brown. Blotches brown, usually well defined (see Fig. 26, opposite Pl. 38). GRAND CANYON RATTLESNAKE, *C. v. abyssus*. Above red or salmon; body blotches often faint in adults. Found within the walls of Grand Canyon, Arizona. ARIZONA BLACK RATTLESNAKE, *C. v. cerberus*. Above dark gray, olive, brown, or black; large dark brown or black blotches; lateral blotches conspicuous. Some individuals nearly solid black; usually 2 loreals. Mts. of Arizona and extreme w. New Mexico. MIDGET FADED RATTLESNAKE, *C. v. concolor*. Above cream or yellowish; blotches of adults often faint or absent. Rarely more than 24 in. total length. SOUTHERN PACIFIC RATTLESNAKE, *C. v. helleri*. Resembles the Arizona Black Rattler but ground color usually lighter and loreal single. Last dark tail ring about twice as wide as the others and poorly defined. Young with bright yellow tail. NORTHERN PACIFIC RATTLESNAKE, *C. v. oreganus*. Resembles the Southern Pacific Rattler but dark tail rings well defined and of uniform width. Young with bright yellow tail. GREAT BASIN RATTLESNAKE, *C. v. lutosus*. Above usually buff or drab, with brown blotches occupying about the same longitudinal distance as the interspaces. HOPI RATTLESNAKE, *C. v. nuntius*. Above pink, red, or reddish brown. Adult rarely over 24 in. total length. The rattler commonly used in the Hopi Indian snake dance.   Map 185

MOJAVE RATTLESNAKE *Crotalus scutulatus*   **Pl. 38**
Identification: 24–51. Well-defined light-edged diamonds or hexagons down middle of the back, the light scales of the pattern usually unmarked, entirely light-colored. Ground color greenish gray, olive-green, or occasionally brownish or yellowish. A white to yellowish stripe from behind the eye to behind the corner of the mouth. Tail with contrasting light and dark rings,

the *dark rings narrower than the light rings. Enlarged scales on snout and between the supraoculars. Young:* Around 9 to 11 in.

Chiefly a snake of high desert and lower mountain slopes, but it ranges to about sea level near the mouth of the Colorado River and to high elevation in the Sierra Madre Occidental. Habitats vary — barren desert, grassland, and brushland; it seems to be most common in areas of scattered scrubby growth such as creosote bush and mesquite. Not common in broken rocky terrain or where vegetation is dense. Live-bearing.

Similar species: See (1) Western Diamondback, (2) Western, and (3) Speckled Rattlesnakes.

Range: S. Nevada to Puebla, near s. edge of Mexican plateau; western edge of Mojave Desert, California, to extreme w. Texas. From near sea level to 8000 ft.

Subspecies: The MOJAVE RATTLESNAKE, *C. s. scutulatus,* occurs in our area.   Map 190

TWIN-SPOTTED RATTLESNAKE *Crotalus pricei*   **Pl. 39**
Identification: 12–26. A small, slender, grayish-brown, or gray rattlesnake with *2 rows of brown spots on its back,* alternating or arranged in pairs and sometimes joined to form transverse blotches. Smaller spots on sides. Fine brown speckling over the dorsum. Tail with distinct brown bands. Throat sometimes salmon. *Young:* 6½–7.

A high-mountain rock dweller of pine-oak woodland and coniferous forest. Its activity is restricted by low night temperatures and thunder showers, but it may be abroad during warm rains. Search well-illuminated rocky slopes on sunny mornings when the snakes are basking or searching for lizards and small mammals. Well camouflaged. Hidden individuals can sometimes be made to rattle by tossing rocks into talus. The sound is weak, resembling a locust or beetle buzzing among leaves. Usually a mild-tempered snake. Live-bearing.

Range: Se. Arizona (Graham, Dos Cabezas, Santa Rita, Huachuca, and Chiricahua Mts.) south in Sierra Madre Occidental to s. Durango; isolated populations in ne. Mexico. From 6300 to above 10,000 ft.

Subspecies: The TWIN-SPOTTED RATTLESNAKE, *C. p. pricei,* occurs in our area.   Map 180

RIDGE-NOSED RATTLESNAKE *Crotalus willardi*   **Pl. 39**
Identification: 15–24. Dorsum reddish, brown, or gray, marked above with *crossbars of whitish, edged with dark brown or black, which merge with color of the sides.* A prominent ridge follows the contour of the snout, as viewed from above. Snout with or without a vertical white stripe. Tail rings usually confined to anterior portion of tail. *Young:* 6½–7½.

A high-mountain snake of the pine-oak and pine-fir belts. May be found basking on well-illuminated rocky slopes in moist woodland and forest or crawling over the forest floor. Frequents canyon bottoms grown to alder, box elder, maple, oak, and other broadleaf deciduous trees. Live-bearing.

Range: Se. Arizona and sw. New Mexico to Durango and Zacatecas. From around 5600 to 9000 ft.

Subspecies: ARIZONA RIDGE-NOSED RATTLESNAKE, *C. w. willardi.* A white vertical line on the rostral and mental. Huachuca (Ramsey and Carr Canyons) and Santa Rita Mts., Arizona. CHIHUAHUAN RIDGE-NOSED RATTLESNAKE, *C. w. silus.* No vertical white line on rostral or mental. In the U.S. known only from upper end of Indian Creek Canyon, Animas Mts., New Mexico, between 6800 and 7000 ft., in pine, oak, and juniper forest.   Map 184

XI

Amphibian Eggs and Larvae

MOST OF the eggs and larvae of western amphibians are illustrated here in Figures 33–39. Omitted species are those that have not been described or are poorly known. Descriptions of some species are brief and not fully diagnostic because of inadequate information. Refer to information on distribution (see maps), habitat, and breeding sites under the main species entries to be found in Chapters VI–X. See page 23 for help in using these keys, which differ only in minor details from the keys in Chapter V.

In making identifications, examine the mouthparts of tadpoles and the gelatinous envelopes of eggs under magnification. Tooth rows are expressed as a fraction — $\frac{2}{3}$, $\frac{3}{4}$, etc. The numerator is the number of rows in the upper labium; the denominator, the number of rows in the lower labium. In examining specimens immerse them in shallow water to eliminate distracting highlights. Color patterns may also be enhanced in this way. A dissecting microscope usually will be required for studying egg capsules.

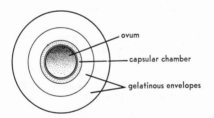

Fig. 30. Amphibian egg

Eggs should be immersed and viewed with transmitted light. To count gill rakers in salamander larvae, enlarge the gill openings of preserved specimens by snipping the tissues between the gill arches. All measurements of salamander larvae and tadpoles are of total length. The keys to eggs and larvae apply only to western species.

Caution: Amphibian eggs and larvae may quickly succumb if overheated. Keep them cool if to be studied fresh; otherwise, preserve in 1 part commercial Formalin to 14 parts of water.

KEY TO AMPHIBIAN EGGS
(see Fig. 30 for explanation of terms)
See Figs. 33 and 34 (pp. 208–209).

1A. Ovum uniformly white or cream, unpigmented   2
1B. Upper surface or entire ovum pigmented olive, brown,
    or black   5

2A. Eggs arranged like string of beads, connected by slender
    strands of jelly; found in cold streams   **Tailed Frog**
2B. Eggs not connected like string of beads, or, if so, found
    on land   3

3A. Each egg suspended by a single slender jelly strand (Fig.
    33, 13–15) or in rosary-like string (Fig. 33, 12); eggs
    may become separated and bear a slender jelly strand
    at one or both ends (Fig. 33, 12)   4
3B. Eggs attached by very short jelly strands or broadly
    adherent to each other or attachment surface (Fig. 33,
    7–11)   **Olympic, Pacific Giant,**
                   Woodland Salamanders, and Ensatina

4A. Eggs suspended by their jelly strands; strands elongate,
    often intertwined (Fig. 33, 13–15)
                              Climbing Salamanders
4B. Eggs more or less connected by their strands, resembling
    a string of beads (Fig. 33, 12)   **Slender Salamanders**

5A. Gelatinous envelope firm, rubberlike; ovum (when fer-
    tilized) moves freely in large capsular chamber (Fig.
    33, 1–4); eggs usually in globular cluster (laid singly in
    Rough-skinned Newt)
               Newts and Northwestern Salamander
5B. Jelly less firm; ovum not in large capsular chamber (Fig.
    34); eggs in rounded clumps, strings, floating rafts, or
    single   6

6A. Eggs in cylindrical strings (Fig. 34, 7, 8, 10–12) or more
    or less connected like string of beads (Fig. 34, 9, 13, 14)
                                           True Toads
6B. Eggs not in strings but in grapelike cluster or single   7

7A. Gelatinous envelope flattened on 1 side (Fig. 34, 3)
                   Great Plains Narrow-mouthed Toad
7B. Gelatinous envelope not flattened   8

8A. Eggs in floating raft, 1 to a few eggs thick
                              Bullfrog and Green Frog

8B. Eggs single or in globular or irregular clusters
Tiger and Long-toed Salamanders, Frogs and Hylids

Eggs of Salamanders

See Fig. 33, p. 208; $\times$ 1¾.

Eggs shown in black have dark pigment on the upper surface
and are usually exposed to sunlight. Those shown in white
are unpigmented and are laid under stones or in
crevices in logs or the ground.

Rough-skinned Newt (*Taricha granulosa*). In this and other newts,
eggs are in firm gelatinous capsules; fertilized egg moves freely
in large capsular chamber. Usually laid singly, attached to
vegetation and other objects in quiet or slowly flowing water.
Map 6

Red-bellied Newt (*Taricha rivularis*). In flattened firm clusters of
about 1-in. diam., often only 1 egg thick, and usually attached
to the undersides of stones in streams.   Map 9

California Newt (*Taricha torosa*). In rounded firm clusters of
about 1 in. diam., attached to sticks, the undersides of stones,
and vegetation, in quiet or flowing water.   Map 8

Northwestern Salamander (*Ambystoma gracile*). In rounded firm
clusters, diam. 2–6 in., individual eggs in large capsular chambers; clusters attached to submerged branches and other firm
supports in ponds, lakes, and slowly flowing streams.   Map 2

Long-toed Salamander (*Ambystoma macrodactylum*). Laid singly
or in clusters of 8 or 10, attached to vegetation or free on bottom
of ponds, lakes, and quiet parts of streams.   Map 3

Tiger Salamander (*Ambystoma tigrinum*). In West usually laid
singly or in small clusters attached to twigs, weeds, and other
objects in ponds, lakes, and quiet parts of streams.   Map 5

Olympic Salamander (*Rhyacotriton olympicus*). Evidently laid
singly, attached to roots and other supports, beneath stones and
other objects in small cold streams and seepages.   Map 4

Pacific Giant Salamander (*Dicamptodon ensatus*). Evidently laid
singly, but close together, attached by short peduncles to objects
in springs and streams; probably deposited underground.
Map 1

Dunn's Salamander (*Plethodon dunni*). In grapelike clusters attached by slender stalk; illustration based on eggs laid in the
laboratory.   Map 12

Western Red-backed Salamander (*Plethodon vehiculum*). In grapelike clusters, attached to sides or roof of hollows in logs and the ground. Eggs of other plethodons unknown or little studied.
Map 11

Ensatina (*Ensatina eschscholtzi*). In grapelike clusters, outer envelopes more or less adherent, deposited in mammal burrows and beneath the bark and in hollows of decayed logs.   Map 10

California Slender Salamander (*Batrachoseps attenuatus*). In clusters, individual eggs connected by slender jelly strands, like string of beads; strands often break and eggs become separated. Under logs, rocks, and other objects on the surface and in hollows in logs or the ground. Eggs and laying sites of other slender salamanders resemble those of the California form.   Map 17

Black Salamander (*Aneides flavipunctatus*). In this and remaining species, eggs in clusters, suspended by intertwined strands united at a common base; attached to the roof and sides of cavities.   Map 23

Arboreal Salamander (*Aneides lugubris*). Suspended beneath objects on the ground and in hollows in trees (coast live oaks, etc.) and the ground.   Map 20

Clouded Salamander (*Aneides ferreus*). In hollows and beneath the bark of logs, especially Douglas fir.   Map 19

Eggs of Frogs and Toads

See Fig. 34, p. 209; × 1⅖.

Eggs shown in black have dark pigment on the upper surface
and are usually exposed to sunlight; those shown in white
are unpigmented. Broken lines indicate indistinct
boundaries between gelatinous envelopes.

Tailed Frog (*Ascaphus truei*). In rosary-like strings arranged in globular clumps and attached to the undersides of stones in cold running water.   Map 28

Western Spadefoot (*Scaphiopus hammondi*). In irregular cylindrical clusters attached to plant stems and other objects in temporary or permanent ponds and quiet parts of streams.
Map 26

Couch's Spadefoot (*Scaphiopus couchi*). Egg resembles Western Spadefoot's, but smaller.   Map 27

Great Plains Narrow-mouthed Toad (*Gastrophryne olivacea*). Laid singly, but often close together in shallow temporary pools or quiet parts of streams; capsules flattened on 1 side.   Map 29

Pacific Treefrog (*Hyla regilla*). In loose irregular clusters attached to plant stems, sticks, or other objects in shallow, quiet water of ponds, lake borders, and streams; 2 envelopes.   Map 44

California Treefrog (*Hyla californiae*). Laid singly, attached to leaves, sticks, rocks, or free on the bottom in quiet water of rocky streams; single envelope.   Map 46

Cricket Frog (*Acris crepitans*). Laid singly and in small clusters attached to leaves, twigs, grass stems or on the bottom in shallow, quiet water of springs, ponds, and streams.   Map 43

Chorus Frog (*Pseudacris triseriata*). In small, loose, irregular clusters, diam. often less than 1 in., attached to vegetation in clear, quiet water of ponds, lakes, and marshy fields.   Map 41

Southwestern Toad (*Bufo microscaphus*). In tangled strings with eggs in 1–3 rows, usually deposited on the bottom in quiet parts of clear streams; single envelope.   Map 33

Western Toad (*Bufo boreas*). In tangled strings with eggs in 1–3 rows, often greatly entwined in vegetation along margins of ponds, reservoirs, and streams; 2 envelopes.   Map 31

Yosemite Toad (*Bufo canorus*). In beadlike strings and clusters, often covered with silt, in the shallows of meadow pools of the Sierra Nevada.   Map 32

Texas Toad (*Bufo speciosus*). In strings coiled about in rain pools, irrigation and cattle tanks, and other quiet water; envelope single, sometimes slightly scalloped.   Map 37

Colorado River Toad (*Bufo alvarius*). In long strings in temporary pools or shallow streams; to be expected after first heavy summer showers; single envelope.   Map 39

Woodhouse's Toad (*Bufo woodhousei*). In strings intertwined about vegetation or debris in almost any type of pool or stream; single envelope.   Map 34

Great Plains Toad (*Bufo cognatus*). In strings attached to vegetation and debris on the bottom of temporary pools, springs, and small streams; 2 envelopes, decidedly scalloped.   Map 36

Red-spotted Toad (*Bufo punctatus*). Laid singly, in short strings, or as loose flat cluster on bottom of small, shallow, often rocky pools.   Map 40

Mountain Yellow-legged Frog (*Rana muscosa*). In somewhat flattened clumps 1–2 in. across, attached to stems of sedge or other vegetation, or to bank itself in ponds, lakes, and streams mostly above 7000 ft. in Sierra Nevada and in streams at lower elevations in mts. or s. California.   Map 54

Foothill Yellow-legged Frog (*Rana boylei*). In a compact grapelike cluster, diam. 2–4 in., deposited in shallow water near margins of clear streams and attached to stones (often on downstream side); may become coated with silt; envelopes firm.   Map 55

Green Frog (*Rana clamitans*). In a floating cluster usually 1 egg thick and less than 1 sq. ft. in area, attached to vegetation or free, usually deposited near the margins of permanent quiet water; 2 envelopes.   Map 52

Bullfrog (*Rana catesbeiana*). Egg resembles Green Frog's, but clusters large, 1–5 ft. across; single envelope.   Map 53

Red-legged Frog (*Rana aurora*). In irregular grapelike clusters, diam. 3–10 in. and jelly loose and viscid, attached to vegetation at or just below surface of lake margins and permanent pools; 3 envelopes.   Map 48

Spotted Frog (*Rana pretiosa*). In clumps, diam. 3–6 in., in shallow water often unattached among grasses at edges of ponds, the top layer of eggs exposed at surface; 1 or 2 envelopes.   Map 50

Wood Frog (*Rana sylvatica*). In firm spherical masses, diam. rarely to 6 in., many often in a small area and in contact; usually in shallow ponds near the surface, occasionally to depths of 2 or 3 ft. attached to vegetation.   Map 47

Cascades Frog (*Rana cascadae*). Egg resembles Red-legged Frog's but clusters usually smaller, deposited in shallow water of pools and lake margins.   Map 49

Leopard Frog (*Rana pipiens*). In globular clusters, attached to vegetation in quiet water of ponds, lake margins, reservoirs, canals, and streams; 2 or 3 envelopes.   Map 51

KEY TO SALAMANDER LARVAE
(see Fig. 31 for explanation of terms)
See Fig. 35, p. 210.

Both front and hind limbs present; external gills.

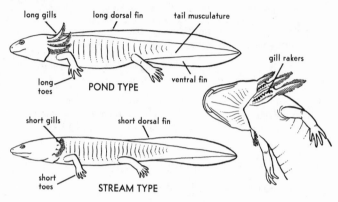

Fig. 31. Salamander larvae

1A. Pond type, usually found in ponds, lakes, or quiet parts
  of streams   3
1B. Stream type, usually found in streams or trickles   2

2A. Prominent light and dark mottling on tail fin; gills short
  but bushy and well developed; eyes small; to over 11 in.
                                Pacific Giant Salamander
2B. Tail fin not colored as in 2A; gills reduced to nubbins;
  eyes large; under 3 in.   **Olympic Salamander**

3A. Head broad and rather flat; eyes set well in from outline
  of head as seen from above; 9–22 gill rakers on anterior
  side of 3rd gill arch   6
3B. Head narrower and less flattened; eyes on or near outline of head as seen from above; 5–7 gill rakers on anterior
  side of 3rd gill arch   4

4A. Dorsal fin does not reach shoulders; dark color rather
  evenly distributed over back and sides; streams of
  Sonoma and Mendocino Co., California; usually under
  2½ in.   **Red-bellied Newt**
4B. Dorsal fin usually reaches shoulders; dark color not
  evenly distributed; usually under 2½ in.   5

5A. 2 irregular black stripes on back, 1 on each side of dorsal
 fin **California Newt**
5B. No black stripes; light spots on sides often arranged in
 longitudinal rows which may join to form light stripes
 Rough-skinned Newt

6A. Rough strip of skin (formed by openings of poison
 glands) along upper side of tail musculature, near base of
 upper fin; similar rough patch behind eyes on each side
 of head; glandular patches in preserved specimens often
 with adherent whitish secretion; to approximately 6 in.
 Northwestern Salamander
6B. No roughened glandular areas 7

7A. 9 to 13 gill rakers on front side of 3rd gill arch; usually
 under 3 in. **Long-toed Salamander**
7B. 15 to 24 gill rakers on front side of 3rd gill arch; to 10 in.
 Tiger Salamander

Salamander Larvae

See Fig. 35, p. 210; relative size not shown.

California Newt (*Taricha torosa*). Pond-type larva; dark dorsolateral stripes; transformation at usually under 2½ in. Map 8

Rough-skinned Newt (*Taricha granulosa*). Pond-type larva; trunk
usually with 2 longitudinal rows of light spots, which may more
or less unite to form a single light stripe; sometimes reaches 3 in.
at transformation. Map 6

Red-bellied Newt (*Taricha rivularis*). Tends toward stream type,
dorsal fin usually failing to reach shoulders; back and sides of
nearly uniform pigmentation; transformation at around 2 in.
Map 9

Olympic Salamander (*Rhyacotriton olympicus*). Stream type; gills
and gill rakers reduced to nubbins; olive or brown above, speckled
with black; may transform at nearly adult size, around 2½ in.
Map 4

Pacific Giant Salamander (*Dicamptodon ensatus*). Stream type;
smoky dark and light mottling on back and fins, light stripe
behind eye; short, bushy, dark red gills; transformation usually
at 6–8 in., but as axolotl may reach 11 in. Map 1

Northwestern Salamander (*Ambystoma gracile*). Pond-type larva;
deep brown, olive-green, or light yellow above, blotched with
sooty and spotted with yellow on sides; glandular strip at base
of tail fin, from which whitish secretion may exude; 7–10 gill

rakers on anterior border of 3rd arch; transformation at 3–6 in.
Map 2

Tiger Salamander (*Ambystoma tigrinum*). Pond-type larva; above usually olive or greenish, mottled with dark brown or black; 17–22 gill rakers on anterior border of 3rd arch; transformation at 3–5 in., but as axolotl may reach 10 in. Map 5

Long-toed Salamander (*Ambystoma macrodactylum*). Pond-type larva; above light olive-gray to brownish gray, mottled with brownish and black; 9–13 gill rakers on 3rd arch; transformation at 2½–4 in. Map 3

KEY TO TADPOLES
(see Fig. 32 for explanation of terms)
See Figs. 36–39 (pp. 211–214).

Forelimbs and gills are concealed.

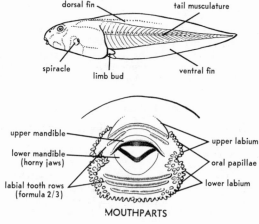

MOUTHPARTS

Fig. 32. Tadpole

1A. No horny jaws or rows of labial teeth
Great Plains Narrow-mouthed Toad
1B. Horny jaws and labial teeth present 2

2A. Large, round suckerlike mouth occupying ⅓ to ½ underside of body **Tailed Frog**
2B. Mouth not greatly enlarged 3

3A. Oral papillae encircle mouth or are interrupted by a very
    small gap in middle of upper labium   **Spadefoot Toads**
3B. Upper labium without oral papillae except at sides;
    middle part of lower labium with or without papillae   **4**

4A. Oral papillae on lower labium confined to sides
    True Toads
4B. Oral papillae present along entire edge of lower labium   **5**

5A. Lip margin indented at sides   **True Frogs**
5B. Lip margin not indented   **Treefrogs and Relatives**

Tailed Frog, Narrow-mouthed and Spadefoot Toads

See Fig. 36, p. 211; × ⅚.

Tailed Frog (*Ascaphus truei*). Large round mouth occupying
nearly ½ ventral surface of body; labial tooth rows $^{2-3}\!\!\frac{}{}\!\!4$-10;
tip of tail often white or rose-colored, set off by dark band; to
2⅓ in.; cold streams.   Map 28

Great Plains Narrow-mouthed Toad (*Gastrophryne olivacea*).
Distinctive mouthparts — upper lip fleshy, notched at midline,
overlying beaklike lower lip; no horny jaws or labial teeth; eyes
widely separated, on lateral outline of head as viewed from
above; under 1½ in.; extr. s. Arizona.   Map 29

Spadefoot Toads (*Scaphiopus*)

Oral papillae encircle mouth (occasionally small gap in middle of
upper labium); labial tooth rows usually $\frac{4}{4}$, $\frac{4}{5}$, or $\frac{5}{5}$; eyes close
together, well inside outline of head as viewed from above.

Plains Spadefoot (*Scaphiopus bombifrons*). Body broadest just
behind eyes, giving "muttonchop" contour; light to medium
gray or brown above; in carnivorous tadpoles upper mandible
beaked, lower mandible notched; to 2¾ in.; often in turbid,
temporary pools.   Map 25

Western Spadefoot (*Scaphiopus hammondi*). Resembles Plains
Spadefoot tadpole, but jaws with less-developed beak and
notch; labial tooth rows usually $\frac{5}{5}$.   Map 26

Couch's Spadefoot (*Scaphiopus couchi*). Smaller and darker than
preceding — dark gray, bronze, to nearly black above; to 1 in.
    Map 27

True Toads (*Bufo*)

See Fig. 37, p. 212; × ⅚.

Tadpoles often small and dark; oral papillae confined to
sides of mouth and indented; labial tooth rows usually ⅔.

Western Toad (*B. boreas*). Body uniformly black, dark brown, or
dark gray, including tail musculature; to around 2 in., but often
much smaller.   Map 31

Yosemite Toad (*B. canorus*). Resembles Western Toad tadpole,
but body and tail musculature darker, snout blunter, and tip of
tail more rounded; to around 1½ in.; Sierra Nevada, California,
usually above 6500 ft.   Map 32

Dakota Toad (*B. hemiophrys*). Resembles Western Toad tadpole.
                                                             Map 35

Red-spotted Toad (*B. punctatus*). Rather coarse spotting on
dorsal fin; upper labium and its tooth rows extend downward
on each side of mouth.   Map 40

Woodhouse's Toad (*B. woodhousei*). Lower part of tail musculature unpigmented; to around 1 in.   Map 34

Southwestern Toad (*B. microscaphus*). Above olive, gray, or tan,
commonly spotted or mottled with blackish to brown; tail
musculature colored like body; below white in life; to around
1½ in.   Map 33

Texas Toad (*B. speciosus*). Tail musculature with irregular, dark-
colored lateral stripe or blotches tending to form a stripe; underside of body light tan to pinkish; extr. se. New Mexico.   Map 37

Treefrogs and Relatives

See Fig. 38, p. 213; × ⅚.

Mouth round, not indented at the sides; middle part of
upper labium without oral papillae; labial tooth rows
usually ⅔.

Pacific Treefrog (*Hyla regilla*). Eyes on lateral outline of head as
viewed from above; intestines not visible; to about 1½ in.
                                                             Map 44

Arizona Treefrog (*Hyla wrightorum*). Resembles Pacific Treefrog tadpole. Map 45

California Treefrog (*Hyla californiae*). Eyes fail to reach lateral outline of head as viewed from above; dorsal surface of tail musculature marked with alternating transverse dark bars (San Gabriel Mts.); intestines visible; $1\frac{3}{4}$ in.; California and Baja California. Map 46

Canyon Treefrog (*Hyla arenicolor*). No dark bars on tail musculature; oral papillae on upper labium more extensive than in Pacific and California Treefrogs. Map 46

Chorus Frog (*Pseudacris triseriata*). Tail fins wide; dorsal fin highly arched; to around $1\frac{1}{2}$ in. Map 41

Cricket Frog (*Acris crepitans*). Tip of tail usually black; labial tooth rows $\frac{2}{2}$ or $\frac{2}{3}$; to around 2 in. Map 43

True Frogs (*Rana*)

See Fig. 39, p. 214; × $\frac{5}{6}$.

Oral papillae absent from median part of upper labium; mouth indented at sides. Eyes situated well in from outline of head as viewed from above.

Red-legged Frog (*R. aurora*). Dark brown or yellowish above; belly with pinkish iridescence; labial tooth rows usually $\frac{2}{3}$; to around 3 in.; ponds or slowly flowing streams. Map 48

Foothill Yellow-legged Frog (*R. boylei*). Body and tail musculature usually mottled; labial tooth rows often $\frac{6}{6}$ or $\frac{7}{6}$; to around 2 in.; rivers and streams. Map 55

Tarahumara Frog (*R. tarahumarae*). Above dark brown; body and tail with numerous dark spots; labial tooth rows usually $\frac{5}{3}$ or $\frac{4}{3}$; to around $2\frac{1}{2}$ in.; streams; in our area known only from extr. s. Arizona Map 56

Wood Frog (*R. sylvatica*). Body and tail rather uniformly pigmented, dusky or brownish, with greenish sheen; belly cream, with pinkish iridescence; tail tip pointed and fins high; labial tooth rows usually $\frac{2}{3}$ or $\frac{3}{4}$; to around 2 in. Map 47

Leopard Frog (*R. pipiens*). Body above dark brown with fine gold spots; belly often weakly pigmented, intestines showing through; labial tooth rows usually $\frac{2}{3}$; to around $3\frac{1}{2}$ in. Map 51

Green Frog (*R. clamitans*). Above olive-green, with numerous distinct dark spots; belly cream, with coppery sheen; labial tooth rows usually ⅔ or ⅓; to 3½ in.; in our area known only from Toad Lake, Whatcom Co., Washington; lower Weber River, Ogden, Utah; and extr. sw. B.C.   Map 52

Bullfrog (*R. catesbeiana*). Resembles Red-legged Frog tadpole, but snout more rounded from above, eyes more widely separated; olive-green above; belly whitish, without iridescence; labial tooth rows usually ⅔ or ¾; to 5½ in.   Map 53

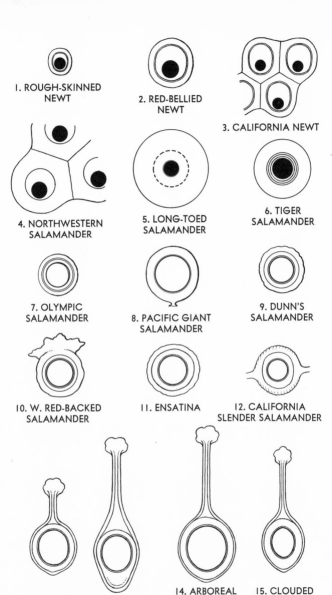

1. ROUGH-SKINNED NEWT

2. RED-BELLIED NEWT

3. CALIFORNIA NEWT

4. NORTHWESTERN SALAMANDER

5. LONG-TOED SALAMANDER

6. TIGER SALAMANDER

7. OLYMPIC SALAMANDER

8. PACIFIC GIANT SALAMANDER

9. DUNN'S SALAMANDER

10. W. RED-BACKED SALAMANDER

11. ENSATINA

12. CALIFORNIA SLENDER SALAMANDER

13. BLACK SALAMANDER

14. ARBOREAL SALAMANDER

15. CLOUDED SALAMANDER

Fig. 33. Eggs of salamanders

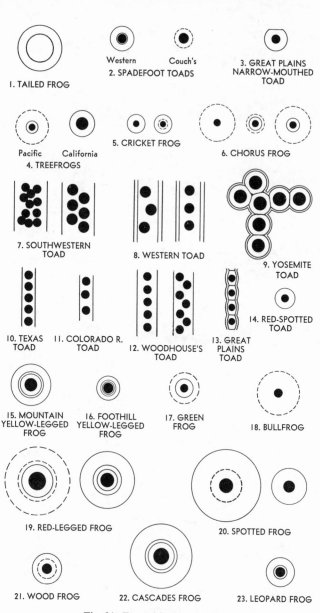

Fig. 34. Eggs of frogs and toads

209

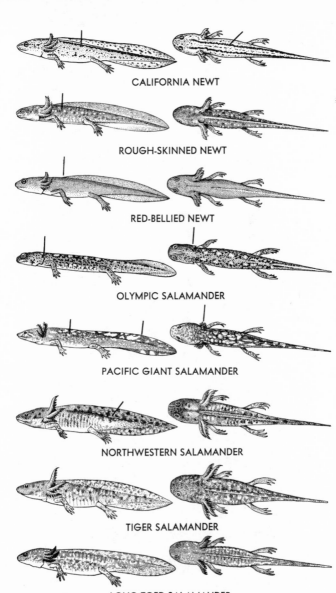

CALIFORNIA NEWT

ROUGH-SKINNED NEWT

RED-BELLIED NEWT

OLYMPIC SALAMANDER

PACIFIC GIANT SALAMANDER

NORTHWESTERN SALAMANDER

TIGER SALAMANDER

LONG-TOED SALAMANDER

Fig. 35. Salamander larvae

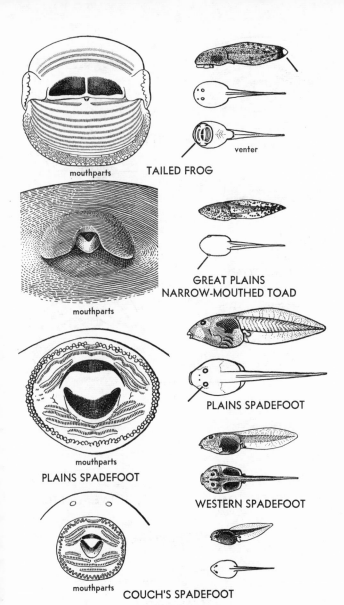

mouthparts

TAILED FROG

venter

GREAT PLAINS
NARROW-MOUTHED TOAD

mouthparts

PLAINS SPADEFOOT

mouthparts

PLAINS SPADEFOOT

WESTERN SPADEFOOT

mouthparts   COUCH'S SPADEFOOT

Fig. 36. Tailed Frog, Great Plains Narrow-mouthed Toad,
and spadefoot toads

211

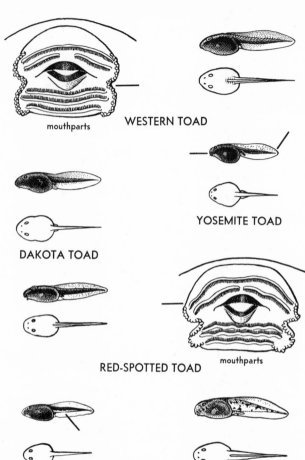

mouthparts

WESTERN TOAD

YOSEMITE TOAD

DAKOTA TOAD

RED-SPOTTED TOAD   mouthparts

WOODHOUSE'S TOAD   SOUTHWESTERN TOAD

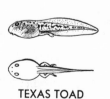

TEXAS TOAD

Fig. 37. True toads

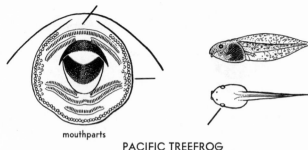

mouthparts

PACIFIC TREEFROG

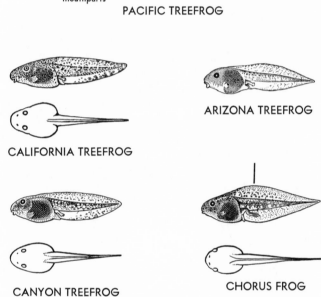

ARIZONA TREEFROG

CALIFORNIA TREEFROG

CANYON TREEFROG

CHORUS FROG

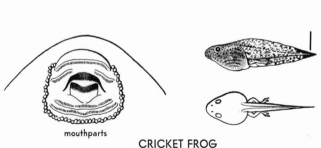

mouthparts

CRICKET FROG

Fig. 38. Treefrogs and relatives

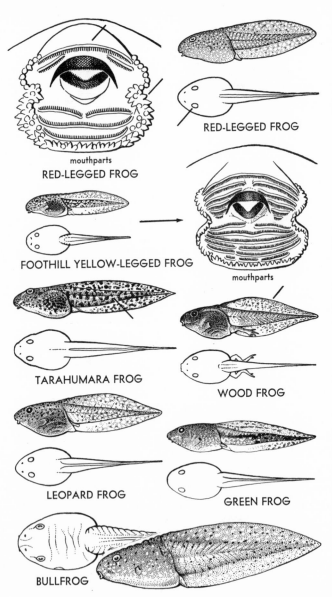

mouthparts
RED-LEGGED FROG

RED-LEGGED FROG

FOOTHILL YELLOW-LEGGED FROG

mouthparts

TARAHUMARA FROG

WOOD FROG

LEOPARD FROG

GREEN FROG

BULLFROG

Fig. 39. True frogs

214

Glossary

References

Credits for Use of Illustrations

Glossary

Adpress. To press close to or against; to lay flat against. As a measure of relative limb length in salamanders, the fore- and hind limbs on one side are laid straight along the side of the body and the amount of overlap of the extended toes, or the distance separating them, is noted. In frogs the hind limb is extended forward, while the body is held straight, and the position of the heel in relation to the nostril is noted. Species accounts refer to condition in adults only.

Alluvial fan. The alluvial deposit of a stream where it issues from a gorge onto an open plain.

Amplexus. An embrace; the sexual embrace of a male amphibian. *Pectoral amplexus:* position of amplexus in which the forelimbs of the male clasp the female from behind in the chest or axillary region. *Pelvic amplexus:* position of amplexus in which the male clasps the female from behind about her waist.

Anal scent glands. Scent glands that open on each side of the vent in certain snakes and lizards.

Anterior. Before, or toward the front.

Apical pits. *See* Scale pits.

Axolotl. Any of several larval salamanders of the genus *Ambystoma.* Such larvae may live and breed in the larval condition but are capable of resorbing their gills and fins, while beginning to breathe air at the surface, and of eventually emerging as adult salamanders.

Bajada. A long outwash slope at the base of a mountain range.

Capsular cavity. In amphibians the chamber occupied by the egg and enclosed by the jelly envelope(s). It is typically filled with a viscous jelly in which the egg moves freely, after fertilization.

Carapace. In turtles the upper part of the shell, including its bony plates and horny shields.

Casque-headed. An armored head. An area of thickened skin and/or bone on the heads of certain amphibians.

Clone. The progeny of uniparental reproduction. All the descendants of a single individual.

Costal folds. In salamanders the vertical folds of skin on the sides of the body set off by the costal grooves.

Costal grooves. In salamanders the vertical furrows on the sides of the body that set off the costal folds.

Countersunk. Sunk beneath the margins of — as in the jaws of burrowing snakes, in which the lower jaw fits snuggly within the margins of the upper jaw.

Cranial boss. A protuberance or rounded swelling between the eyes in some spadefoot toads and true toads. It may be glandular or bony.

Cranial crests. The ridges that frame the inner border of the upper eyelids in toads.

Cusp. A toothlike projection, as on the jaw of a turtle.

Cycloid scales. Scales whose free borders are circular.

Dorsal. Pertaining to the upper surface of the body.

Dorsolateral. Pertaining to the upper sides.

Dorsolateral fold. A longitudinal glandular ridge or fold between the side of the body and midback of certain frogs.

Dorsum. The upper, or dorsal, surface.

Egg capsule. In amphibians the covering of the egg, consisting of the jelly envelopes.

Egg envelope. In amphibians, a jellylike membrane that surrounds the egg. There may be 1 to 3 envelopes, depending on the species.

Exfoliation. Scaling off in flakes.

Femoral pores. Pores containing a waxlike material, found on the underside of the thighs in certain lizards.

Gill arch. One of the bony or cartilaginous arches or curved bars extending dorsoventrally, and placed one behind the other on each side of the pharynx, supporting the gills of fishes and amphibians.

Gill raker. One of the bony or cartilaginous filaments or processes, on the inside of the gill arches of fishes and certain amphibians (larvae, etc.), which help to prevent solid substances from being carried out through the gill clefts.

Gular fold. Fold of skin across the posterior portion of the throat; well developed in salamanders and some lizards.

Hemipenis (pl. hemipenes). One of the paired copulatory organs of lizards and snakes.

Hybrid. The offspring of the union of a male of one race, variety, species, genus, etc., with the female of another; a crossbred animal or plant.

Inset lower jaw. *See* Countersunk.

Intergrade. To merge gradually one with another through a series of intermediate forms.

Interspace. The area of color between two pattern elements on the back of lizards and snakes.

Juvenile. A young or immature individual, often displaying proportions and coloration differing from that of the adult.

Keel. A longitudinal ridge on the scales of certain lizards and snakes or down the back or venter of a turtle.

Labial teeth. Small horny teeth arranged like the teeth of a comb and attached in transverse rows to the lips (labia) of tadpoles. The number of rows in the upper and lower lips is expressed by a number above and below a diagonal line. The upper digit indicates the number of rows (a row divided at the midline is counted as one) on the upper lip, the lower is the number on the lower lip. A common formula is $\frac{2}{3}$.

Lamellae. In reference to the toes of lizards, the transverse plates or straplike scales that extend across the underside of the toes.

Larva. The early form of an animal which, while immature, is unlike its parent and must pass through more or less of a metamorphosis before assuming the adult characters. The tadpole of a frog is an example among amphibians.

Lateral stripe. A longitudinal stripe on the side of the body.

Melanistic. The condition in which black pigment is accentuated, sometimes to the point of obscuring all other color.

Mental gland. A gland on the chin of certain male salamanders. Its secretion appears to make the female receptive to mating.

Microenvironment. The immediate surroundings of an organism.

Nasolabial groove. A hairline groove extending from the nostril to the edge of the upper lip in all salamanders of the family Plethodontidae. A hand lens usually will be required to see it.

Neotenic. Having the period of immaturity indefinitely prolonged. Some salamanders may remain permanently in the larval condition.

Nuptial pad. In amphibians a patch of roughened, usually darkly pigmented skin that appears in males during the breeding period. Such pads generally develop on certain of the digits and aid the male in holding the female during amplexus.

Ocellus (pl. ocelli). A small eye; an eyelike spot.

Oculars. In blind snakes the scales beneath which the vestigial eyes are found.

Oral papillae. In tadpoles the small nipplelike projections that commonly form a fringe encircling the mouth. They are tactile and perhaps chemoreceptive in function.

Oviparous. Producing eggs that hatch after laying.

Ovoviviparous. Producing eggs that have a well-developed shell or membranous covering, but which hatch before or at the time of laying, as in certain reptiles.

Ovum. A female germ cell; an egg cell or egg apart from any investing membrane.

Paravertebral stripe. A stripe to one side and parallel to the dorsal midline.

Parotoid. One of a pair of large wartlike glands at the back of the head in toads.

Parthenogenesis. Reproduction by the development of an unfertilized egg.

Pectoral. Pertaining to the chest.

Peduncle. A stem or stalk.

Plastron. The ventral part of the shell of a tortoise or turtle, consisting typically of 9 symmetrically placed bones overlain by horny shields.

Playa. The flat-floored bottom of an undrained desert basin which much of the time may lack water.

Plethodons. Lungless salamanders of the genus *Plethodon*.

Postanal scale. A scale situated posterior to the anus. In the males of most iguanid lizards 2 or more of these scales are enlarged.

Posterior. Situated behind or to the rear; at or toward the hinder end of the body.

Postrostral scales. Scales between the rostral and internasals, as in certain rattlesnakes.

Preanal scale. A scale situated in the pelvic region anterior to the anus. In certain lizards several of these scales may have pores that secrete a waxlike substance.

Prehensile. Adapted for seizing or grasping, especially by wrapping around.

Premaxillary teeth. Teeth attached to the premaxillary bones, which are situated at the front of the upper jaw.

Prenasal. In rattlesnakes the scale located immediately in front of the nostril.

Relict. A survivor, especially of a vanishing race, type, or species; belonging to a nearly extinct class.

Riparian. Of, pertaining to, or living on, the bank of a river, lake, or tidewater.

Scale pits. Small paired pits or oval-shaped modifications near the free (apical) end of the scales of certain snakes.

Shield. In reference to turtles, any one of the plates of horn that cover the shell.

Sibling species. Two or more species that have been derived from a common parental stock. They often resemble each other closely and replace one another geographically; their ranges may or may not overlap at points of contact.

Subspecies. A subdivision of a species; a variety or race; a category (usually the lowest category recognized in classification) ranking next below a species. The differences separating subspecies are usually slight and are commonly bridged in zones of intergradation. Some systematists insist that intergradation should be the criterion in deciding whether two adjacent, slightly different animal populations should be considered as subspecies or species. If intergradation (or intermixture of characters) does not exist, they are regarded as species.

Supraorbital ridges. Ridges above the eyes.

Temporal horns. In horned lizards, the horns toward the sides of the crown.

Transformation. A marked and more or less abrupt change in the form and structure (and usually also in the habits, food, etc.) of an animal during postembryonic development, as when the larva of an insect becomes a pupa, or a tadpole changes to a frog.

Tubercle. Any of various small knoblike prominences or projections.

Unisexual. Consisting of only one sex.

Vent. The opening on the surface of the body of the cloaca which in reptiles and amphibians is the common chamber into which the intestinal, urinary, and reproductive canals discharge.

Vent lobes. Fleshy lobes on each side and usually to the rear of the vent. Found in certain male salamanders.

Venter. The belly or underside of an animal.

Ventral. The underside, or lower surface, of the body.

Vertebral line or stripe. A stripe down the midline of the back, overlying the position of the vertebral column.

Vertical pupil. An elliptical pupil with its long axis vertical.

Villi. Fine hairlike processes.

Vocal sac. A sac of loose skin on the throat of frogs and toads which becomes distended and acts as a resonating chamber when these animals vocalize.

Wedged preocular. The condition in racers and whipsnakes in which the lower preocular projects downward between the adjacent labial scales.

References

LISTED below are selected general references among which will be found further information on species covered by this book and general information on the biology of reptiles and amphibians. Many additional references are cited in the bibliographies of most of these publications.

Allen, E. Ross, and Wilfred T. Neill. *Keep Them Alive* (manual on the care of reptiles in captivity). Ross Allen Reptile Institute, Special Publication No. 1, 1950.

Bishop, Sherman C. *Handbook of Salamanders*. Ithaca, N. Y.: Comstock Publishing Co., Inc., 1947.

Blair, Albert P., and Fred R. Cagle (for sections on amphibians and reptiles). *Vertebrates of the United States,* New York: McGraw-Hill Book Co., 1957.

Carr, Archie. *Handbook of Turtles*. Ithaca, N. Y.: Comstock Publishing Associates, Cornell University Press, 1952.

Cochran, Doris M. *Living Amphibians of the World*. Garden City, N. Y.: Doubleday & Co. Inc., 1961.

Goin, Coleman J., and Olive B. Goin. *Introduction to Herpetology*. San Francisco and London: W. H. Freeman & Co., 1962.

Kauffeld, Carl. *Snakes and Snake Hunting*. Garden City, N. Y.: Hanover House, 1957.

Klauber, Laurence M. *Rattlesnakes: Their Habits, Life Histories, and Influence on Mankind*. Berkeley and Los Angeles: University of California Press, 1956. 2 vols.

Noble, G. Kingsley. *The Biology of the Amphibia*. New York: McGraw-Hill Book Co., Inc., 1931.

Oliver, James A. *The Natural History of North American Amphibians and Reptiles*. Princeton: D. Van Nostrand Co., Inc., 1955.

Pope, Clifford H. *Snakes Alive and How They Live*. New York: Viking Press, 1937.

——. *Turtles of the United States and Canada*. New York: Alfred A. Knopf, 1939.

——. *The Reptile World*. New York: Alfred A. Knopf, 1955.

Schmidt, Karl P. *A Check List of North American Amphibians and Reptiles*, 6th ed. Chicago: American Society of Ichthyologists and Herpetologists, 1953. (Procurable from Professor N. Bayard Green, Dept. of Zoology, Marshall College, Huntington, W. Va.)

——, and D. Dwight Davis. *Field Book of Snakes of the United States and Canada*. New York: G. P. Putnam's Sons, 1941.

——, and Robert F. Inger. *Living Reptiles of the World*. Garden City, N. Y.: Hanover House, 1957.

Smith, Hobart M. *Handbook of Lizards*. Ithaca, N. Y.: Comstock Publishing Co., Inc., 1946.

Stebbins, Robert C. *Amphibians of Western North America*. Berkeley and Los Angeles: University of California Press, 1951.

——. *Amphibians and Reptiles of Western North America*. New York: McGraw-Hill Book Co., Inc., 1954.

Wright, Albert Hazen, and Anna Allen Wright. *Handbook of Frogs and Toads of the United States and Canada*, 3rd ed. Ithaca, N. Y.: Comstock Publishing Co., Inc., 1949.

——. *Handbook of Snakes of the United States and Canada*. Ithaca, N. Y.: Comstock Publishing Associates, Cornell University Press, 1957. 2 vols.

SOUND RECORDING OF FROG AND TOAD CALLS

Bogert, Charles M. *Sounds of North American Frogs: The Biological Significance of Voice in Frogs*. Folkways Records & Service Corp., 117 West 46th Street, New York, N. Y. 10036. (12-in. LP record; 92 calls of 50 species of frogs and toads; accompanied by a profusely illustrated essay on the subject.)

Credits for Use of Illustrations

PARENTHETICAL numbers indicate positions of drawings in plates and figures. Count from top downward or from left to right when there are two or more columns of illustrations. The three books are by Robert C. Stebbins.

Amphibians of Western North America
(University of California Press, 1951)

Plates
7 (7–9), 10 (1–7), 11 (all).
Figures
1, 2, 5, 6, 8–15, 30–39.
Endpapers
Salamanders (except 3 and 5), frogs, and toads.

Reptiles and Amphibians of the San Francisco Bay Region
(University of California Press, 1959)

Plates
1 (1, 2, 4), 2 (1, 2), 5 (8), 6 (1–7), 8 (2–4), 9 (1–5), 12 (1–4, 7), 13 (5, 6), 22 (3–6), 24 (3–6), 25 (5, 6), 28 (1), 29 (5), 30 (2, 4–6, 9), 31 (2, 4, 6–8), 33 (1–3, 7), 37 (1–4), 38 (1).

Amphibians and Reptiles of Western North America
(McGraw-Hill, 1954)

Plates
7 (1–6), 14 (all), 15 (all), 16 (1, 2, 4), 17 (all), 18 (all), 19 (all), 20 (all), 21 (all), 26 (all), 27 (1–3, 5, 6), 34 (1–10, 13, 14), 35 (1–5, 7–9).
Figures
4 (inset of lizard), 7, 8, 16–18, 20, 21 (1–4), 22–26, 28, 29.
Endpapers
Lizards (except 6), turtles, snakes.

Maps

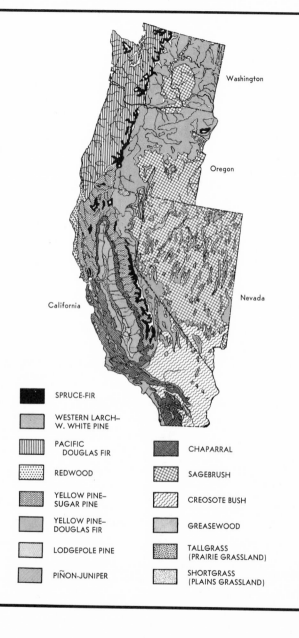

	SPRUCE-FIR
	WESTERN LARCH– W. WHITE PINE
	PACIFIC DOUGLAS FIR
	REDWOOD
	YELLOW PINE– SUGAR PINE
	YELLOW PINE– DOUGLAS FIR
	LODGEPOLE PINE
	PIÑON-JUNIPER

	CHAPARRAL
	SAGEBRUSH
	CREOSOTE BUSH
	GREASEWOOD
	TALLGRASS (PRAIRIE GRASSLAND)
	SHORTGRASS (PLAINS GRASSLAND)

Washington

Oregon

Nevada

California

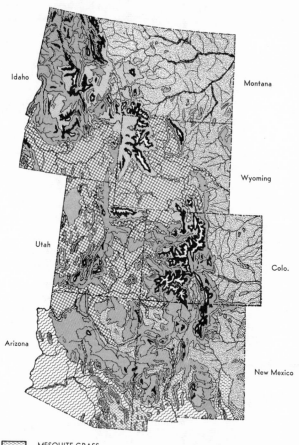

Idaho

Montana

Wyoming

Utah

Colo.

Arizona

New Mexico

MESQUITE GRASS
(DESERT GRASSLAND)

BUNCH GRASS
(PACIFIC GRASSLAND)

ALPINE MEADOW

MARSH GRASS
(MARSH GRASSLAND)

OAK-HICKORY

KEY TO RANGE MAPS
(on following pages)

X   Isolated record or
    locality

?   Record questionable
    or data inadequate

    Range boundaries of
    adjacent eastern or
    Mexican subspecies

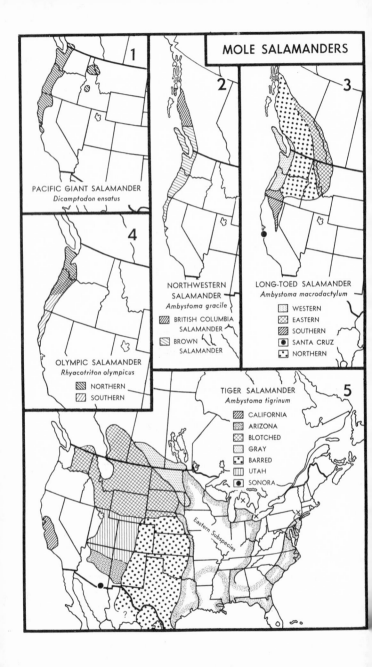

MOLE SALAMANDERS

1

PACIFIC GIANT SALAMANDER
Dicamptodon ensatus

2

NORTHWESTERN
SALAMANDER
Ambystoma gracile

▨ BRITISH COLUMBIA
    SALAMANDER
▧ BROWN
    SALAMANDER

3

LONG-TOED SALAMANDER
Ambystoma macrodactylum

▢ WESTERN
⊠ EASTERN
▨ SOUTHERN
● SANTA CRUZ
⚬ NORTHERN

4

OLYMPIC SALAMANDER
Rhyacotriton olympicus

▨ NORTHERN
▧ SOUTHERN

5

TIGER SALAMANDER
Ambystoma tigrinum

▨ CALIFORNIA
▨ ARIZONA
▨ BLOTCHED
▨ GRAY
⚬ BARRED
▥ UTAH
● SONORA

Eastern Subspecies

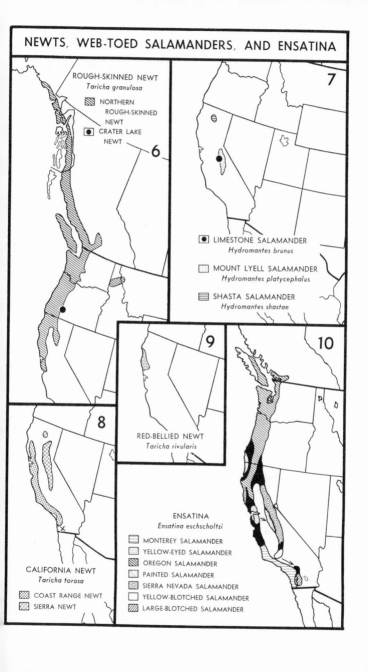

NEWTS, WEB-TOED SALAMANDERS, AND ENSATINA

ROUGH-SKINNED NEWT
Taricha granulosa

⬚ NORTHERN
ROUGH-SKINNED
NEWT

⬤ CRATER LAKE
NEWT

6

7

LIMESTONE SALAMANDER
Hydromantes brunus

MOUNT LYELL SALAMANDER
Hydromantes platycephalus

SHASTA SALAMANDER
Hydromantes shastae

8

9

RED-BELLIED NEWT
Taricha rivularis

10

CALIFORNIA NEWT
Taricha torosa

▨ COAST RANGE NEWT

▧ SIERRA NEWT

ENSATINA
Ensatina eschscholtzi

⬚ MONTEREY SALAMANDER

⬚ YELLOW-EYED SALAMANDER

⬚ OREGON SALAMANDER

⬚ PAINTED SALAMANDER

⬚ SIERRA NEVADA SALAMANDER

⬚ YELLOW-BLOTCHED SALAMANDER

⬚ LARGE-BLOTCHED SALAMANDER

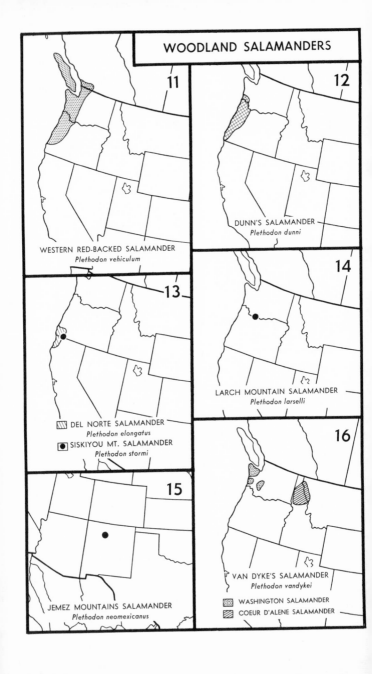

WOODLAND SALAMANDERS

11
WESTERN RED-BACKED SALAMANDER
Plethodon vehiculum

12
DUNN'S SALAMANDER
Plethodon dunni

13
⧄ DEL NORTE SALAMANDER
Plethodon elongatus
⬤ SISKIYOU MT. SALAMANDER
Plethodon stormi

14
LARCH MOUNTAIN SALAMANDER
Plethodon larselli

15
JEMEZ MOUNTAINS SALAMANDER
Plethodon neomexicanus

16
VAN DYKE'S SALAMANDER
Plethodon vandykei
▨ WASHINGTON SALAMANDER
⧄ COEUR D'ALENE SALAMANDER

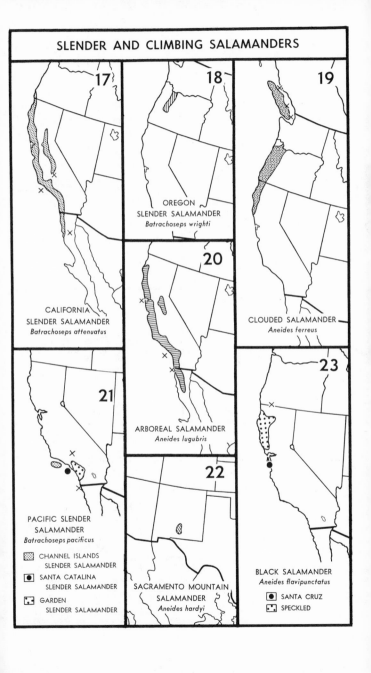

SLENDER AND CLIMBING SALAMANDERS

17

CALIFORNIA
SLENDER SALAMANDER
Batrachoseps attenuatus

18

OREGON
SLENDER SALAMANDER
Batrachoseps wrighti

19

CLOUDED SALAMANDER
Aneides ferreus

20

ARBOREAL SALAMANDER
Aneides lugubris

21

PACIFIC SLENDER
SALAMANDER
Batrachoseps pacificus

▦ CHANNEL ISLANDS
SLENDER SALAMANDER
◉ SANTA CATALINA
SLENDER SALAMANDER
▞ GARDEN
SLENDER SALAMANDER

22

SACRAMENTO MOUNTAIN
SALAMANDER
Aneides hardyi

23

BLACK SALAMANDER
Aneides flavipunctatus

◉ SANTA CRUZ
▞ SPECKLED

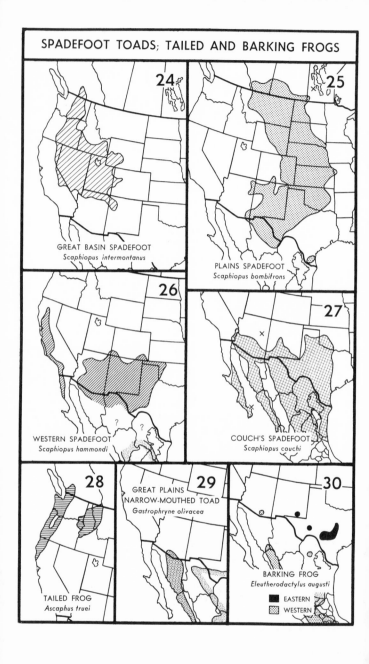

SPADEFOOT TOADS; TAILED AND BARKING FROGS

24
GREAT BASIN SPADEFOOT
Scaphiopus intermontanus

25
PLAINS SPADEFOOT
Scaphiopus bombifrons

26
WESTERN SPADEFOOT
Scaphiopus hammondi

27
COUCH'S SPADEFOOT
Scaphiopus couchi

28
TAILED FROG
Ascaphus truei

29
GREAT PLAINS
NARROW-MOUTHED TOAD
Gastrophryne olivacea

30
BARKING FROG
Eleutherodactylus augusti

■ EASTERN
▧ WESTERN

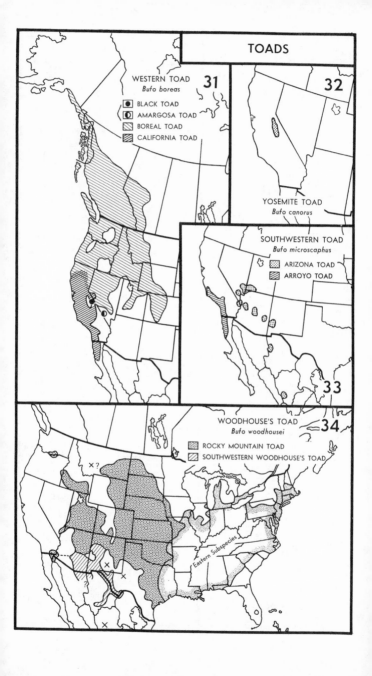

TOADS

WESTERN TOAD
Bufo boreas   31   32
   ● BLACK TOAD
   ◐ AMARGOSA TOAD
   ▨ BOREAL TOAD
   ▩ CALIFORNIA TOAD

YOSEMITE TOAD
Bufo canorus

SOUTHWESTERN TOAD
Bufo microscaphus
   ▨ ARIZONA TOAD
   ▨ ARROYO TOAD

                                        33

WOODHOUSE'S TOAD   34
Bufo woodhousei
   ▦ ROCKY MOUNTAIN TOAD
   ▨ SOUTHWESTERN WOODHOUSE'S TOAD

Eastern Subspecies

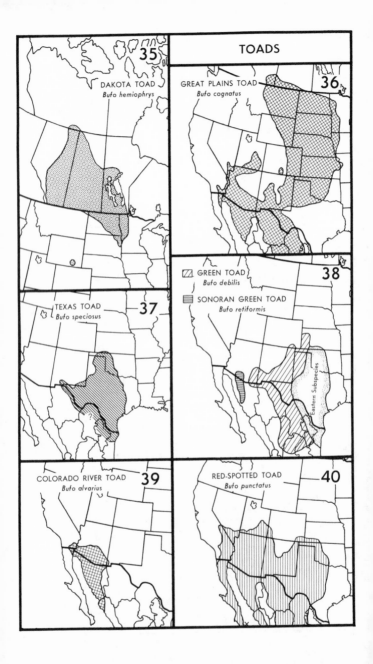

TOADS

DAKOTA TOAD
Bufo hemiophrys
35

GREAT PLAINS TOAD
Bufo cognatus
36

TEXAS TOAD
Bufo speciosus
37

GREEN TOAD
Bufo debilis

SONORAN GREEN TOAD
Bufo retiformis
38

Eastern Subspecies

COLORADO RIVER TOAD
Bufo alvarius
39

RED-SPOTTED TOAD
Bufo punctatus
40

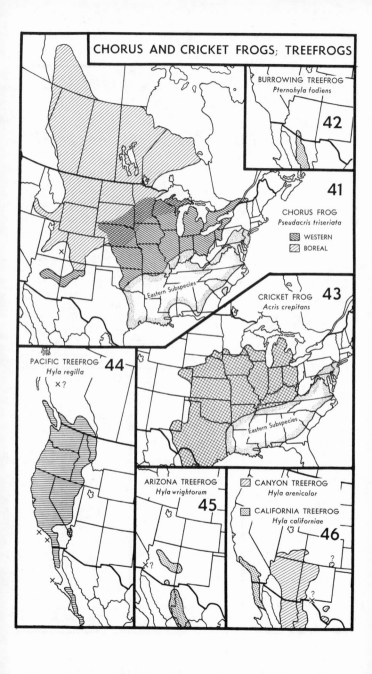

CHORUS AND CRICKET FROGS; TREEFROGS

BURROWING TREEFROG
Pternohyla fodiens
42

41

CHORUS FROG
Pseudacris triseriata
⬛ WESTERN
▨ BOREAL

Eastern Subspecies

CRICKET FROG 43
Acris crepitans

PACIFIC TREEFROG 44
Hyla regilla
×?

Eastern Subspecies

ARIZONA TREEFROG 45
Hyla wrightorum
×?

▨ CANYON TREEFROG
Hyla arenicolor
▦ CALIFORNIA TREEFROG 46
Hyla californiae

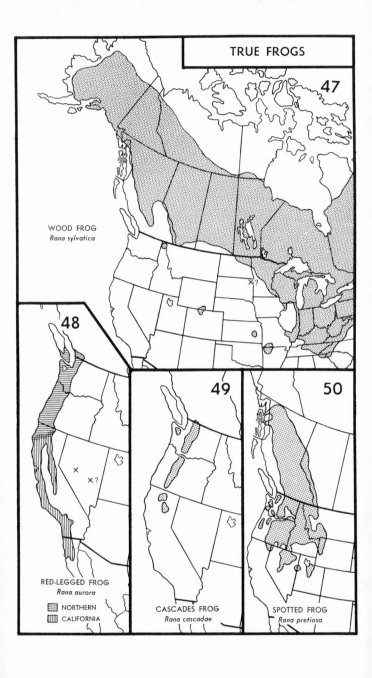

TRUE FROGS

47

WOOD FROG
Rana sylvatica

48

RED-LEGGED FROG
Rana aurora

☰ NORTHERN
▥ CALIFORNIA

49

CASCADES FROG
Rana cascadae

50

SPOTTED FROG
Rana pretiosa

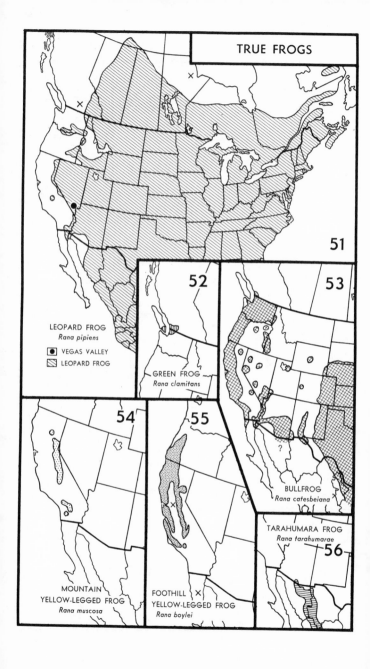

TRUE FROGS

51

LEOPARD FROG
Rana pipiens

⊙ VEGAS VALLEY
▨ LEOPARD FROG

52

GREEN FROG
Rana clamitans

53

BULLFROG
Rana catesbeiana

54

MOUNTAIN
YELLOW-LEGGED FROG
Rana muscosa

55

FOOTHILL
YELLOW-LEGGED FROG
Rana boylei

TARAHUMARA FROG
Rana tarahumarae

56

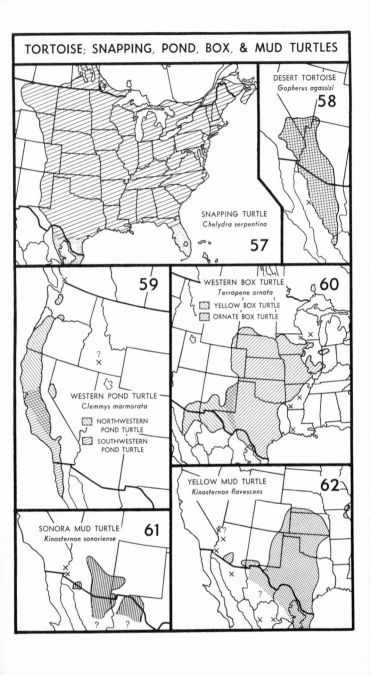

TORTOISE; SNAPPING, POND, BOX, & MUD TURTLES

DESERT TORTOISE
Gopherus agassizi
58

SNAPPING TURTLE
Chelydra serpentina
57

59

WESTERN POND TURTLE
Clemmys marmorata

NORTHWESTERN
POND TURTLE

SOUTHWESTERN
POND TURTLE

WESTERN BOX TURTLE **60**
Terrapene ornata

YELLOW BOX TURTLE

ORNATE BOX TURTLE

YELLOW MUD TURTLE **62**
Kinosternon flavescens

SONORA MUD TURTLE **61**
Kinosternon sonoriense

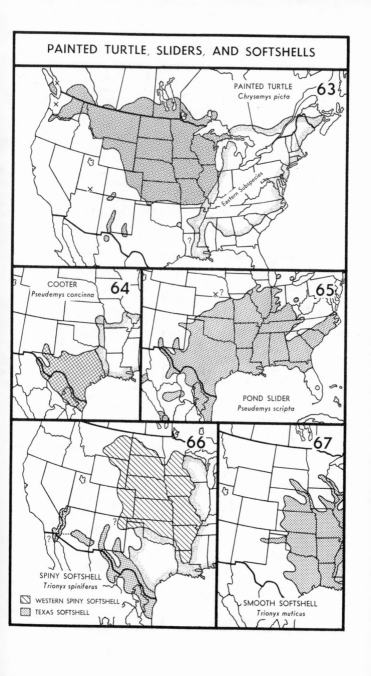

PAINTED TURTLE, SLIDERS, AND SOFTSHELLS

63
PAINTED TURTLE
Chrysemys picta

Eastern Subspecies

64
COOTER
Pseudemys concinna

65
POND SLIDER
Pseudemys scripta

66
SPINY SOFTSHELL
Trionyx spiniferus

◩ WESTERN SPINY SOFTSHELL
▧ TEXAS SOFTSHELL

67
SMOOTH SOFTSHELL
Trionyx muticus

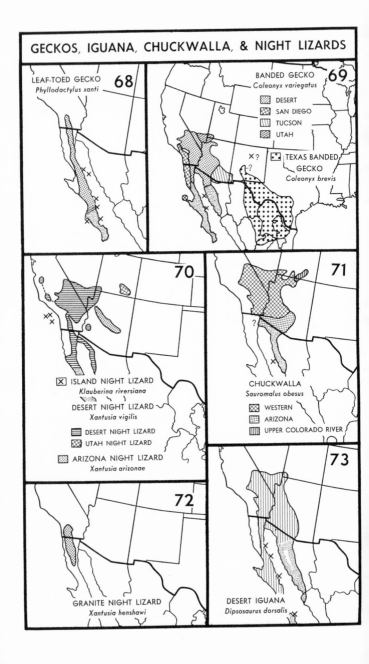

GECKOS, IGUANA, CHUCKWALLA, & NIGHT LIZARDS

LEAF-TOED GECKO **68**
Phyllodactylus xanti

BANDED GECKO **69**
Coleonyx variegatus

- ⊠ DESERT
- ⊠ SAN DIEGO
- ⊠ TUCSON
- ⊠ UTAH

X?
?

▪ TEXAS BANDED GECKO
Coleonyx brevis

70

- ☒ ISLAND NIGHT LIZARD
  Klauberina riversiana
- DESERT NIGHT LIZARD
  Xantusia vigilis
  - ▤ DESERT NIGHT LIZARD
  - ⊠ UTAH NIGHT LIZARD
- ☒ ARIZONA NIGHT LIZARD
  Xantusia arizonae

71

?

CHUCKWALLA
Sauromalus obesus

- ⊠ WESTERN
- ▦ ARIZONA
- ⦀ UPPER COLORADO RIVER

72

GRANITE NIGHT LIZARD
Xantusia henshawi

73

DESERT IGUANA
Dipsosaurus dorsalis

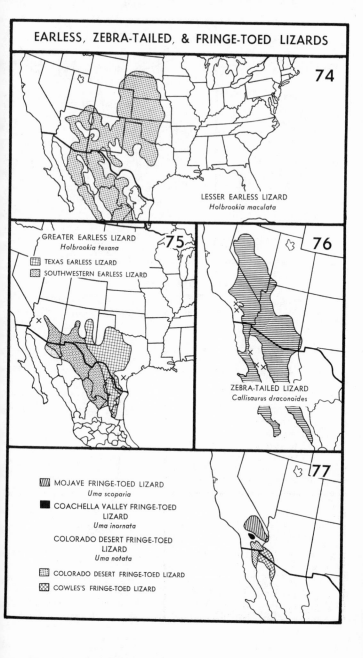

EARLESS, ZEBRA-TAILED, & FRINGE-TOED LIZARDS

74

LESSER EARLESS LIZARD
Holbrookia maculata

GREATER EARLESS LIZARD
Holbrookia texana
75
⊞ TEXAS EARLESS LIZARD
▦ SOUTHWESTERN EARLESS LIZARD

76

ZEBRA-TAILED LIZARD
Callisaurus draconoides

▨ MOJAVE FRINGE-TOED LIZARD
Uma scoparia
■ COACHELLA VALLEY FRINGE-TOED
LIZARD
Uma inornata

COLORADO DESERT FRINGE-TOED
LIZARD
Uma notata

⊞ COLORADO DESERT FRINGE-TOED LIZARD
⊠ COWLES'S FRINGE-TOED LIZARD

77

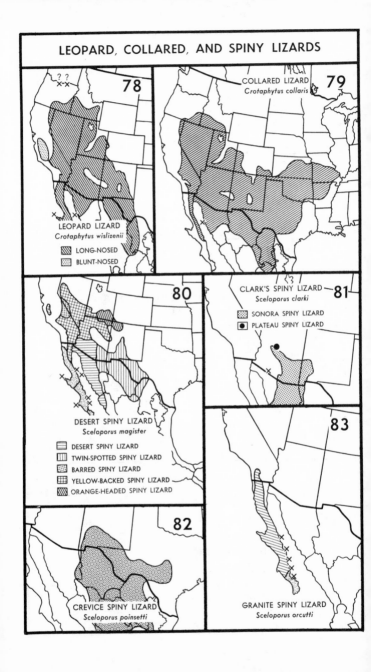

LEOPARD, COLLARED, AND SPINY LIZARDS

78

LEOPARD LIZARD
Crotaphytus wislizenii

▨ LONG-NOSED
▧ BLUNT-NOSED

79

COLLARED LIZARD
Crotaphytus collaris

80

DESERT SPINY LIZARD
Sceloporus magister

☰ DESERT SPINY LIZARD
▥ TWIN-SPOTTED SPINY LIZARD
▨ BARRED SPINY LIZARD
▦ YELLOW-BACKED SPINY LIZARD
▧ ORANGE-HEADED SPINY LIZARD

CLARK'S SPINY LIZARD — 81
Sceloporus clarki

▧ SONORA SPINY LIZARD
● PLATEAU SPINY LIZARD

83

GRANITE SPINY LIZARD
Sceloporus orcutti

82

CREVICE SPINY LIZARD
Sceloporus poinsetti

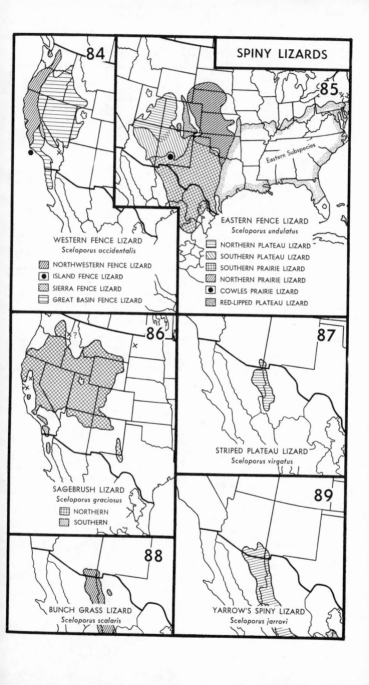

SPINY LIZARDS

84

WESTERN FENCE LIZARD
Sceloporus occidentalis

▨ NORTHWESTERN FENCE LIZARD
⬤ ISLAND FENCE LIZARD
▧ SIERRA FENCE LIZARD
☰ GREAT BASIN FENCE LIZARD

85

Eastern Subspecies

EASTERN FENCE LIZARD
Sceloporus undulatus

☰ NORTHERN PLATEAU LIZARD
⬔ SOUTHERN PLATEAU LIZARD
▦ SOUTHERN PRAIRIE LIZARD
▨ NORTHERN PRAIRIE LIZARD
⬤ COWLES PRAIRIE LIZARD
▦ RED-LIPPED PLATEAU LIZARD

86

SAGEBRUSH LIZARD
Sceloporus graciosus

▦ NORTHERN
▦ SOUTHERN

88

BUNCH GRASS LIZARD
Sceloporus scalaris

87

STRIPED PLATEAU LIZARD
Sceloporus virgatus

89

YARROW'S SPINY LIZARD
Sceloporus jarrovi

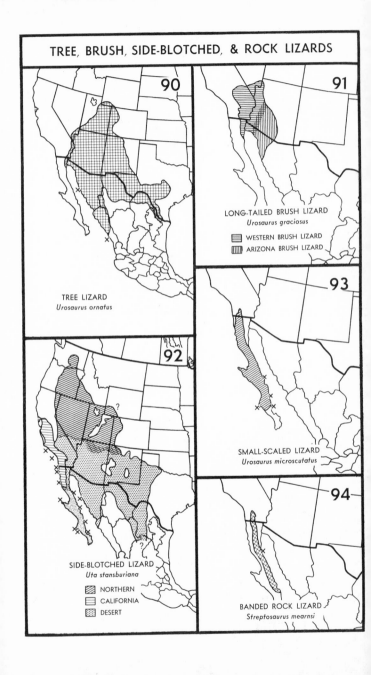

TREE, BRUSH, SIDE-BLOTCHED, & ROCK LIZARDS

90

TREE LIZARD
Urosaurus ornatus

91

LONG-TAILED BRUSH LIZARD
Urosaurus graciosus

- ▤ WESTERN BRUSH LIZARD
- ▥ ARIZONA BRUSH LIZARD

92

SIDE-BLOTCHED LIZARD
Uta stansburiana

- ▨ NORTHERN
- ▤ CALIFORNIA
- ▦ DESERT

93

SMALL-SCALED LIZARD
Urosaurus microscutatus

94

BANDED ROCK LIZARD
Streptosaurus mearnsi

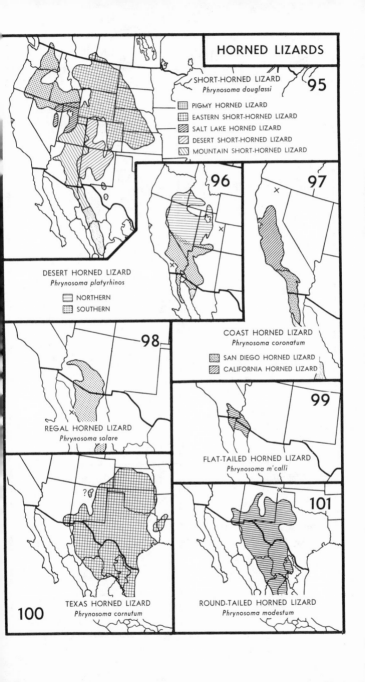

HORNED LIZARDS

SHORT-HORNED LIZARD *Phrynosoma douglassi* **95**

⊞ PIGMY HORNED LIZARD
⊞ EASTERN SHORT-HORNED LIZARD
▨ SALT LAKE HORNED LIZARD
▨ DESERT SHORT-HORNED LIZARD
▨ MOUNTAIN SHORT-HORNED LIZARD

96

97

DESERT HORNED LIZARD *Phrynosoma platyrhinos*

☐ NORTHERN
⊞ SOUTHERN

COAST HORNED LIZARD *Phrynosoma coronatum*

▨ SAN DIEGO HORNED LIZARD
▨ CALIFORNIA HORNED LIZARD

98

REGAL HORNED LIZARD *Phrynosoma solare*

99

FLAT-TAILED HORNED LIZARD *Phrynosoma m'calli*

100 **TEXAS HORNED LIZARD** *Phrynosoma cornutum*

101

ROUND-TAILED HORNED LIZARD *Phrynosoma modestum*

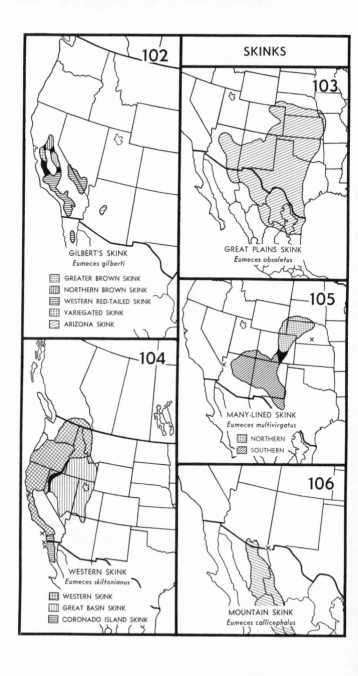

102

SKINKS

103

GILBERT'S SKINK
Eumeces gilberti

GREATER BROWN SKINK
NORTHERN BROWN SKINK
WESTERN RED-TAILED SKINK
VARIEGATED SKINK
ARIZONA SKINK

GREAT PLAINS SKINK
Eumeces obsoletus

104

105

WESTERN SKINK
Eumeces skiltonianus

WESTERN SKINK
GREAT BASIN SKINK
CORONADO ISLAND SKINK

MANY-LINED SKINK
Eumeces multivirgatus

NORTHERN
SOUTHERN

106

MOUNTAIN SKINK
Eumeces callicephalus

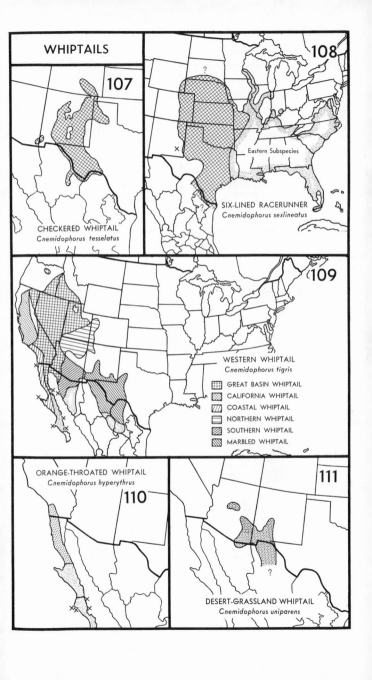

WHIPTAILS

107
CHECKERED WHIPTAIL
Cnemidophorus tesselatus

108
SIX-LINED RACERUNNER
Cnemidophorus sexlineatus

Eastern Subspecies

109
WESTERN WHIPTAIL
Cnemidophorus tigris

⊞ GREAT BASIN WHIPTAIL
▒ CALIFORNIA WHIPTAIL
▨ COASTAL WHIPTAIL
⊟ NORTHERN WHIPTAIL
▨ SOUTHERN WHIPTAIL
▨ MARBLED WHIPTAIL

110
ORANGE-THROATED WHIPTAIL
Cnemidophorus hyperythrus

111
DESERT-GRASSLAND WHIPTAIL
Cnemidophorus uniparens

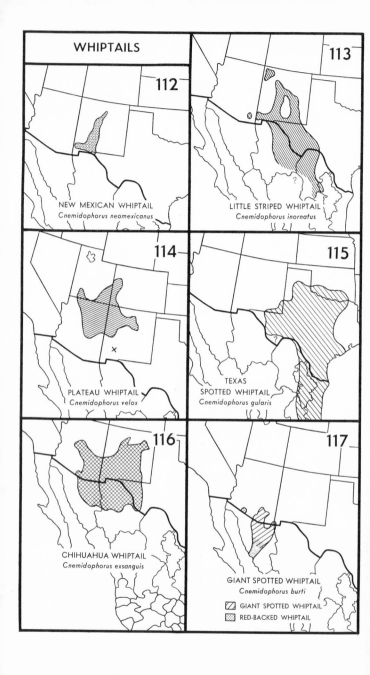

WHIPTAILS

112

NEW MEXICAN WHIPTAIL
Cnemidophorus neomexicanus

113

LITTLE STRIPED WHIPTAIL
Cnemidophorus inornatus

114

PLATEAU WHIPTAIL
Cnemidophorus velox

115

TEXAS
SPOTTED WHIPTAIL
Cnemidophorus gularis

116

CHIHUAHUA WHIPTAIL
Cnemidophorus exsanguis

117

GIANT SPOTTED WHIPTAIL
Cnemidophorus burti

◩ GIANT SPOTTED WHIPTAIL
▨ RED-BACKED WHIPTAIL

ALLIGATOR & LEGLESS LIZARDS; GILA MONSTER

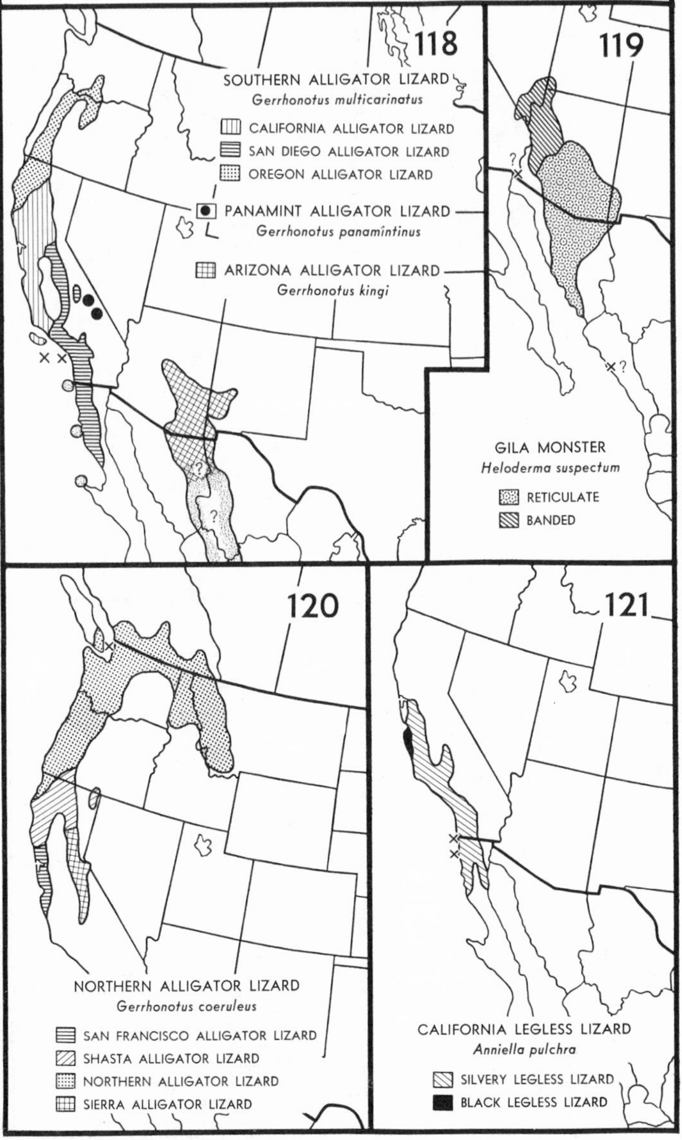
118
SOUTHERN ALLIGATOR LIZARD
Gerrhonotus multicarinatus
CALIFORNIA ALLIGATOR LIZARD
SAN DIEGO ALLIGATOR LIZARD
OREGON ALLIGATOR LIZARD
PANAMINT ALLIGATOR LIZARD
Gerrhonotus panamintinus
ARIZONA ALLIGATOR LIZARD
Gerrhonotus kingi
119
GILA MONSTER
Heloderma suspectum
RETICULATE
BANDED
120
NORTHERN ALLIGATOR LIZARD
Gerrhonotus coeruleus
SAN FRANCISCO ALLIGATOR LIZARD
SHASTA ALLIGATOR LIZARD
NORTHERN ALLIGATOR LIZARD
SIERRA ALLIGATOR LIZARD
121
CALIFORNIA LEGLESS LIZARD
Anniella pulchra
SILVERY LEGLESS LIZARD
BLACK LEGLESS LIZARD

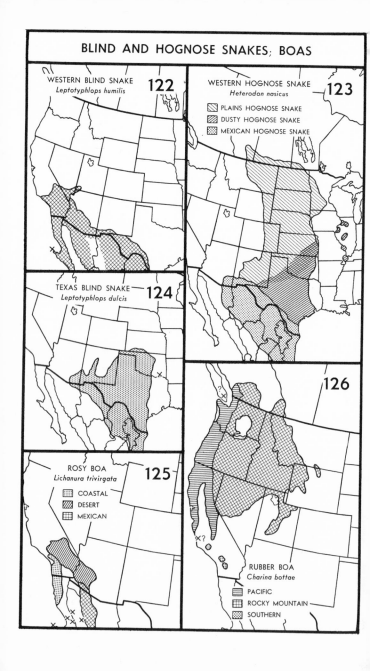

BLIND AND HOGNOSE SNAKES; BOAS

WESTERN BLIND SNAKE **122**
Leptotyphlops humilis

WESTERN HOGNOSE SNAKE **123**
Heterodon nasicus

- PLAINS HOGNOSE SNAKE
- DUSTY HOGNOSE SNAKE
- MEXICAN HOGNOSE SNAKE

TEXAS BLIND SNAKE **124**
Leptotyphlops dulcis

126

ROSY BOA **125**
Lichanura trivirgata

- COASTAL
- DESERT
- MEXICAN

RUBBER BOA
Charina bottae

- PACIFIC
- ROCKY MOUNTAIN
- SOUTHERN

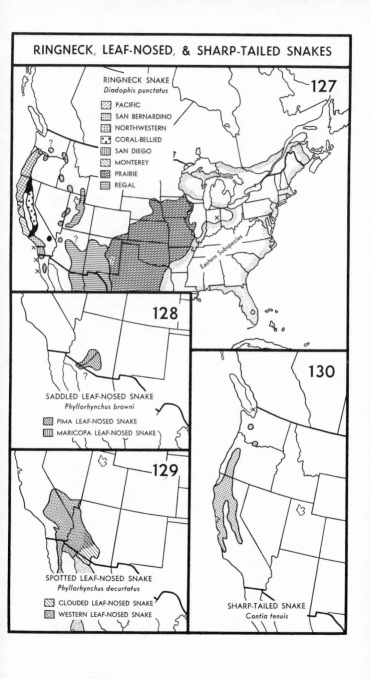

RINGNECK, LEAF-NOSED, & SHARP-TAILED SNAKES

127

RINGNECK SNAKE
Diadophis punctatus

- PACIFIC
- SAN BERNARDINO
- NORTHWESTERN
- CORAL-BELLIED
- SAN DIEGO
- MONTEREY
- PRAIRIE
- REGAL

Eastern Subspecies

128

SADDLED LEAF-NOSED SNAKE
Phyllorhynchus browni

- PIMA LEAF-NOSED SNAKE
- MARICOPA LEAF-NOSED SNAKE

129

SPOTTED LEAF-NOSED SNAKE
Phyllorhynchus decurtatus

- CLOUDED LEAF-NOSED SNAKE
- WESTERN LEAF-NOSED SNAKE

130

SHARP-TAILED SNAKE
Contia tenuis

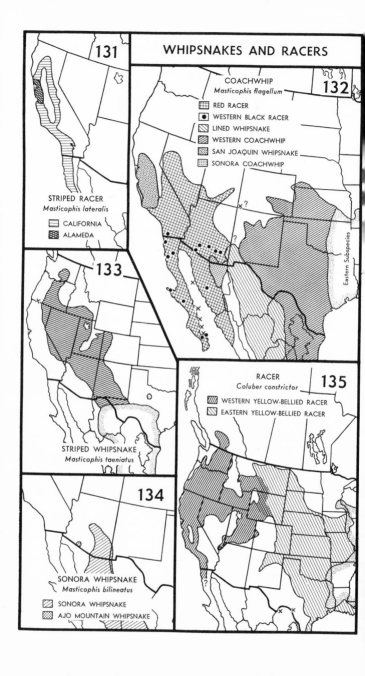

WHIPSNAKES AND RACERS

131

STRIPED RACER
Masticophis lateralis

⬜ CALIFORNIA
▨ ALAMEDA

COACHWHIP
Masticophis flagellum
132

⊞ RED RACER
⦿ WESTERN BLACK RACER
▨ LINED WHIPSNAKE
▨ WESTERN COACHWHIP
▨ SAN JOAQUIN WHIPSNAKE
▦ SONORA COACHWHIP

Eastern Subspecies

133

STRIPED WHIPSNAKE
Masticophis taeniatus

RACER
Coluber constrictor
135

▨ WESTERN YELLOW-BELLIED RACER
▨ EASTERN YELLOW-BELLIED RACER

134

SONORA WHIPSNAKE
Masticophis bilineatus

▨ SONORA WHIPSNAKE
▦ AJO MOUNTAIN WHIPSNAKE

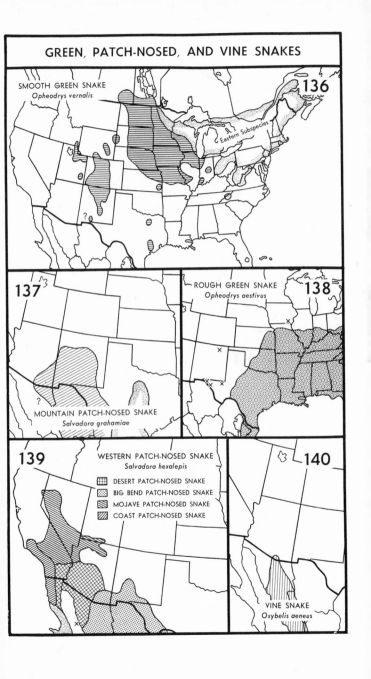

GREEN, PATCH-NOSED, AND VINE SNAKES

136
SMOOTH GREEN SNAKE
Opheodrys vernalis
Eastern Subspecies

137
MOUNTAIN PATCH-NOSED SNAKE
Salvadora grahamiae

138
ROUGH GREEN SNAKE
Opheodrys aestivus

139
WESTERN PATCH-NOSED SNAKE
Salvadora hexalepis

DESERT PATCH-NOSED SNAKE
BIG BEND PATCH-NOSED SNAKE
MOJAVE PATCH-NOSED SNAKE
COAST PATCH-NOSED SNAKE

140
VINE SNAKE
Oxybelis aeneus

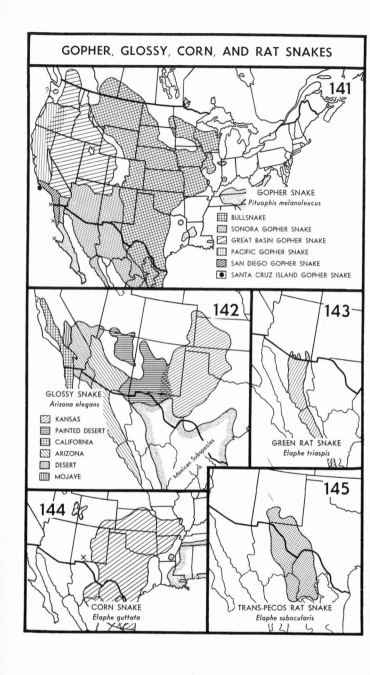

GOPHER, GLOSSY, CORN, AND RAT SNAKES

141

GOPHER SNAKE
Pituophis melanoleucus

⊞ BULLSNAKE
▦ SONORA GOPHER SNAKE
▨ GREAT BASIN GOPHER SNAKE
▥ PACIFIC GOPHER SNAKE
▧ SAN DIEGO GOPHER SNAKE
● SANTA CRUZ ISLAND GOPHER SNAKE

142

GLOSSY SNAKE
Arizona elegans

▨ KANSAS
▤ PAINTED DESERT
⊞ CALIFORNIA
▨ ARIZONA
▦ DESERT
▥ MOJAVE

Mexican Subspecies

143

GREEN RAT SNAKE
Elaphe triaspis

144

CORN SNAKE
Elaphe guttata

145

TRANS-PECOS RAT SNAKE
Elaphe subocularis

KING, MILK, AND LONG-NOSED SNAKES

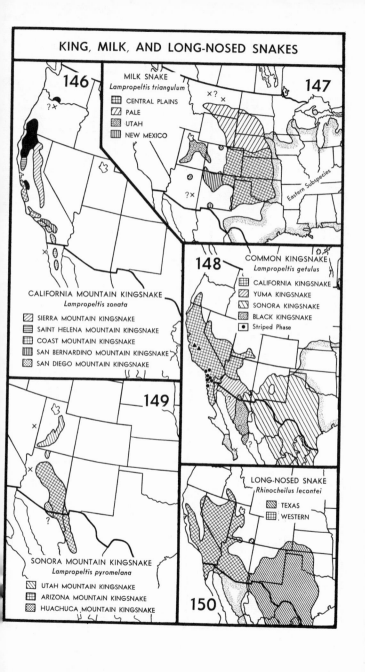

146

MILK SNAKE
Lampropeltis triangulum

▦ CENTRAL PLAINS
▨ PALE
▩ UTAH
▥ NEW MEXICO

147

Eastern Subspecies

CALIFORNIA MOUNTAIN KINGSNAKE
Lampropeltis zonata

▨ SIERRA MOUNTAIN KINGSNAKE
▤ SAINT HELENA MOUNTAIN KINGSNAKE
▦ COAST MOUNTAIN KINGSNAKE
▥ SAN BERNARDINO MOUNTAIN KINGSNAKE
▩ SAN DIEGO MOUNTAIN KINGSNAKE

148

COMMON KINGSNAKE
Lampropeltis getulus

▦ CALIFORNIA KINGSNAKE
▨ YUMA KINGSNAKE
▧ SONORA KINGSNAKE
▩ BLACK KINGSNAKE
● Striped Phase

149

SONORA MOUNTAIN KINGSNAKE
Lampropeltis pyromelana

▨ UTAH MOUNTAIN KINGSNAKE
▦ ARIZONA MOUNTAIN KINGSNAKE
▩ HUACHUCA MOUNTAIN KINGSNAKE

LONG-NOSED SNAKE
Rhinocheilus lecontei

▨ TEXAS
▦ WESTERN

150

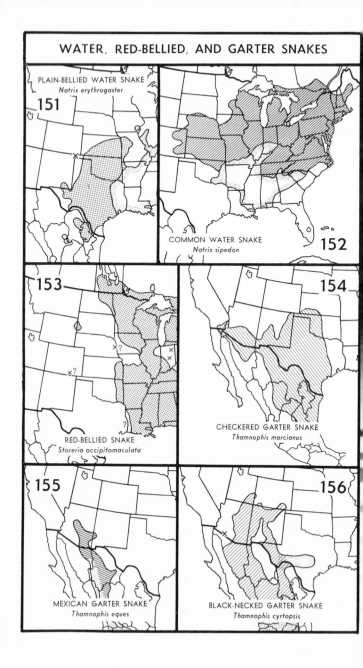

WATER, RED-BELLIED, AND GARTER SNAKES

PLAIN-BELLIED WATER SNAKE
Natrix erythrogaster
151

COMMON WATER SNAKE
Natrix sipedon
152

153
RED-BELLIED SNAKE
Storeria occipitomaculata

154
CHECKERED GARTER SNAKE
Thamnophis marcianus

155
MEXICAN GARTER SNAKE
Thamnophis eques

156
BLACK-NECKED GARTER SNAKE
Thamnophis cyrtopsis

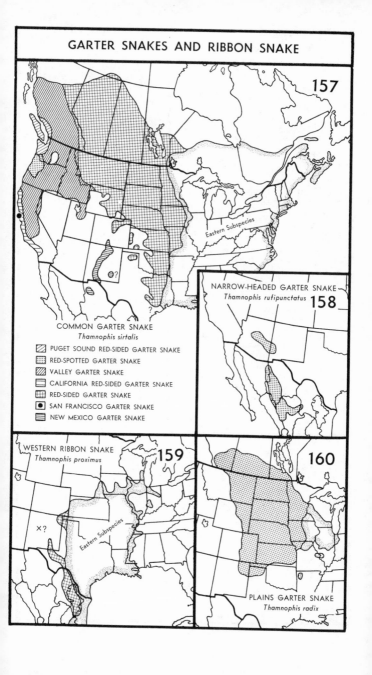

GARTER SNAKES AND RIBBON SNAKE

157

Eastern Subspecies

COMMON GARTER SNAKE
Thamnophis sirtalis

- PUGET SOUND RED-SIDED GARTER SNAKE
- RED-SPOTTED GARTER SNAKE
- VALLEY GARTER SNAKE
- CALIFORNIA RED-SIDED GARTER SNAKE
- RED-SIDED GARTER SNAKE
- SAN FRANCISCO GARTER SNAKE
- NEW MEXICO GARTER SNAKE

NARROW-HEADED GARTER SNAKE
Thamnophis rufipunctatus **158**

WESTERN RIBBON SNAKE
Thamnophis proximus **159**

×?

Eastern Subspecies

160

PLAINS GARTER SNAKE
Thamnophis radix

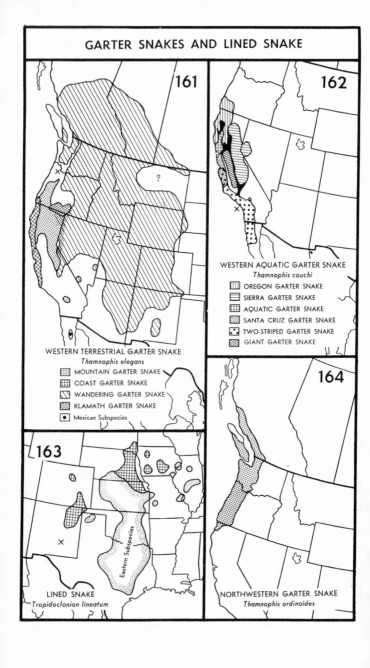

GARTER SNAKES AND LINED SNAKE

161

WESTERN TERRESTRIAL GARTER SNAKE
Thamnophis elegans
- MOUNTAIN GARTER SNAKE
- COAST GARTER SNAKE
- WANDERING GARTER SNAKE
- KLAMATH GARTER SNAKE
- • Mexican Subspecies

162

WESTERN AQUATIC GARTER SNAKE
Thamnophis couchi
- OREGON GARTER SNAKE
- SIERRA GARTER SNAKE
- AQUATIC GARTER SNAKE
- SANTA CRUZ GARTER SNAKE
- TWO-STRIPED GARTER SNAKE
- GIANT GARTER SNAKE

163

LINED SNAKE
Tropidoclonion lineatum

Eastern Subspecies

164

NORTHWESTERN GARTER SNAKE
Thamnophis ordinoides

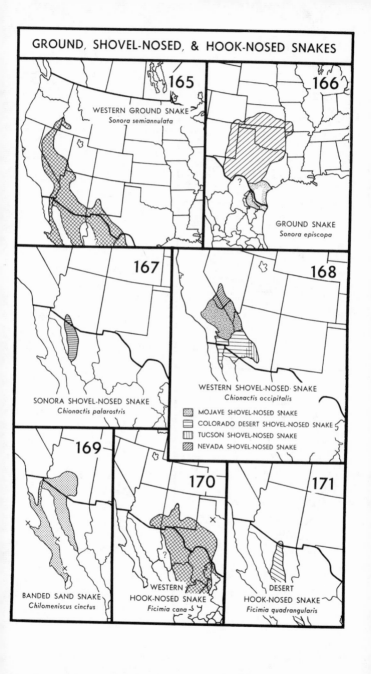

GROUND, SHOVEL-NOSED, & HOOK-NOSED SNAKES

165
WESTERN GROUND SNAKE
Sonora semiannulata

166
GROUND SNAKE
Sonora episcopa

167
SONORA SHOVEL-NOSED SNAKE
Chionactis palarostris

168
WESTERN SHOVEL-NOSED SNAKE
Chionactis occipitalis

MOJAVE SHOVEL-NOSED SNAKE
COLORADO DESERT SHOVEL-NOSED SNAKE
TUCSON SHOVEL-NOSED SNAKE
NEVADA SHOVEL-NOSED SNAKE

169
BANDED SAND SNAKE
Chilomeniscus cinctus

170
WESTERN
HOOK-NOSED SNAKE
Ficimia cana

171
DESERT
HOOK-NOSED SNAKE
Ficimia quadrangularis

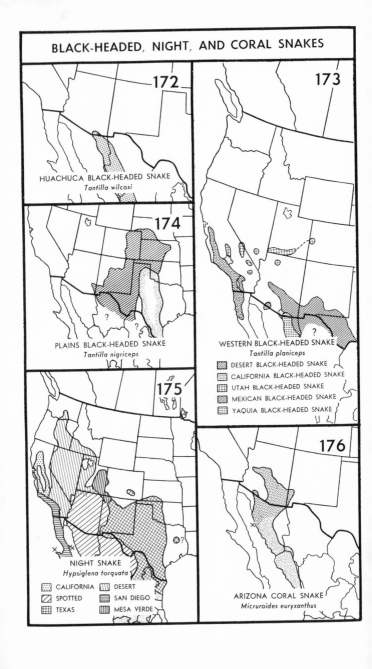

BLACK-HEADED, NIGHT, AND CORAL SNAKES

172
HUACHUCA BLACK-HEADED SNAKE
Tantilla wilcoxi

174
PLAINS BLACK-HEADED SNAKE
Tantilla nigriceps

175
NIGHT SNAKE
Hypsiglena torquata

CALIFORNIA — DESERT
SPOTTED — SAN DIEGO
TEXAS — MESA VERDE

173
WESTERN BLACK-HEADED SNAKE
Tantilla planiceps

DESERT BLACK-HEADED SNAKE
CALIFORNIA BLACK-HEADED SNAKE
UTAH BLACK-HEADED SNAKE
MEXICAN BLACK-HEADED SNAKE
YAQUIA BLACK-HEADED SNAKE

176
ARIZONA CORAL SNAKE
Micruroides euryxanthus

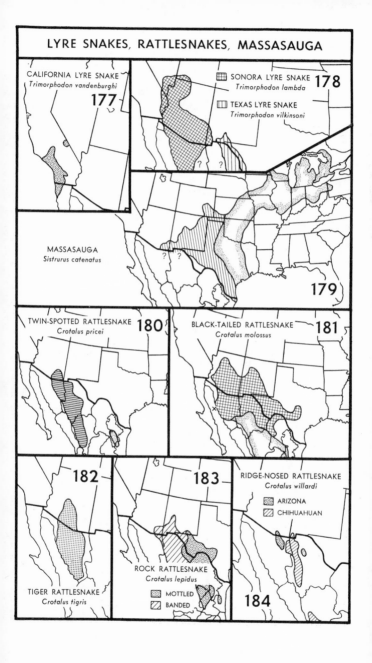

LYRE SNAKES, RATTLESNAKES, MASSASAUGA

CALIFORNIA LYRE SNAKE
Trimorphodon vandenburghi
177

SONORA LYRE SNAKE ⊞ *Trimorphodon lambda*
TEXAS LYRE SNAKE ⊟ *Trimorphodon vilkinsoni*
178

MASSASAUGA
Sistrurus catenatus
179

TWIN-SPOTTED RATTLESNAKE 180
Crotalus pricei

BLACK-TAILED RATTLESNAKE 181
Crotalus molossus

182

TIGER RATTLESNAKE
Crotalus tigris

183

ROCK RATTLESNAKE
Crotalus lepidus
▦ MOTTLED
▨ BANDED

RIDGE-NOSED RATTLESNAKE
Crotalus willardi
▦ ARIZONA
▨ CHIHUAHUAN
184

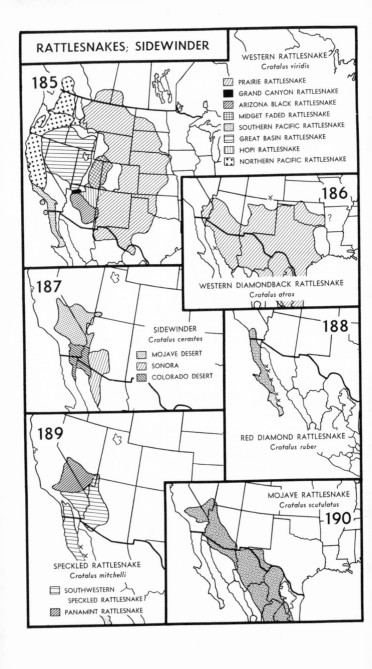

RATTLESNAKES; SIDEWINDER

185

WESTERN RATTLESNAKE
Crotalus viridis

- PRAIRIE RATTLESNAKE
- GRAND CANYON RATTLESNAKE
- ARIZONA BLACK RATTLESNAKE
- MIDGET FADED RATTLESNAKE
- SOUTHERN PACIFIC RATTLESNAKE
- GREAT BASIN RATTLESNAKE
- HOPI RATTLESNAKE
- NORTHERN PACIFIC RATTLESNAKE

186

WESTERN DIAMONDBACK RATTLESNAKE
Crotalus atrox

187

SIDEWINDER
Crotalus cerastes

- MOJAVE DESERT
- SONORA
- COLORADO DESERT

188

RED DIAMOND RATTLESNAKE
Crotalus ruber

189

SPECKLED RATTLESNAKE
Crotalus mitchelli

- SOUTHWESTERN
  SPECKLED RATTLESNAKE
- PANAMINT RATTLESNAKE

MOJAVE RATTLESNAKE
Crotalus scutulatus

190

Index

Index

This is primarily a species index; all headings of family, subfamily, and genus are also included. The chapters preceding the species descriptions are not covered here because the material in those chapters can be found easily from the table of contents and the boldface headings within the chapters. The last chapter is indexed only relative to the main descriptions of eggs and larvae and their illustrations. When a subspecies has the same common name as the species, its text-description page number is preceded by "ssp." in the index to differentiate it from the species text-page number.

The illustrations are referred to by boldface type, the text descriptions by lightface. Range maps are indexed by map number rather than by page number. When a species has more than one illustration, only the main ones are listed, since the others are cross-referenced in the text or on the legend page opposite the plate.

LIZARDS

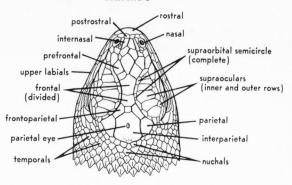

postrostral — rostral
internasal — nasal
prefrontal
upper labials — supraorbital semicircle (complete)
frontal (divided) — supraoculars (inner and outer rows)
frontoparietal
parietal eye — parietal
temporals — interparietal
— nuchals

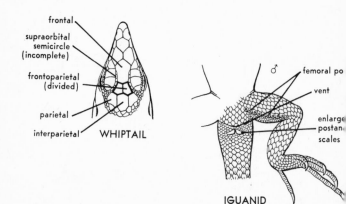

frontal
supraorbital semicircle (incomplete)
frontoparietal (divided)
parietal
interparietal **WHIPTAIL**

♂ — femoral po
vent
enlarge postan scales
IGUANID

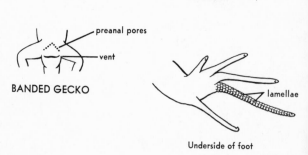

preanal pores
vent
BANDED GECKO

lamellae

Underside of foot

Scales with apical pits
(*Natrix*)   Cycloid   Keeled mucronate   Granular

SCALE TYPES
(Lizards and Snakes)

SNAKES

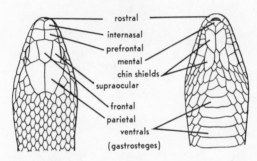

rostral
internasal
prefrontal
mental
chin shields
supraocular
frontal
parietal
ventrals
(gastrosteges)

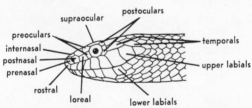

supraocular
postoculars
preoculars
internasal
postnasal
prenasal
rostral
loreal
lower labials
temporals
upper labials

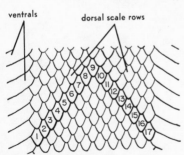

ventrals
dorsal scale rows

9
8
7
10
6
11
5
12
4
13
3
14
2
15
1
16
17

Method of counting
dorsal scale rows

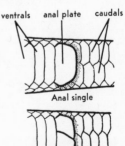

ventrals   anal plate   caudals

Anal single

Anal divided